# MODEL

## *Model Vol. 3*
## Created by Lee So-Young

Translation - Grace Min
English Adaptation - Sam Stormcrow Hayes
Copy Editor - Hope Donovan
Retouch and Lettering - Joseph Mariano
Production Artist - Vicente Rivera, Jr.
Cover Layout - Annna Kernbaum

Editor - Bryce P. Coleman
Digital Imaging Manager - Chris Buford
Pre-Press Manager - Antonio DePietro
Production Managers - Jennifer Miller and Mutsumi Miyazaki
Art Director - Matt Alford
Managing Editor - Jill Freshney
VP of Production - Ron Klamert
President and C.O.O. - John Parker
Publisher and C.E.O. - Stuart Levy

A  Manga

TOKYOPOP Inc.
5900 Wilshire Blvd. Suite 2000
Los Angeles, CA 90036

E-mail: info@TOKYOPOP.com
Come visit us online at www.TOKYOPOP.com

ISBN: 1-59182-713-2

First TOKYOPOP printing: September 2004
10  9  8  7  6  5  4  3
Printed in the USA

# VOLUME THREE

# BY
# LEE SO-YOUNG

HAMBURG // LONDON // LOS ANGELES // TOKYO

# MODEL: THREE

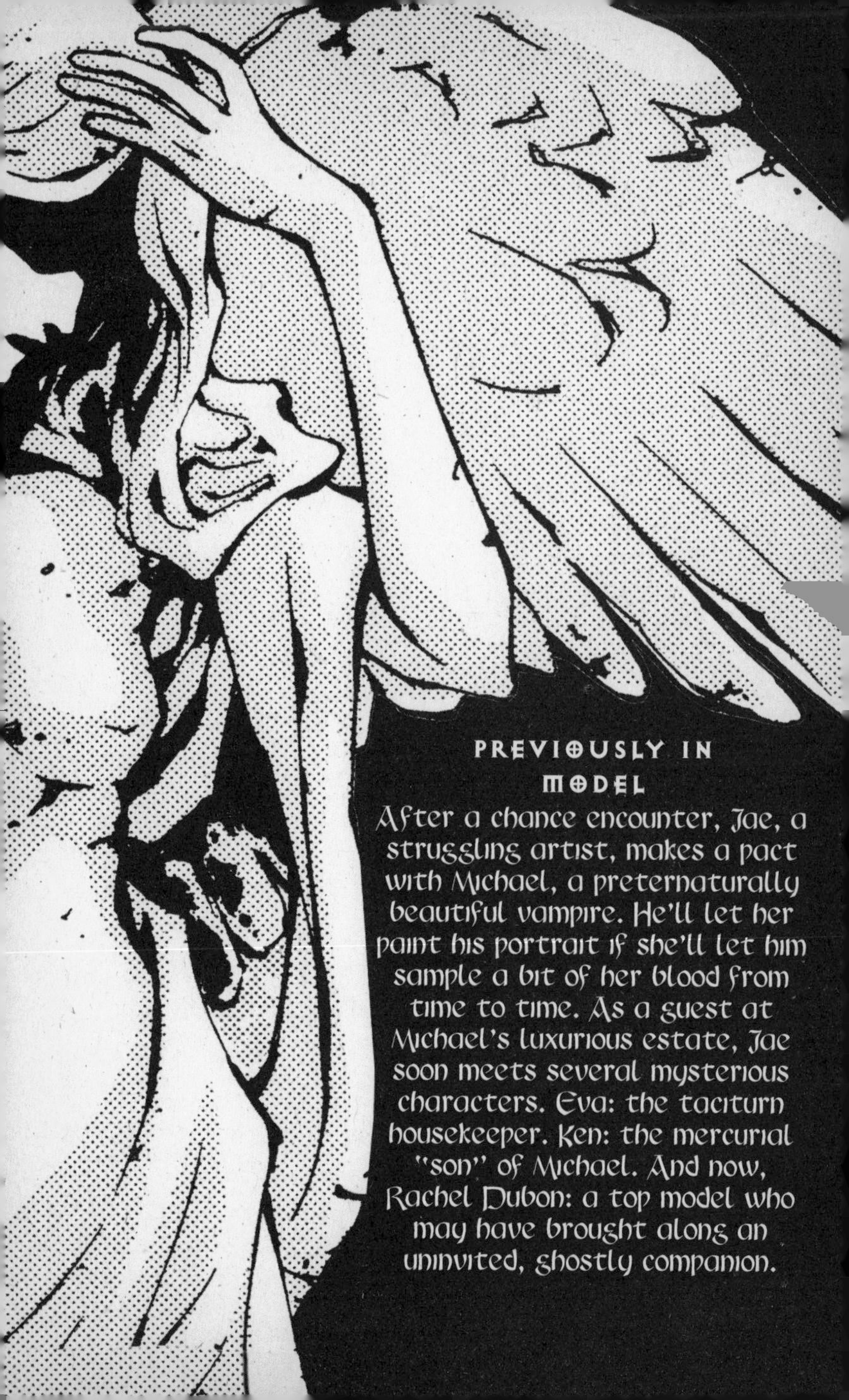
PREVIOUSLY IN MODEL
After a chance encounter, Jae, a struggling artist, makes a pact with Michael, a preternaturally beautiful vampire. He'll let her paint his portrait if she'll let him sample a bit of her blood from time to time. As a guest at Michael's luxurious estate, Jae soon meets several mysterious characters. Eva: the taciturn housekeeper. Ken: the mercurial "son" of Michael. And now, Rachel Dubon: a top model who may have brought along an uninvited, ghostly companion.

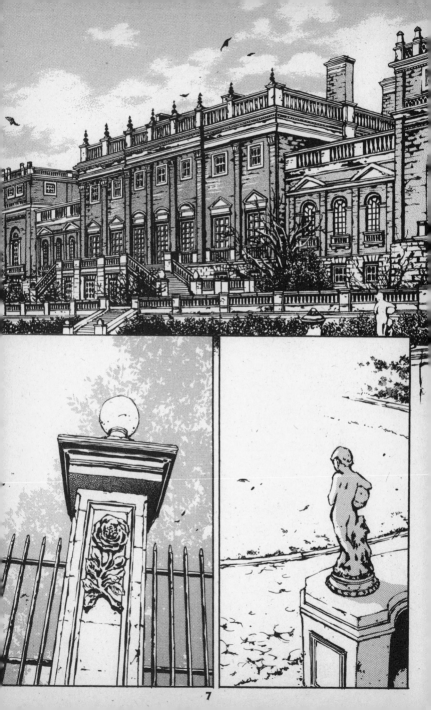

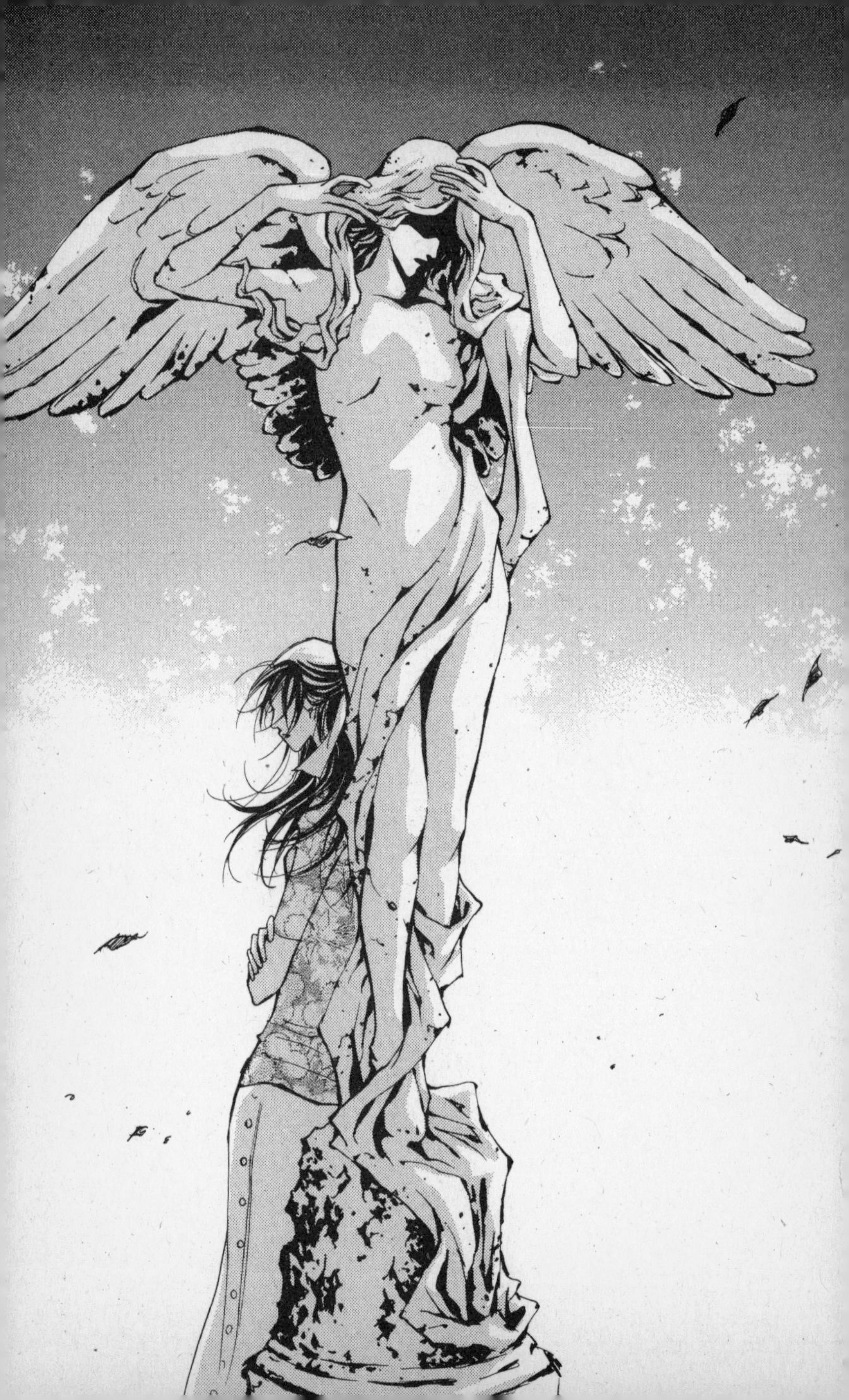

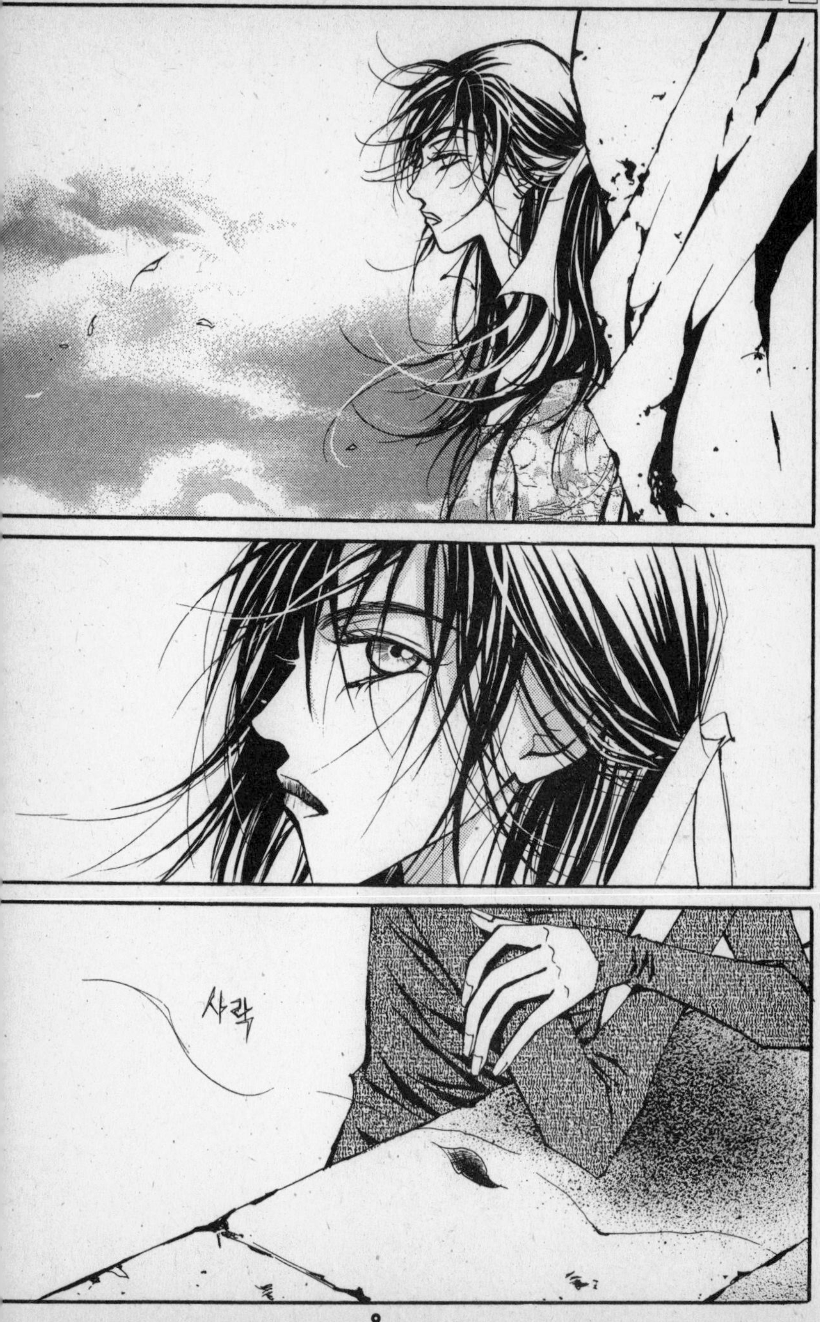
사락

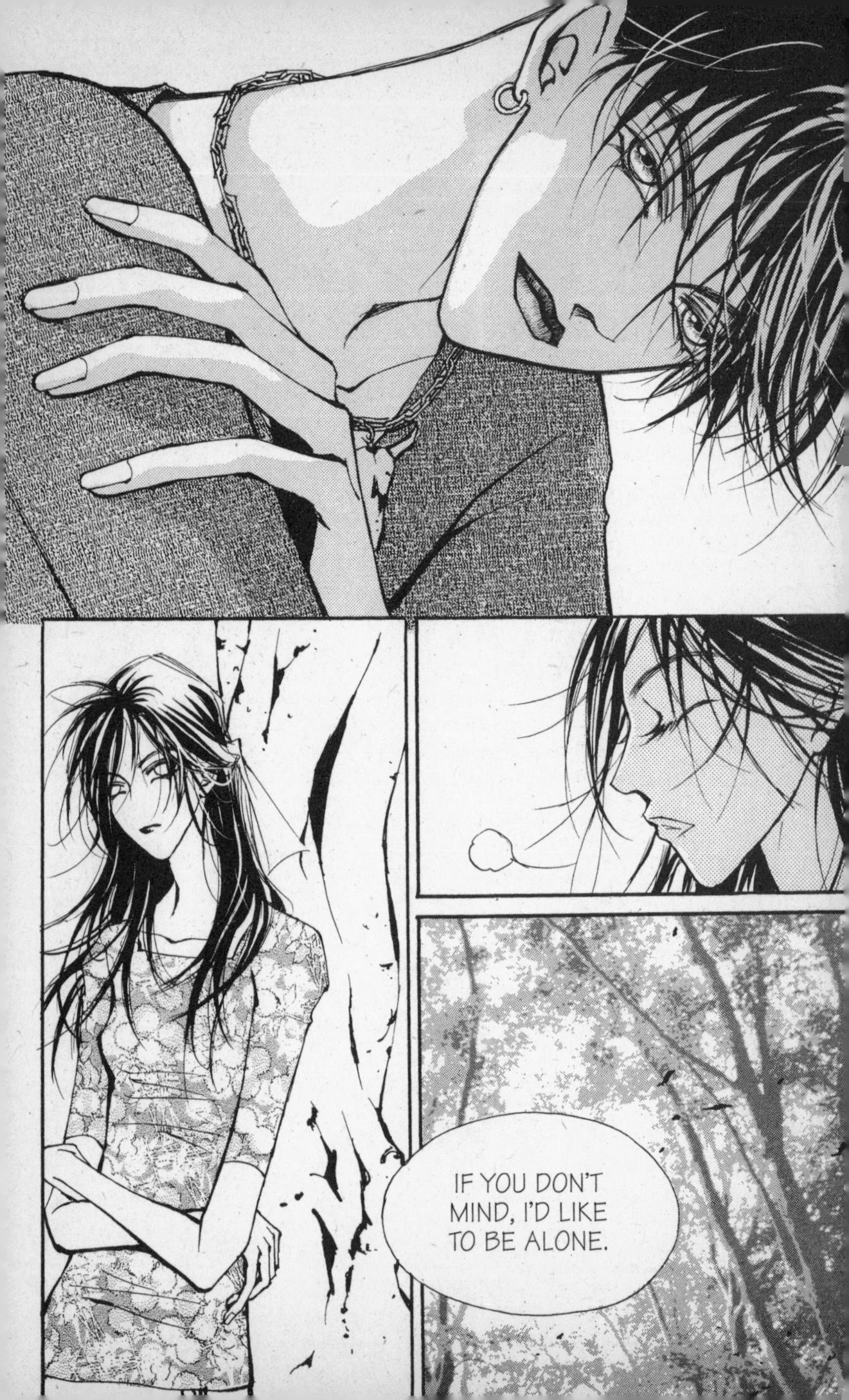
IF YOU DON'T MIND, I'D LIKE TO BE ALONE.

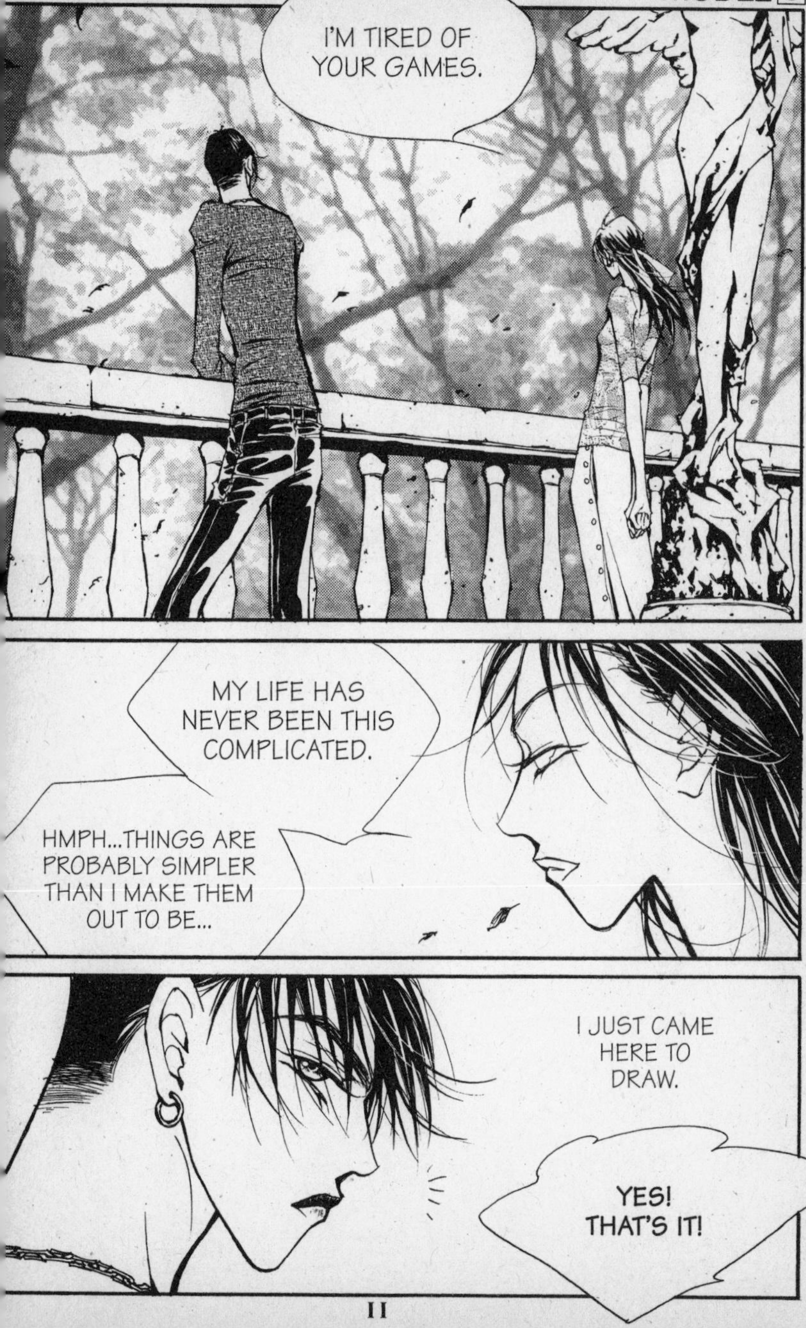
I'M TIRED OF YOUR GAMES.
MY LIFE HAS NEVER BEEN THIS COMPLICATED.
HMPH...THINGS ARE PROBABLY SIMPLER THAN I MAKE THEM OUT TO BE...
I JUST CAME HERE TO DRAW.
YES! THAT'S IT!

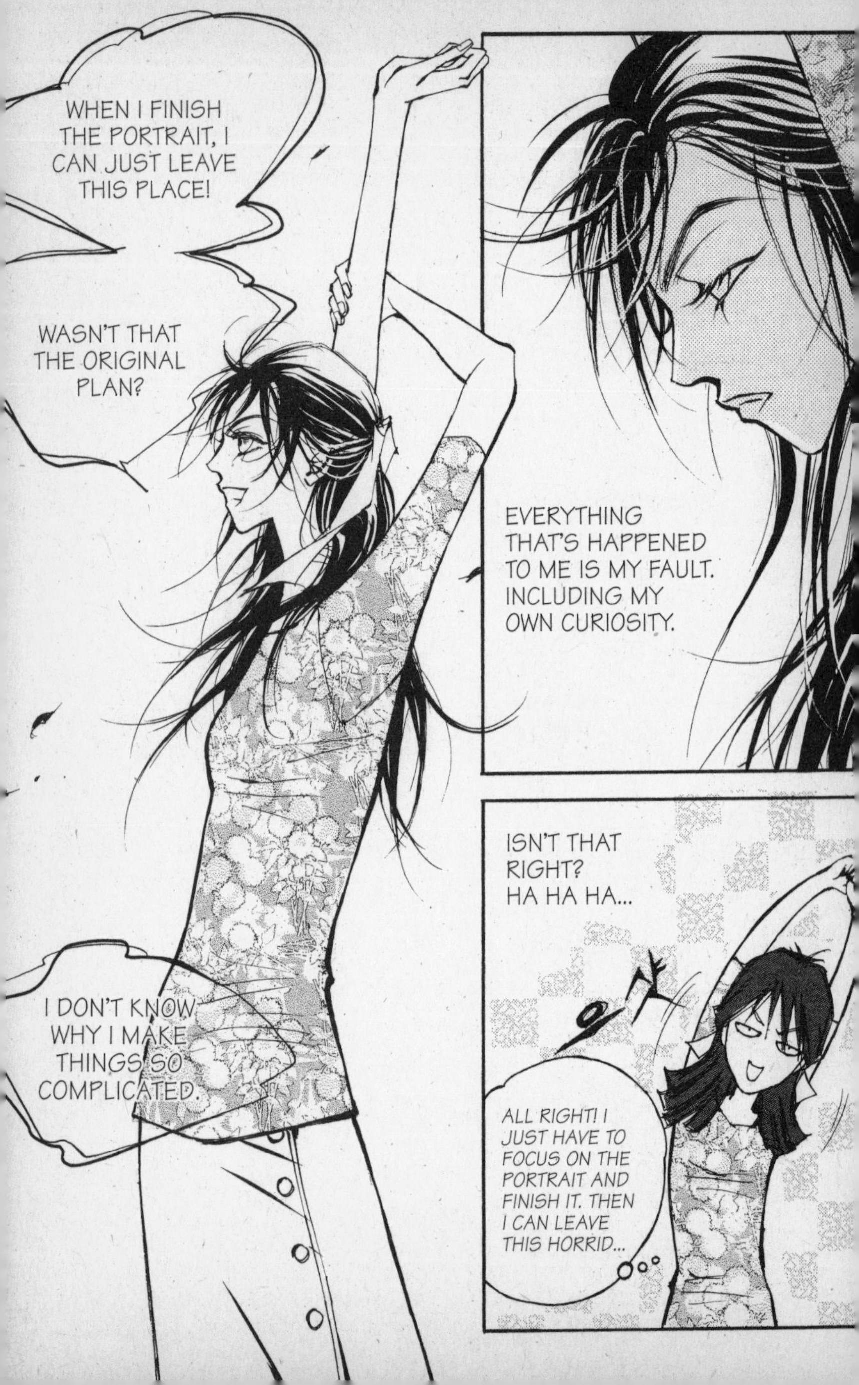
WHEN I FINISH THE PORTRAIT, I CAN JUST LEAVE THIS PLACE!
WASN'T THAT THE ORIGINAL PLAN?
I DON'T KNOW WHY I MAKE THINGS SO COMPLICATED.
EVERYTHING THAT'S HAPPENED TO ME IS MY FAULT. INCLUDING MY OWN CURIOSITY.
ISN'T THAT RIGHT? HA HA HA...
ALL RIGHT! I JUST HAVE TO FOCUS ON THE PORTRAIT AND FINISH IT. THEN I CAN LEAVE THIS HORRID...

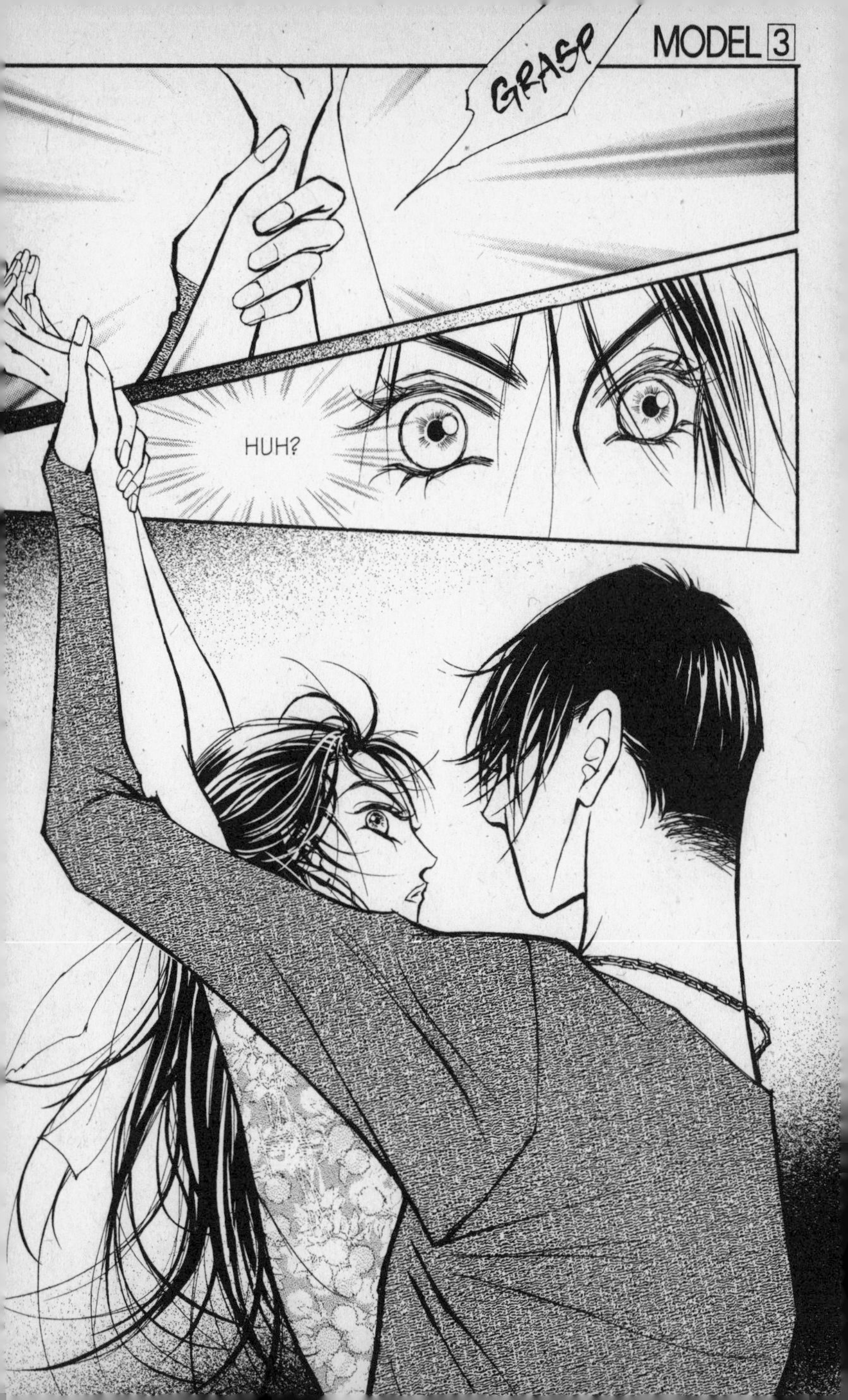
GRASP
HUH?

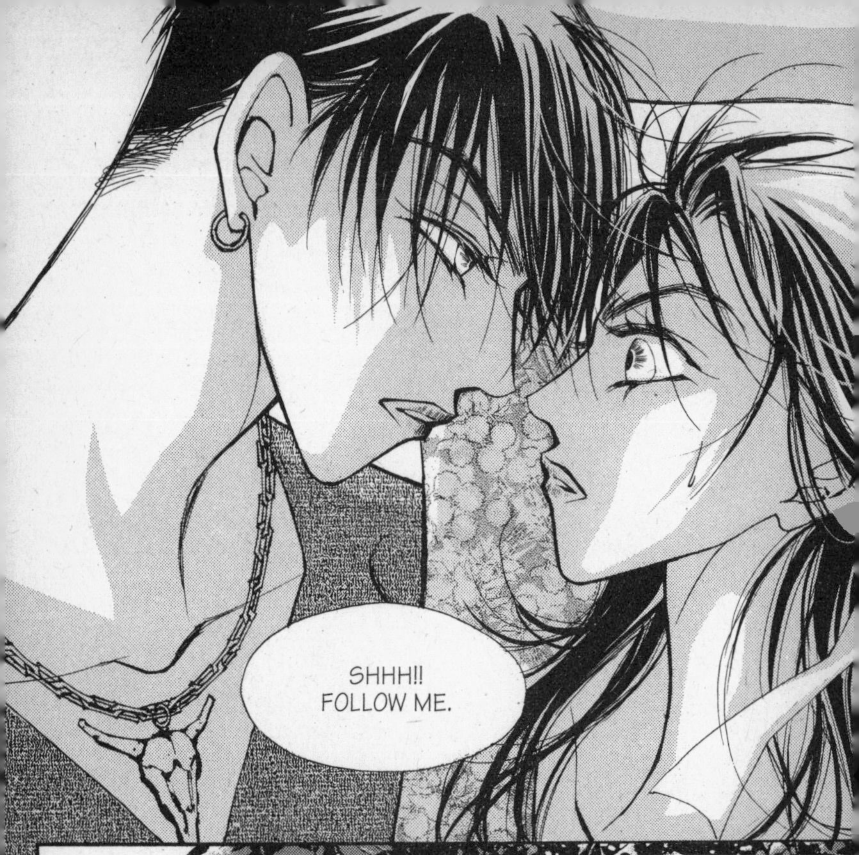
SHHH!! FOLLOW ME.

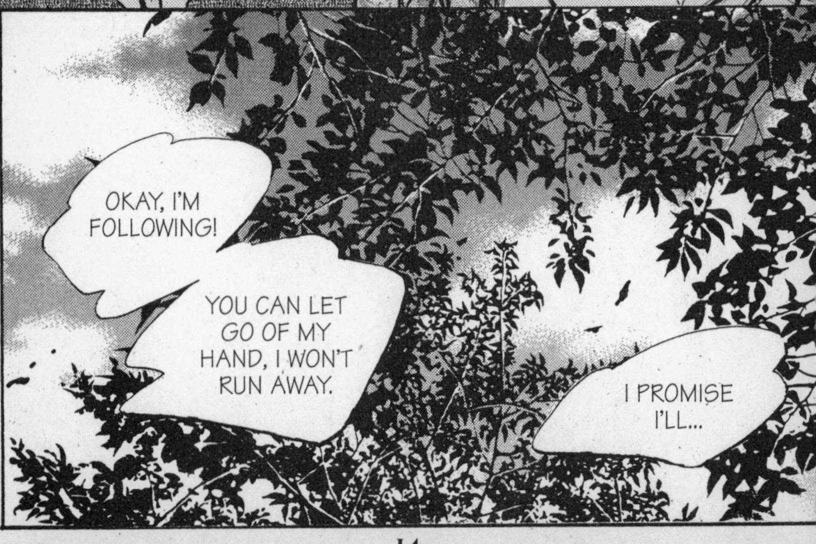
OKAY, I'M FOLLOWING!
YOU CAN LET GO OF MY HAND, I WON'T RUN AWAY.
I PROMISE I'LL...

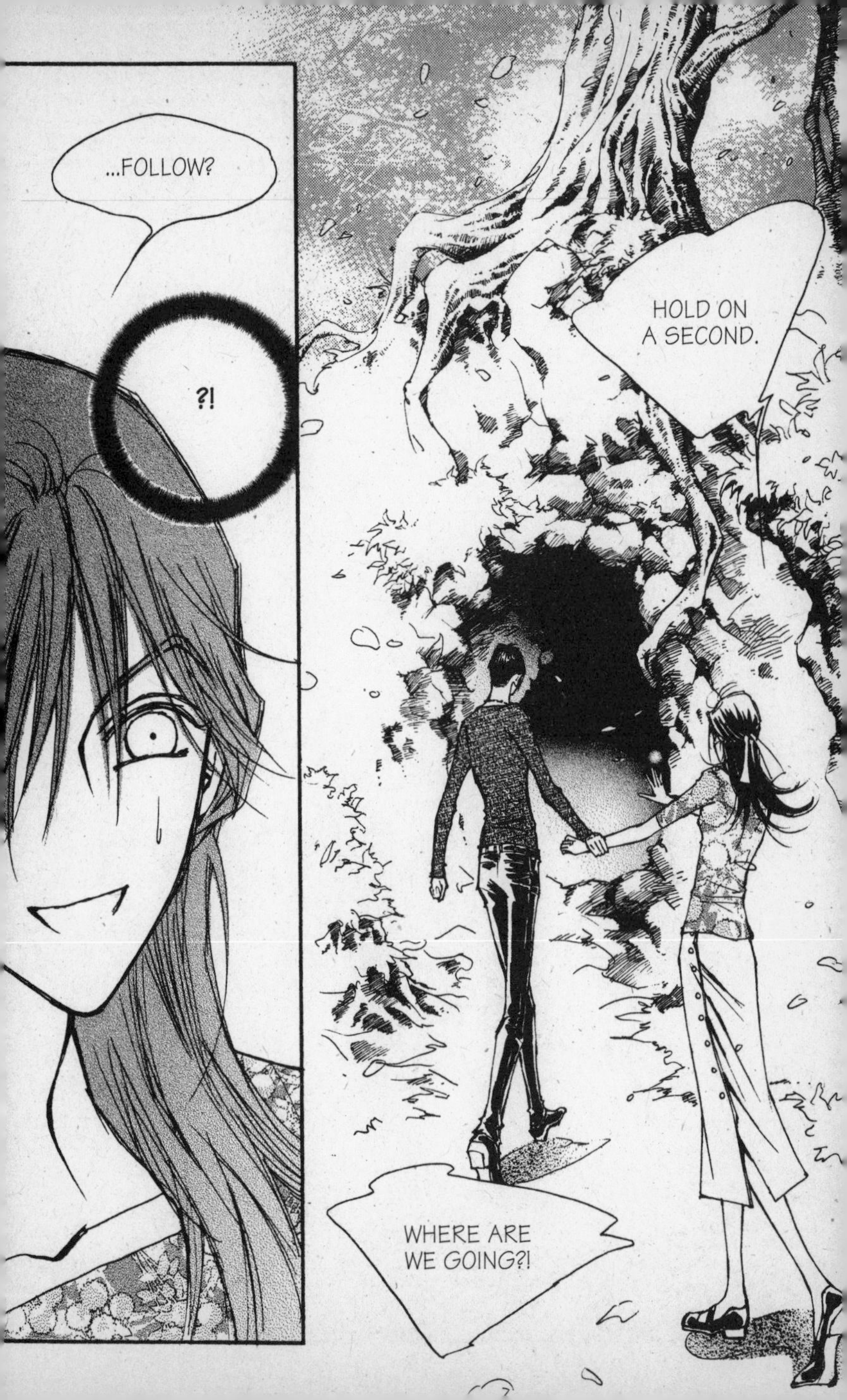
...FOLLOW?
?!
HOLD ON A SECOND.
WHERE ARE WE GOING?!

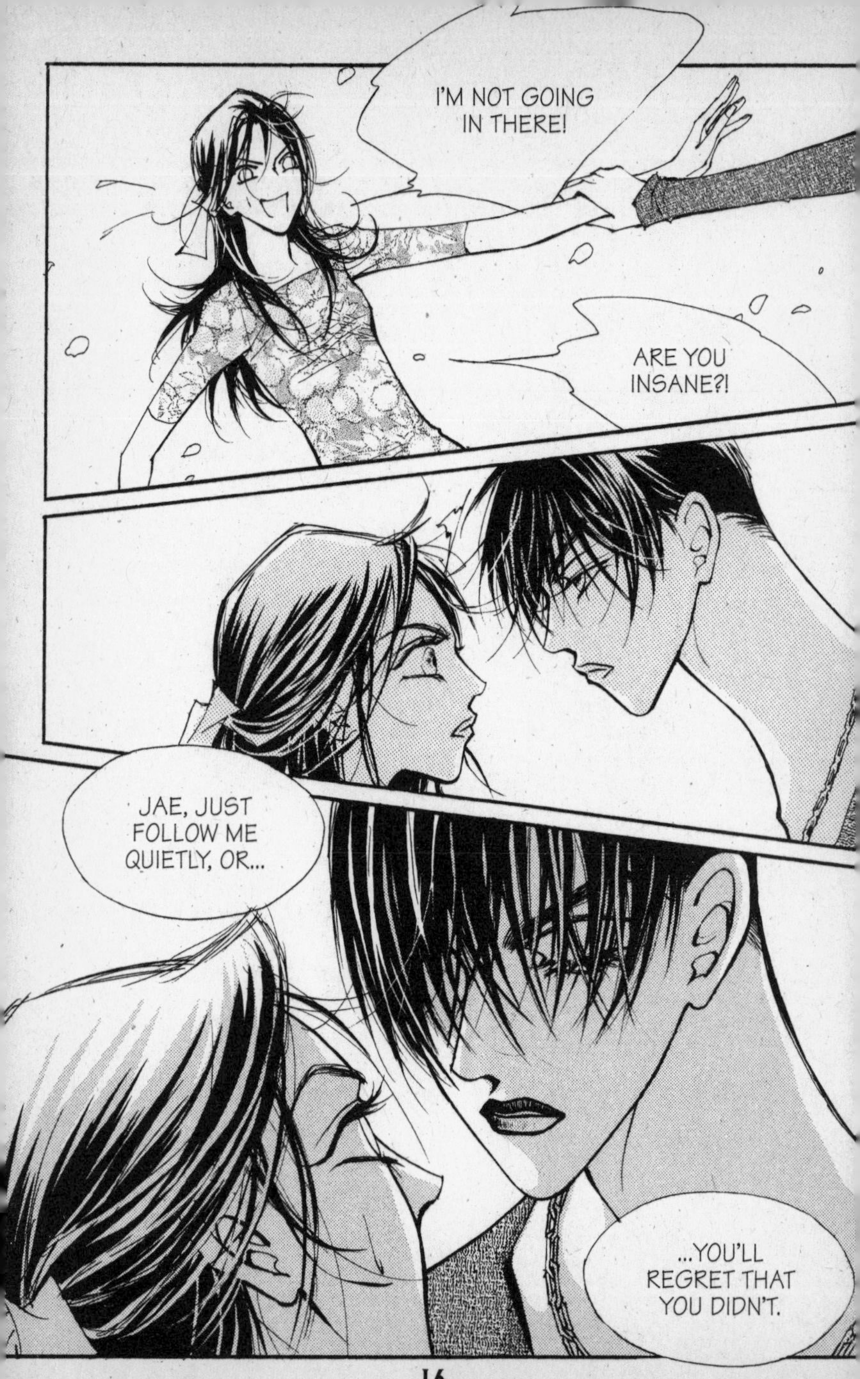
I'M NOT GOING IN THERE!
ARE YOU INSANE?!
JAE, JUST FOLLOW ME QUIETLY, OR...
...YOU'LL REGRET THAT YOU DIDN'T.

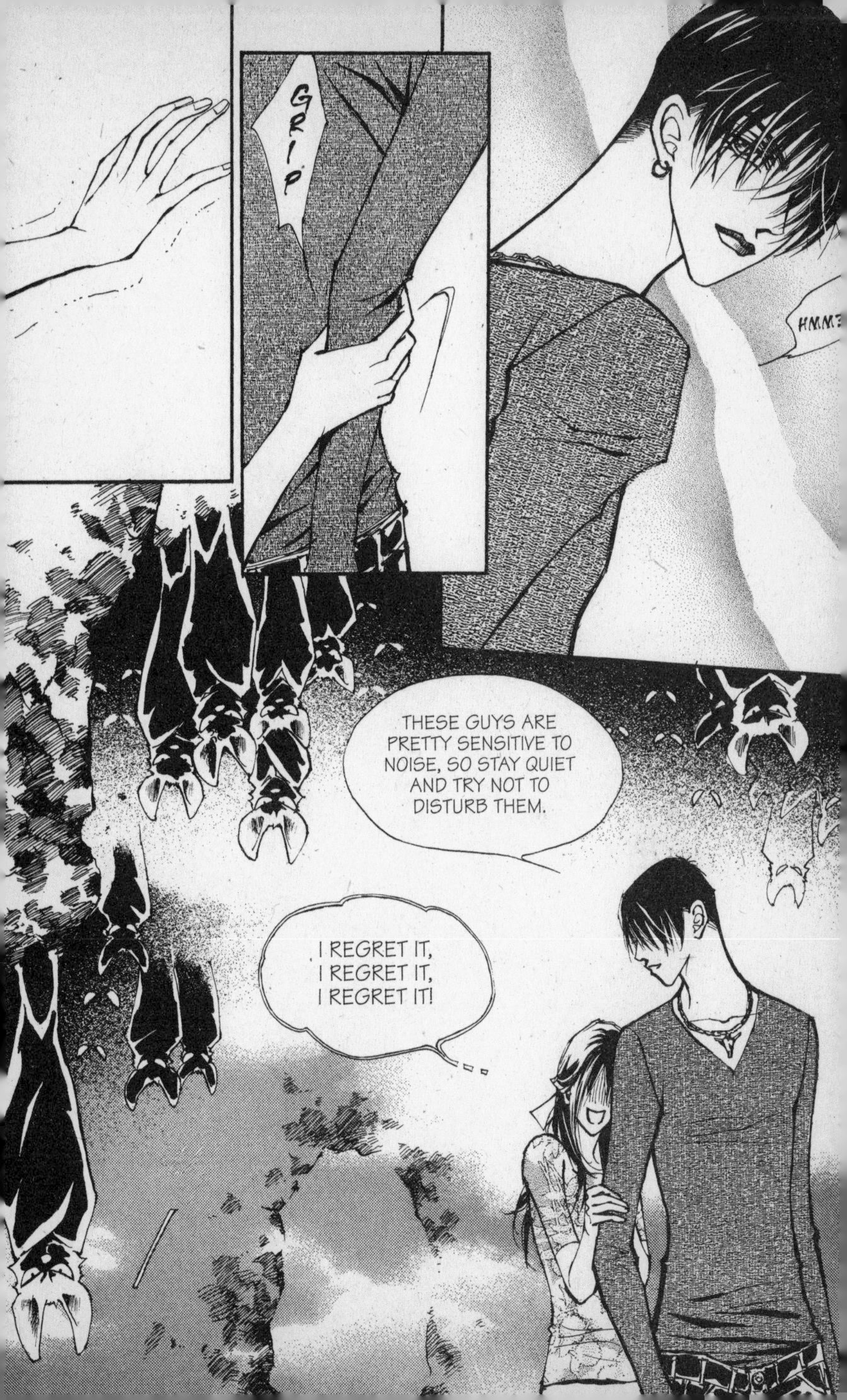
GRIP
HNN
THESE GUYS ARE PRETTY SENSITIVE TO NOISE, SO STAY QUIET AND TRY NOT TO DISTURB THEM.
I REGRET IT, I REGRET IT, I REGRET IT!

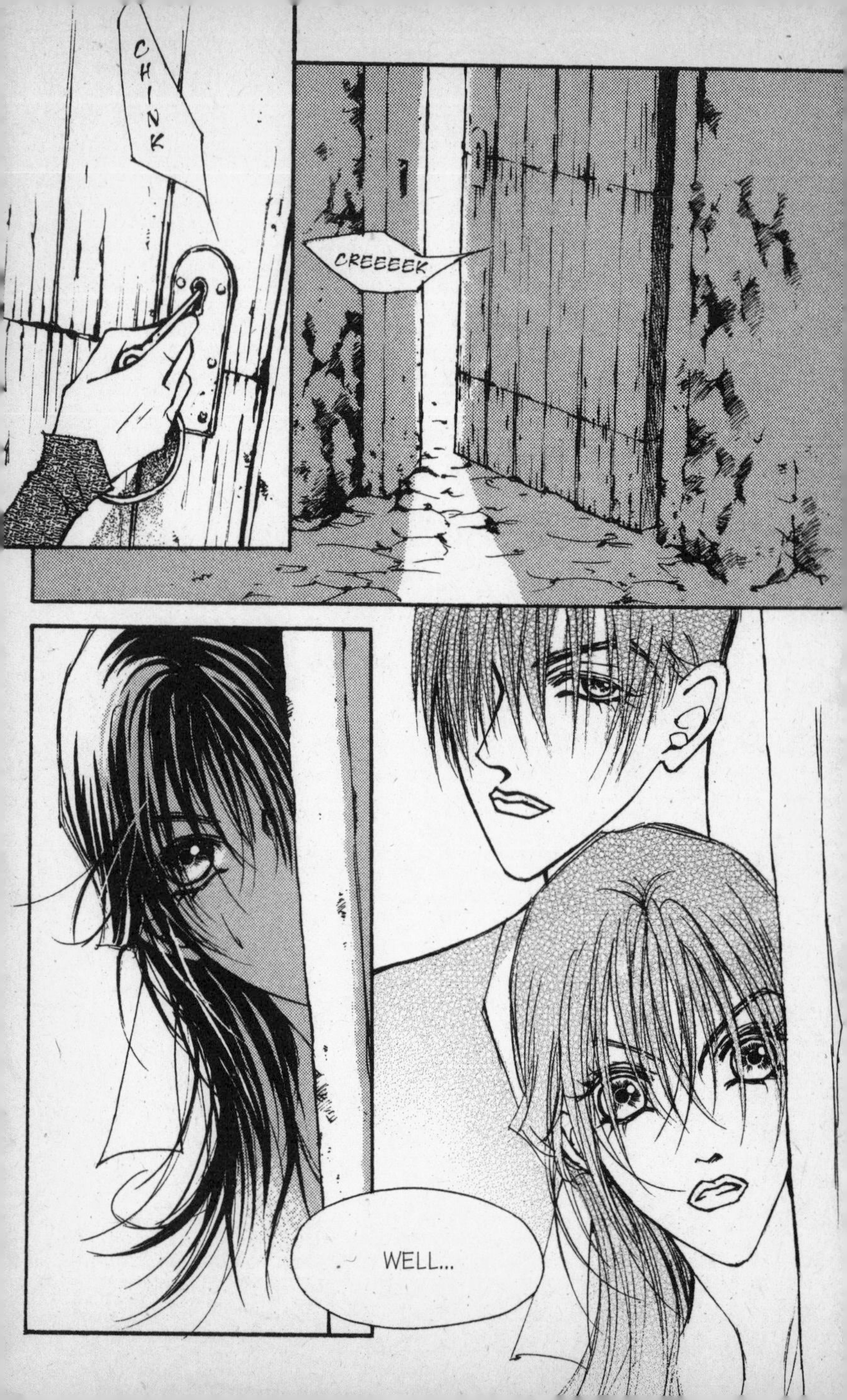
CHINK
CREEEEK
WELL...

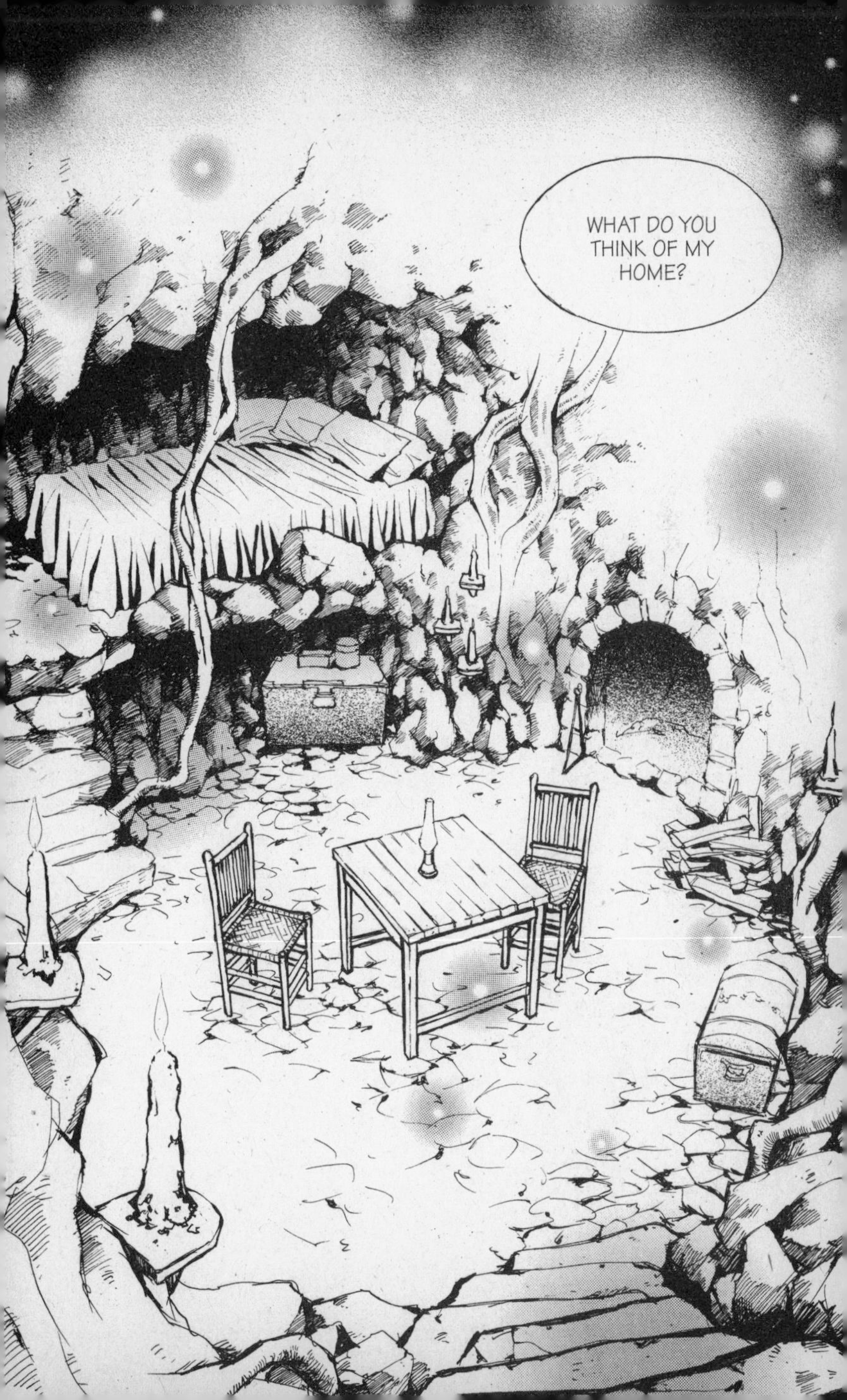
WHAT DO YOU THINK OF MY HOME?

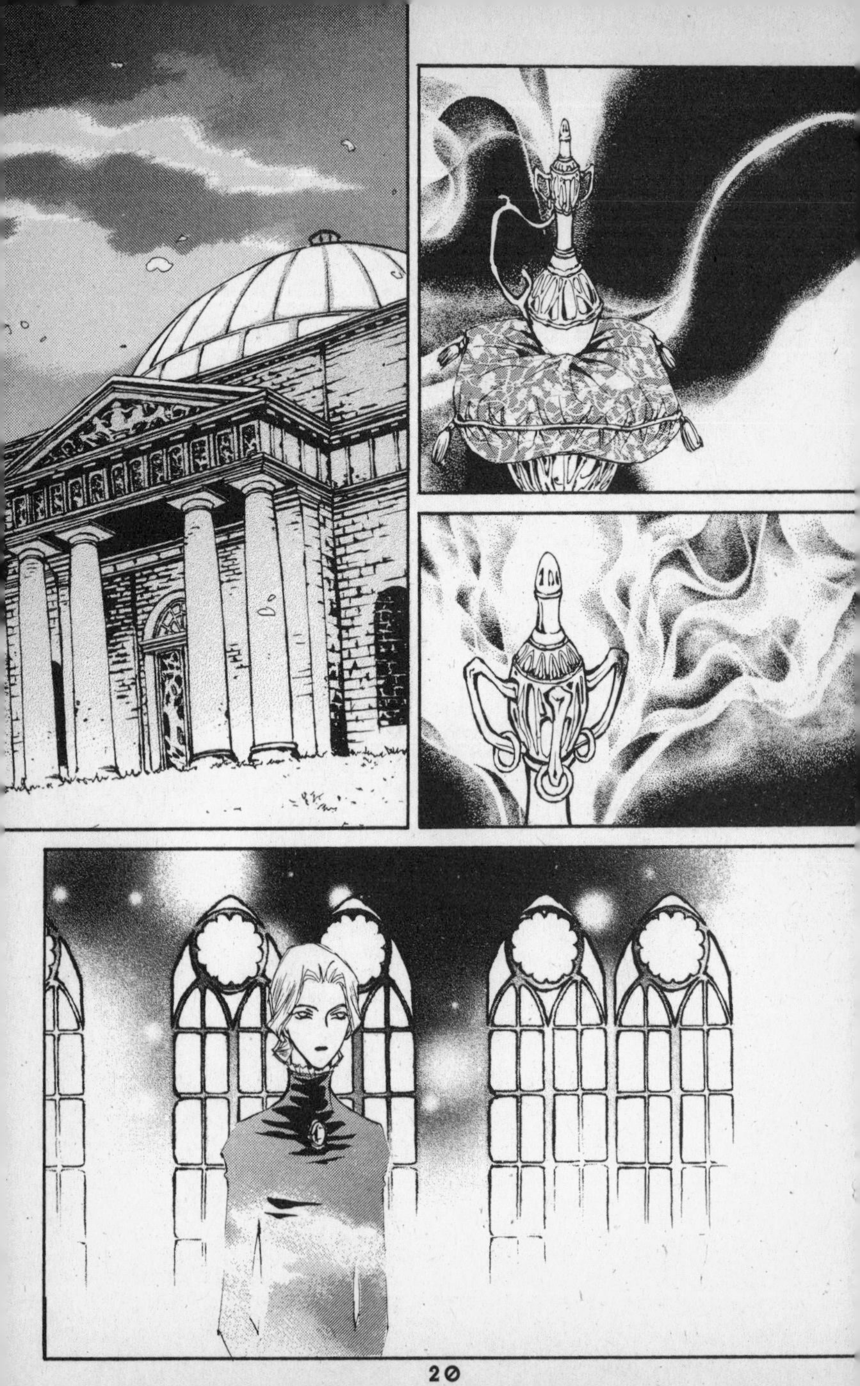

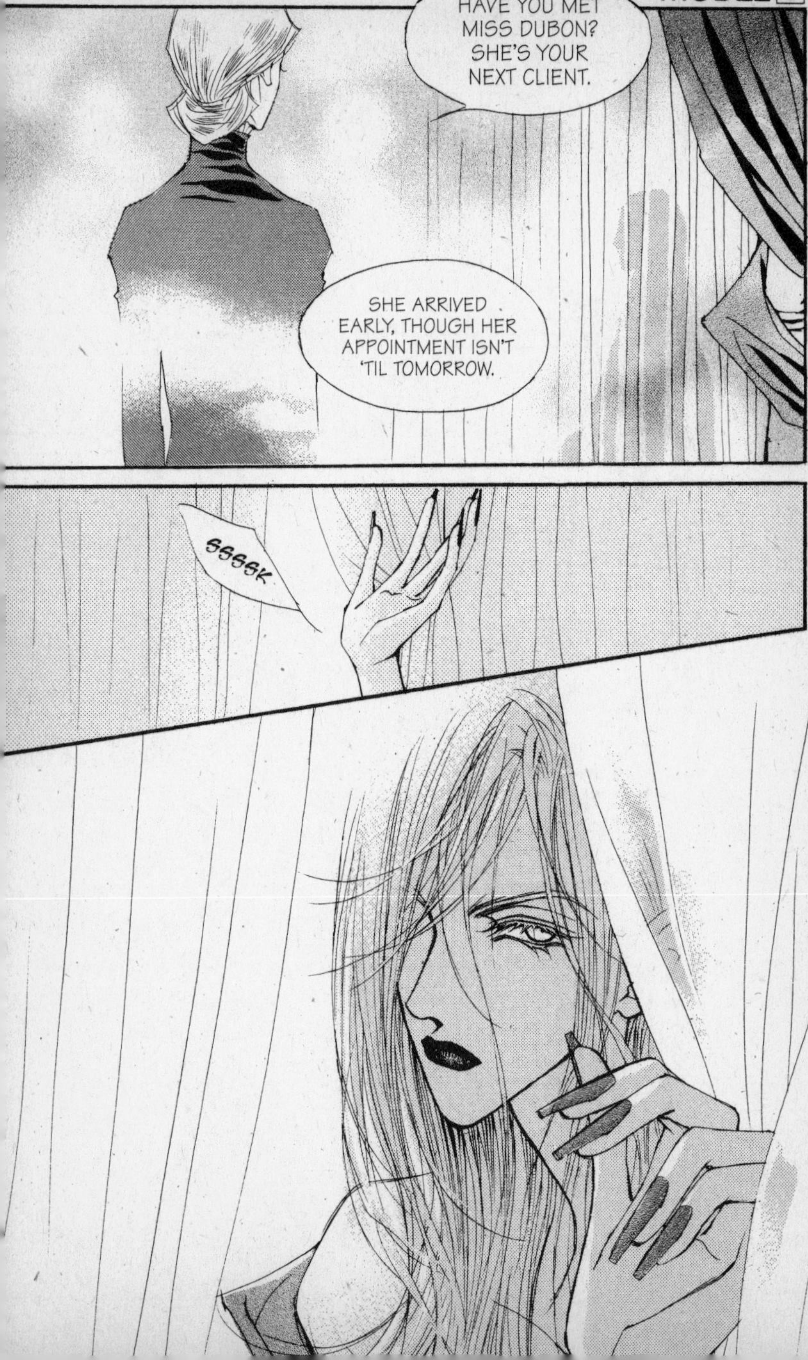
HAVE YOU MET MISS DUBON? SHE'S YOUR NEXT CLIENT.
SHE ARRIVED EARLY, THOUGH HER APPOINTMENT ISN'T 'TIL TOMORROW.
SSSSK

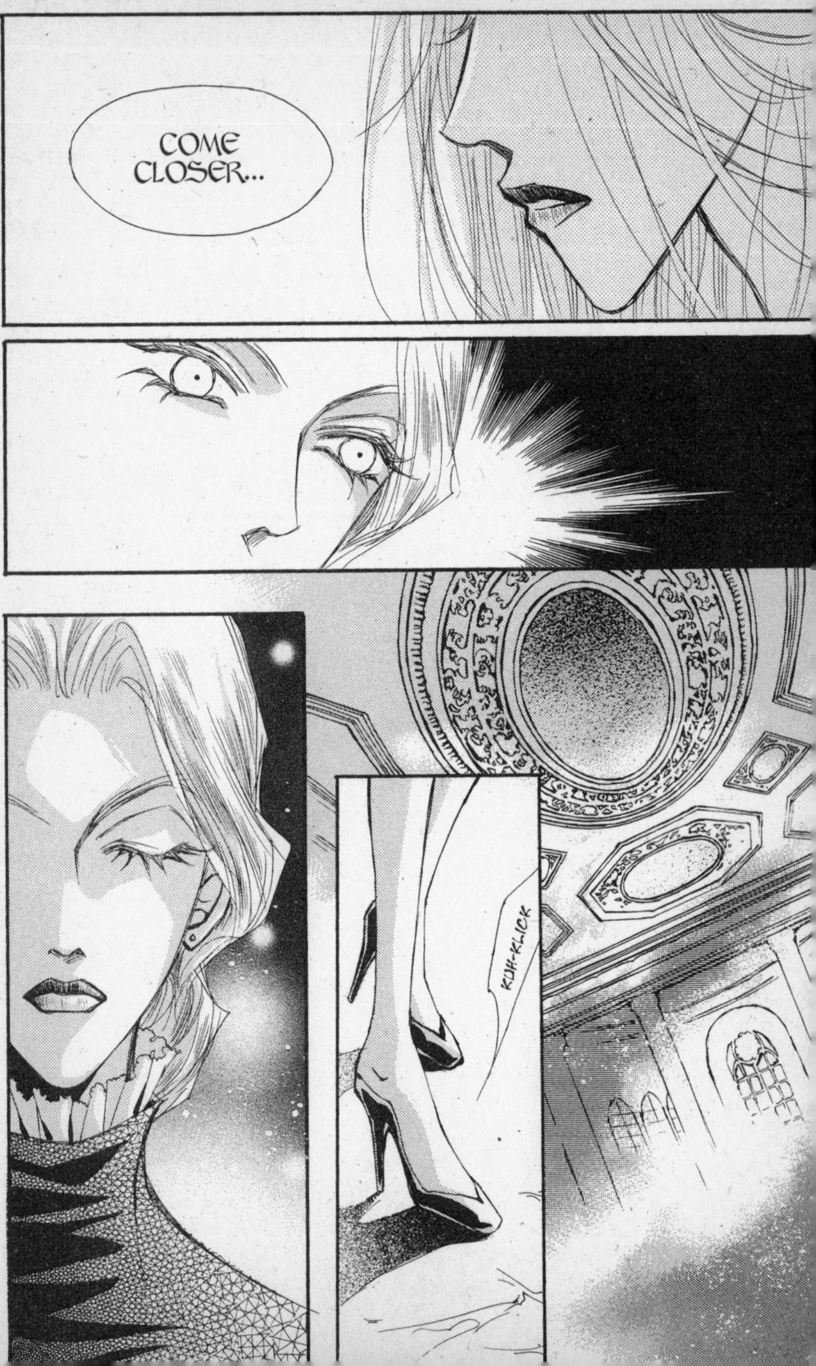
COME CLOSER...
KUH-KLICK

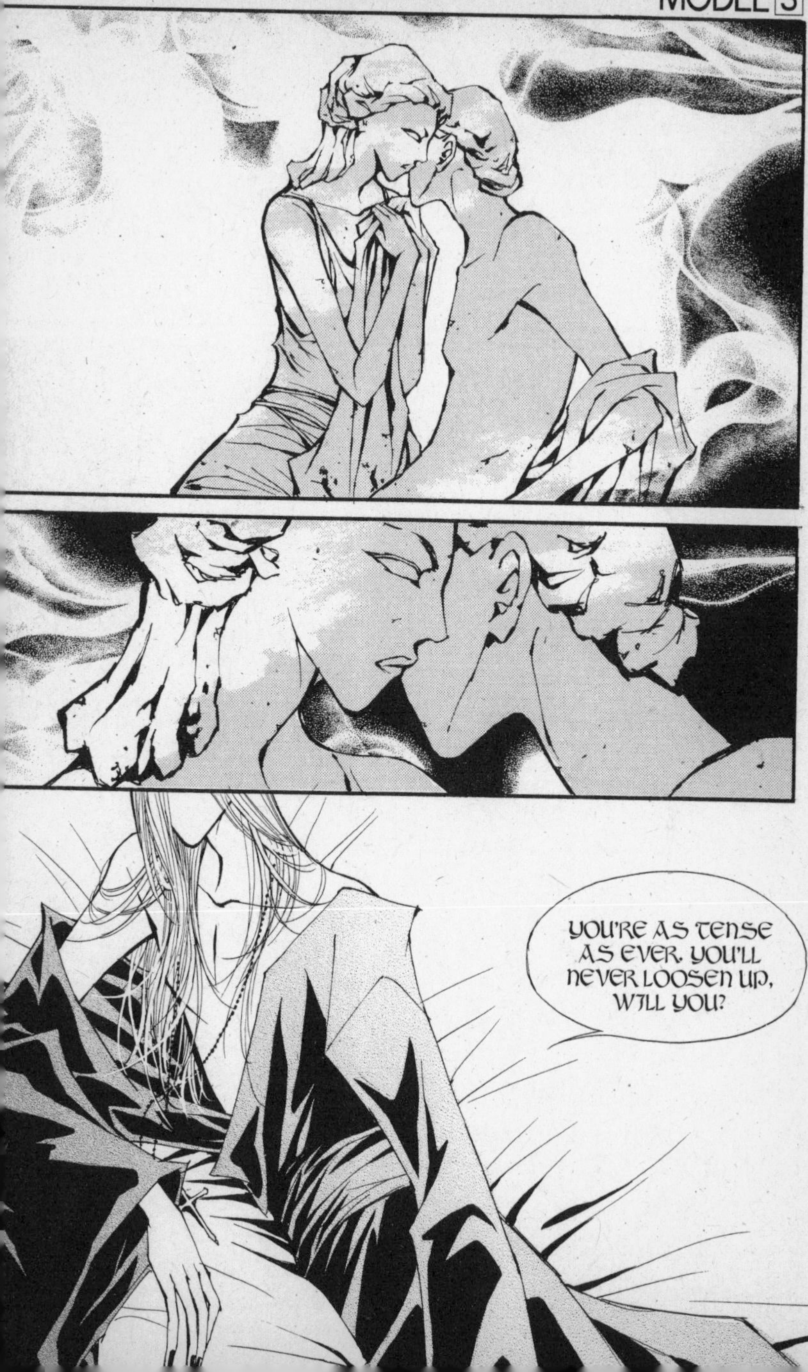
YOU'RE AS TENSE AS EVER. YOU'LL NEVER LOOSEN UP, WILL YOU?

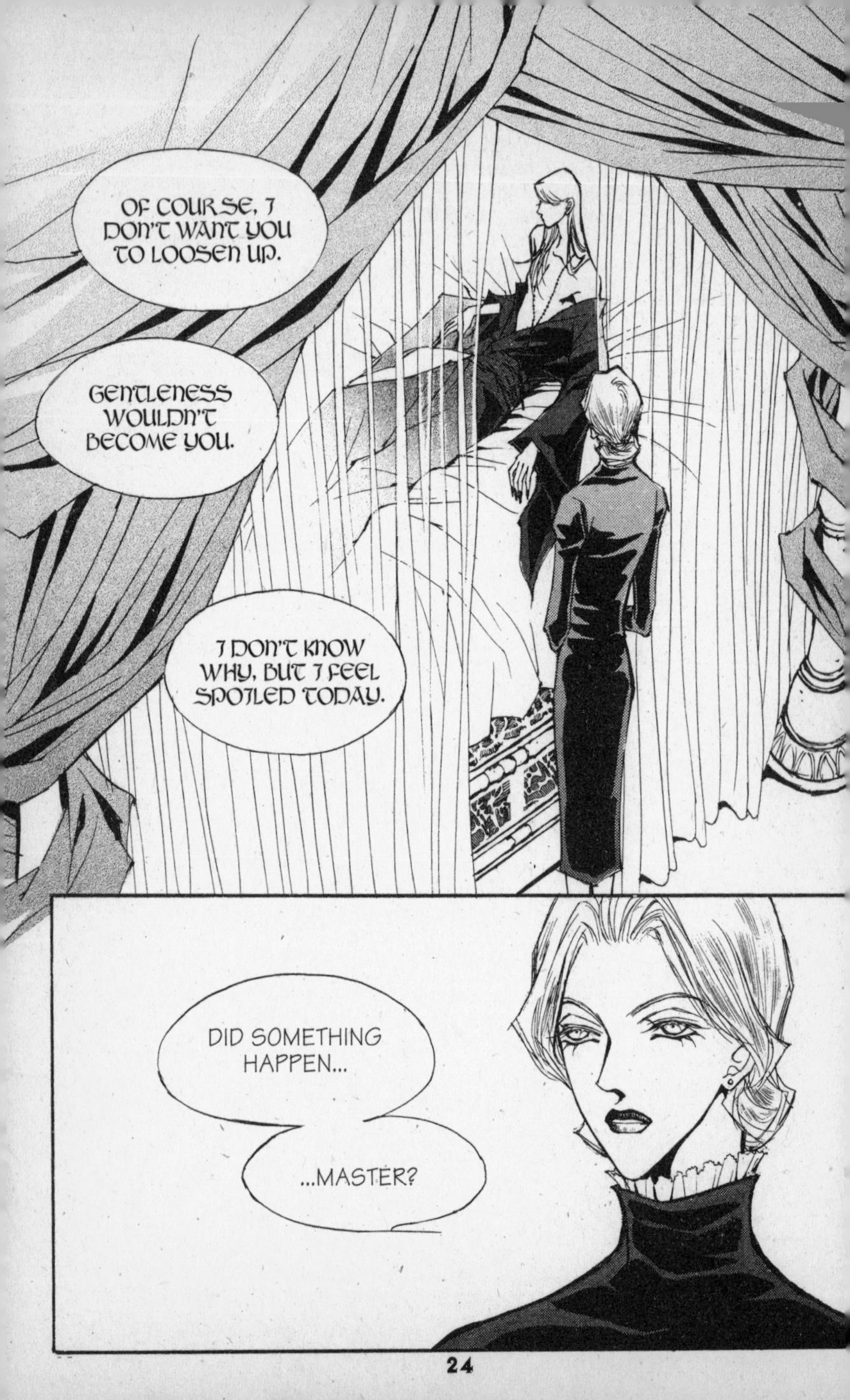
OF COURSE, I DON'T WANT YOU TO LOOSEN UP.
GENTLENESS WOULDN'T BECOME YOU.
I DON'T KNOW WHY, BUT I FEEL SPOILED TODAY.
DID SOMETHING HAPPEN...
...MASTER?

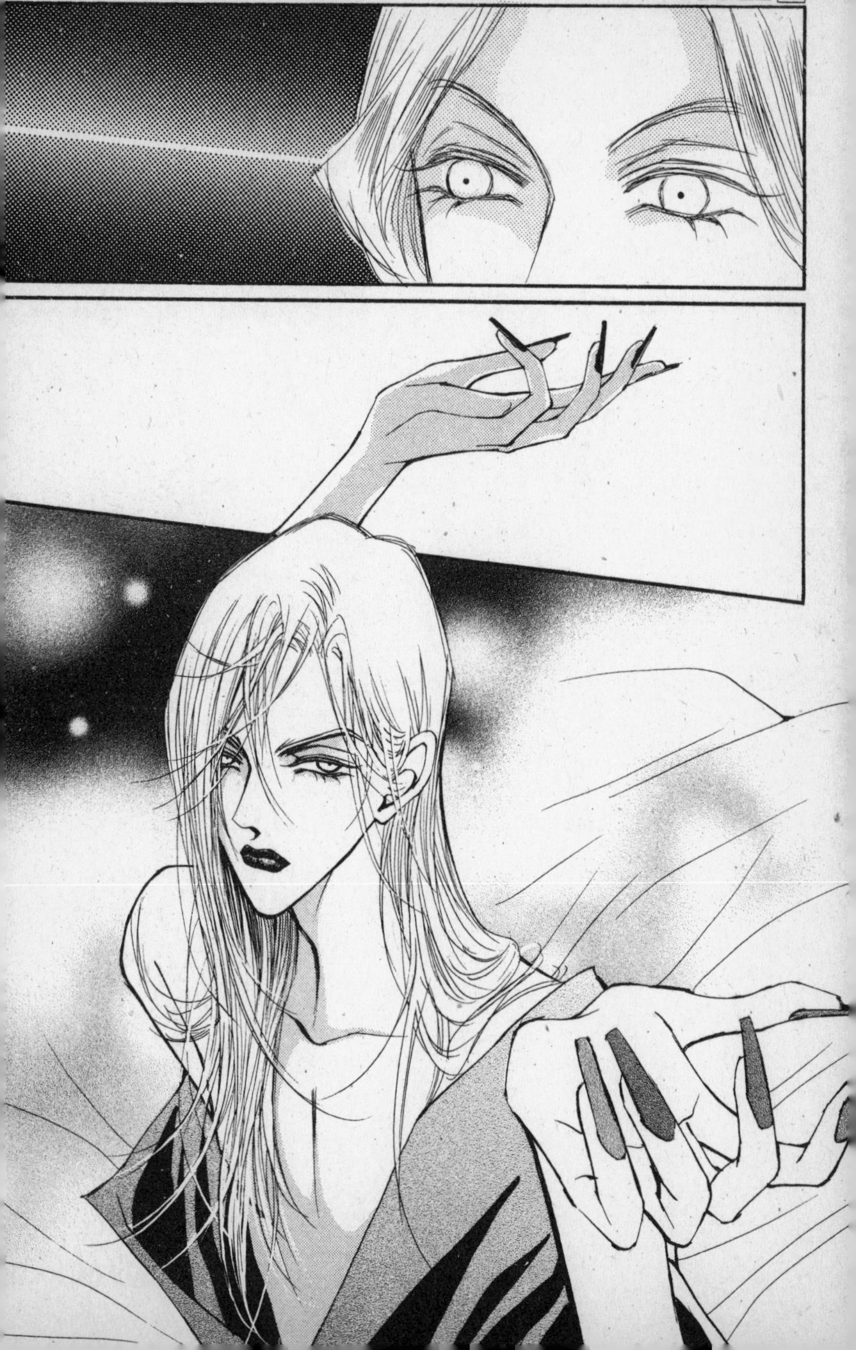

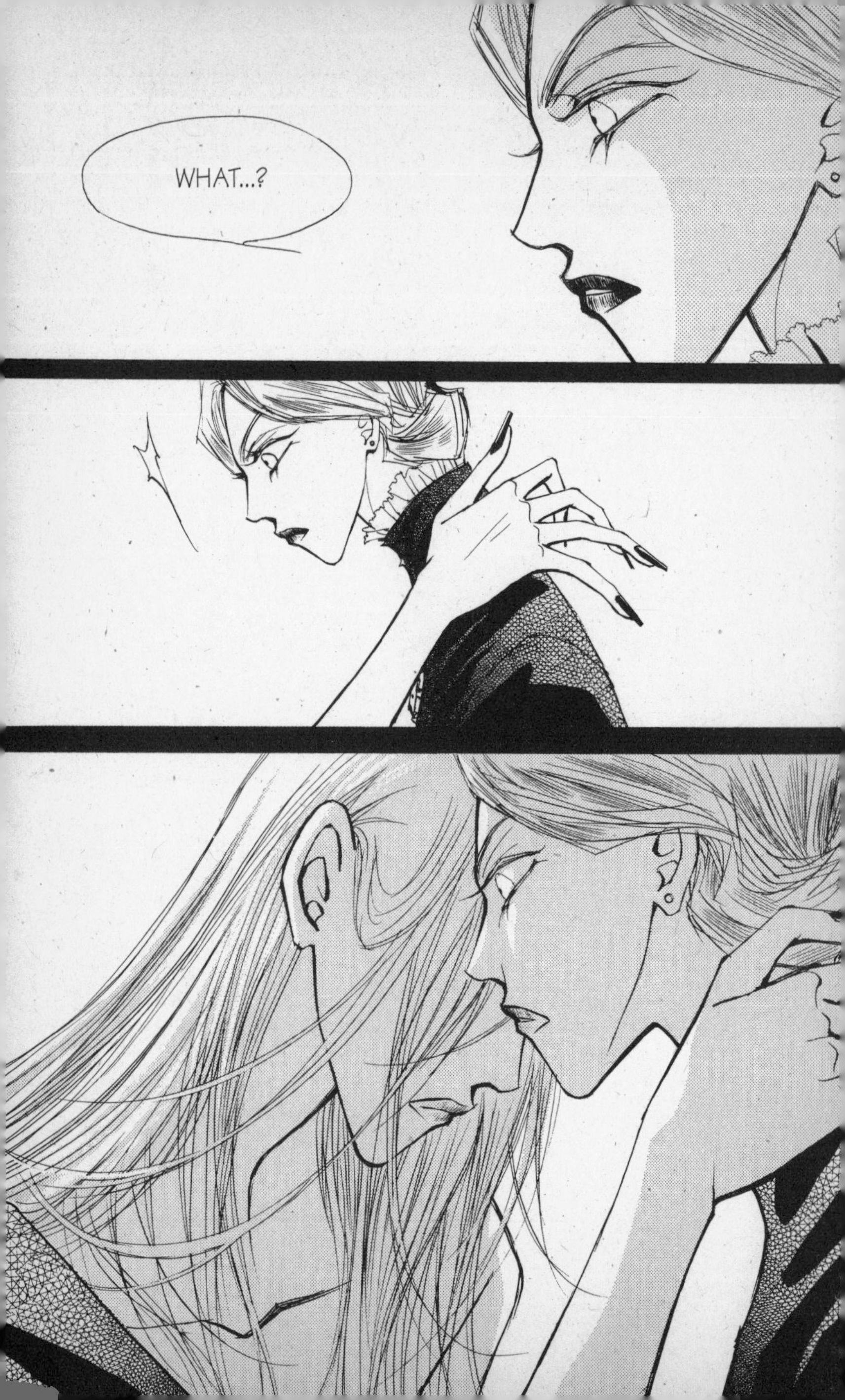
WHAT...?

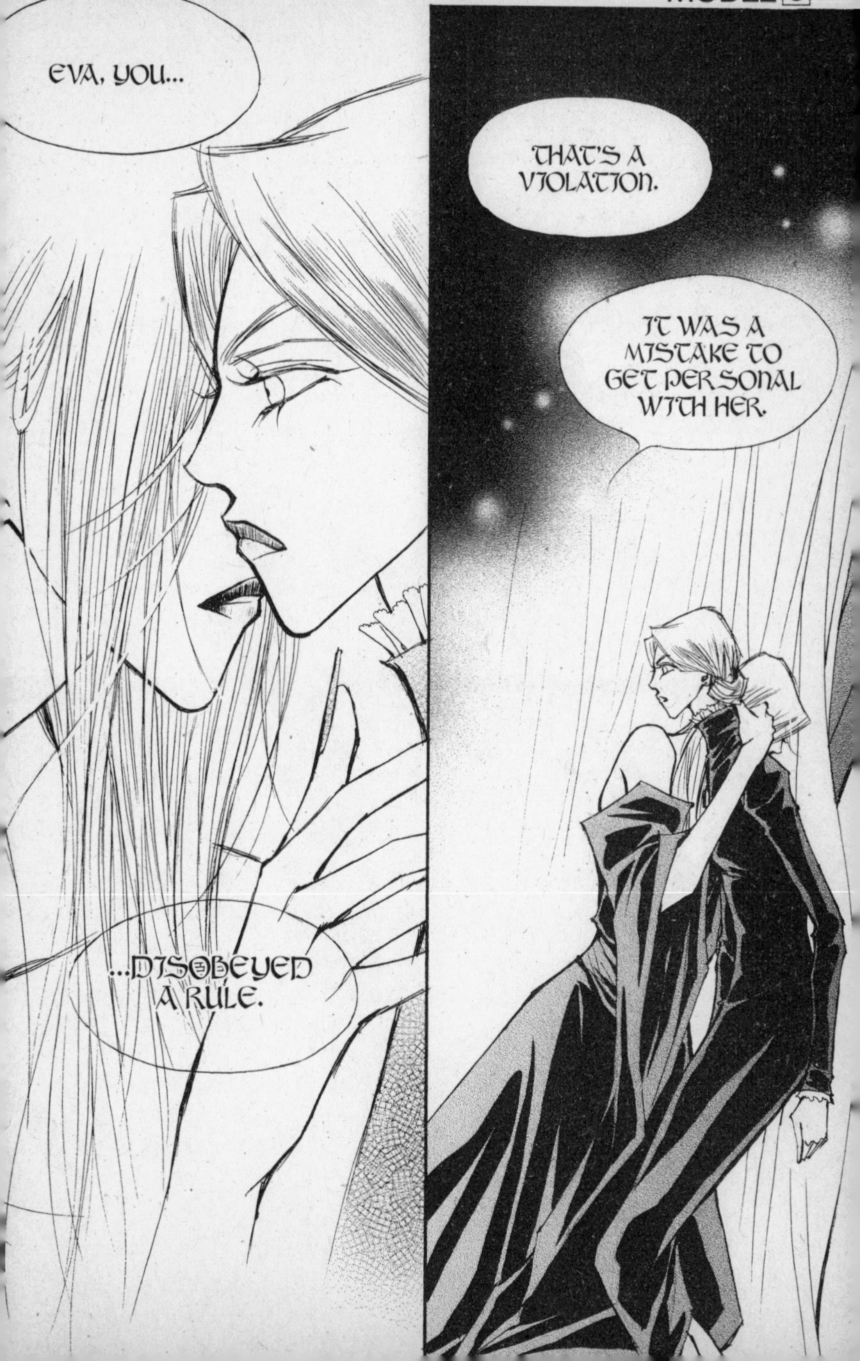
EVA, YOU...
...DISOBEYED A RULE.
THAT'S A VIOLATION.
IT WAS A MISTAKE TO GET PERSONAL WITH HER.

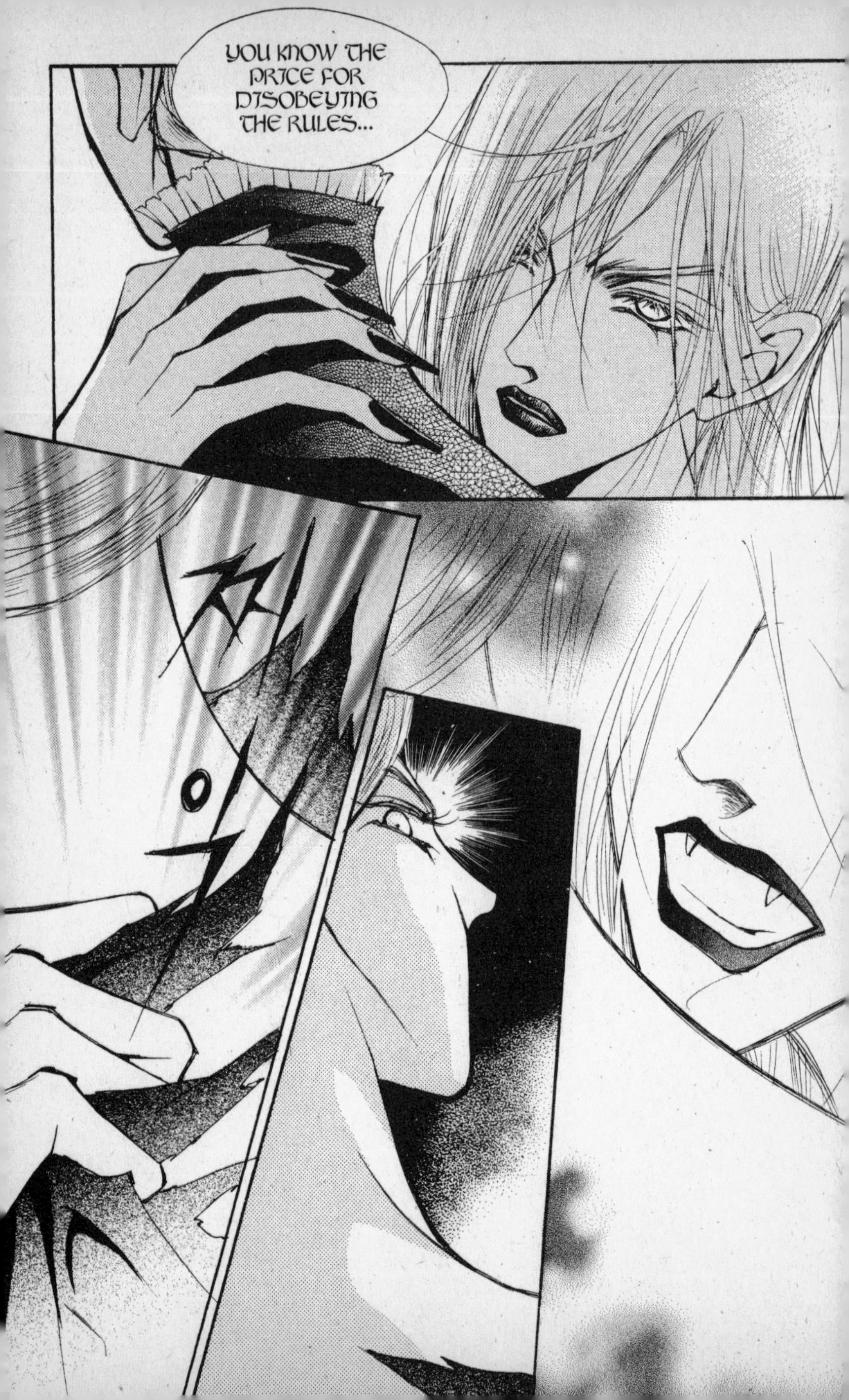
YOU KNOW THE PRICE FOR DISOBEYING THE RULES...

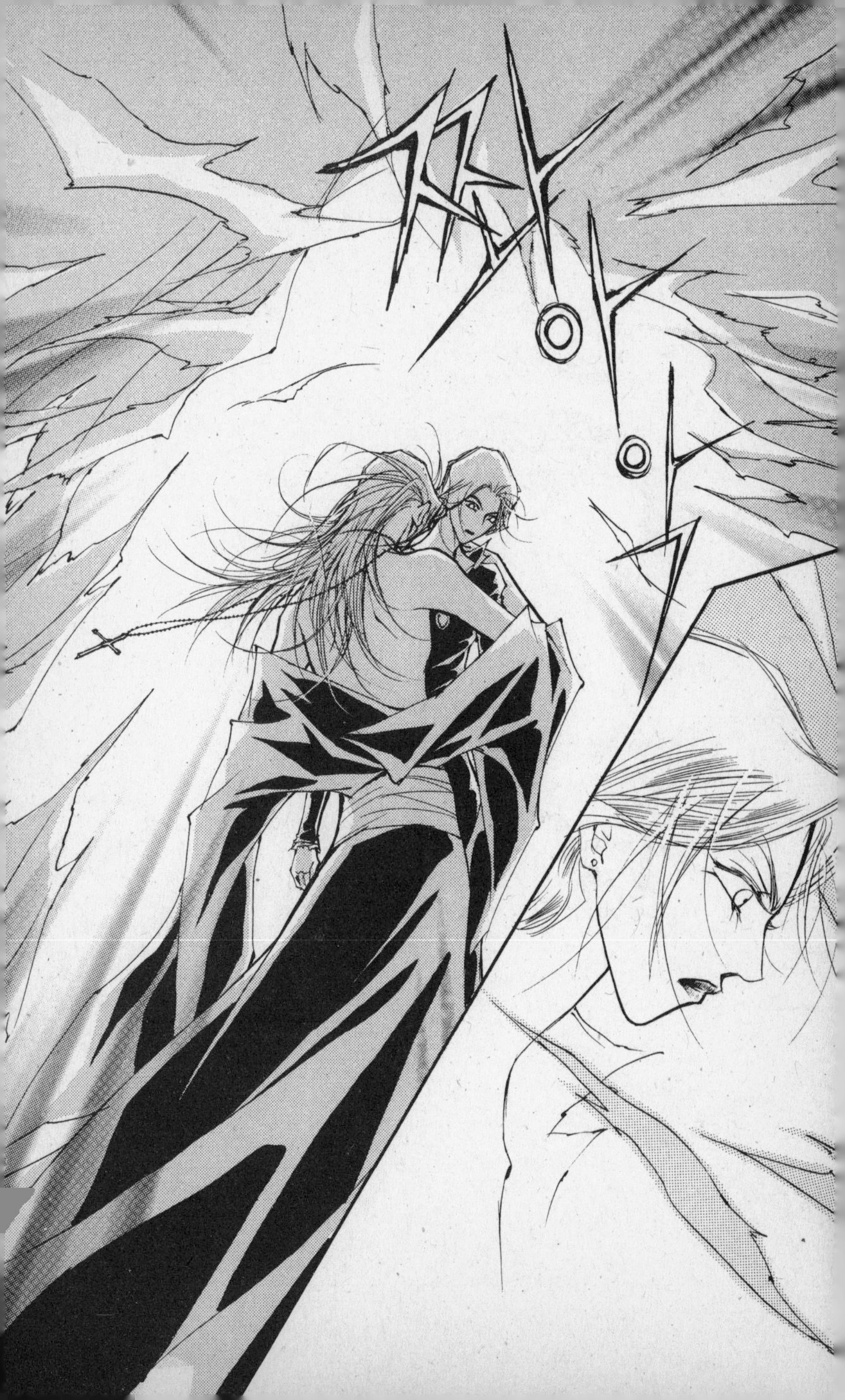

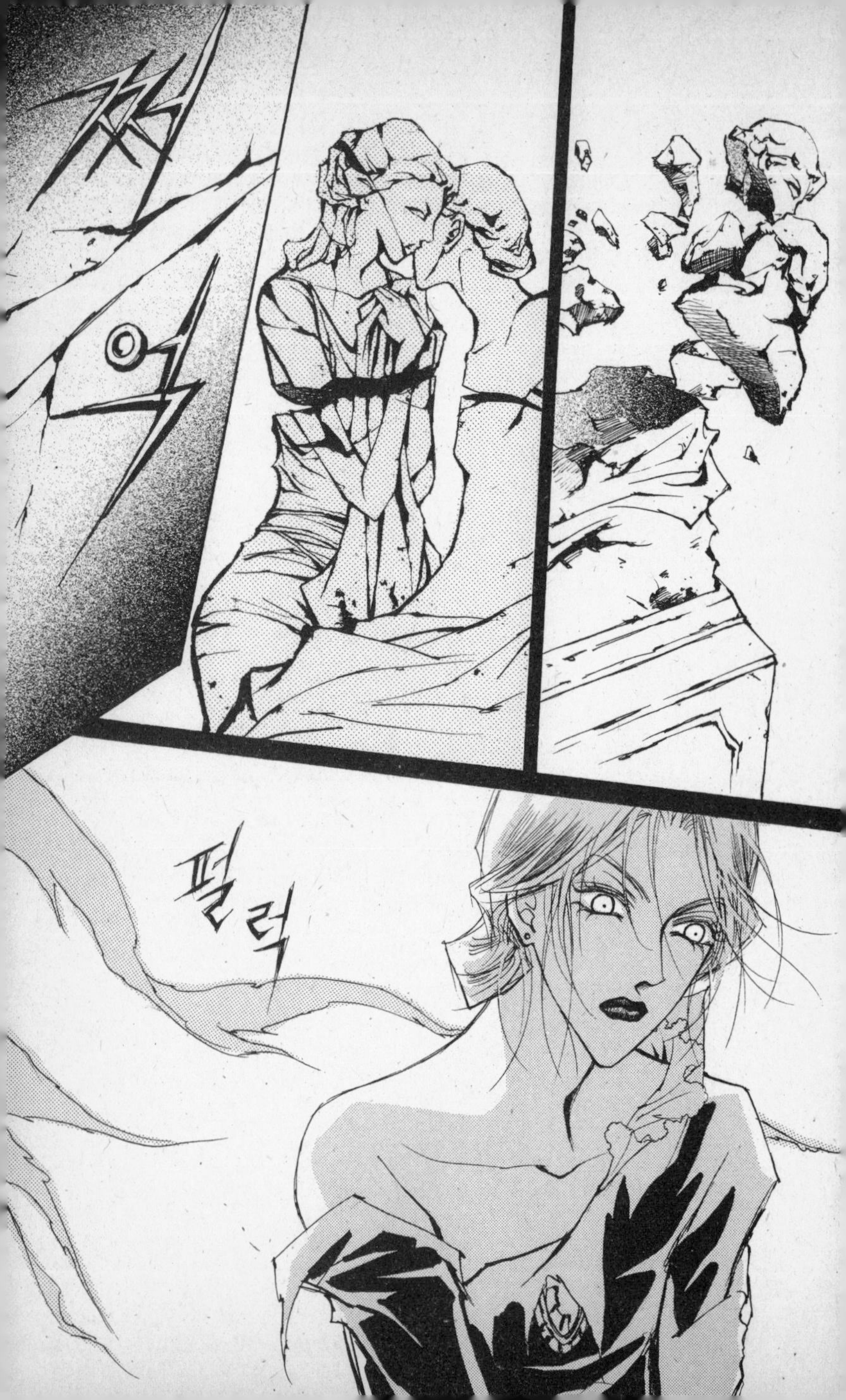
쩌억
펄럭

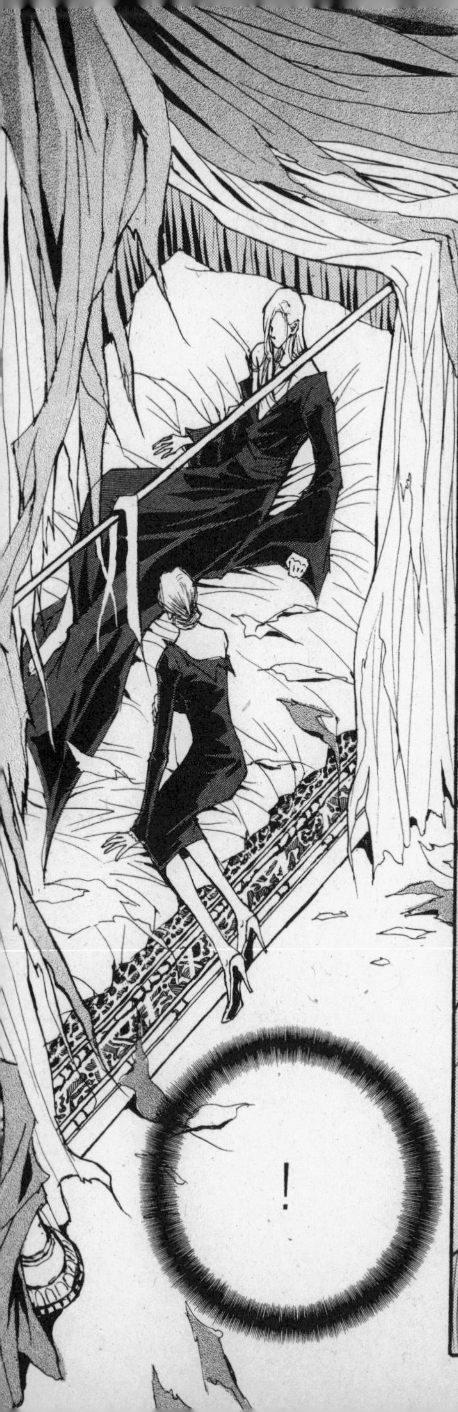
!
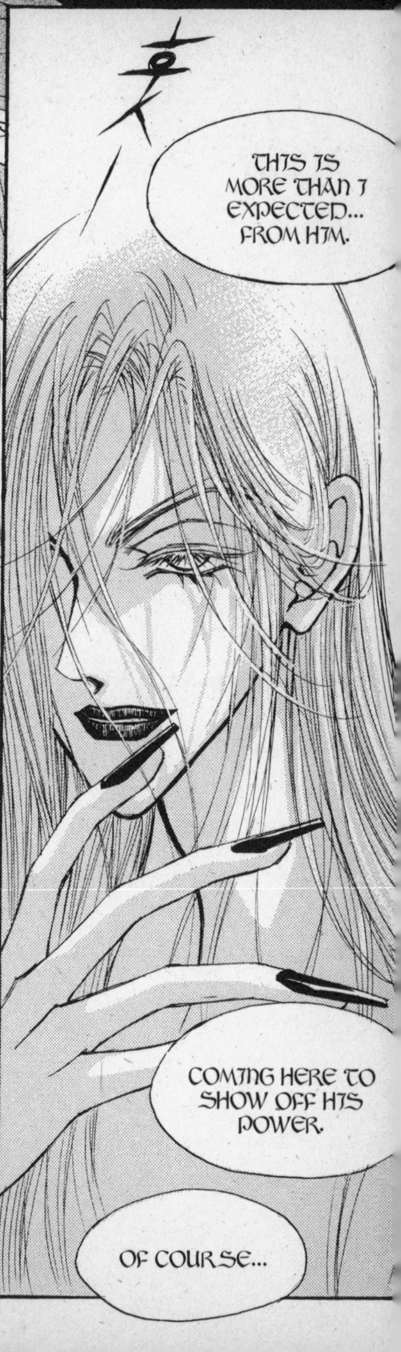
THIS IS MORE THAN I EXPECTED... FROM HIM.
COMING HERE TO SHOW OFF HIS POWER.
OF COURSE...

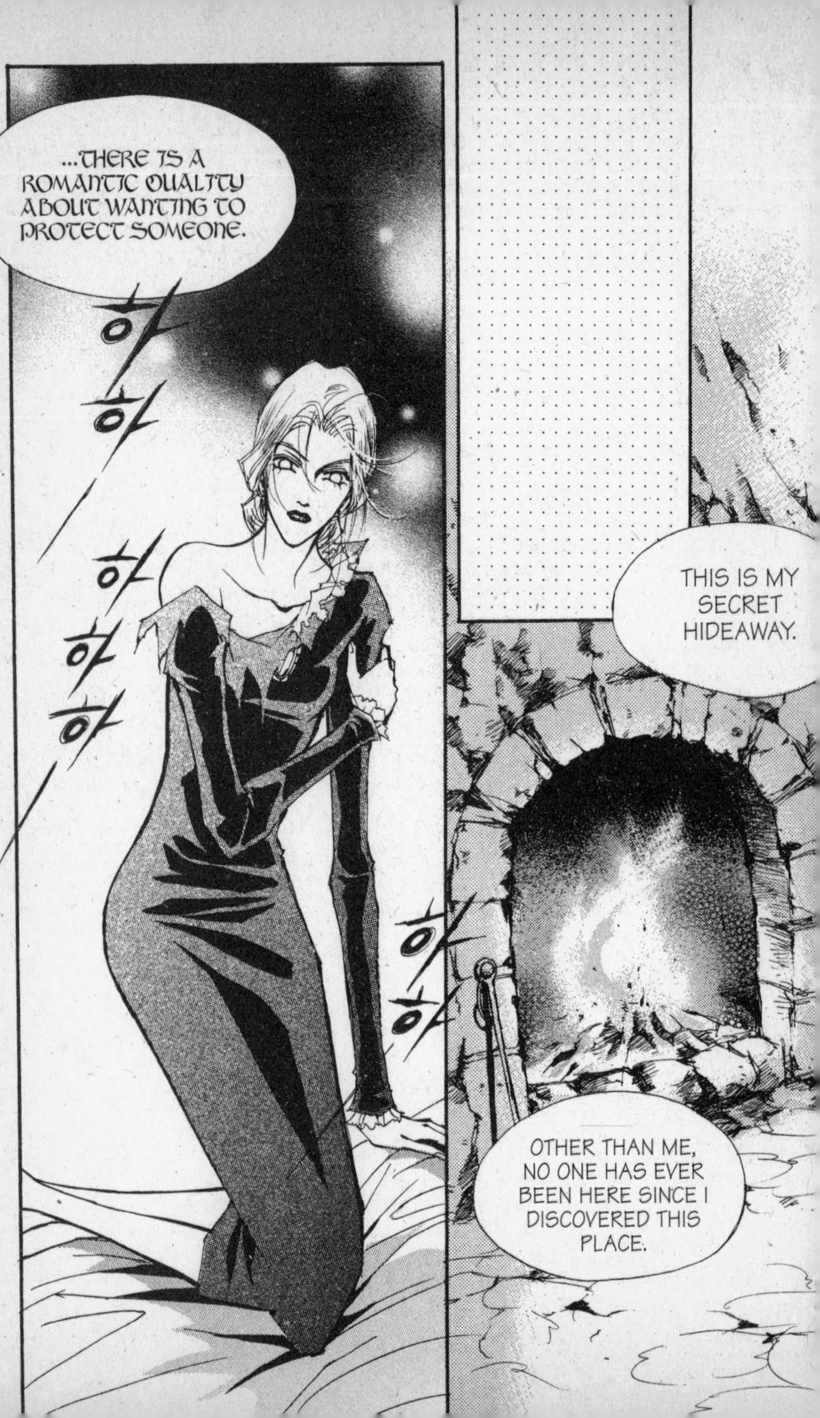
...THERE IS A ROMANTIC QUALITY ABOUT WANTING TO PROTECT SOMEONE.
하하
하하하
하하
THIS IS MY SECRET HIDEAWAY.
OTHER THAN ME, NO ONE HAS EVER BEEN HERE SINCE I DISCOVERED THIS PLACE.

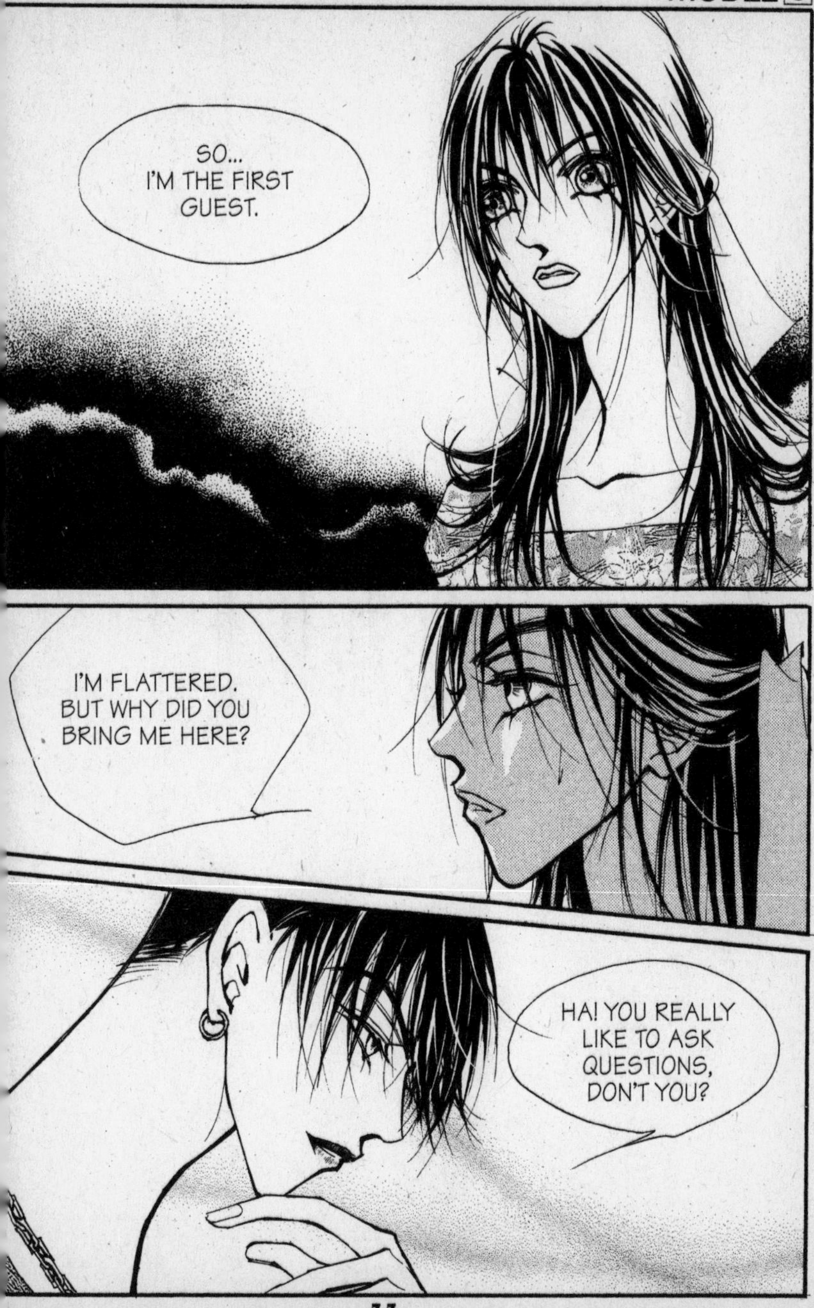
SO...
I'M THE FIRST GUEST.
I'M FLATTERED. BUT WHY DID YOU BRING ME HERE?
HA! YOU REALLY LIKE TO ASK QUESTIONS, DON'T YOU?

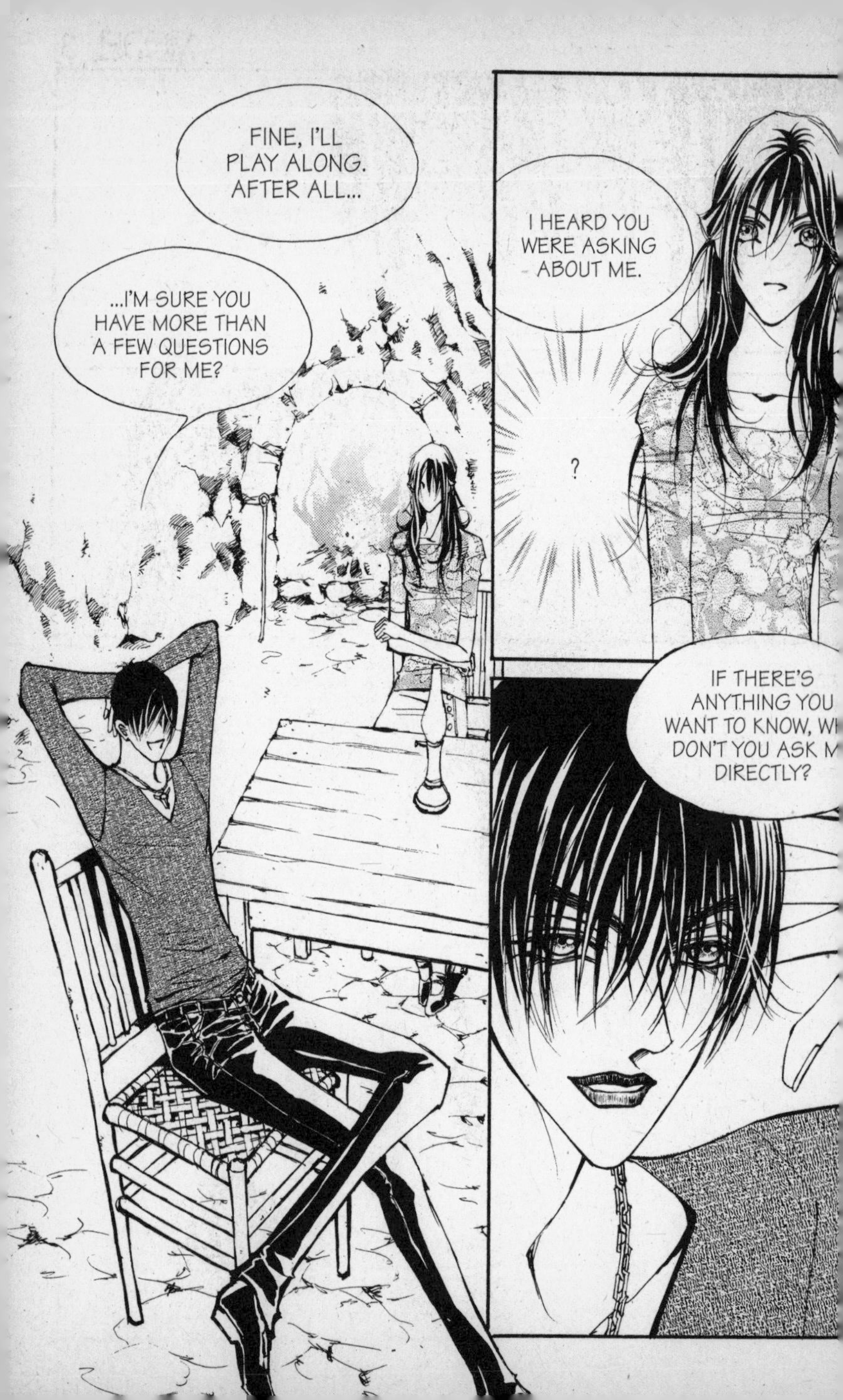
FINE, I'LL PLAY ALONG. AFTER ALL...
...I'M SURE YOU HAVE MORE THAN A FEW QUESTIONS FOR ME?
I HEARD YOU WERE ASKING ABOUT ME.
?
IF THERE'S ANYTHING YOU WANT TO KNOW, WH
DON'T YOU ASK M
DIRECTLY?

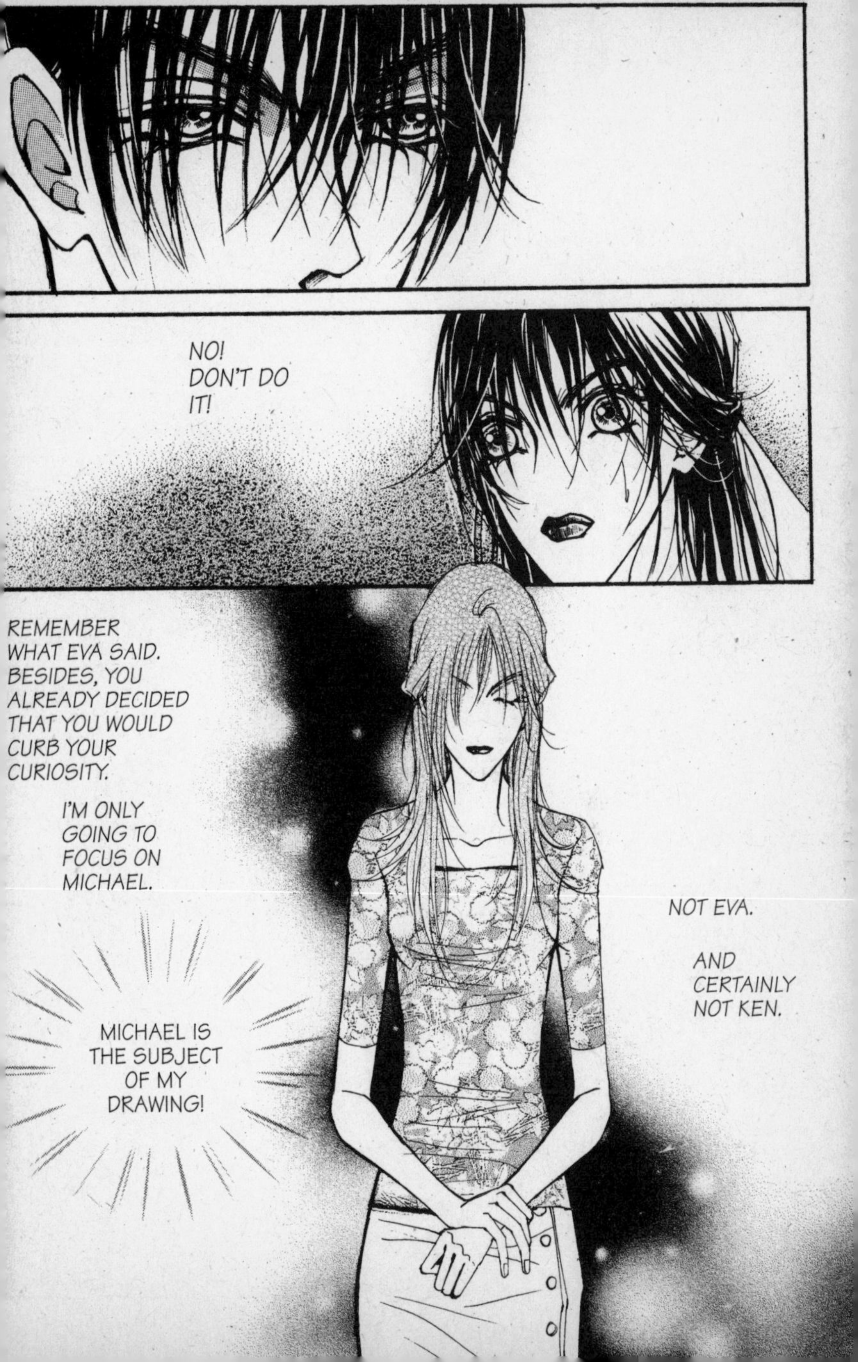
NO!
DON'T DO IT!
REMEMBER WHAT EVA SAID. BESIDES, YOU ALREADY DECIDED THAT YOU WOULD CURB YOUR CURIOSITY.
I'M ONLY GOING TO FOCUS ON MICHAEL.
NOT EVA.
AND CERTAINLY NOT KEN.
MICHAEL IS THE SUBJECT OF MY DRAWING!

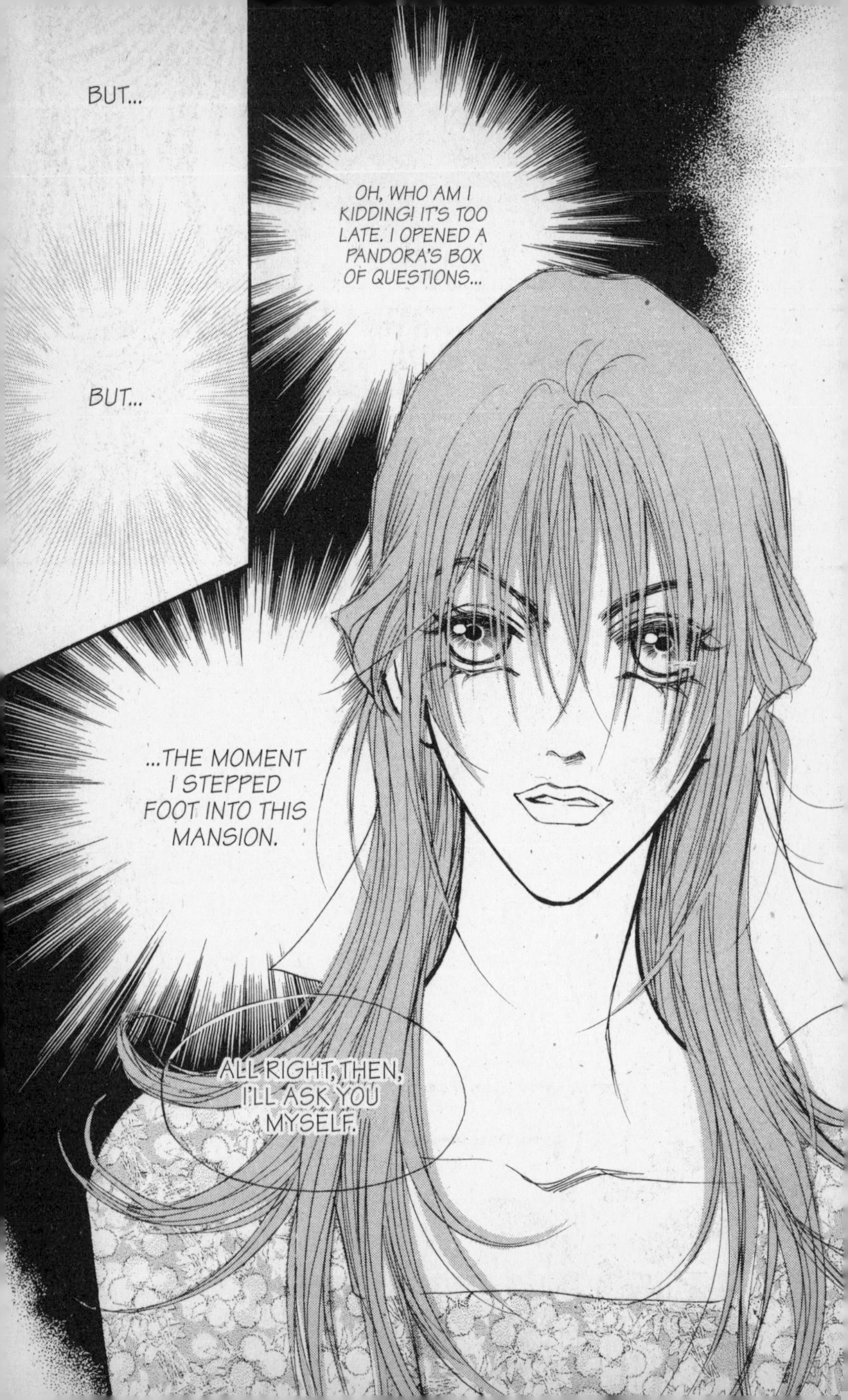
BUT...
BUT...
OH, WHO AM I KIDDING! IT'S TOO LATE. I OPENED A PANDORA'S BOX OF QUESTIONS...
...THE MOMENT I STEPPED FOOT INTO THIS MANSION.
ALL RIGHT, THEN, I'LL ASK YOU MYSELF.

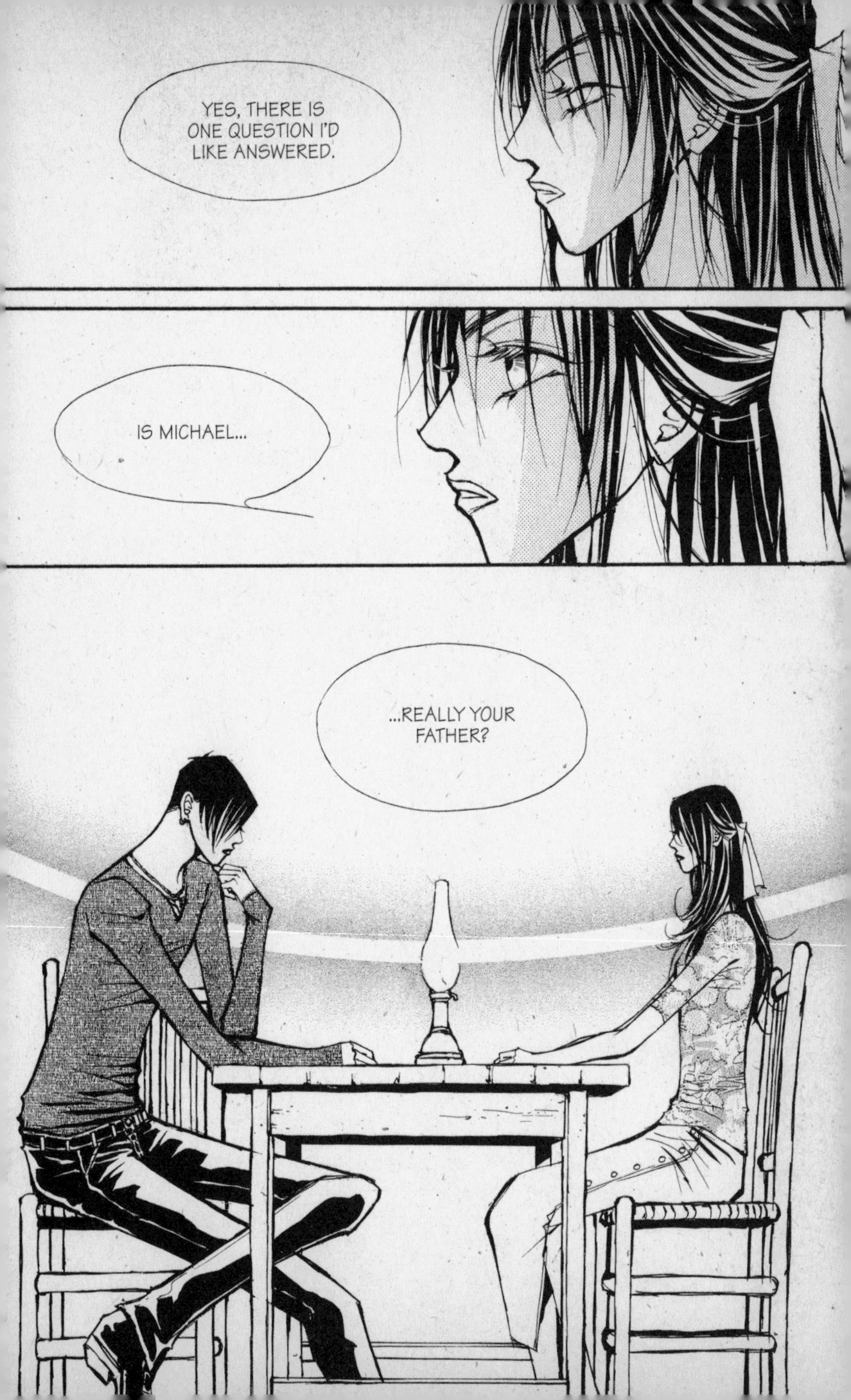
YES, THERE IS ONE QUESTION I'D LIKE ANSWERED.
IS MICHAEL...
...REALLY YOUR FATHER?

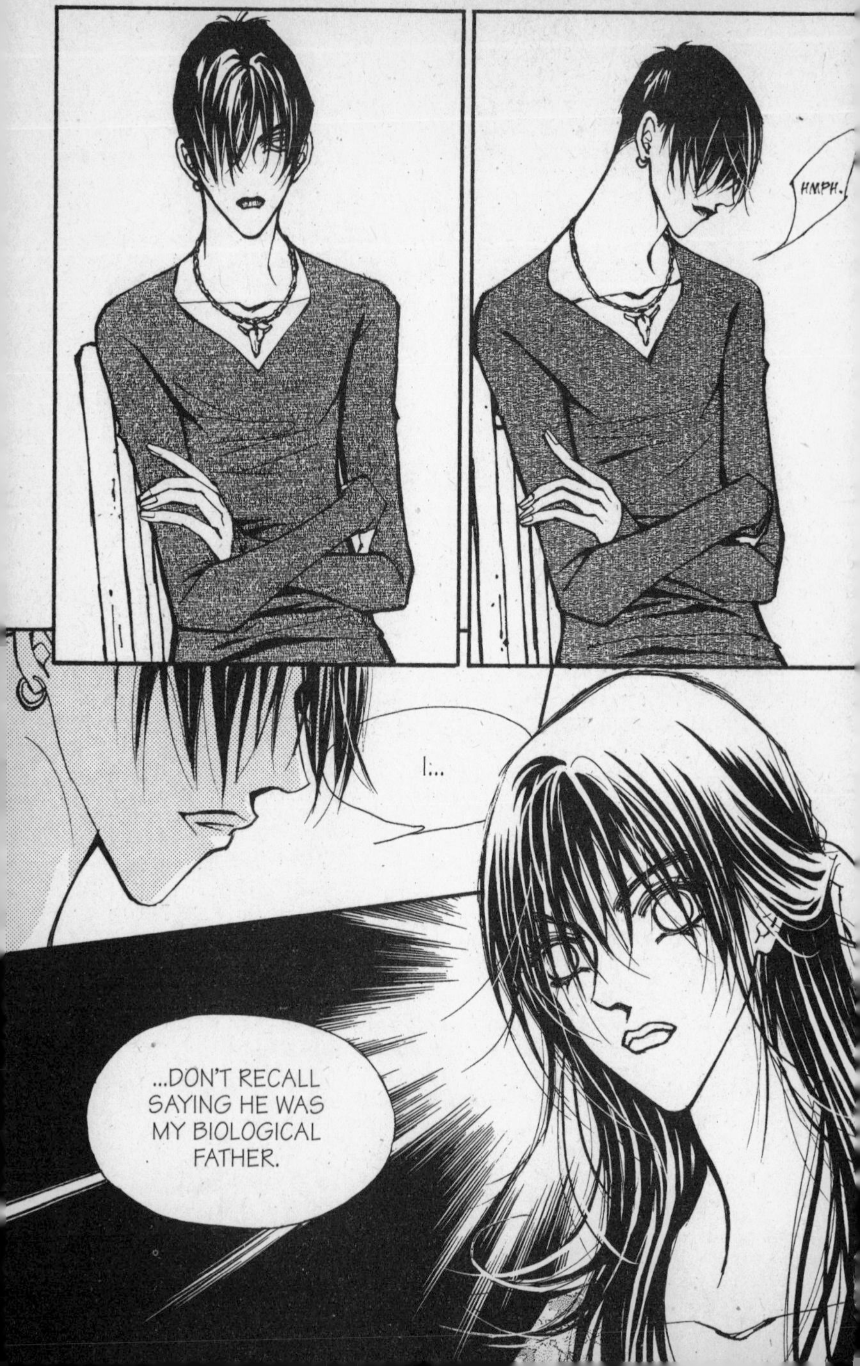
HMPH.
I...
...DON'T RECALL SAYING HE WAS MY BIOLOGICAL FATHER.

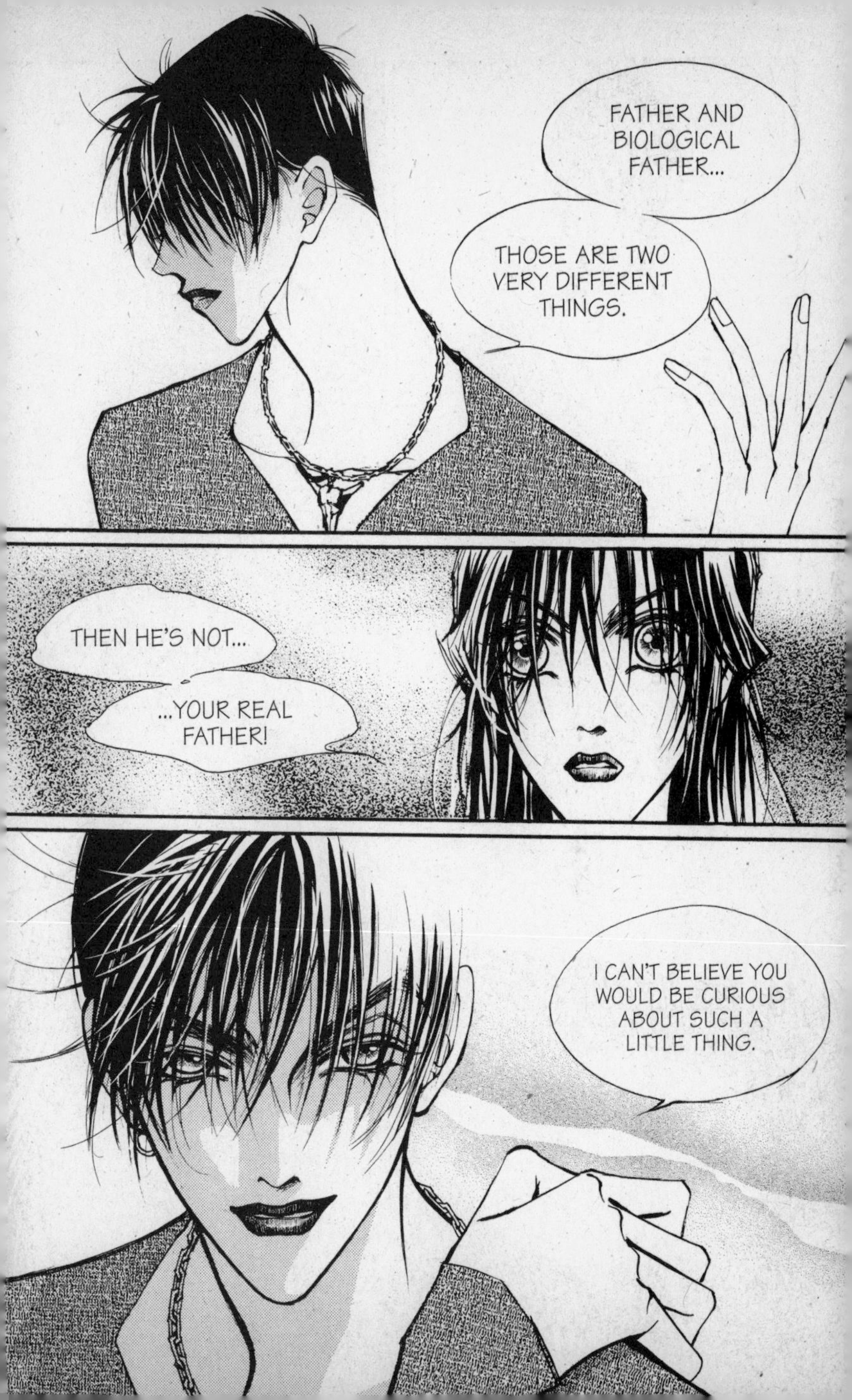
FATHER AND BIOLOGICAL FATHER...
THOSE ARE TWO VERY DIFFERENT THINGS.
THEN HE'S NOT...
...YOUR REAL FATHER!
I CAN'T BELIEVE YOU WOULD BE CURIOUS ABOUT SUCH A LITTLE THING.

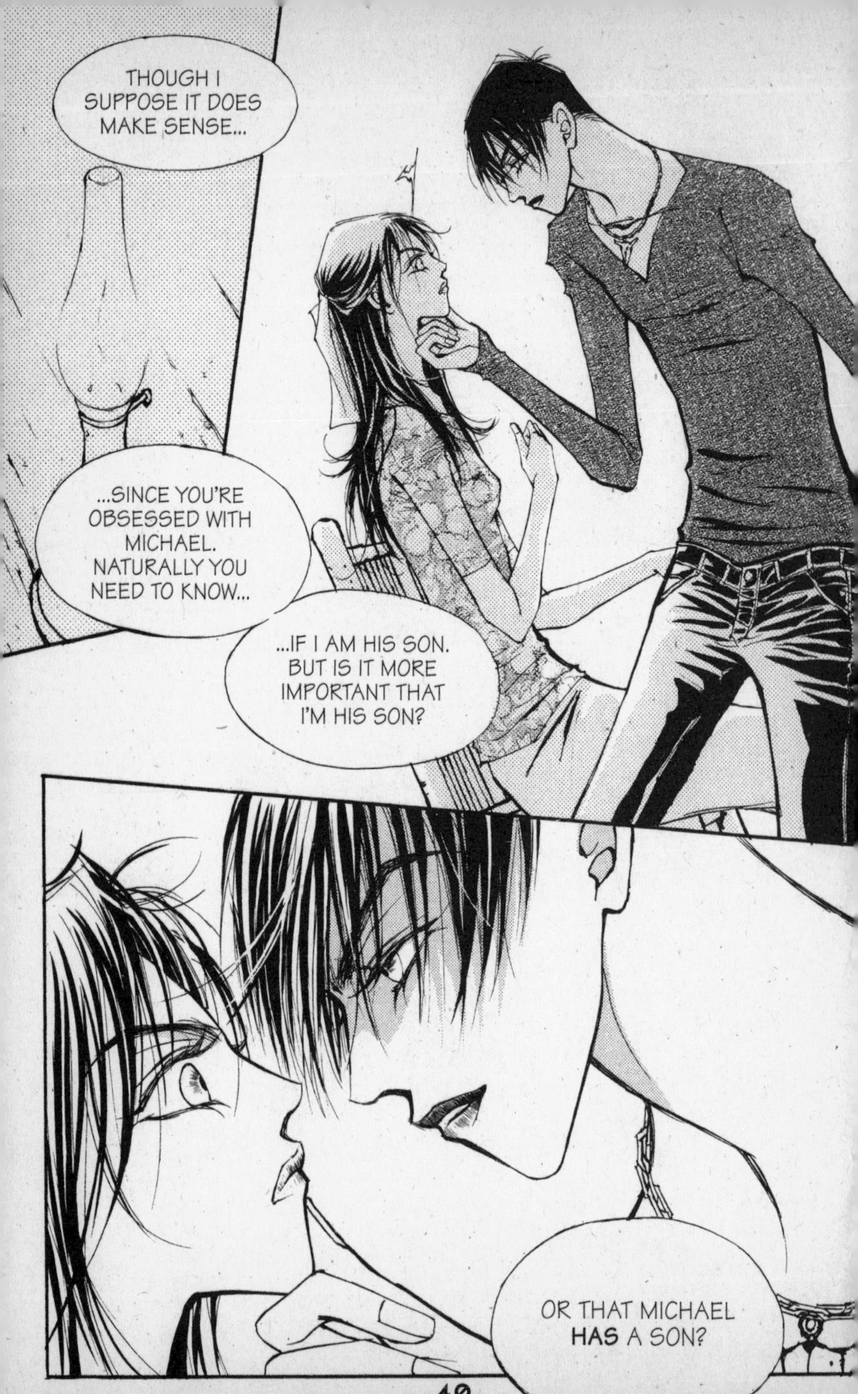
THOUGH I SUPPOSE IT DOES MAKE SENSE...
...SINCE YOU'RE OBSESSED WITH MICHAEL. NATURALLY YOU NEED TO KNOW...
...IF I AM HIS SON. BUT IS IT MORE IMPORTANT THAT I'M HIS SON?
OR THAT MICHAEL **HAS** A SON?

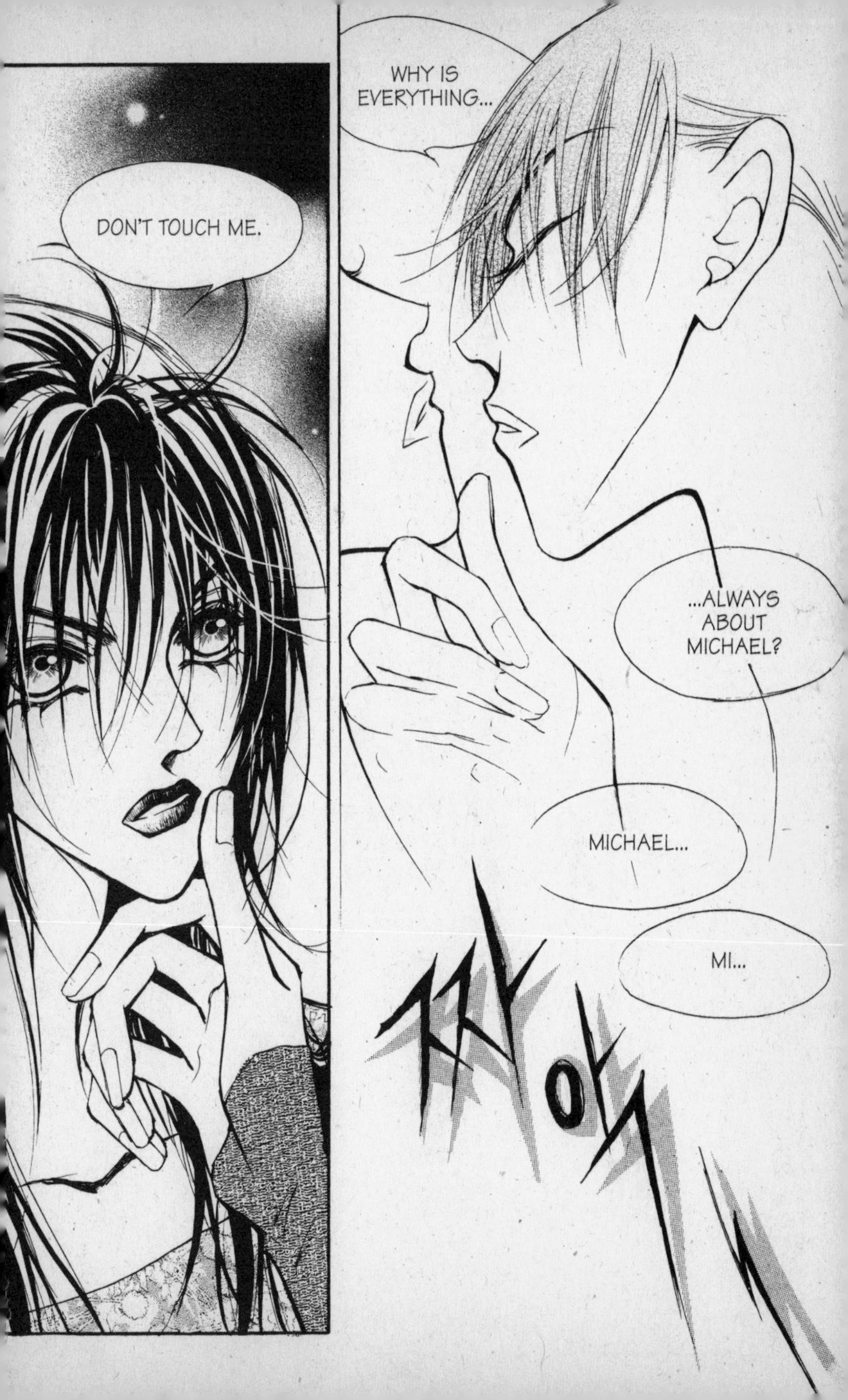
DON'T TOUCH ME.
WHY IS EVERYTHING...
...ALWAYS ABOUT MICHAEL?
MICHAEL...
MI...

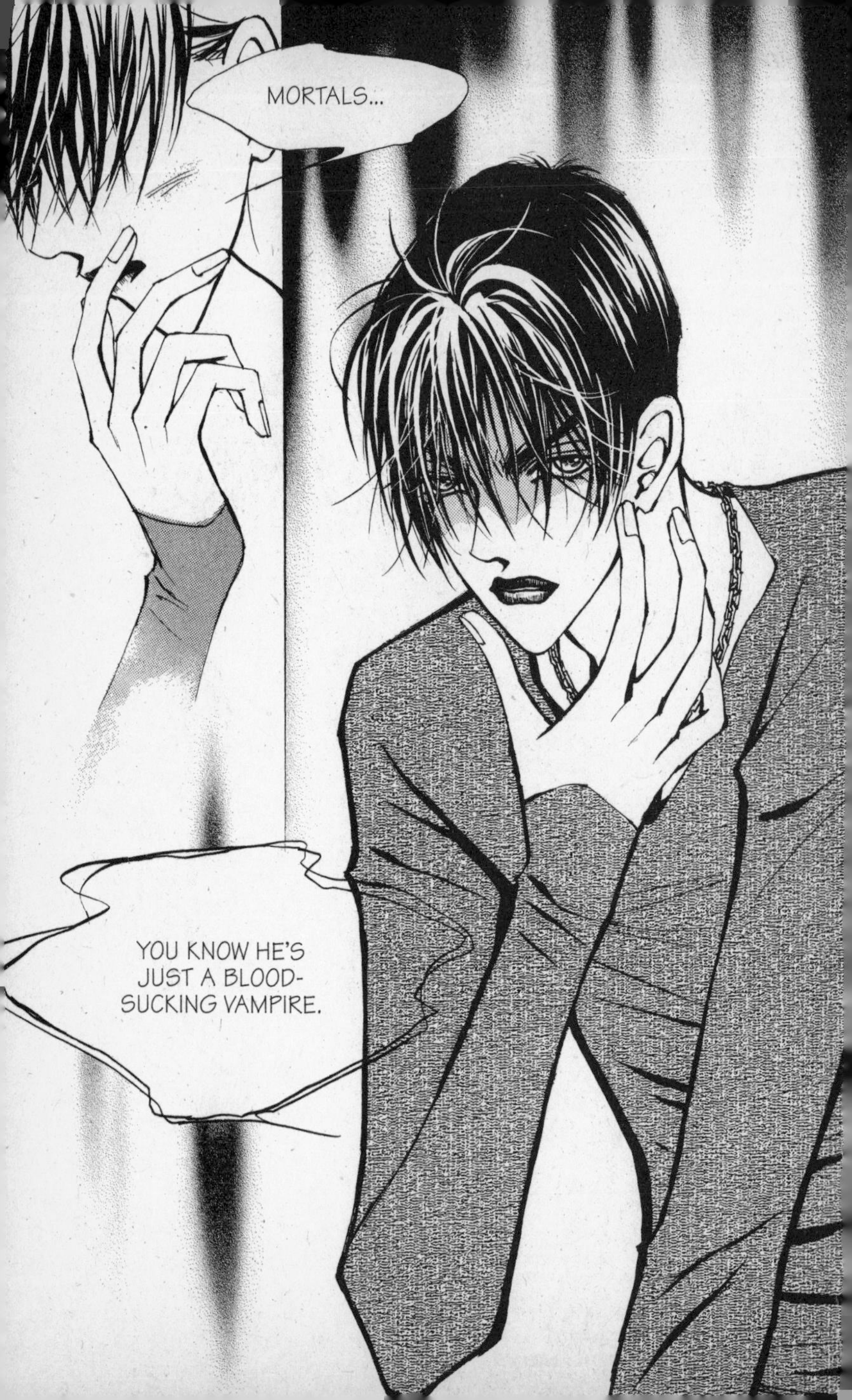
MORTALS...
YOU KNOW HE'S JUST A BLOOD-SUCKING VAMPIRE.

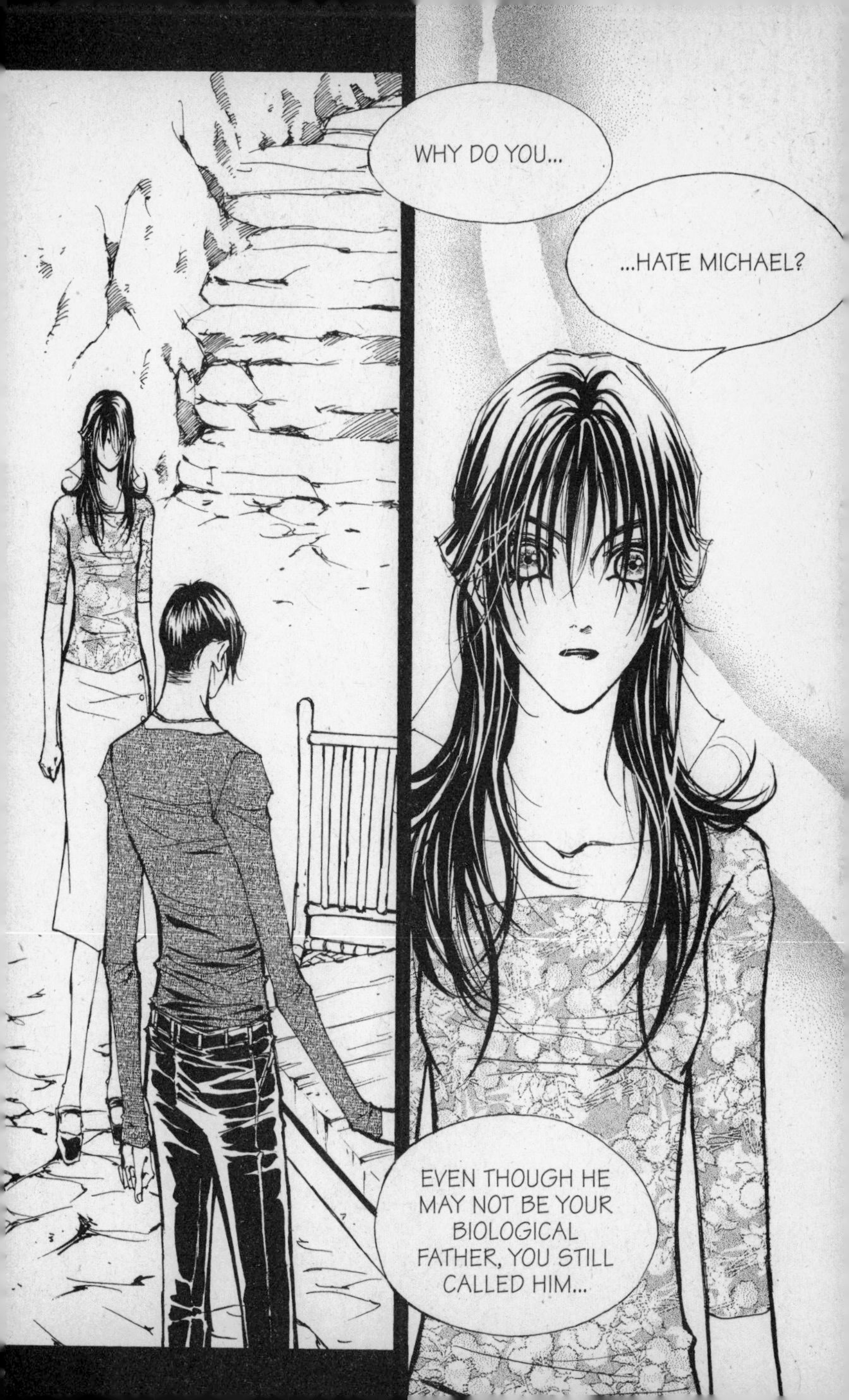
WHY DO YOU...
...HATE MICHAEL?
EVEN THOUGH HE MAY NOT BE YOUR BIOLOGICAL FATHER, YOU STILL CALLED HIM...

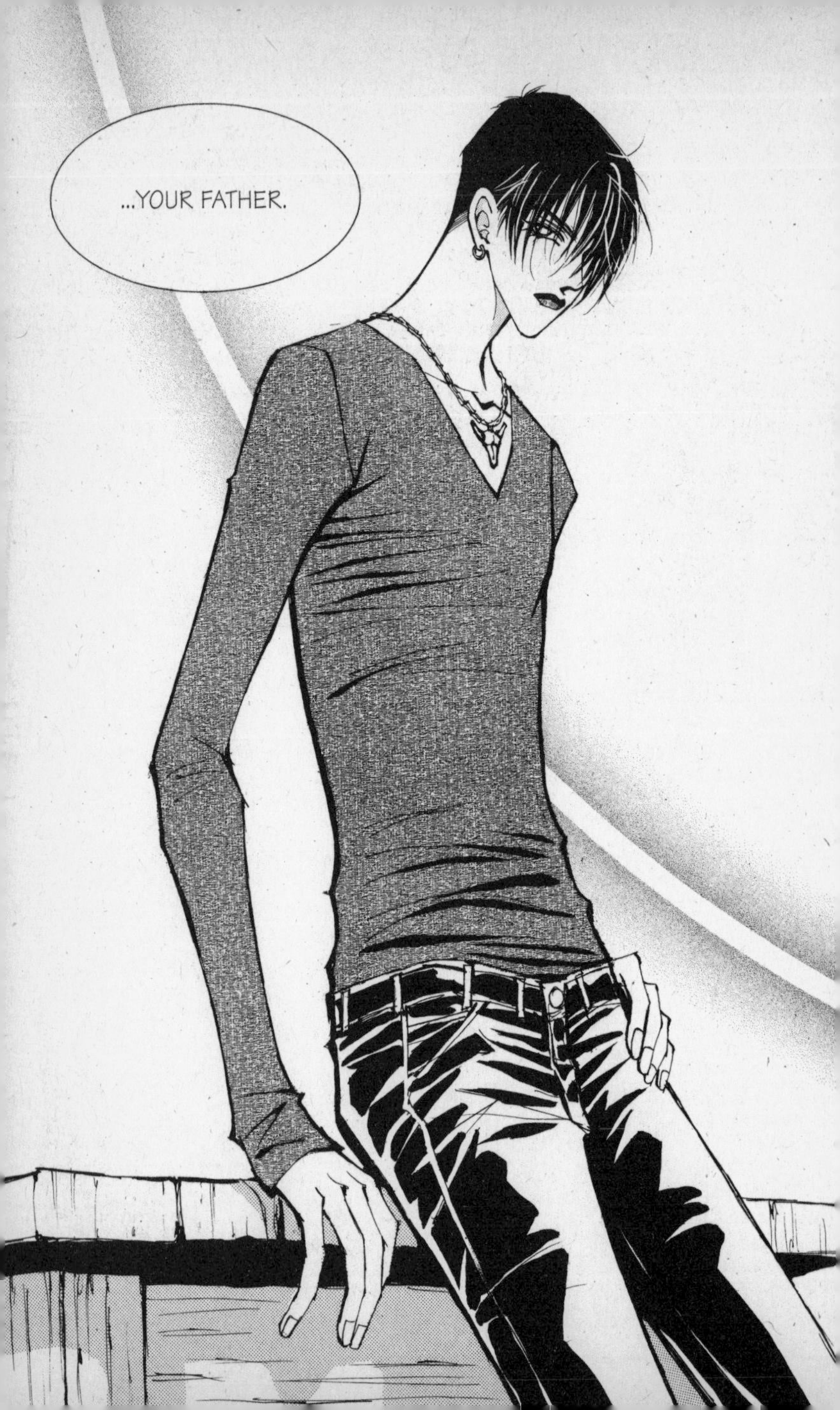
...YOUR FATHER.

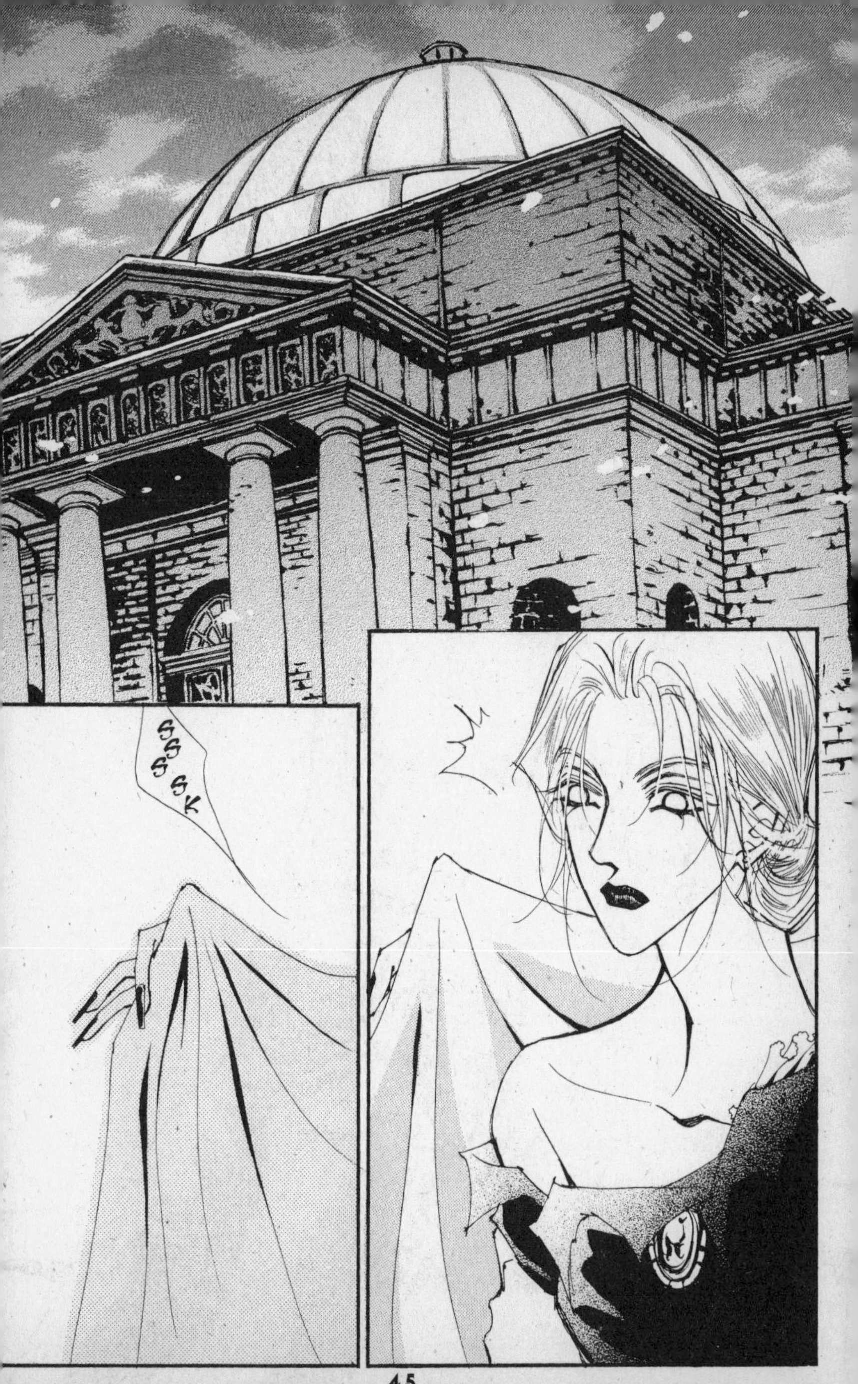
SSSSK

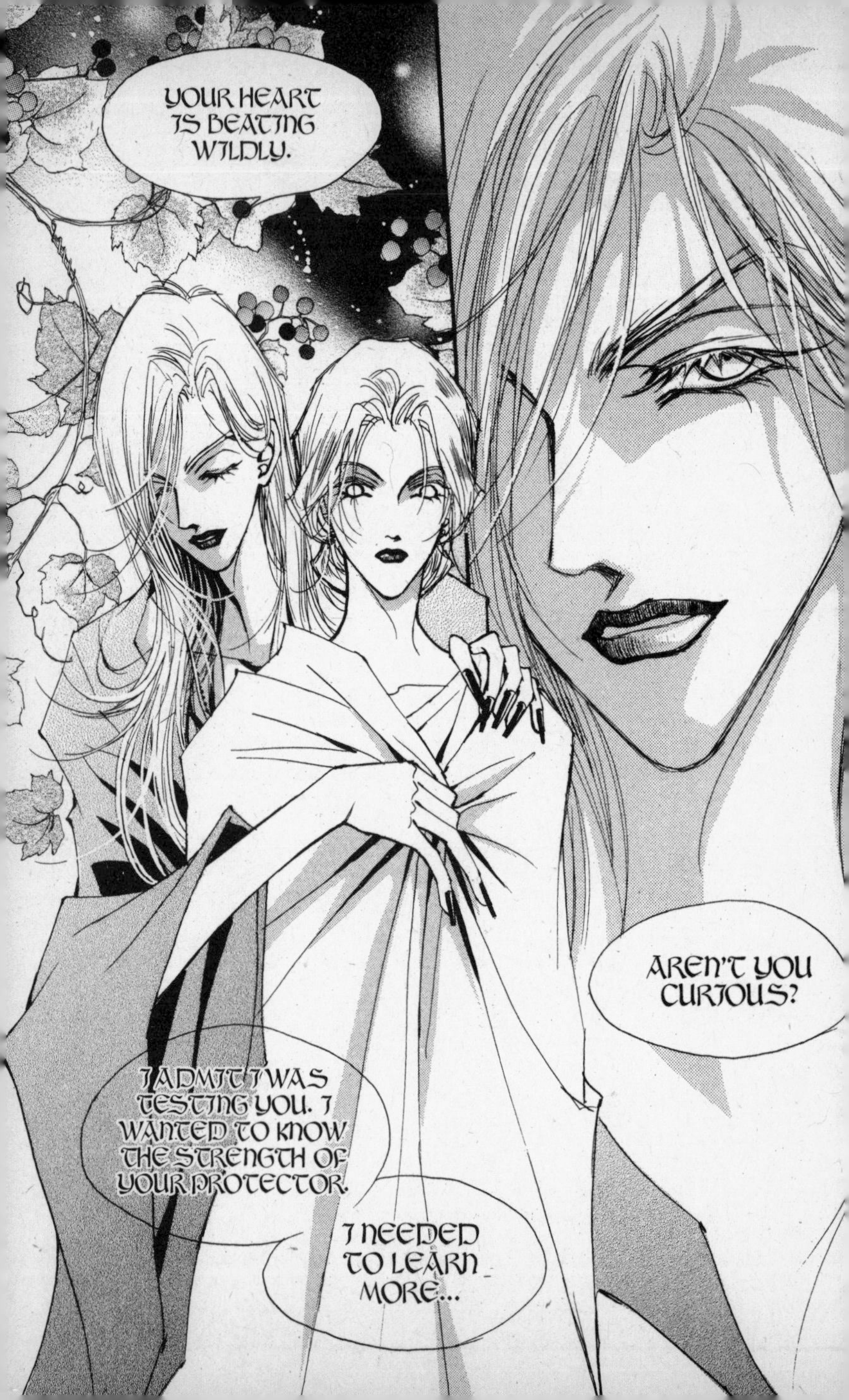
YOUR HEART IS BEATING WILDLY.
AREN'T YOU CURIOUS?
I ADMIT I WAS TESTING YOU. I WANTED TO KNOW THE STRENGTH OF YOUR PROTECTOR.
I NEEDED TO LEARN MORE...

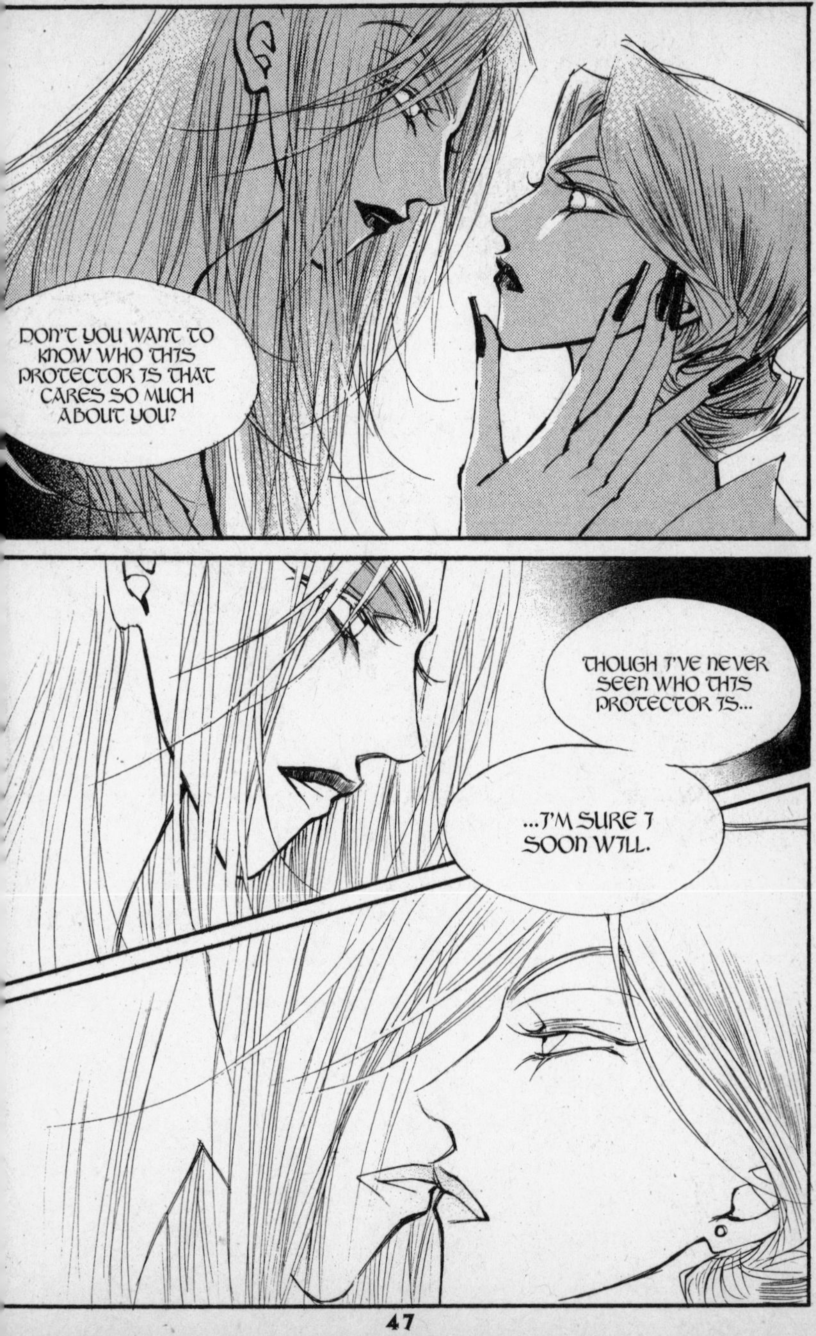
DON'T YOU WANT TO KNOW WHO THIS PROTECTOR IS THAT CARES SO MUCH ABOUT YOU?
THOUGH I'VE NEVER SEEN WHO THIS PROTECTOR IS...
...I'M SURE I SOON WILL.

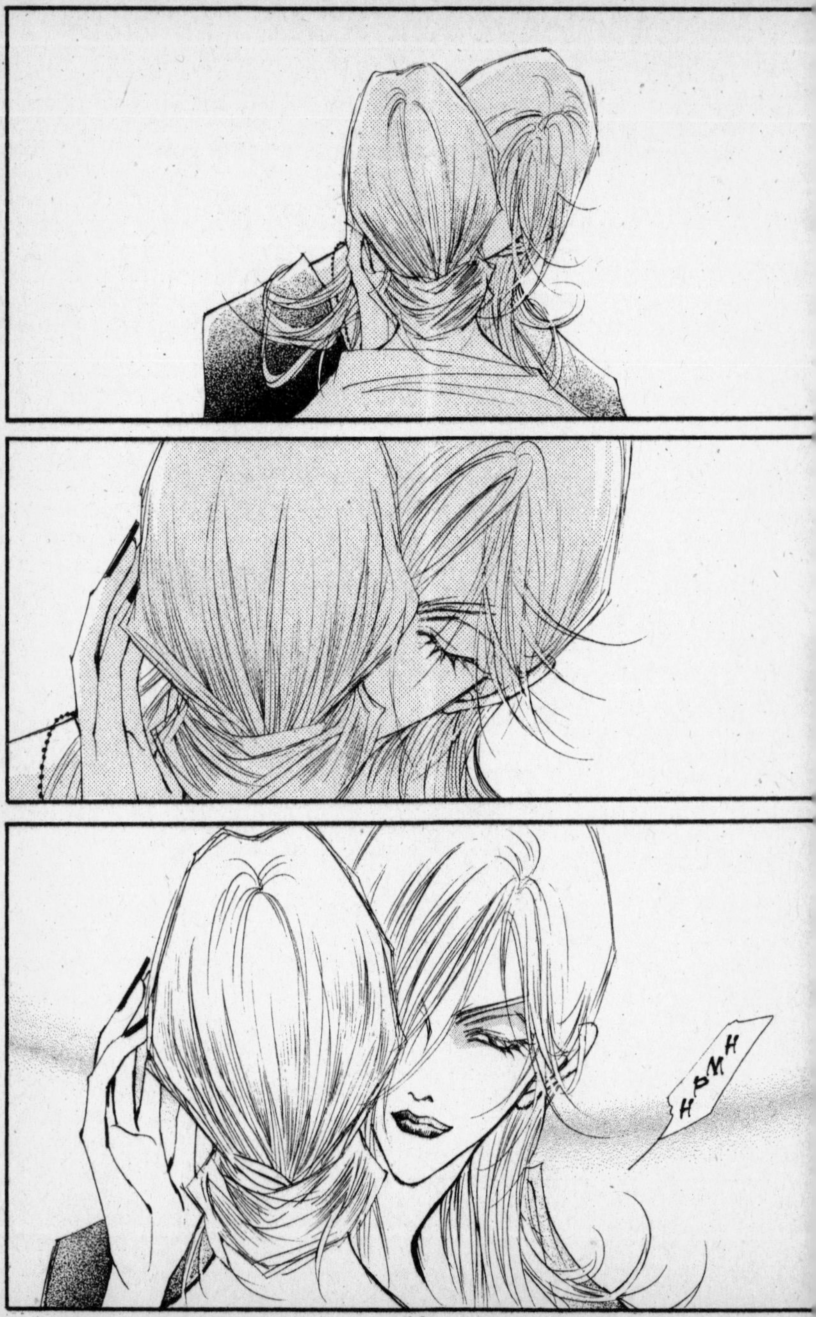
HMMH

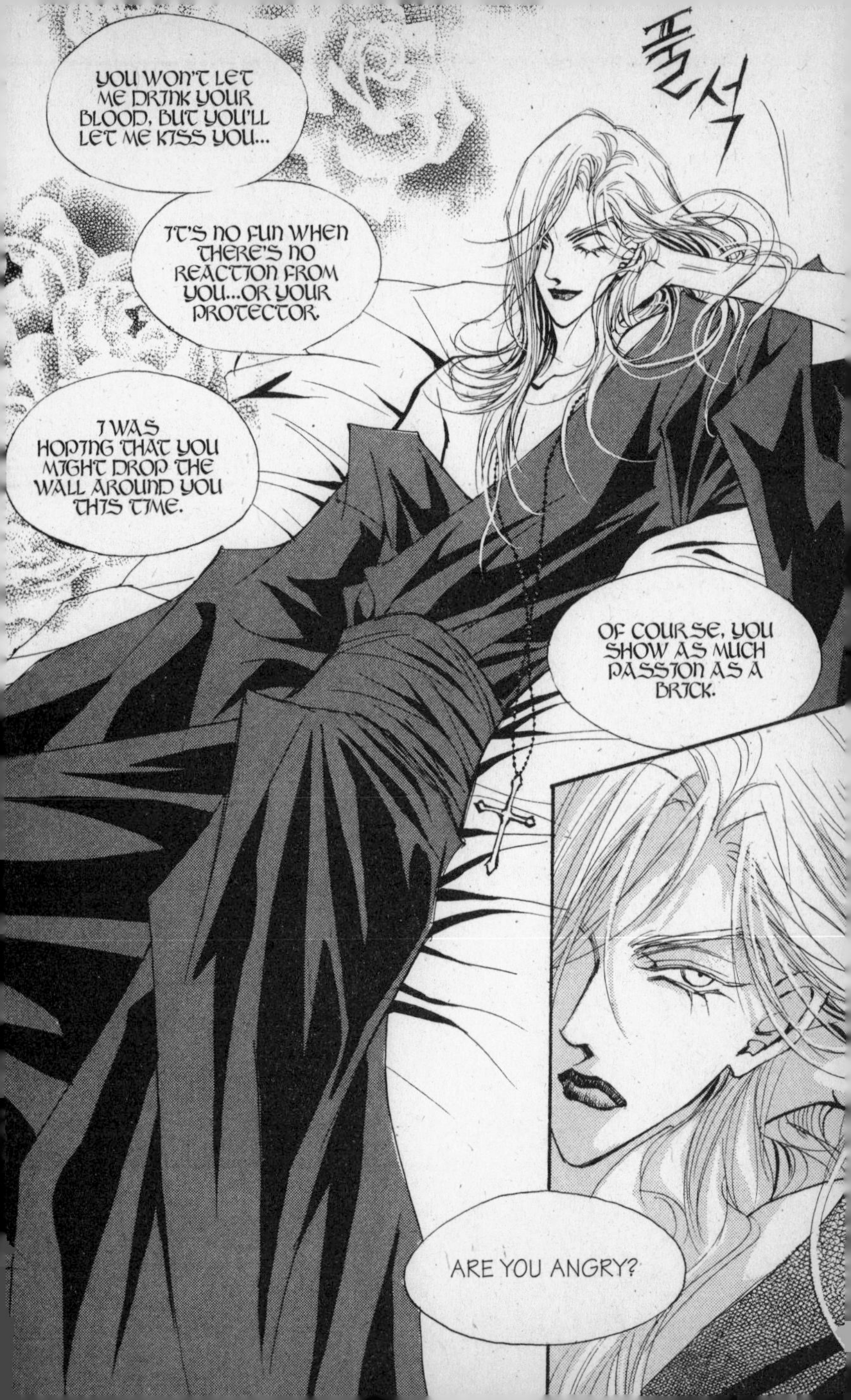

풀석
YOU WON'T LET ME DRINK YOUR BLOOD, BUT YOU'LL LET ME KISS YOU...
IT'S NO FUN WHEN THERE'S NO REACTION FROM YOU...OR YOUR PROTECTOR.
I WAS HOPING THAT YOU MIGHT DROP THE WALL AROUND YOU THIS TIME.
OF COURSE, YOU SHOW AS MUCH PASSION AS A BRICK.
ARE YOU ANGRY?

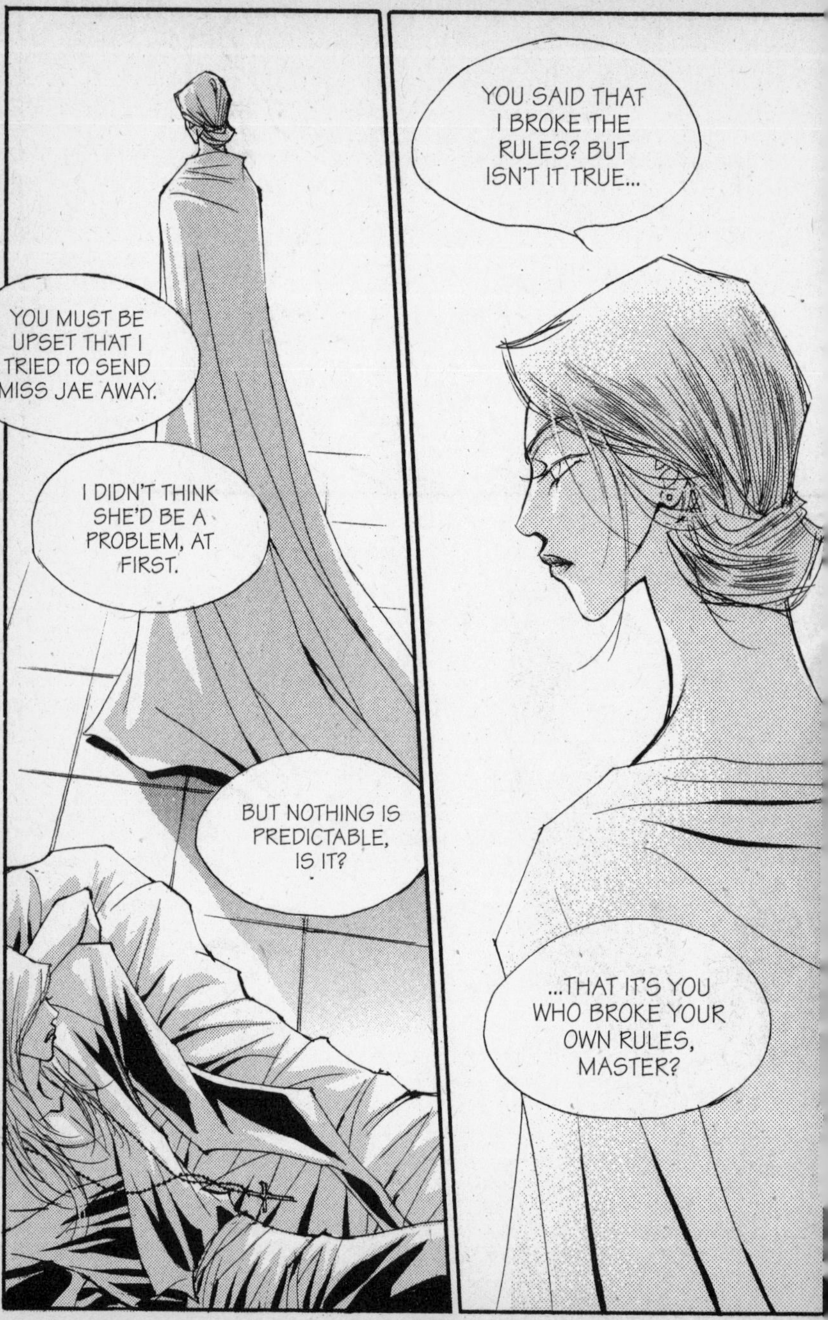
YOU MUST BE UPSET THAT I TRIED TO SEND MISS JAE AWAY.
I DIDN'T THINK SHE'D BE A PROBLEM, AT FIRST.
BUT NOTHING IS PREDICTABLE, IS IT?
YOU SAID THAT I BROKE THE RULES? BUT ISN'T IT TRUE...
...THAT IT'S YOU WHO BROKE YOUR OWN RULES, MASTER?

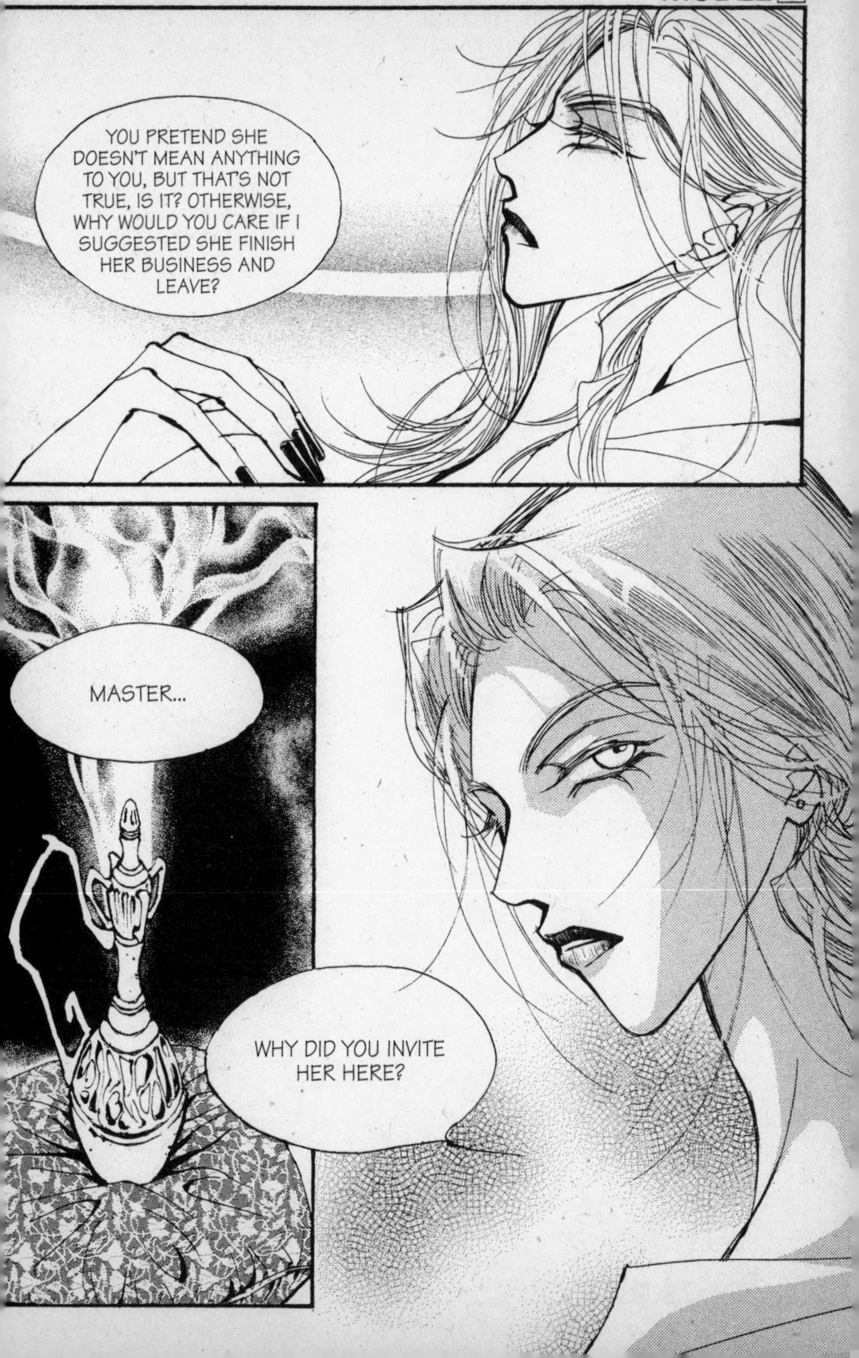
YOU PRETEND SHE DOESN'T MEAN ANYTHING TO YOU, BUT THAT'S NOT TRUE, IS IT? OTHERWISE, WHY WOULD YOU CARE IF I SUGGESTED SHE FINISH HER BUSINESS AND LEAVE?
MASTER...
WHY DID YOU INVITE HER HERE?

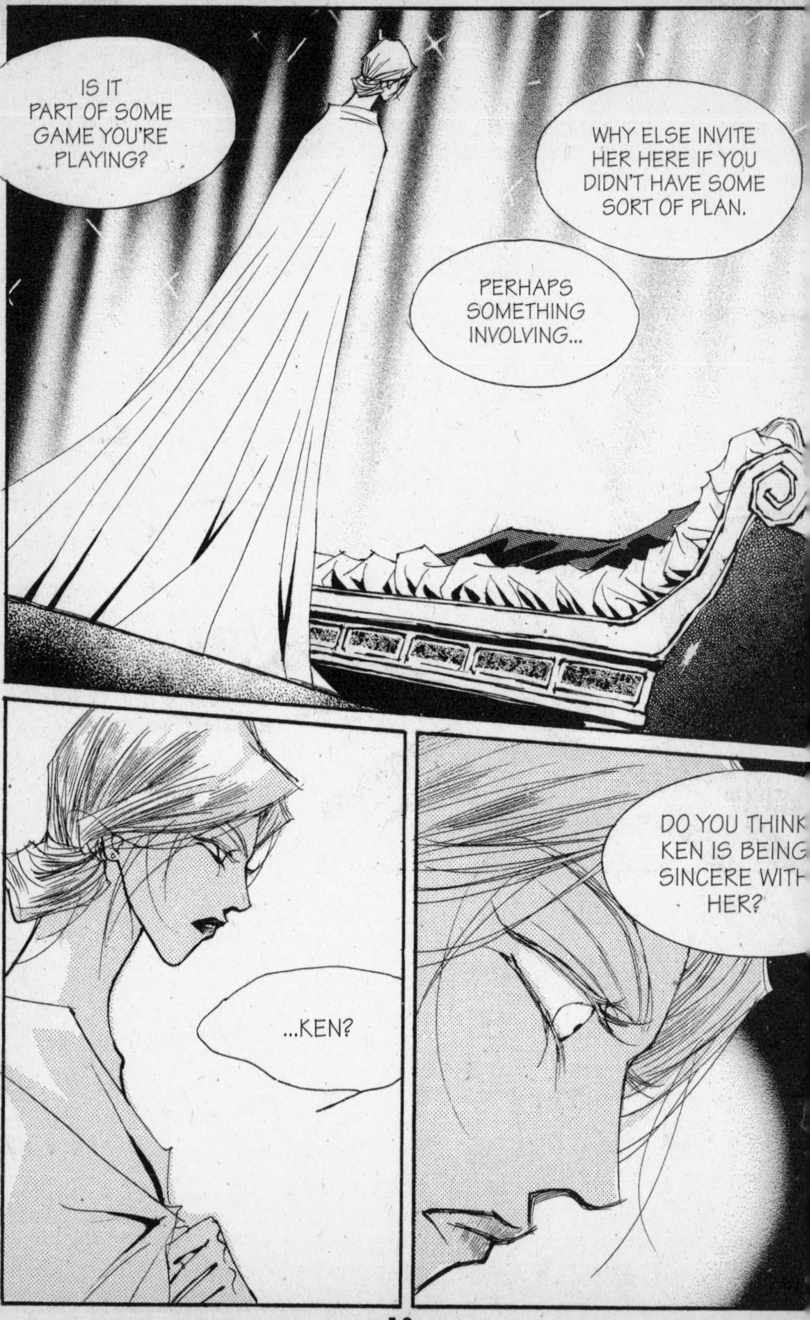
IS IT PART OF SOME GAME YOU'RE PLAYING?
WHY ELSE INVITE HER HERE IF YOU DIDN'T HAVE SOME SORT OF PLAN.
PERHAPS SOMETHING INVOLVING...
...KEN?
DO YOU THINK KEN IS BEING SINCERE WITH HER?

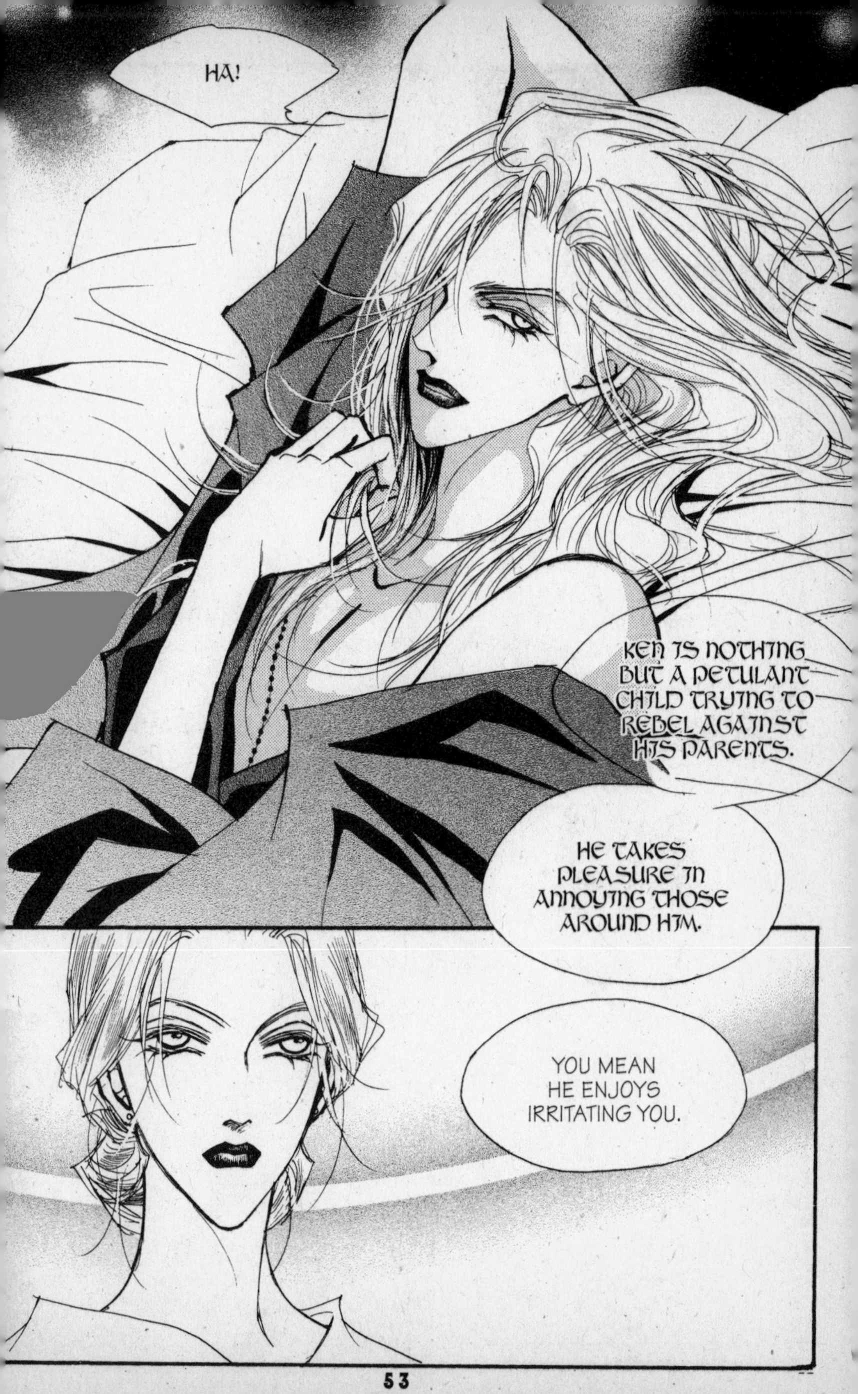
HA!
KEN IS NOTHING BUT A PETULANT CHILD TRYING TO REBEL AGAINST HIS PARENTS.
HE TAKES PLEASURE IN ANNOYING THOSE AROUND HIM.
YOU MEAN HE ENJOYS IRRITATING YOU.

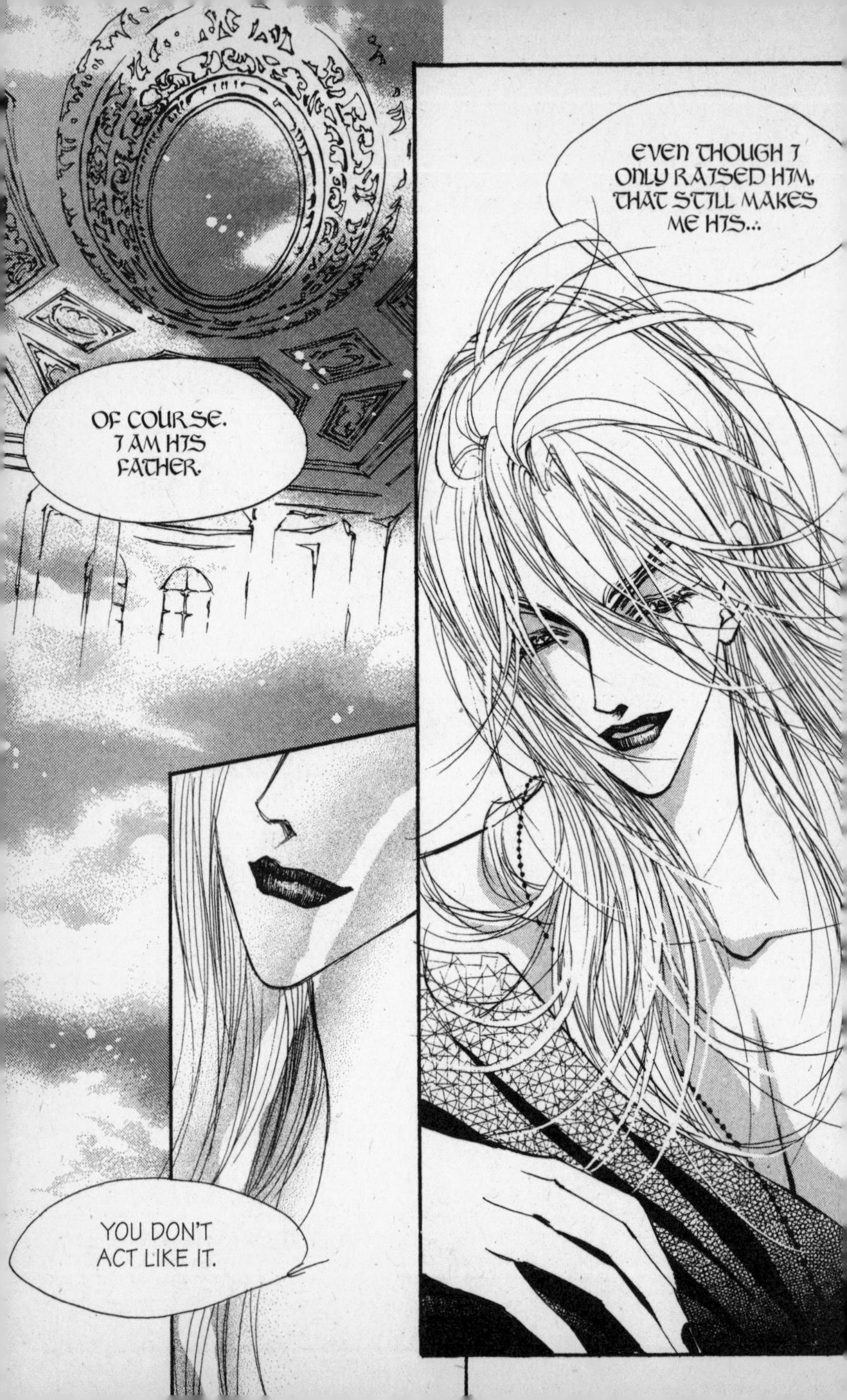
OF COURSE. I AM HIS FATHER.
YOU DON'T ACT LIKE IT.
EVEN THOUGH I ONLY RAISED HIM, THAT STILL MAKES ME HIS...

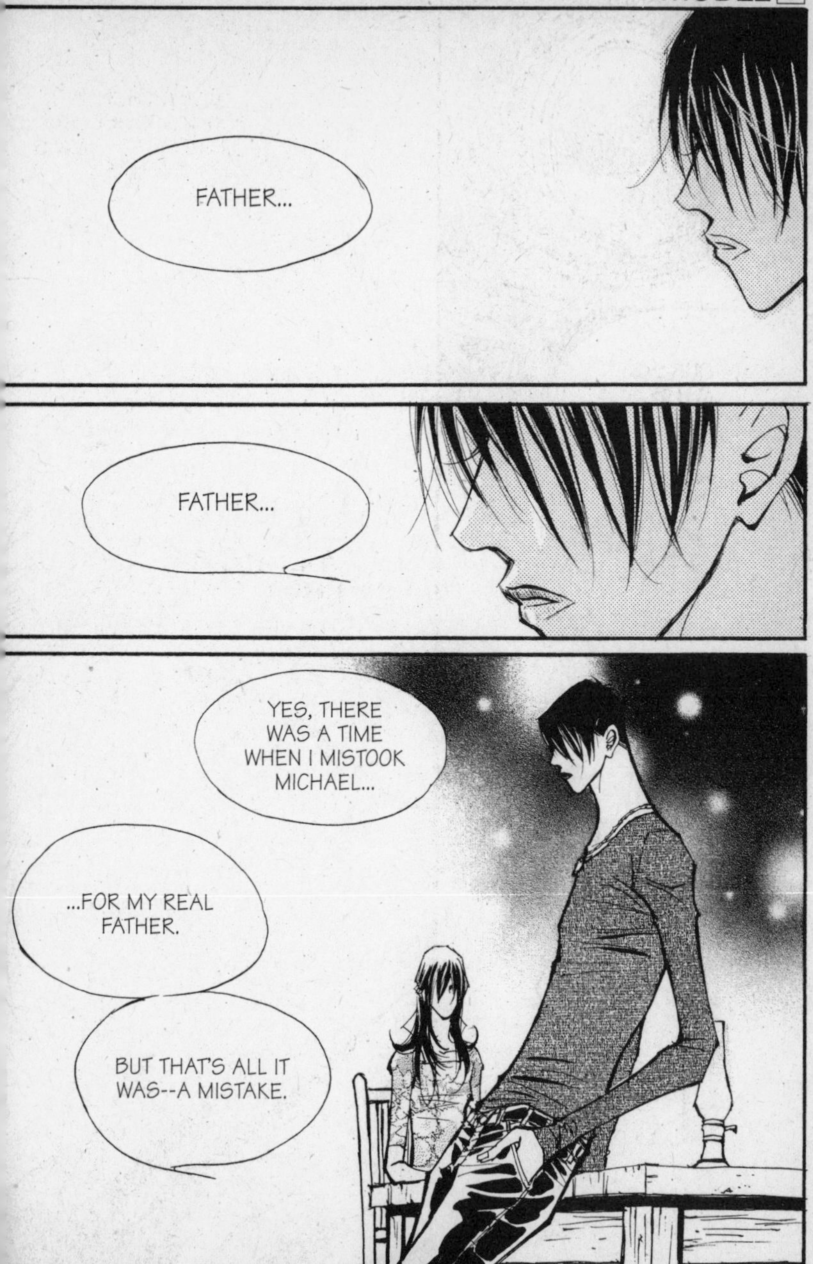
FATHER...
FATHER...
YES, THERE WAS A TIME WHEN I MISTOOK MICHAEL...
...FOR MY REAL FATHER.
BUT THAT'S ALL IT WAS--A MISTAKE.

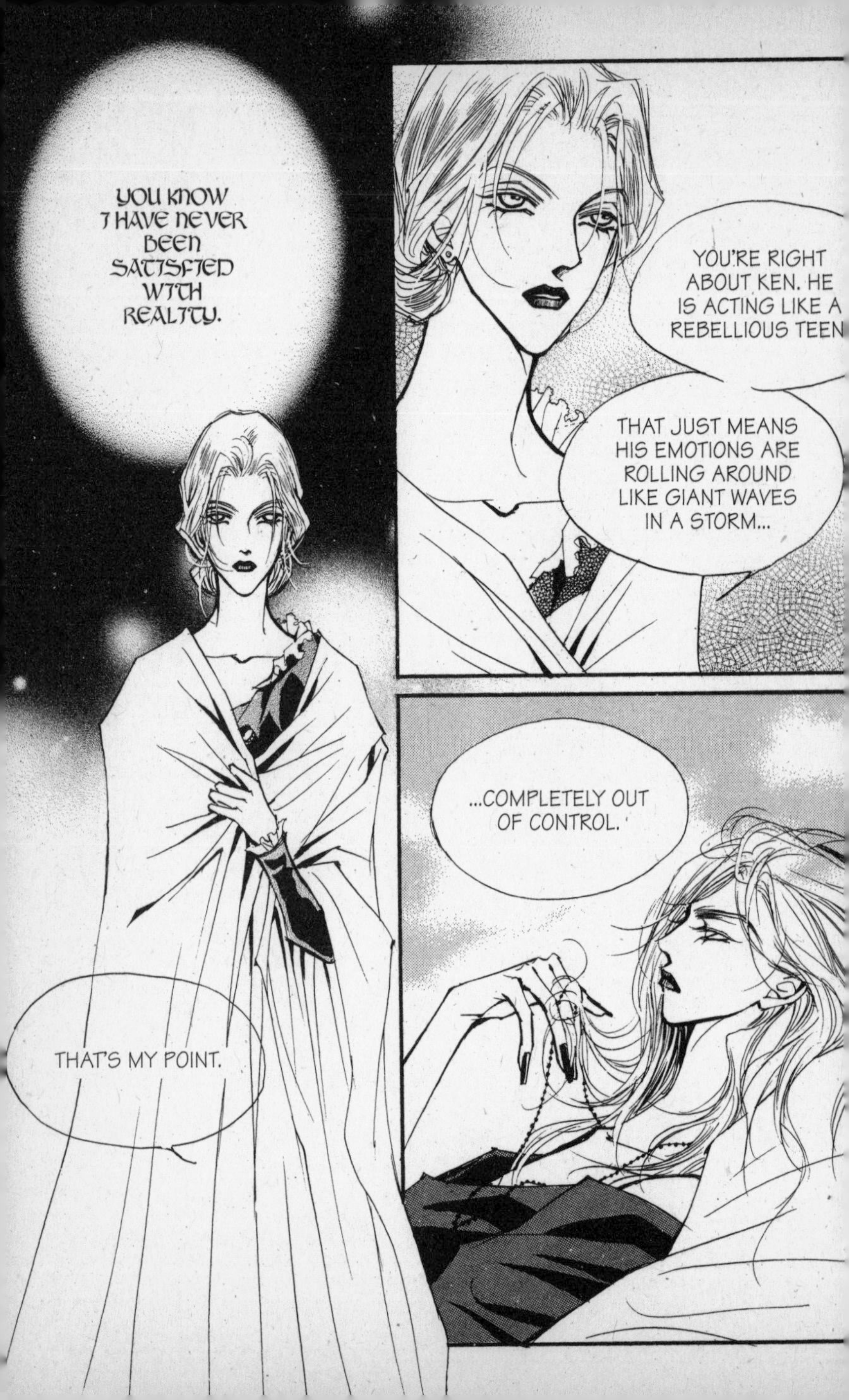
YOU KNOW I HAVE NEVER BEEN SATISFIED WITH REALITY.
THAT'S MY POINT.
YOU'RE RIGHT ABOUT KEN. HE IS ACTING LIKE A REBELLIOUS TEEN
THAT JUST MEANS HIS EMOTIONS ARE ROLLING AROUND LIKE GIANT WAVES IN A STORM...
...COMPLETELY OUT OF CONTROL.

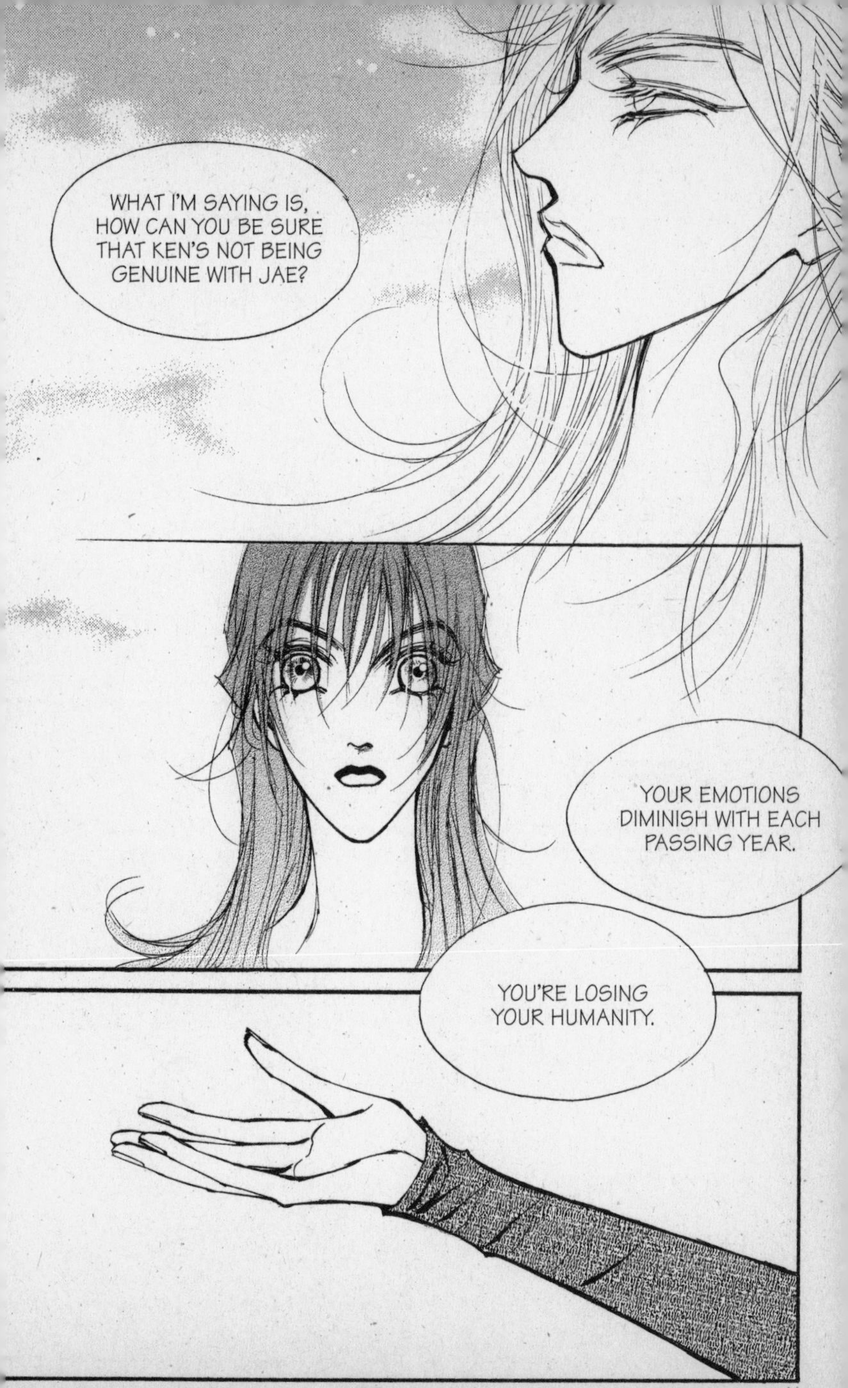
WHAT I'M SAYING IS, HOW CAN YOU BE SURE THAT KEN'S NOT BEING GENUINE WITH JAE?
YOUR EMOTIONS DIMINISH WITH EACH PASSING YEAR.
YOU'RE LOSING YOUR HUMANITY.

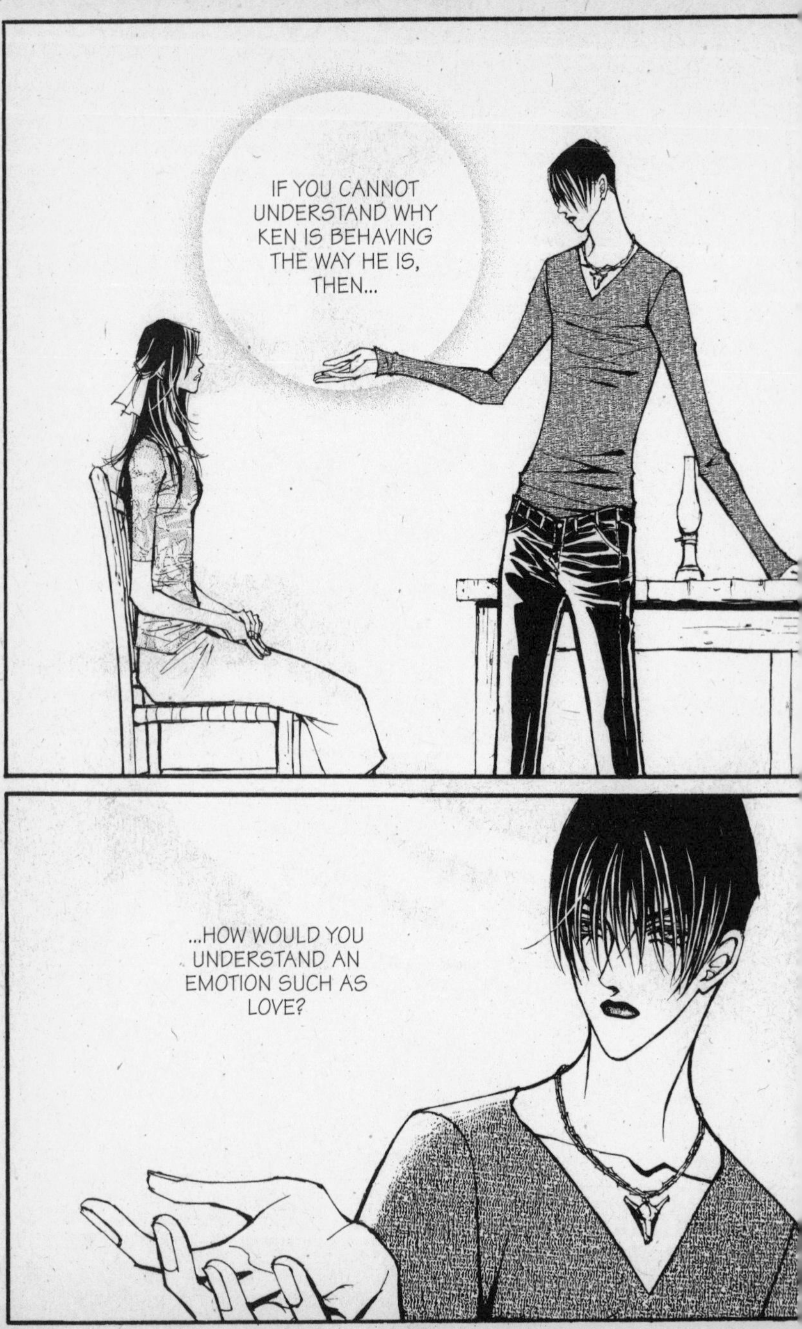
IF YOU CANNOT UNDERSTAND WHY KEN IS BEHAVING THE WAY HE IS, THEN...
...HOW WOULD YOU UNDERSTAND AN EMOTION SUCH AS LOVE?

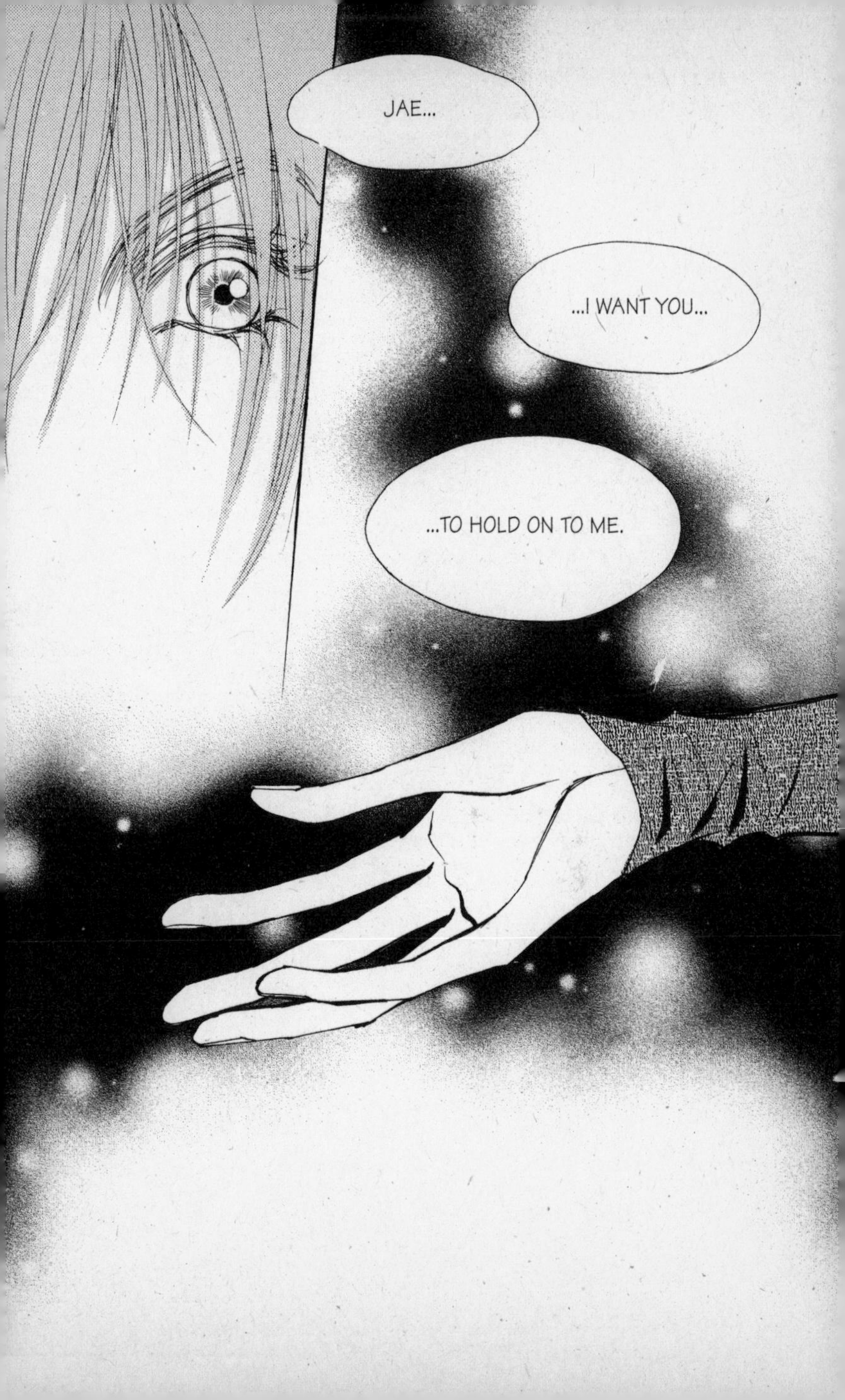
JAE...
...I WANT YOU...
...TO HOLD ON TO ME.

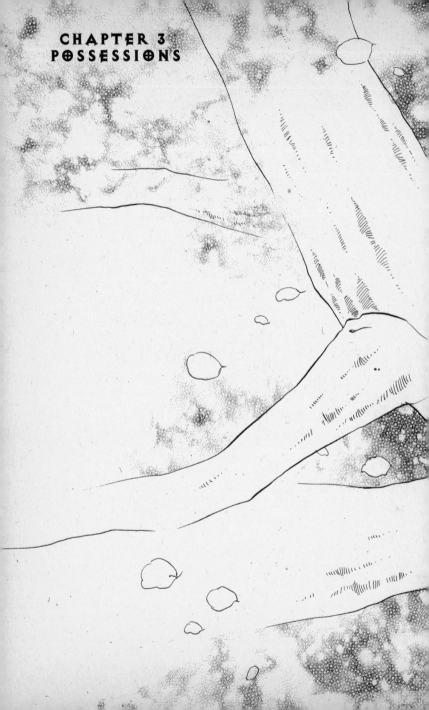

# CHAPTER 3
## POSSESSIONS

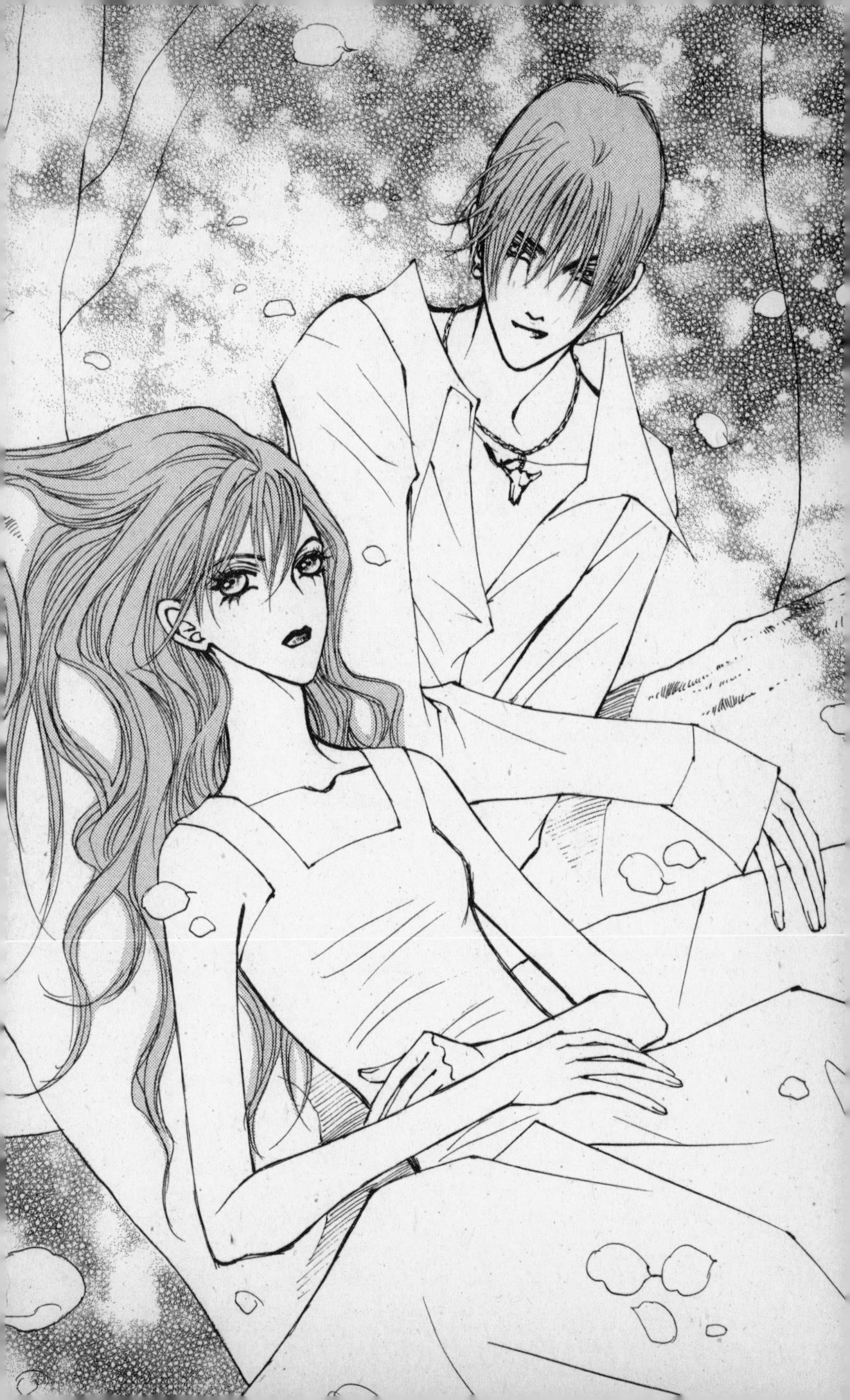

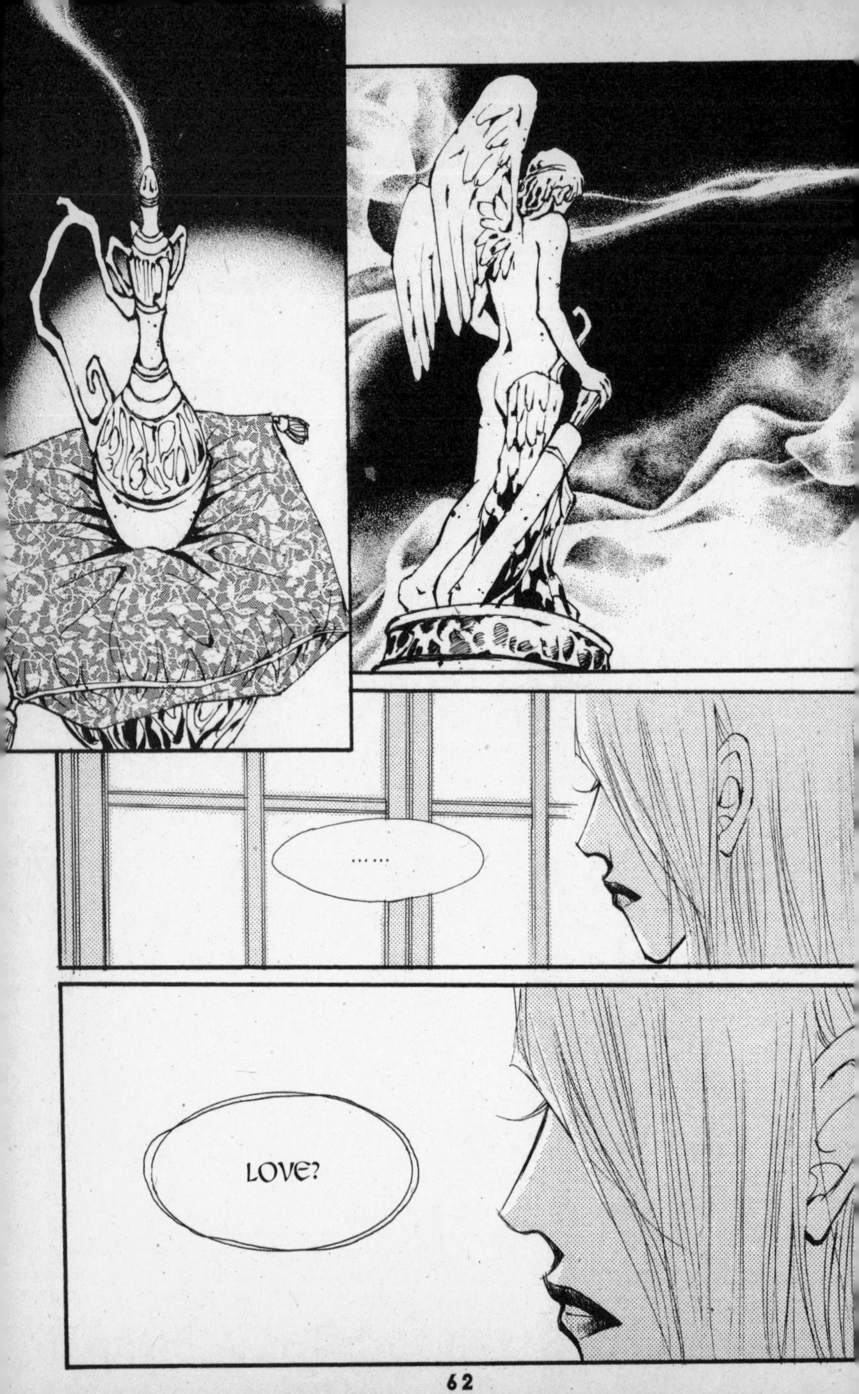
......
LOVE?

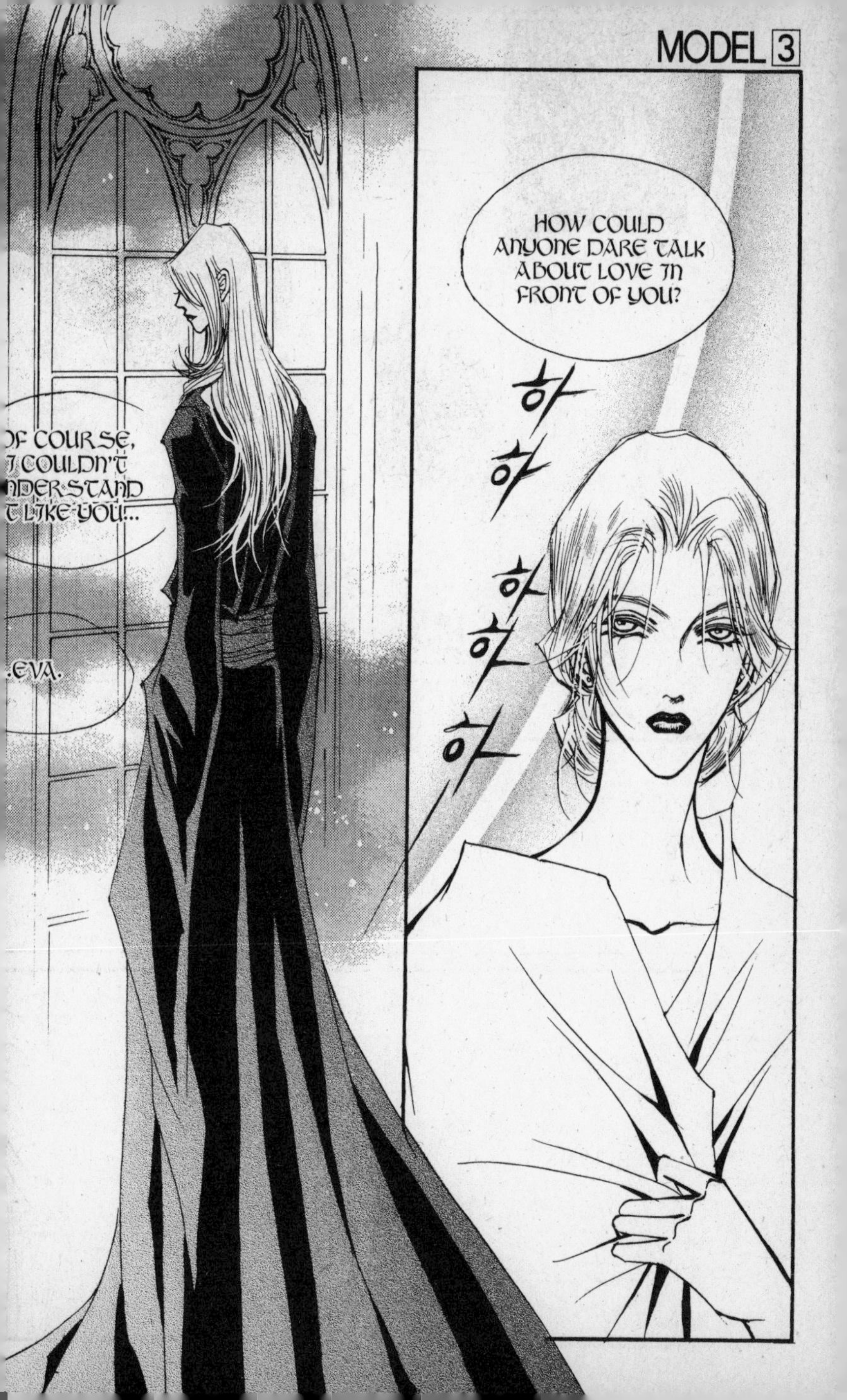
OF COURSE, I COULDN'T NDERSTAND T LIKE YOU!...
.EVA.
HOW COULD ANYONE DARE TALK ABOUT LOVE IN FRONT OF YOU?
하하
하하하

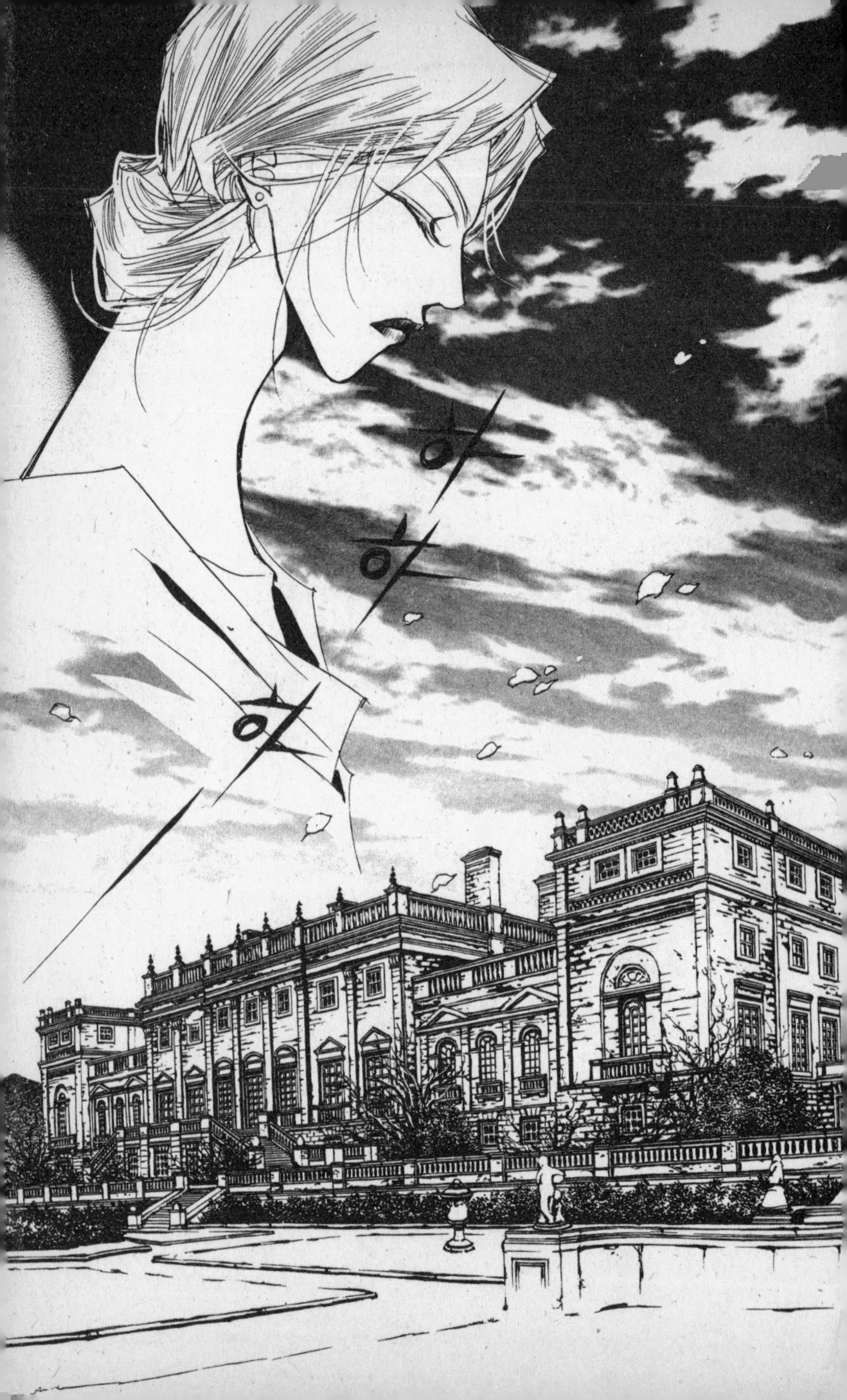
하
하
하

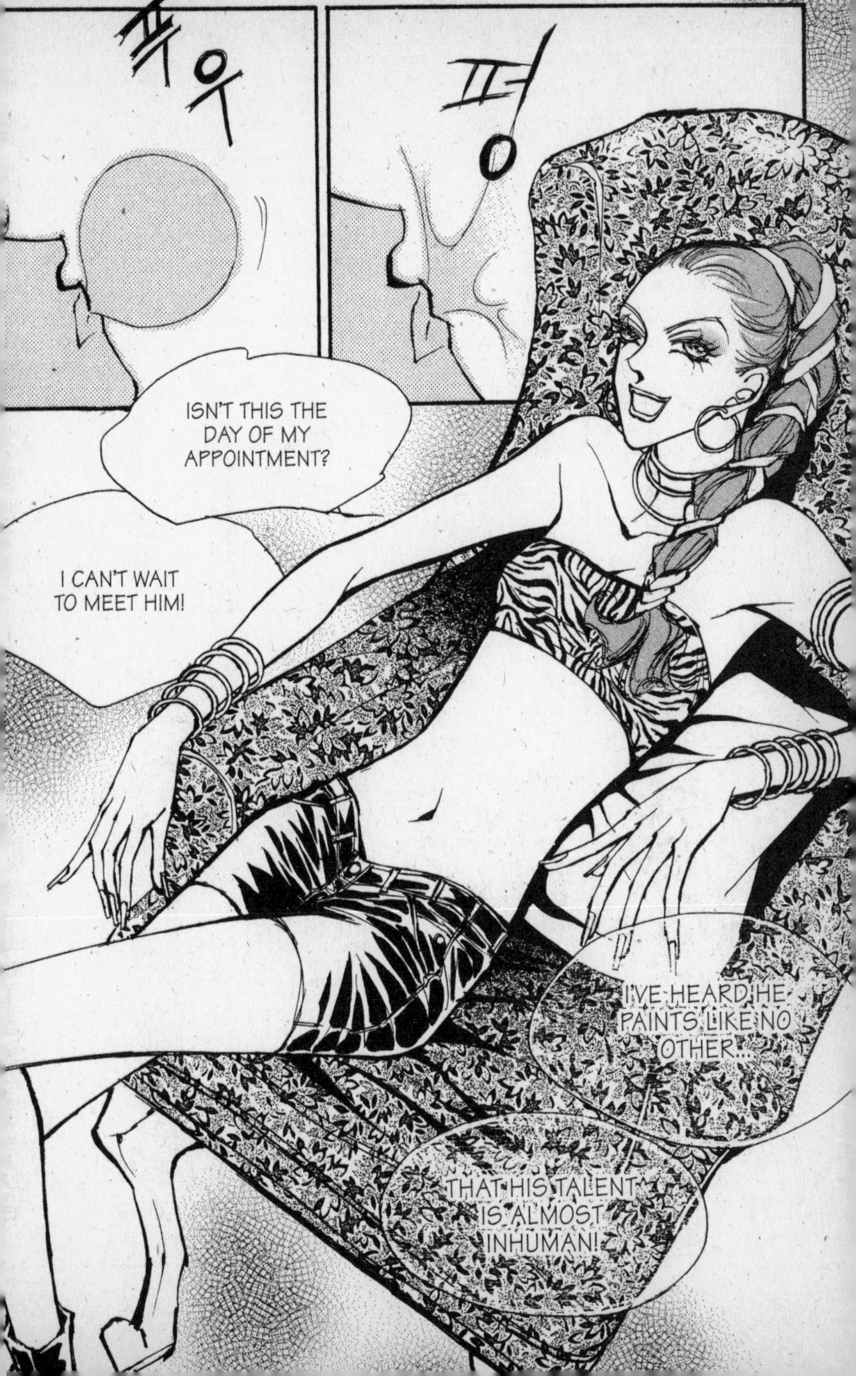
푸우
평
ISN'T THIS THE DAY OF MY APPOINTMENT?
I CAN'T WAIT TO MEET HIM!
I'VE HEARD HE PAINTS LIKE NO OTHER...
THAT HIS TALENT IS ALMOST INHUMAN!

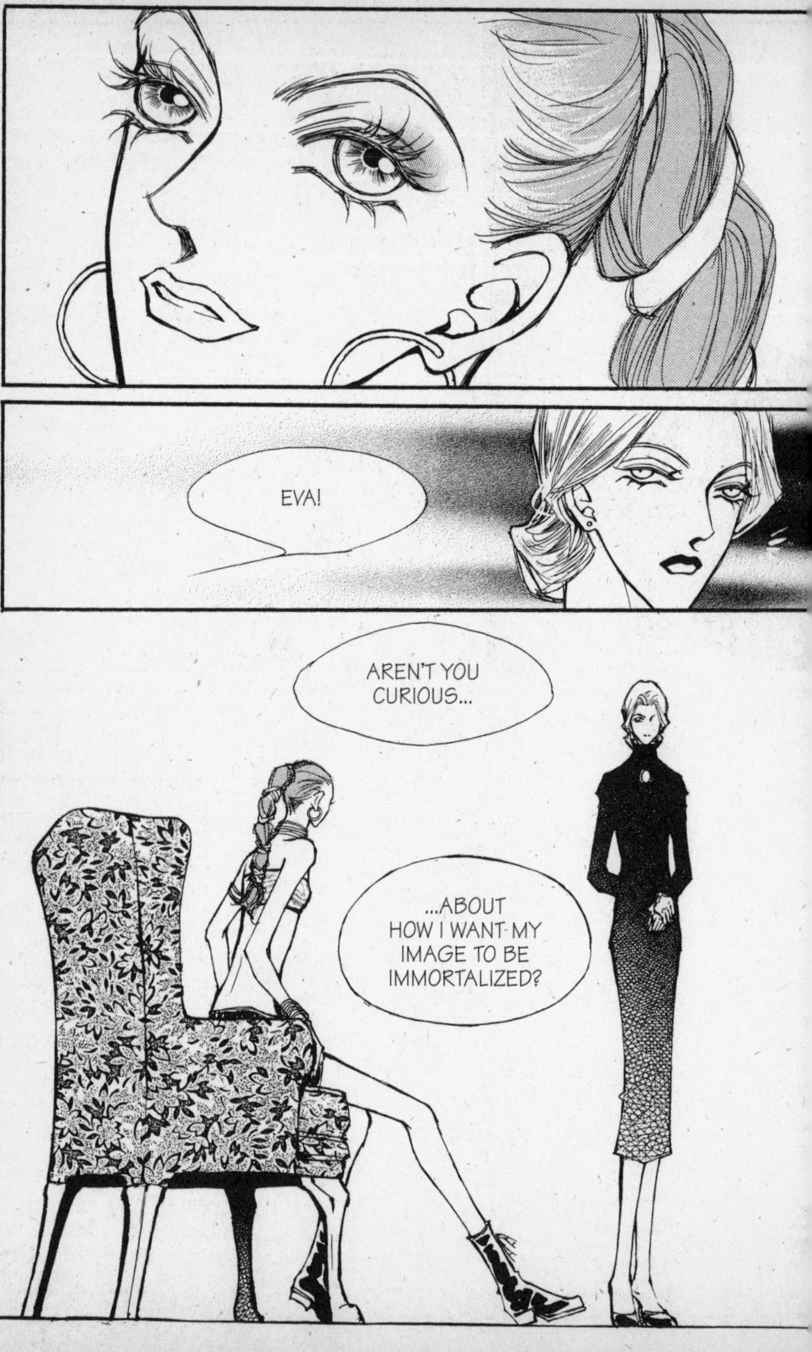
EVA!
AREN'T YOU CURIOUS...
...ABOUT HOW I WANT MY IMAGE TO BE IMMORTALIZED?

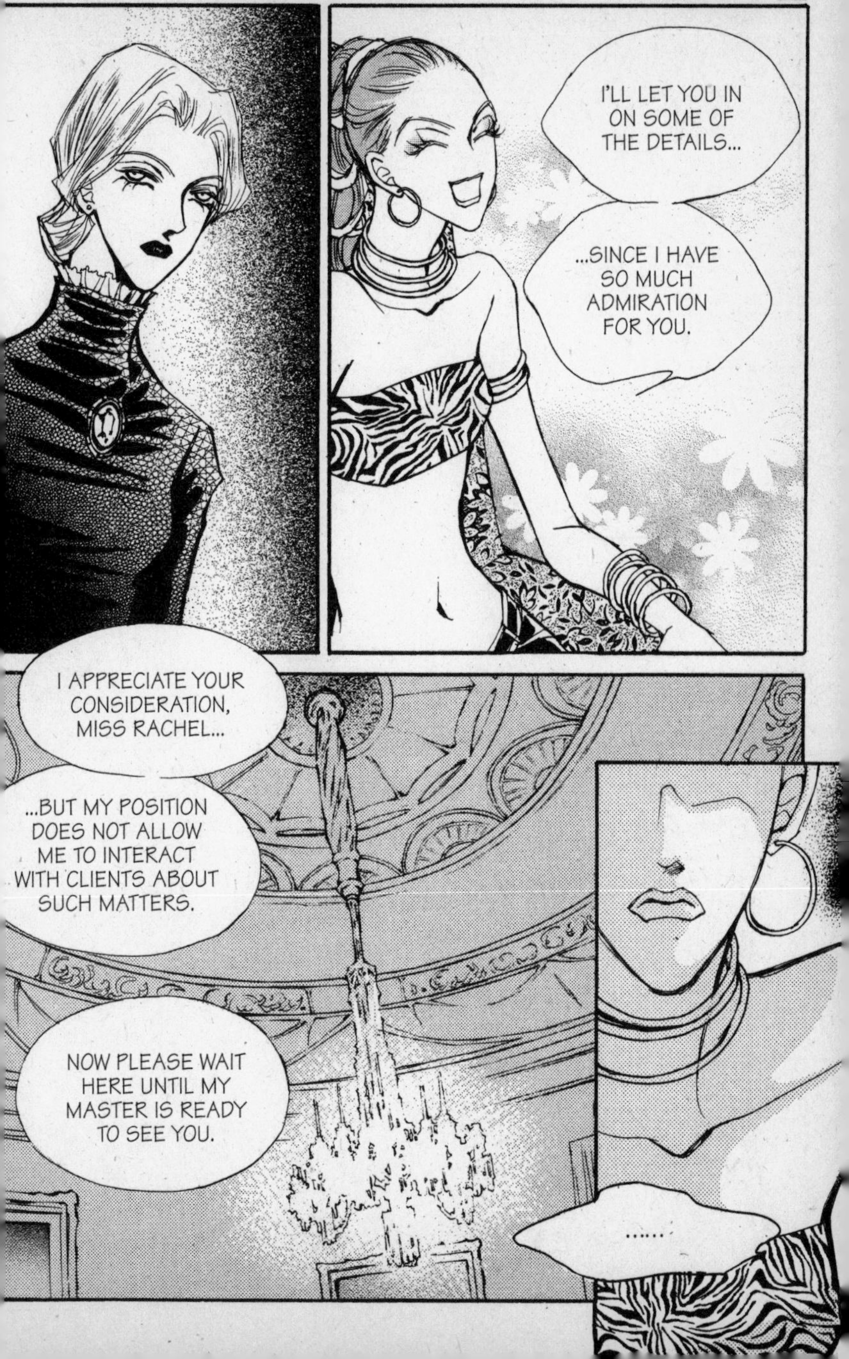
I'LL LET YOU IN ON SOME OF THE DETAILS...
...SINCE I HAVE SO MUCH ADMIRATION FOR YOU.
I APPRECIATE YOUR CONSIDERATION, MISS RACHEL...
...BUT MY POSITION DOES NOT ALLOW ME TO INTERACT WITH CLIENTS ABOUT SUCH MATTERS.
NOW PLEASE WAIT HERE UNTIL MY MASTER IS READY TO SEE YOU.
......

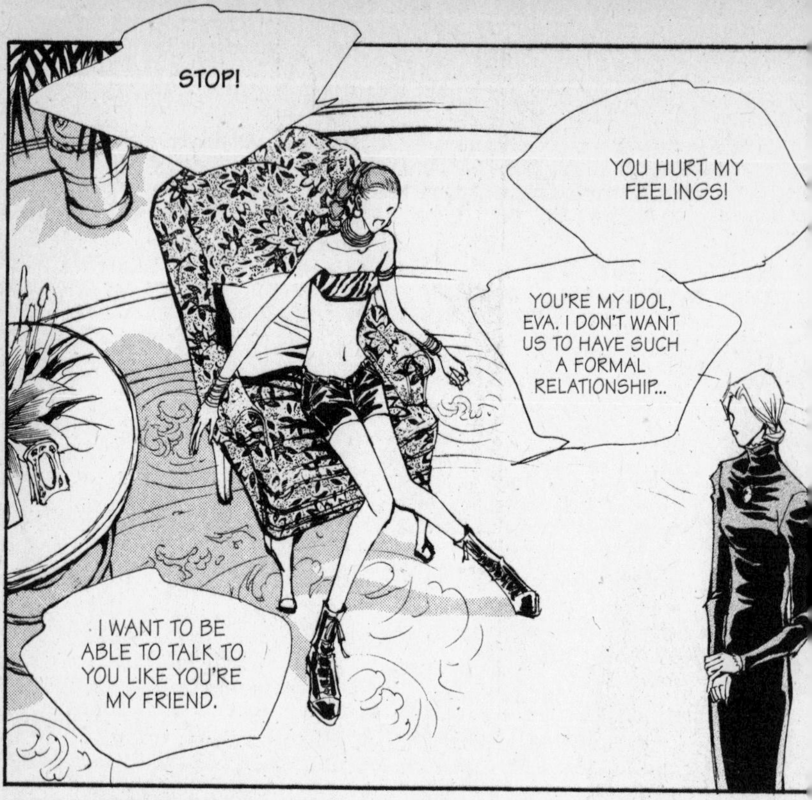
STOP!
YOU HURT MY FEELINGS!
YOU'RE MY IDOL, EVA. I DON'T WANT US TO HAVE SUCH A FORMAL RELATIONSHIP...
I WANT TO BE ABLE TO TALK TO YOU LIKE YOU'RE MY FRIEND.
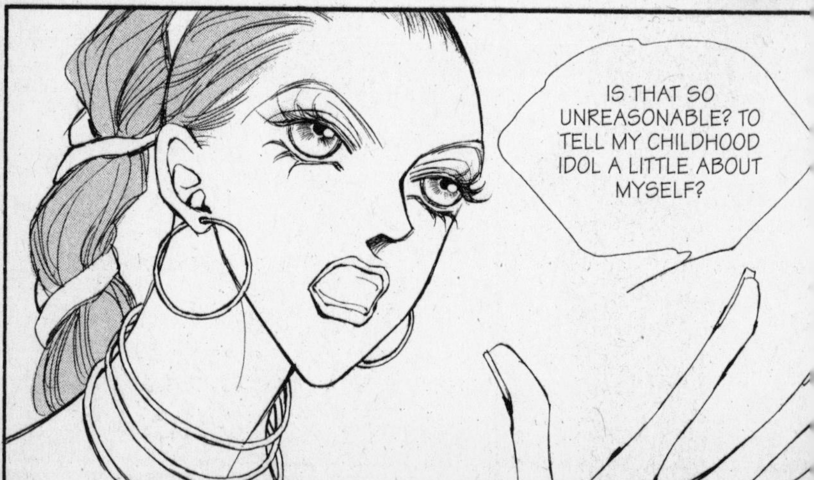
IS THAT SO UNREASONABLE? TO TELL MY CHILDHOOD IDOL A LITTLE ABOUT MYSELF?

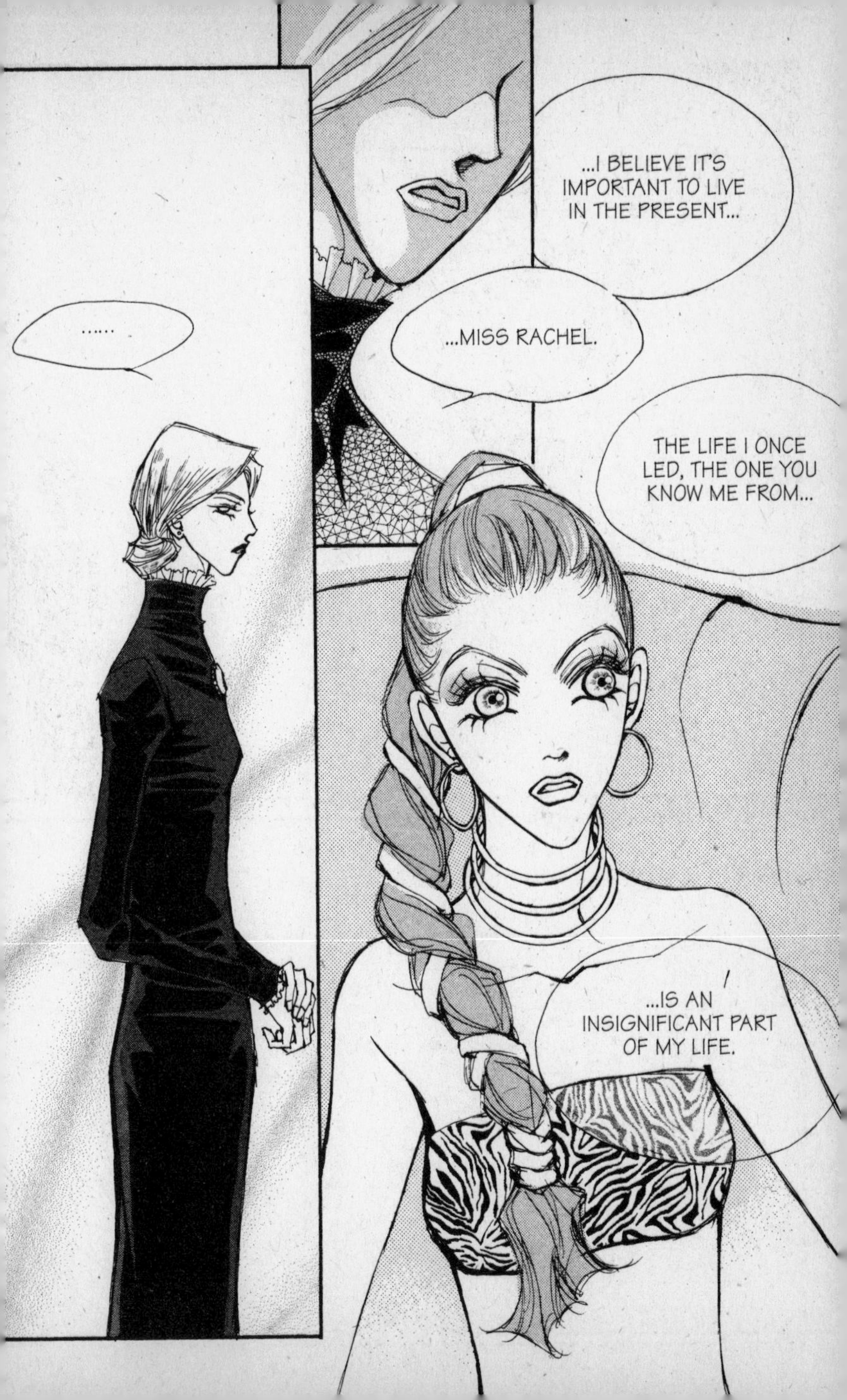
......
...I BELIEVE IT'S IMPORTANT TO LIVE IN THE PRESENT...
...MISS RACHEL.
THE LIFE I ONCE LED, THE ONE YOU KNOW ME FROM...
...IS AN INSIGNIFICANT PART OF MY LIFE.

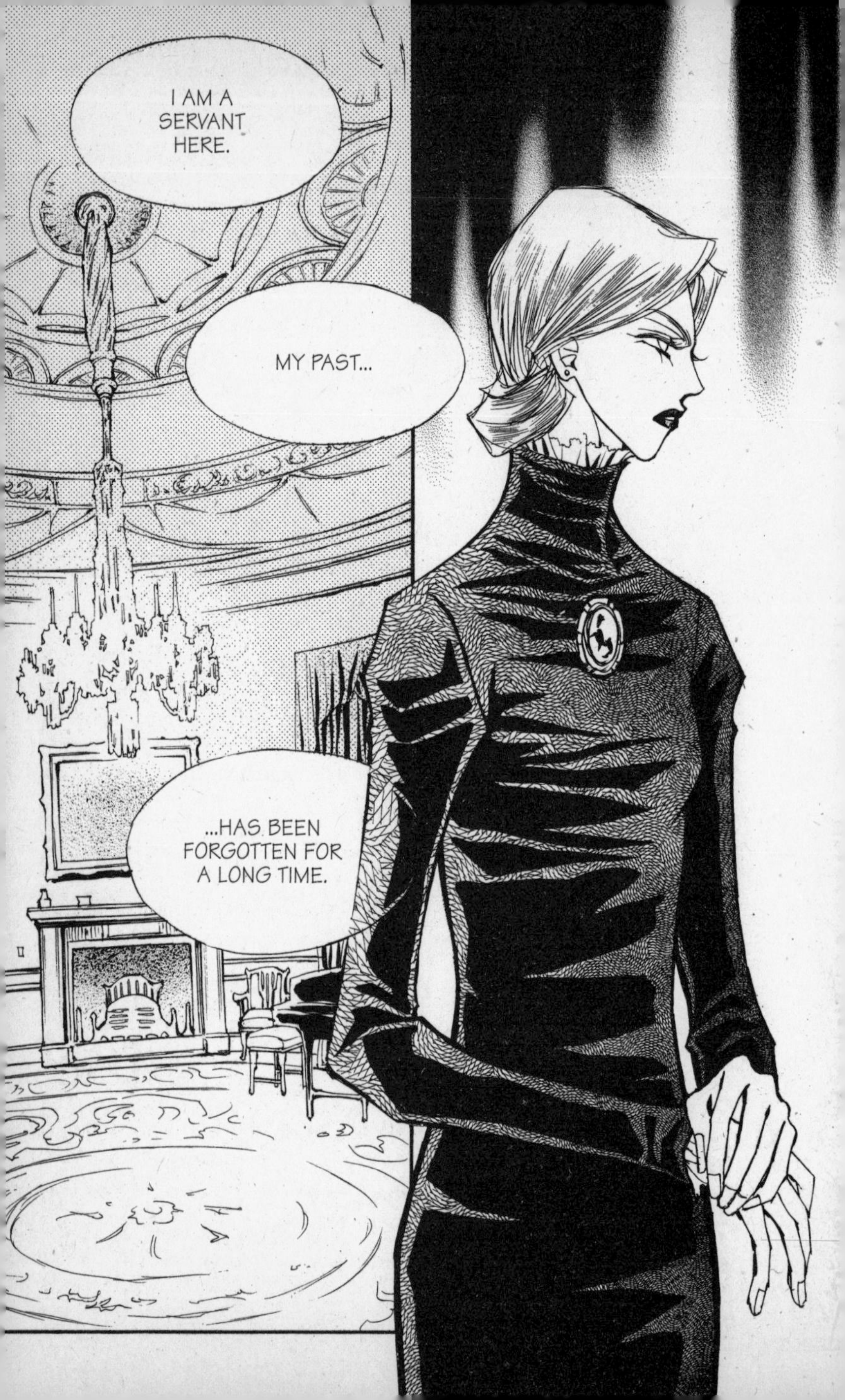
I AM A SERVANT HERE.
MY PAST...
...HAS BEEN FORGOTTEN FOR A LONG TIME.

EXACTLY HOW MUCH OF YOUR PAST HAS BEEN FORGOTTEN?

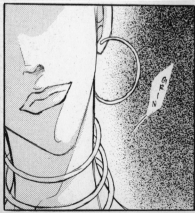

GRIN

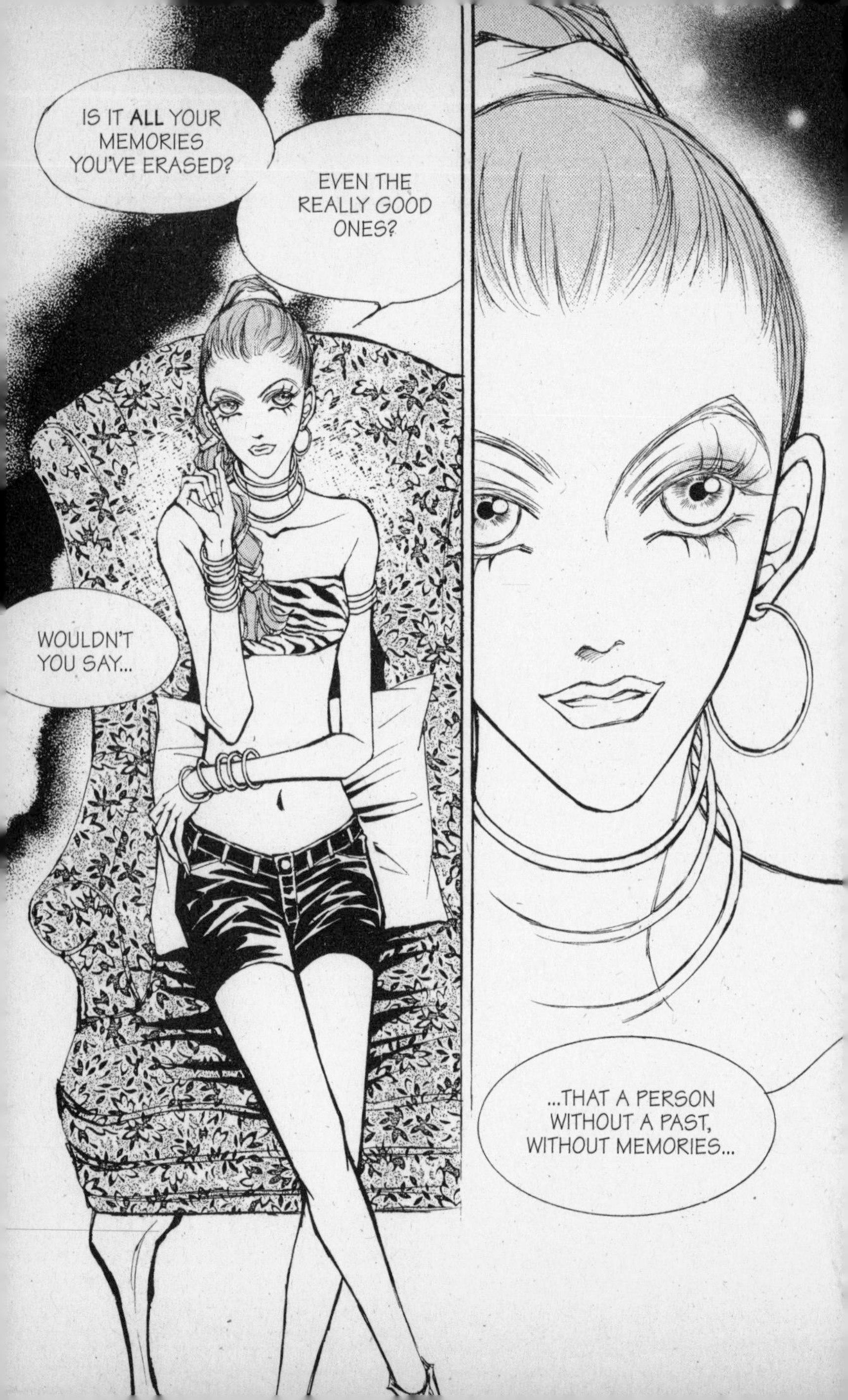
IS IT **ALL** YOUR MEMORIES YOU'VE ERASED?
EVEN THE REALLY *GOOD* ONES?
WOULDN'T YOU SAY...
...THAT A PERSON WITHOUT A PAST, WITHOUT MEMORIES...

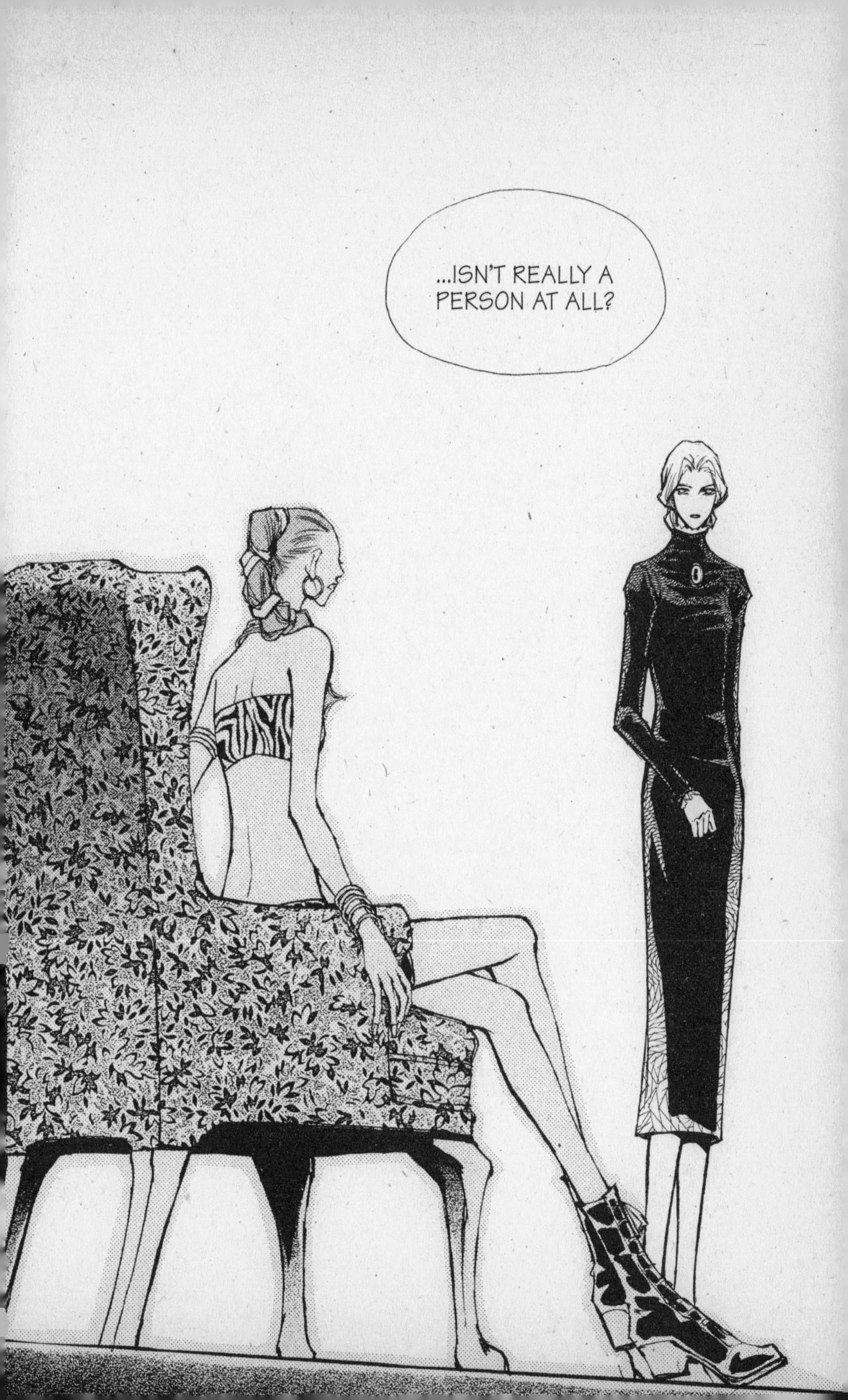
...ISN'T REALLY A PERSON AT ALL?

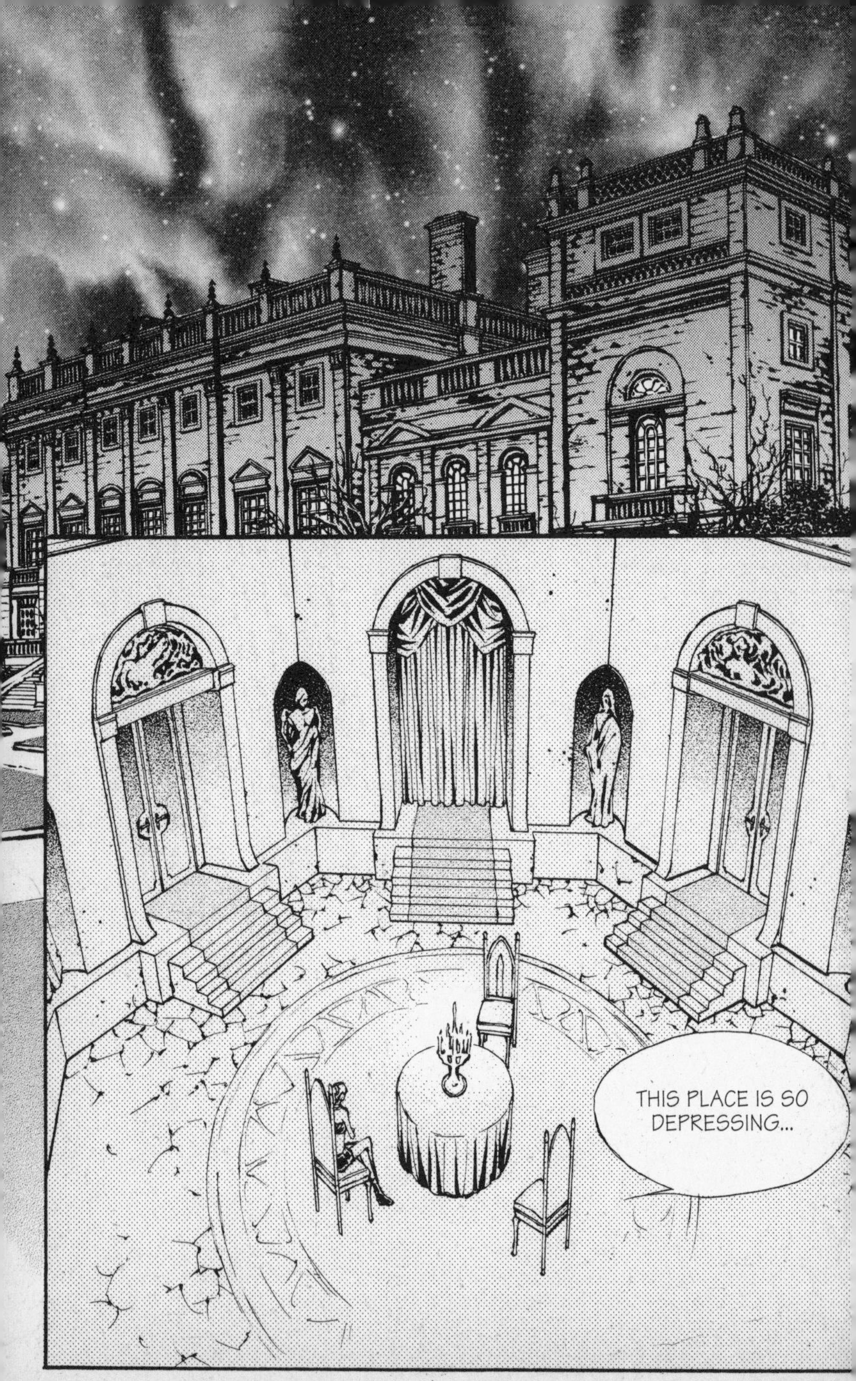
THIS PLACE IS SO DEPRESSING...

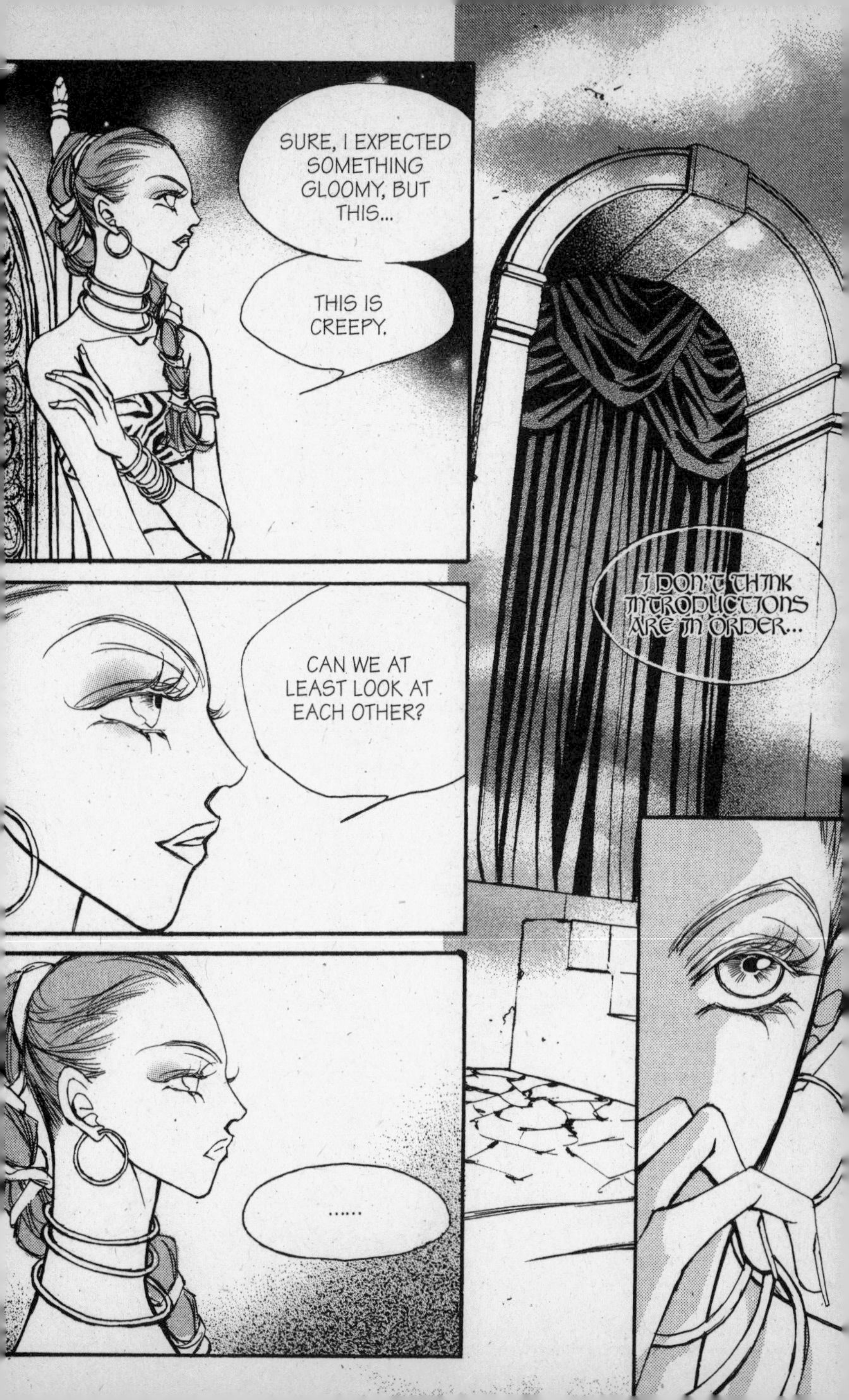
SURE, I EXPECTED SOMETHING GLOOMY, BUT THIS...
THIS IS CREEPY.
I DON'T THINK INTRODUCTIONS ARE IN ORDER...
CAN WE AT LEAST LOOK AT EACH OTHER?
......

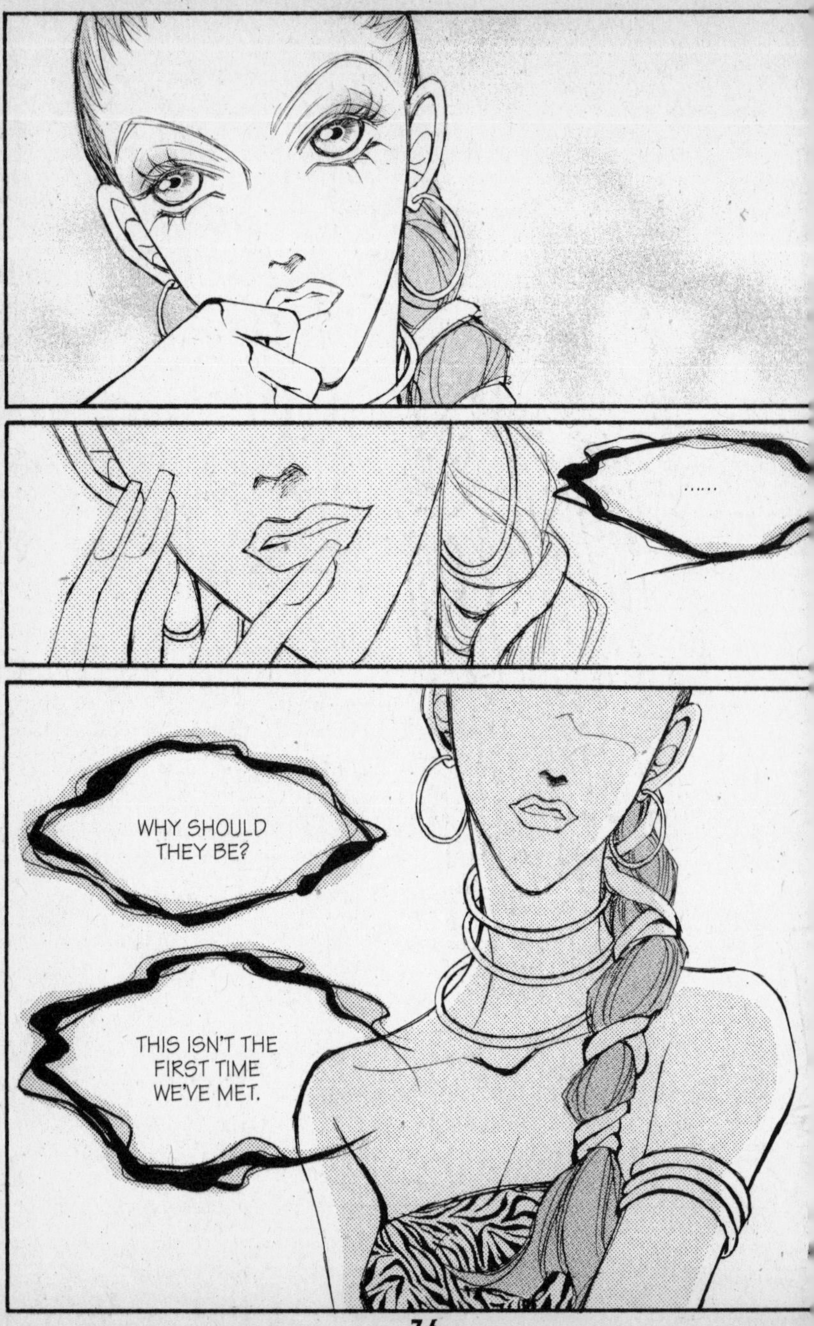
......
WHY SHOULD THEY BE?
THIS ISN'T THE FIRST TIME WE'VE MET.

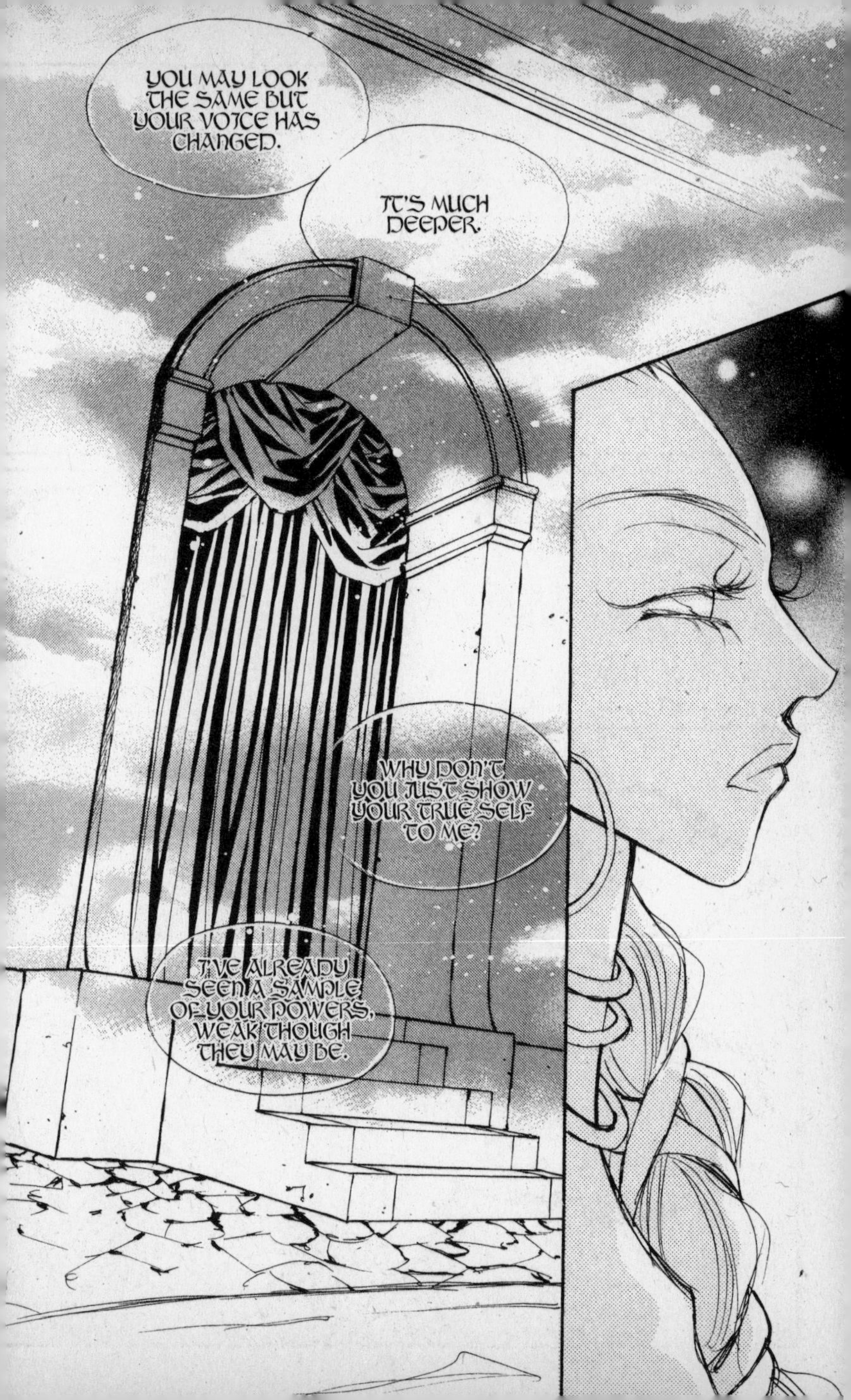
YOU MAY LOOK THE SAME BUT YOUR VOICE HAS CHANGED.
IT'S MUCH DEEPER.
WHY DON'T YOU JUST SHOW YOUR TRUE SELF TO ME?
I'VE ALREADY SEEN A SAMPLE OF YOUR POWERS, WEAK THOUGH THEY MAY BE.

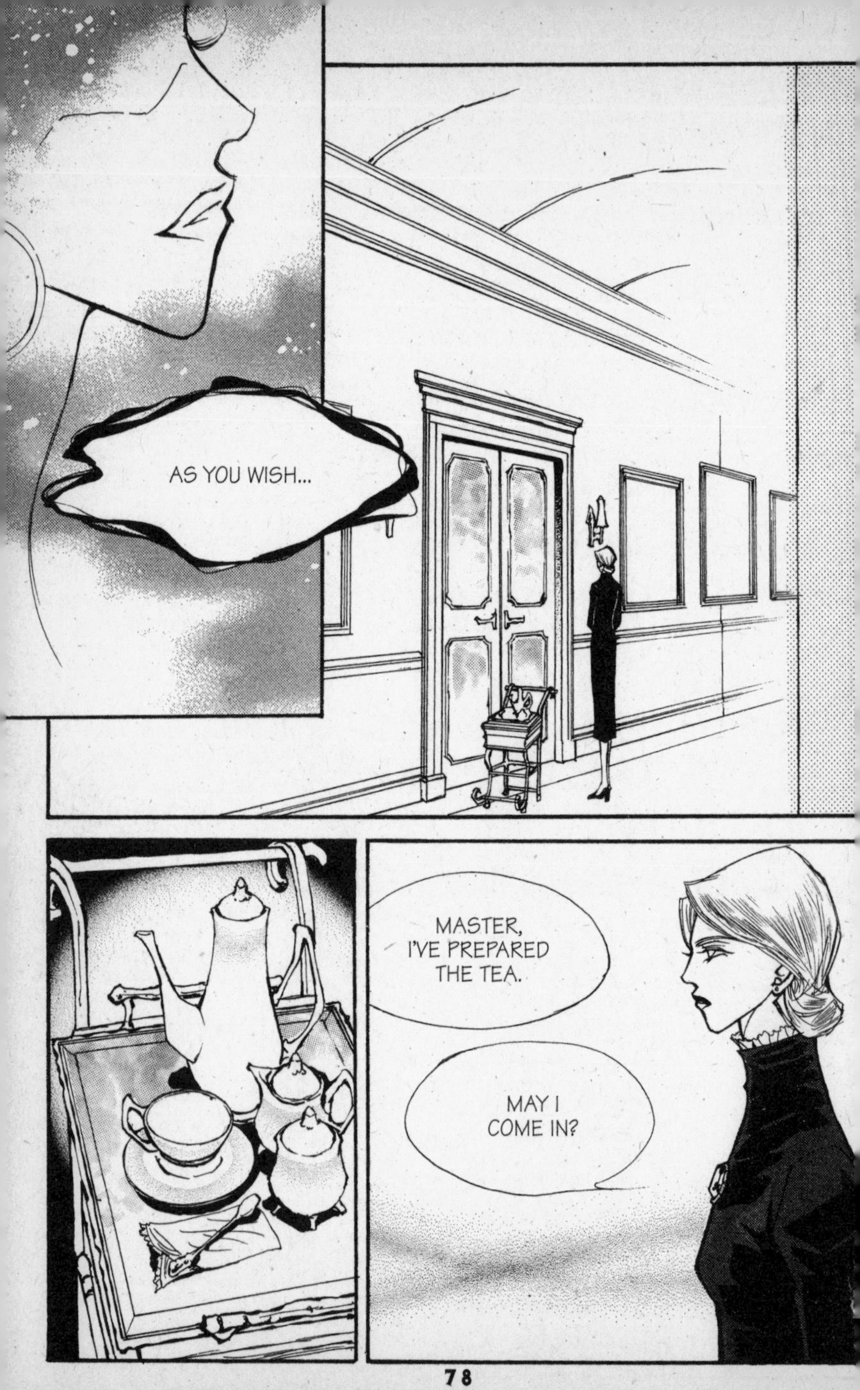
AS YOU WISH...
MASTER, I'VE PREPARED THE TEA.
MAY I COME IN?

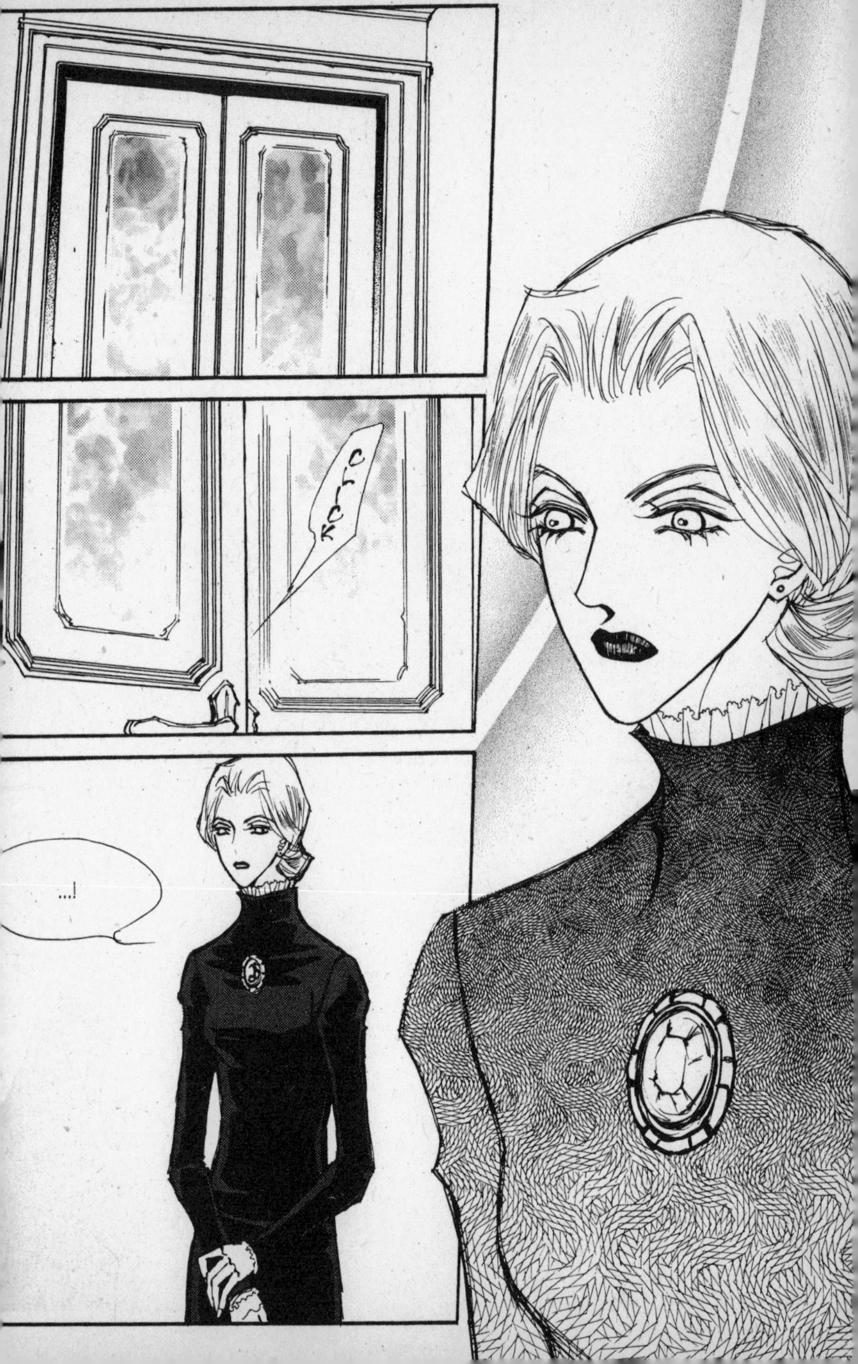
CLICK
...!

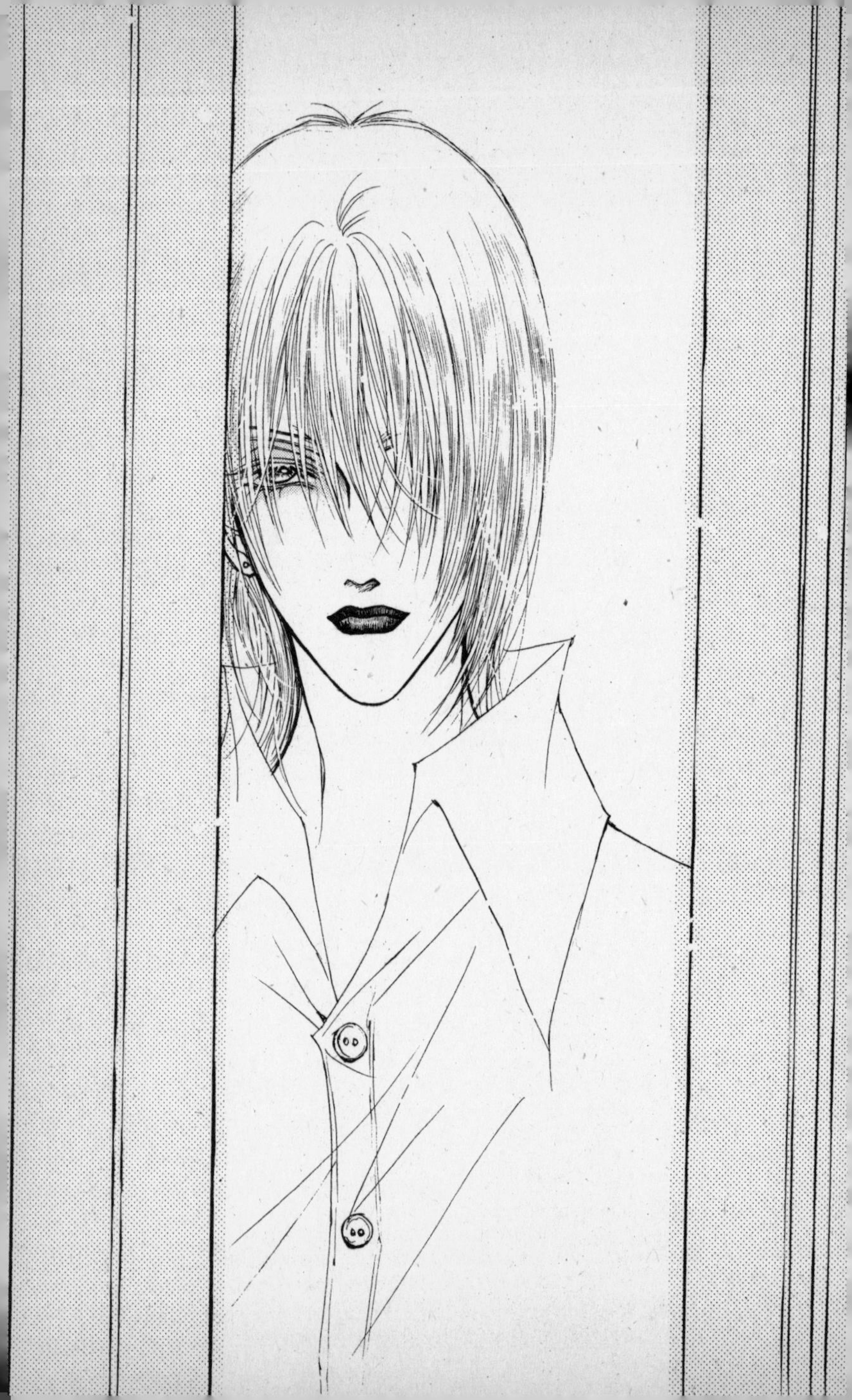

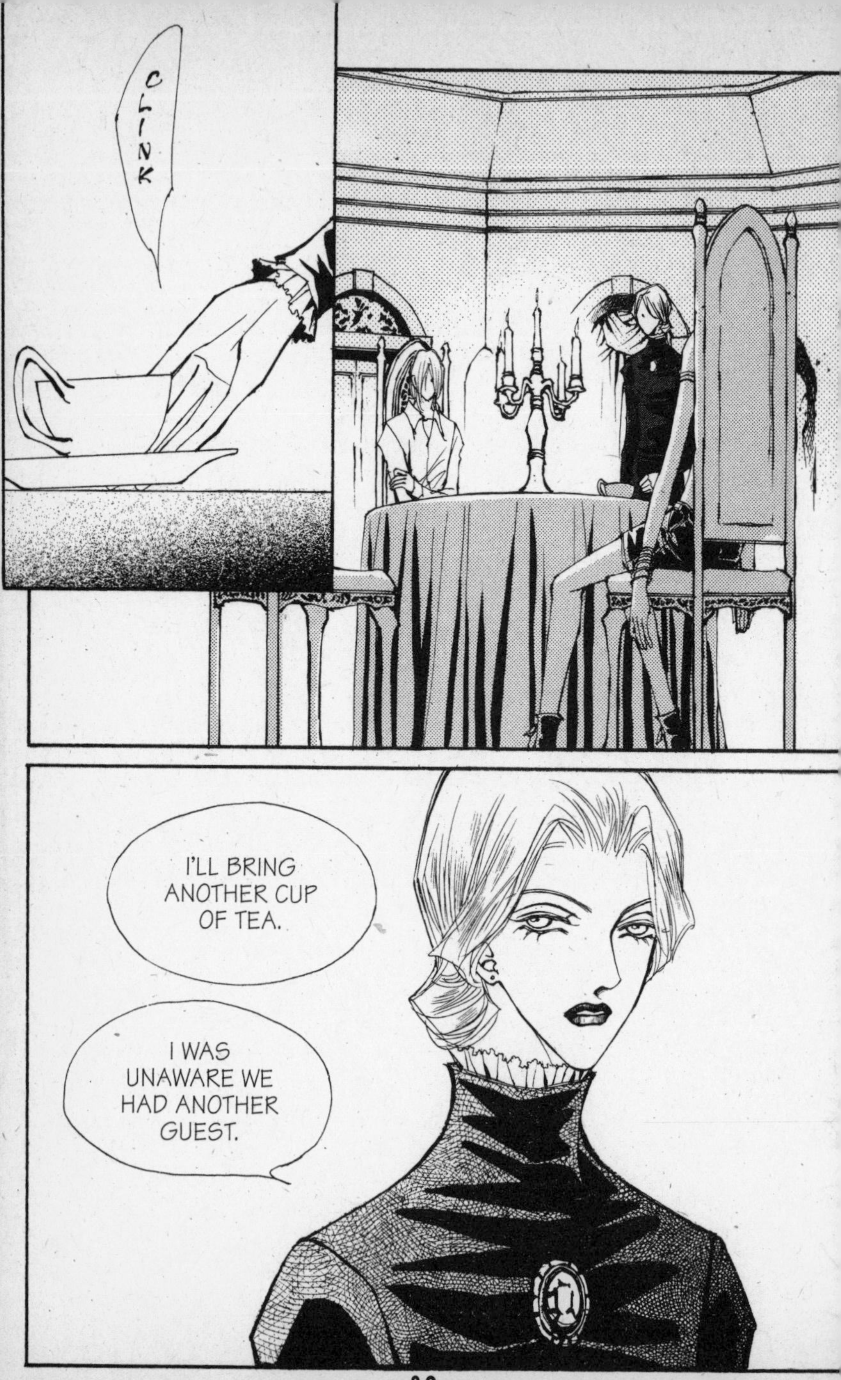
CLINK
I'LL BRING ANOTHER CUP OF TEA.
I WAS UNAWARE WE HAD ANOTHER GUEST.

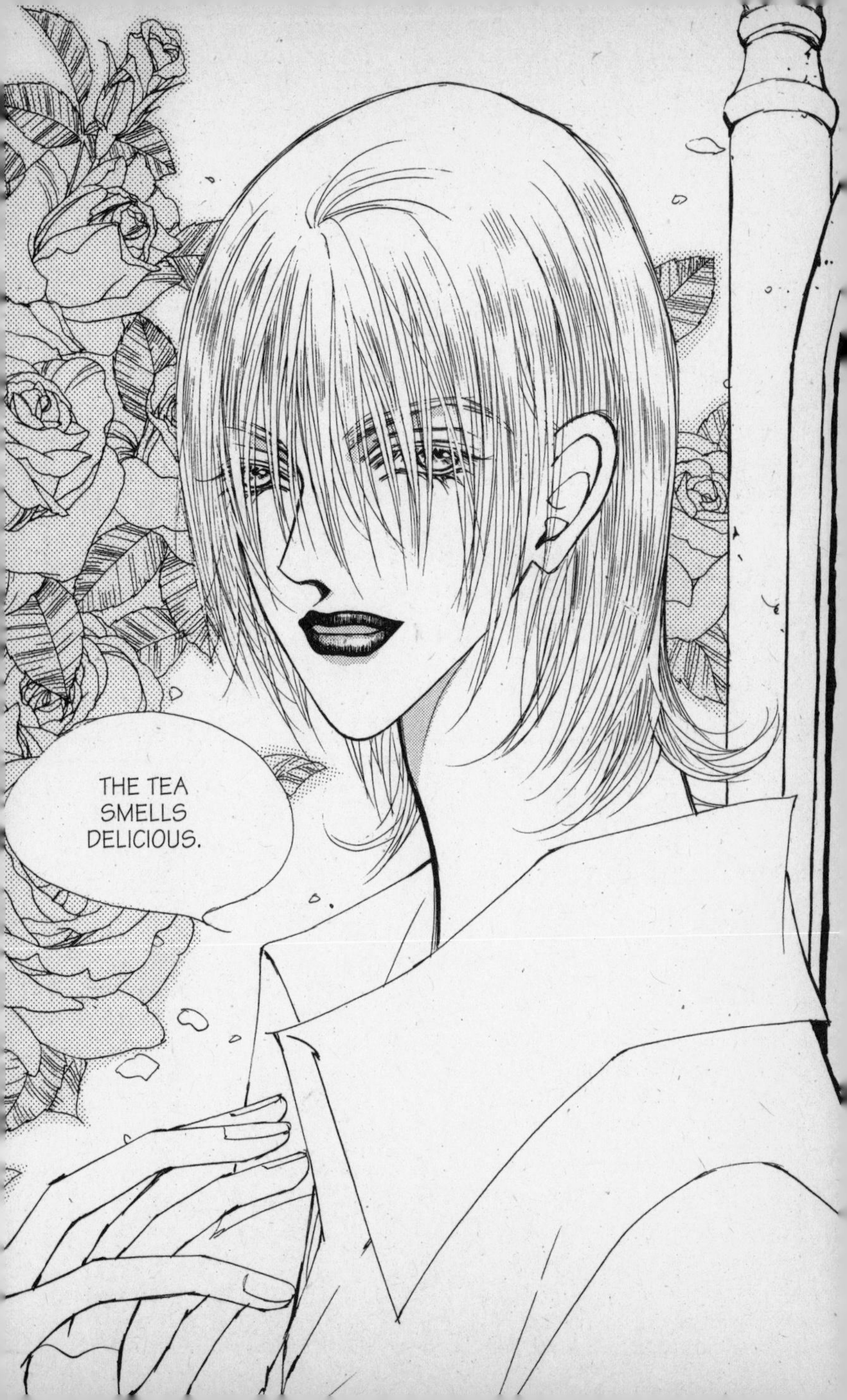
THE TEA SMELLS DELICIOUS.

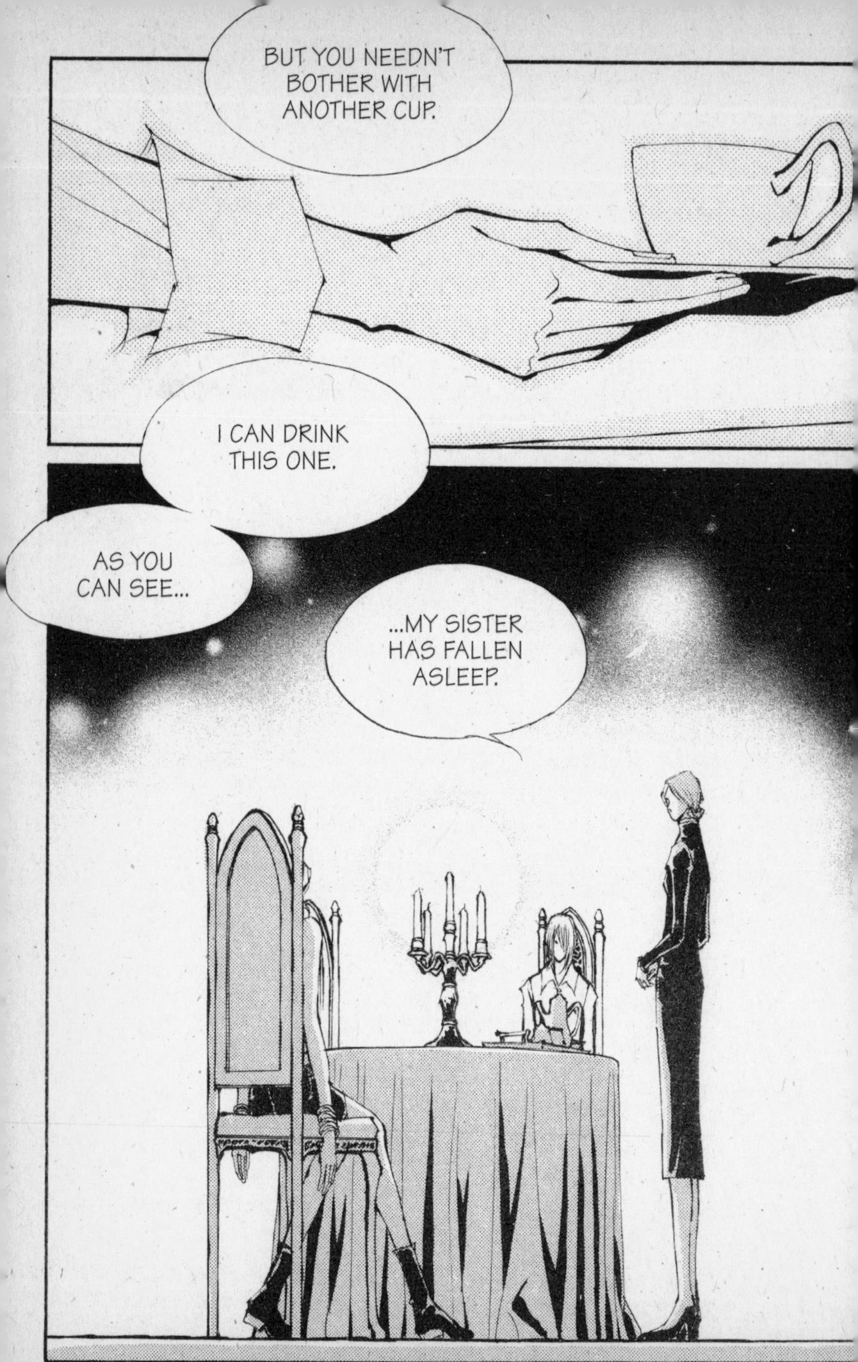
BUT YOU NEEDN'T BOTHER WITH ANOTHER CUP.
I CAN DRINK THIS ONE.
AS YOU CAN SEE...
...MY SISTER HAS FALLEN ASLEEP.

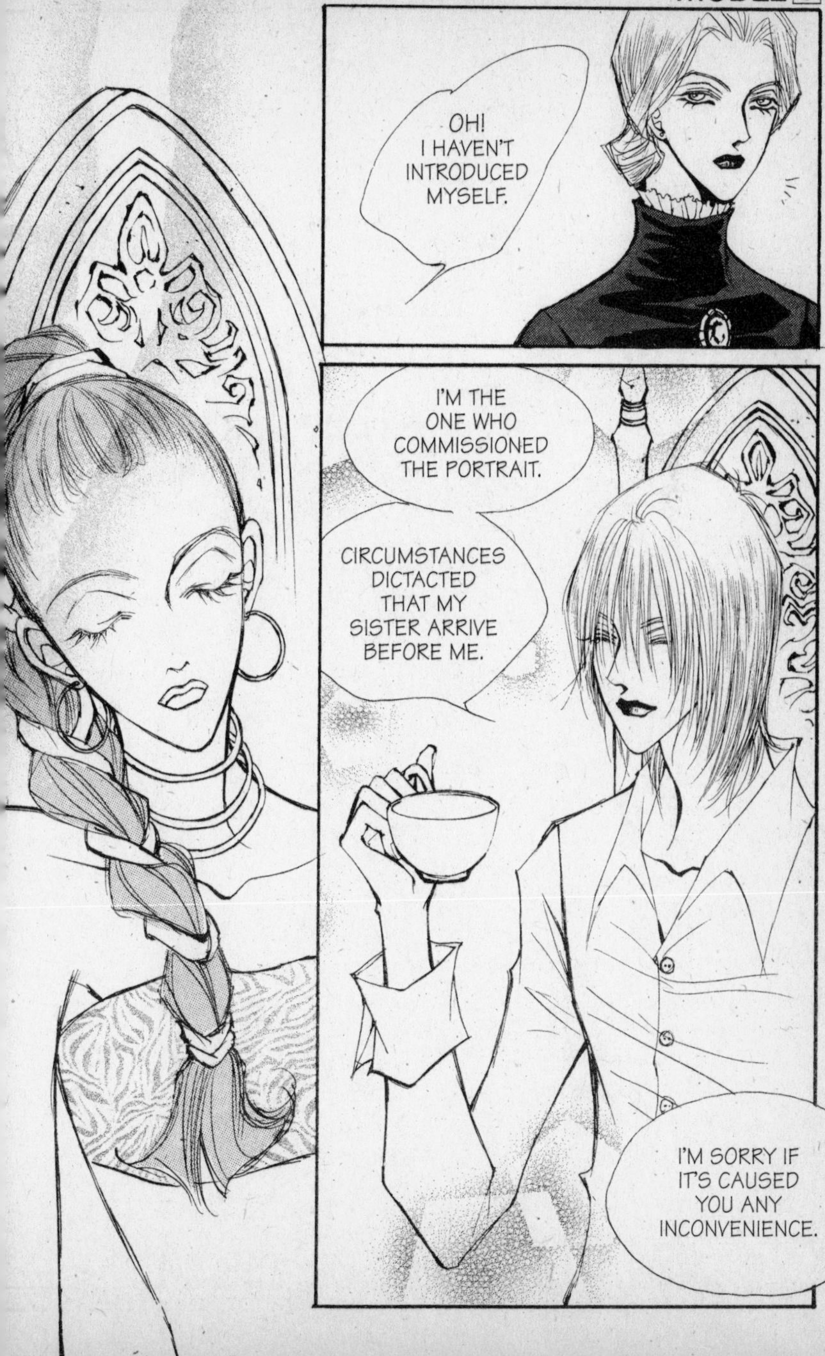
OH!
I HAVEN'T INTRODUCED MYSELF.
I'M THE ONE WHO COMMISSIONED THE PORTRAIT.
CIRCUMSTANCES DICTACTED THAT MY SISTER ARRIVE BEFORE ME.
I'M SORRY IF IT'S CAUSED YOU ANY INCONVENIENCE.

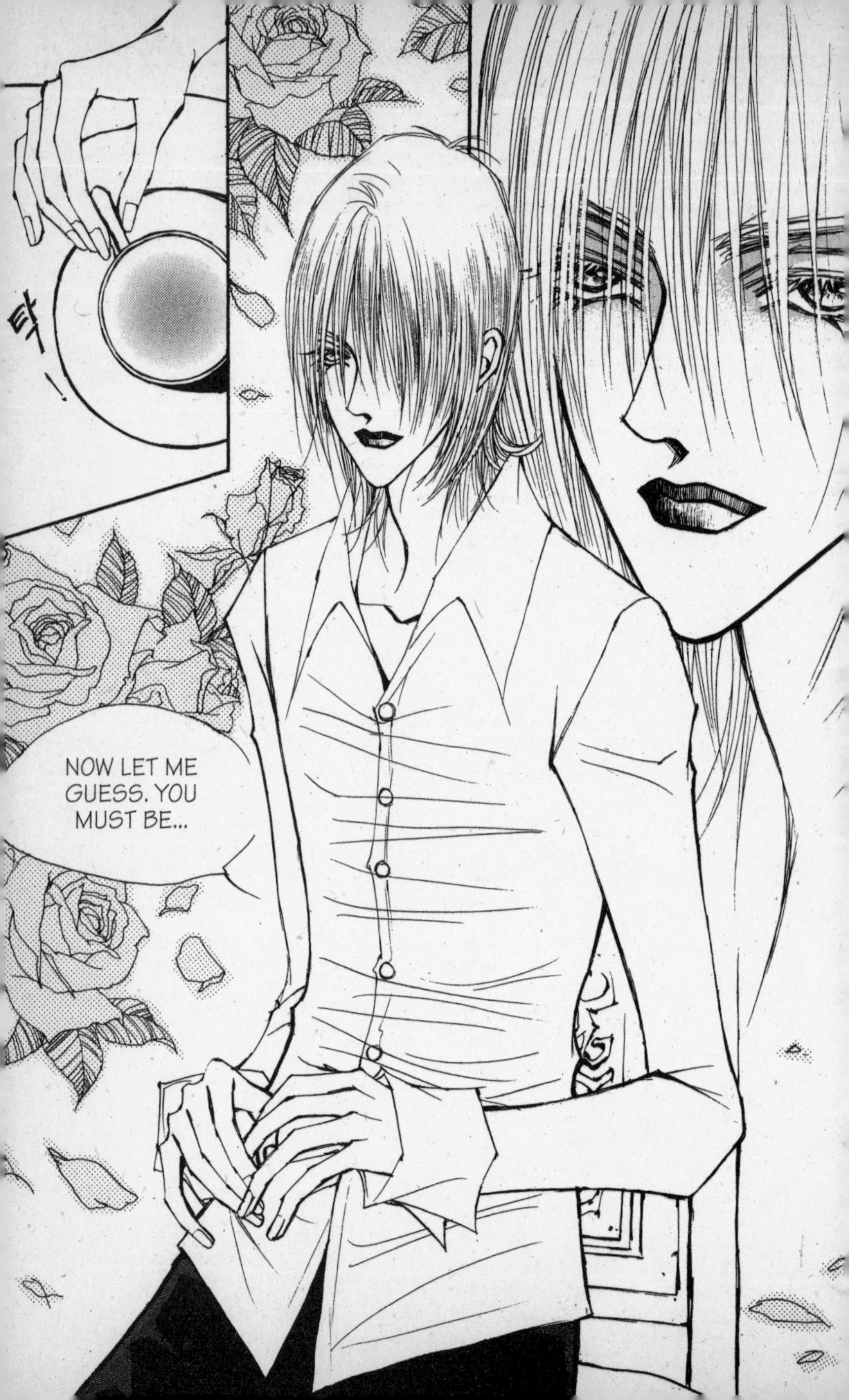
탁!
NOW LET ME GUESS. YOU MUST BE...

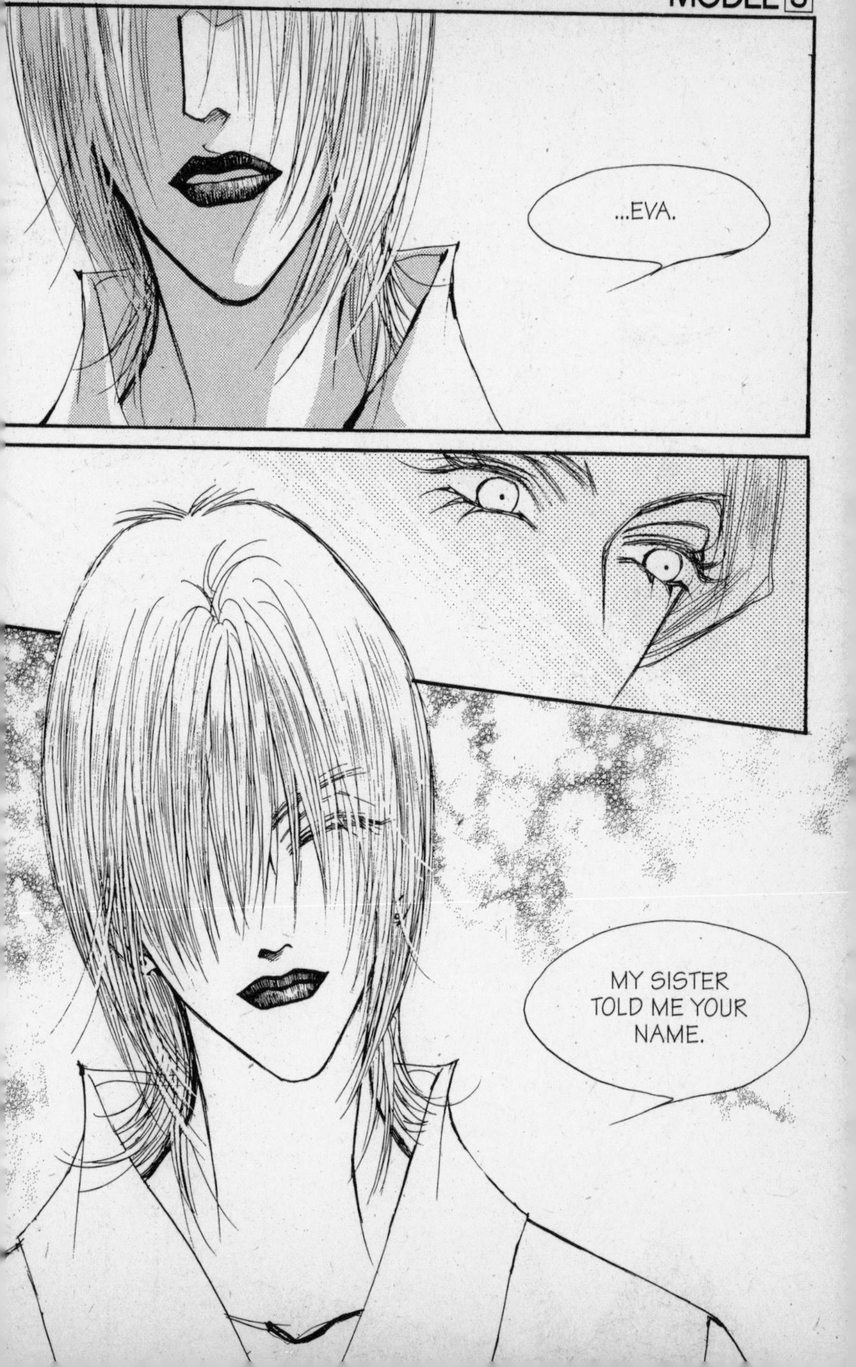
...EVA.
MY SISTER TOLD ME YOUR NAME.

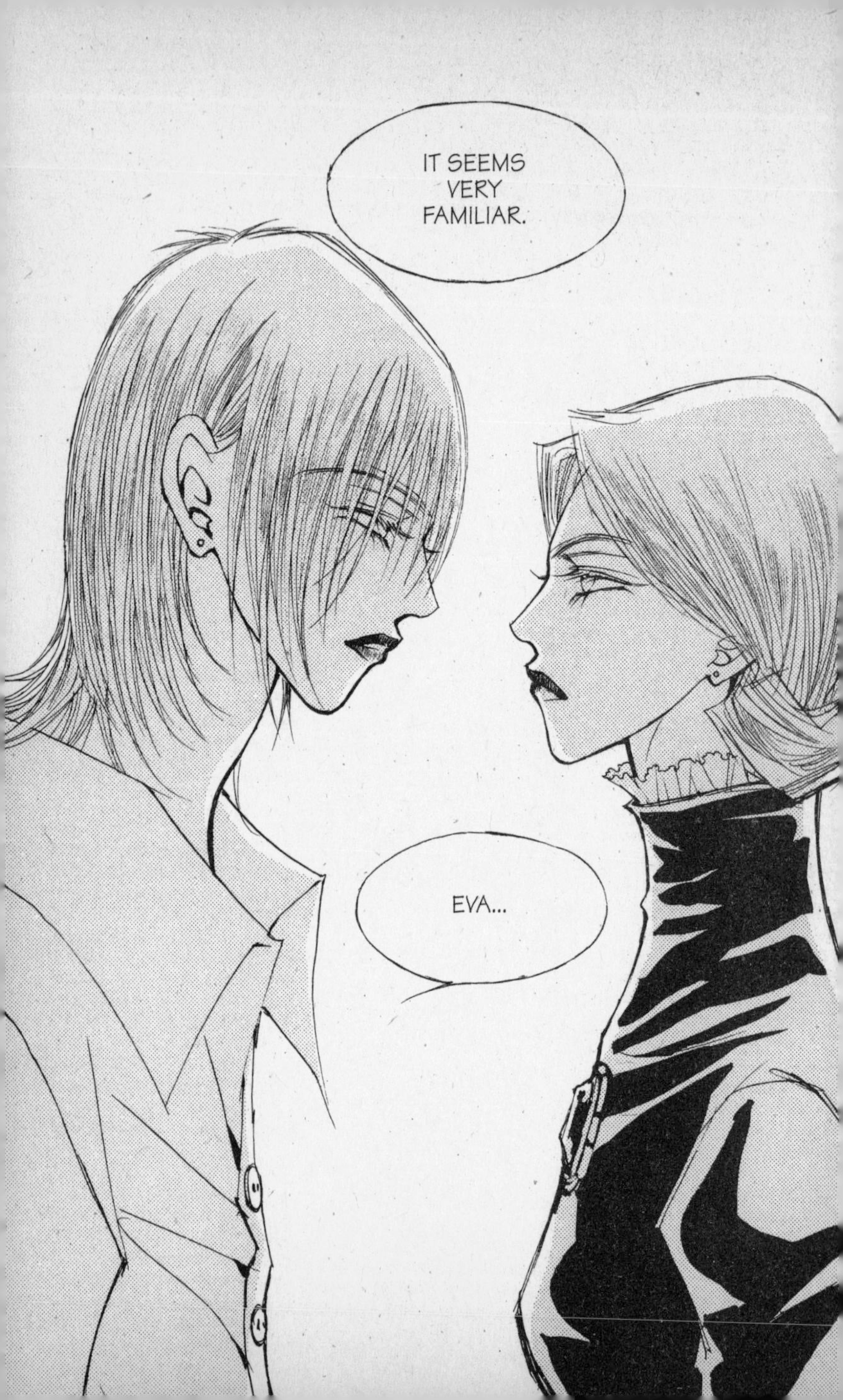
IT SEEMS VERY FAMILIAR.
EVA...

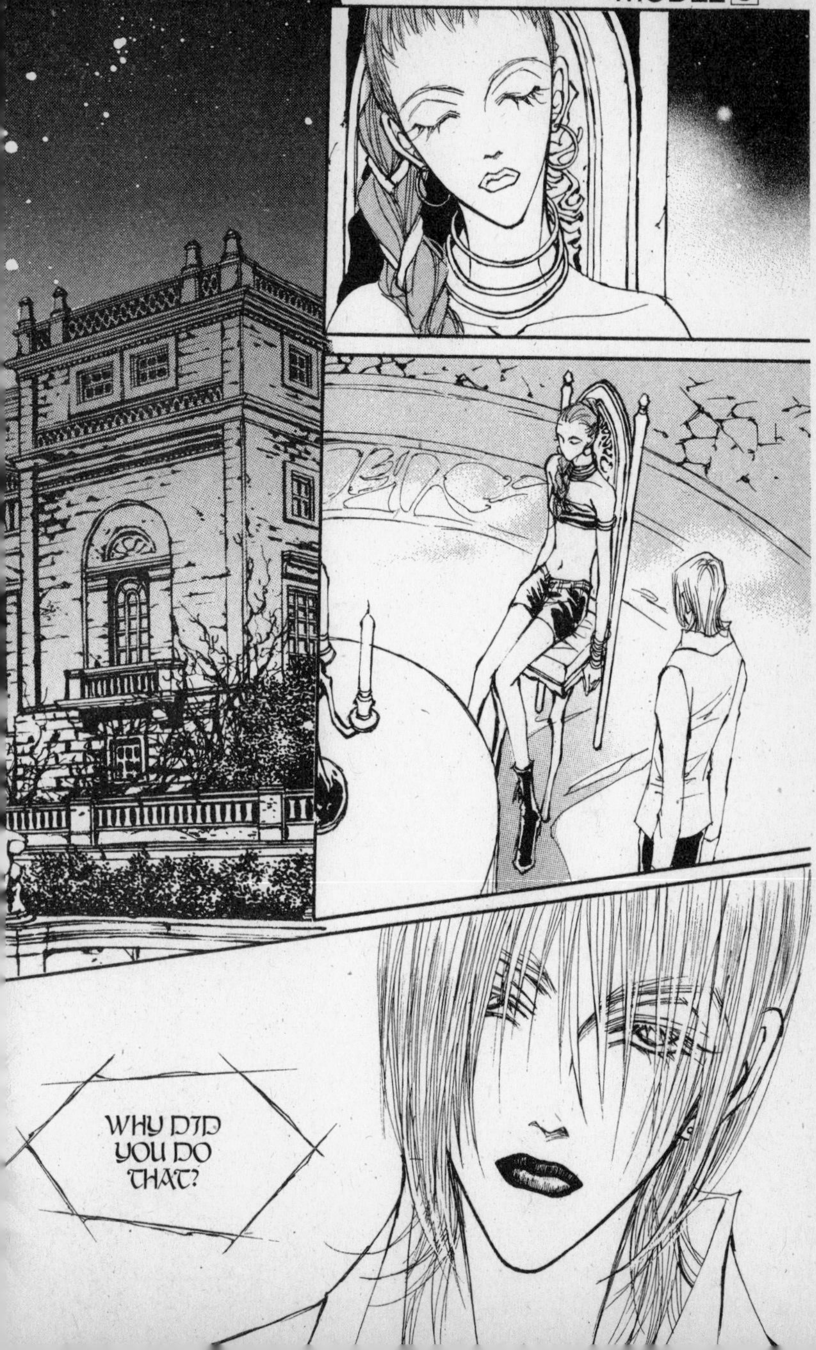
WHY DID YOU DO THAT?

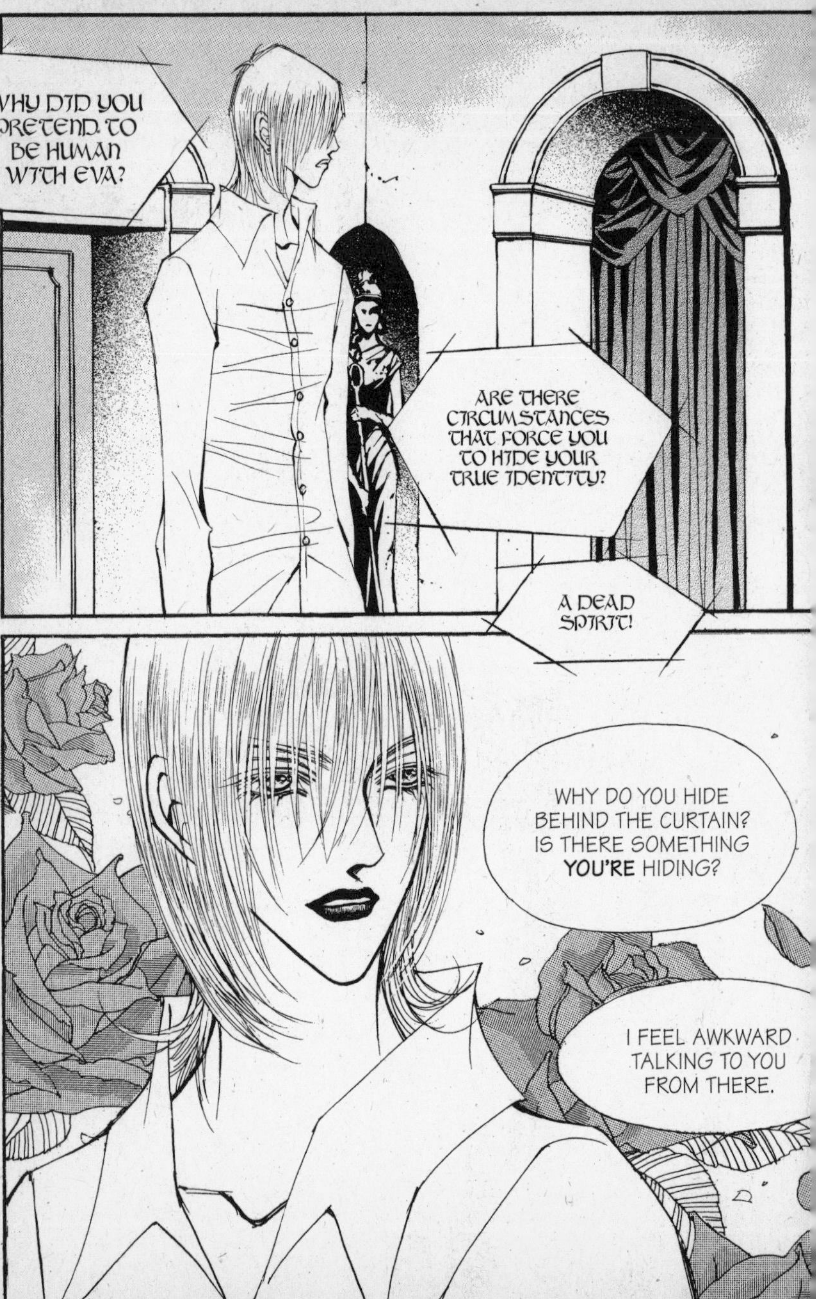
WHY DID YOU PRETEND TO BE HUMAN WITH EVA?
ARE THERE CIRCUMSTANCES THAT FORCE YOU TO HIDE YOUR TRUE IDENTITY?
A DEAD SPIRIT!
WHY DO YOU HIDE BEHIND THE CURTAIN? IS THERE SOMETHING **YOU'RE** HIDING?
I FEEL AWKWARD TALKING TO YOU FROM THERE.

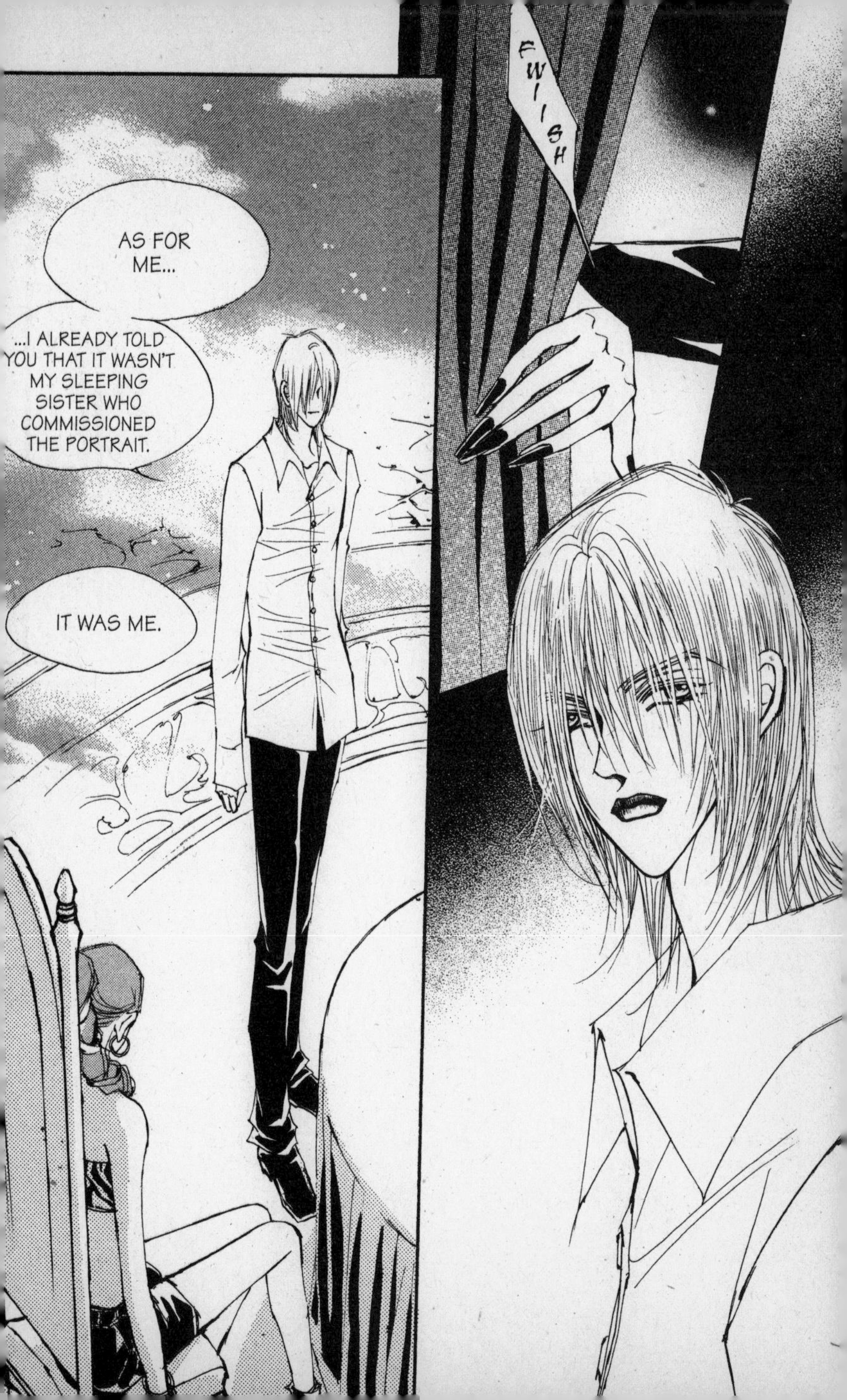
AS FOR ME...
...I ALREADY TOLD YOU THAT IT WASN'T MY SLEEPING SISTER WHO COMMISSIONED THE PORTRAIT.
IT WAS ME.
FWISH

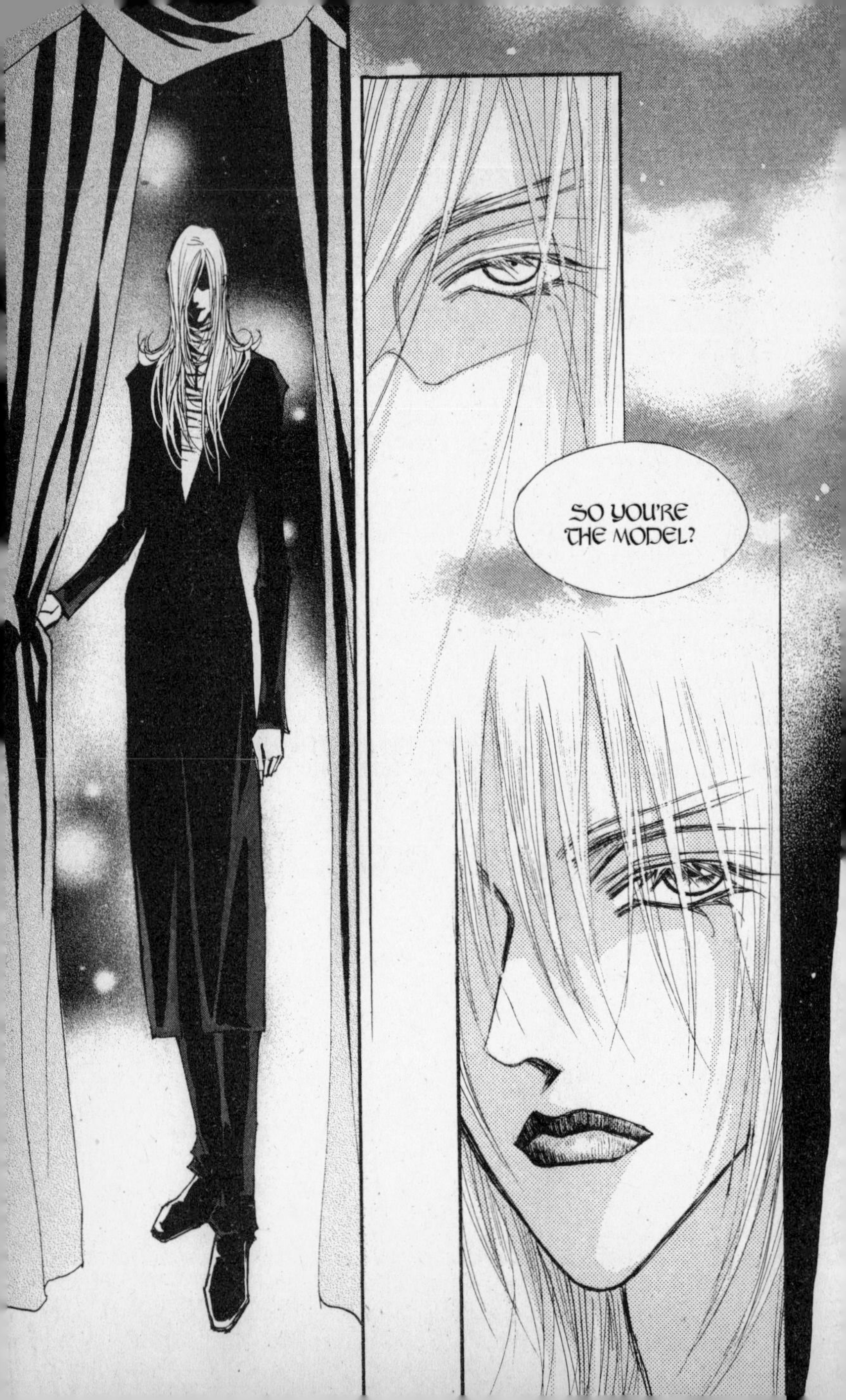
SO YOU'RE THE MODEL?

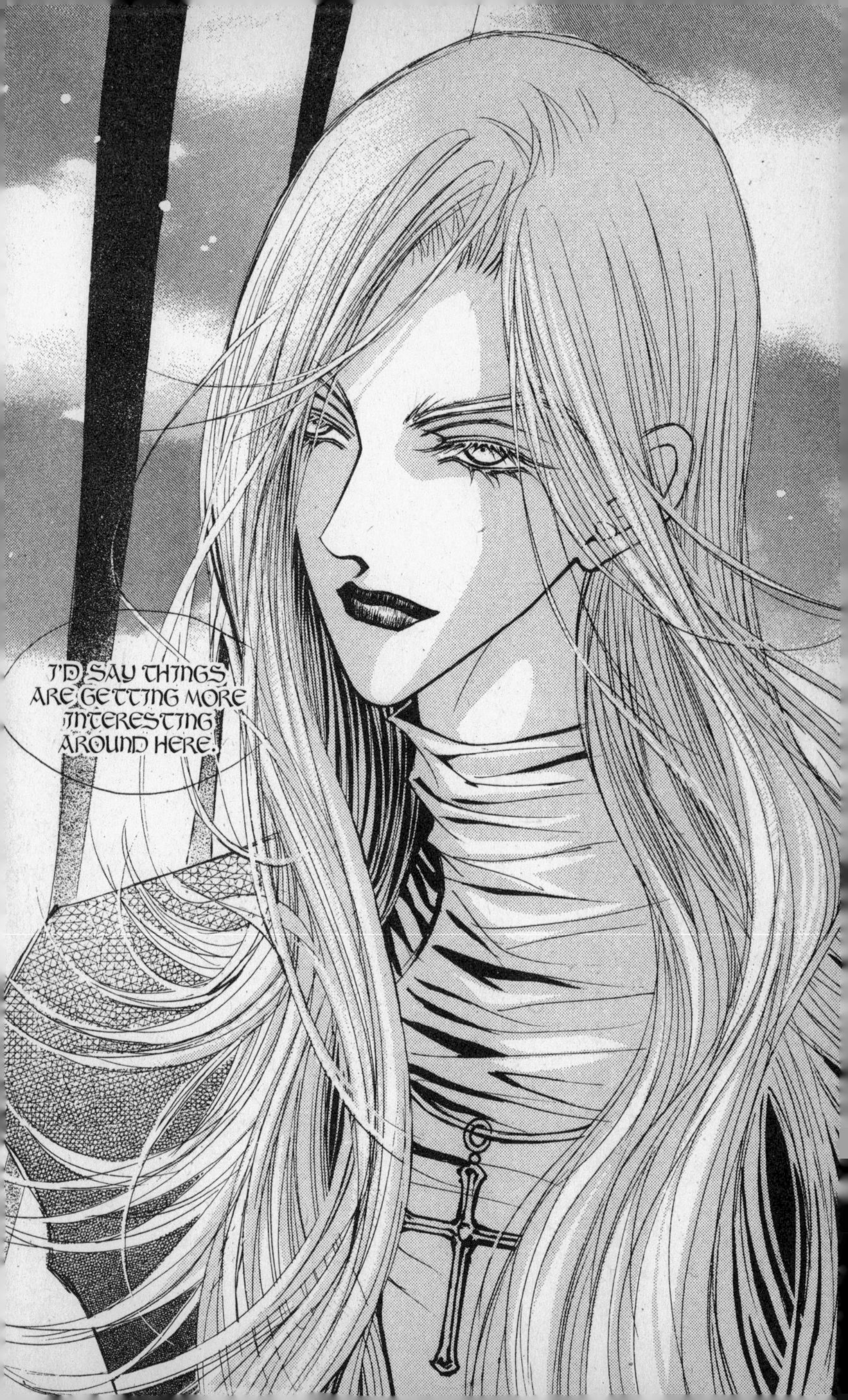
I'D SAY THINGS ARE GETTING MORE INTERESTING AROUND HERE.

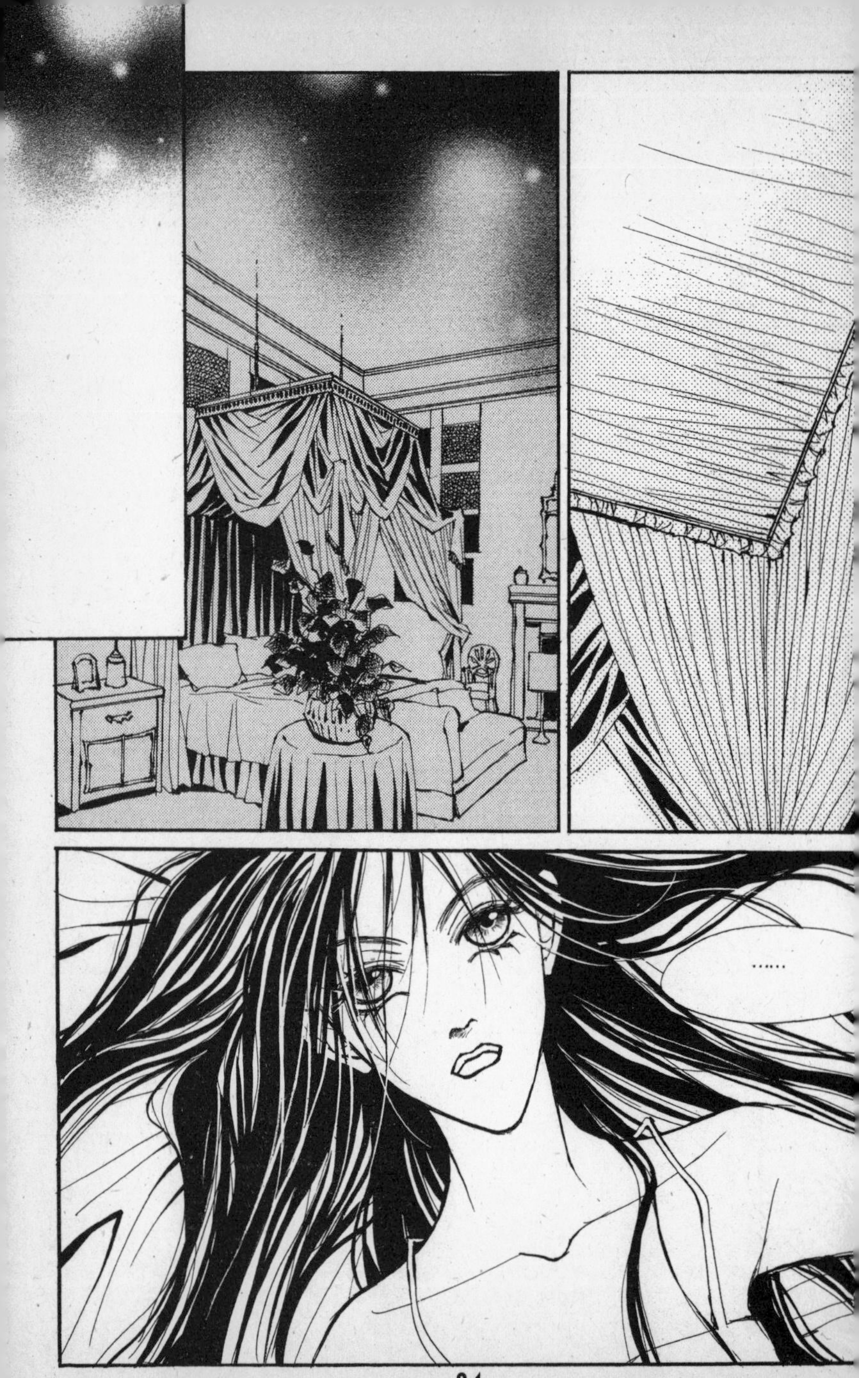
......

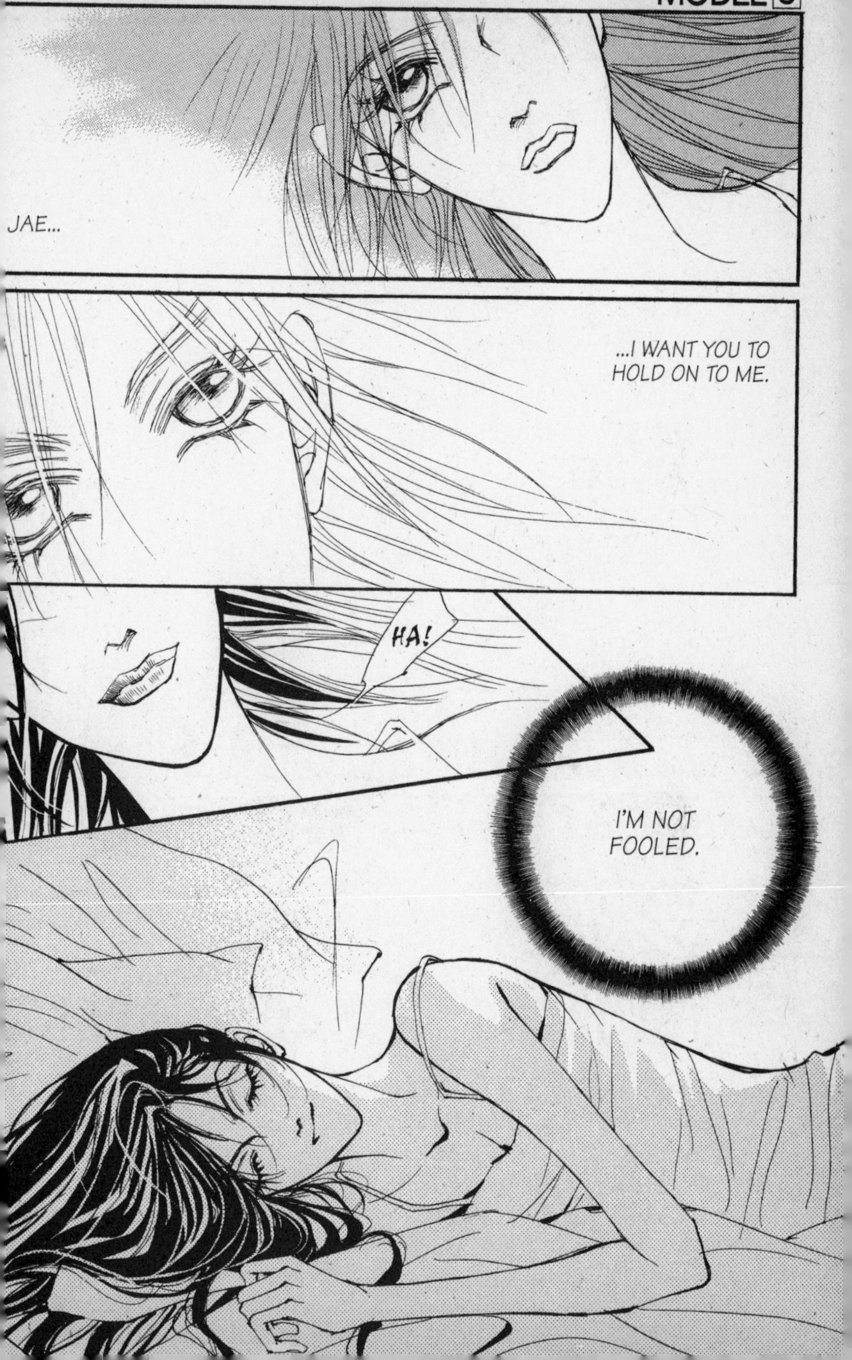
JAE...
...I WANT YOU TO HOLD ON TO ME.
HA!
I'M NOT FOOLED.

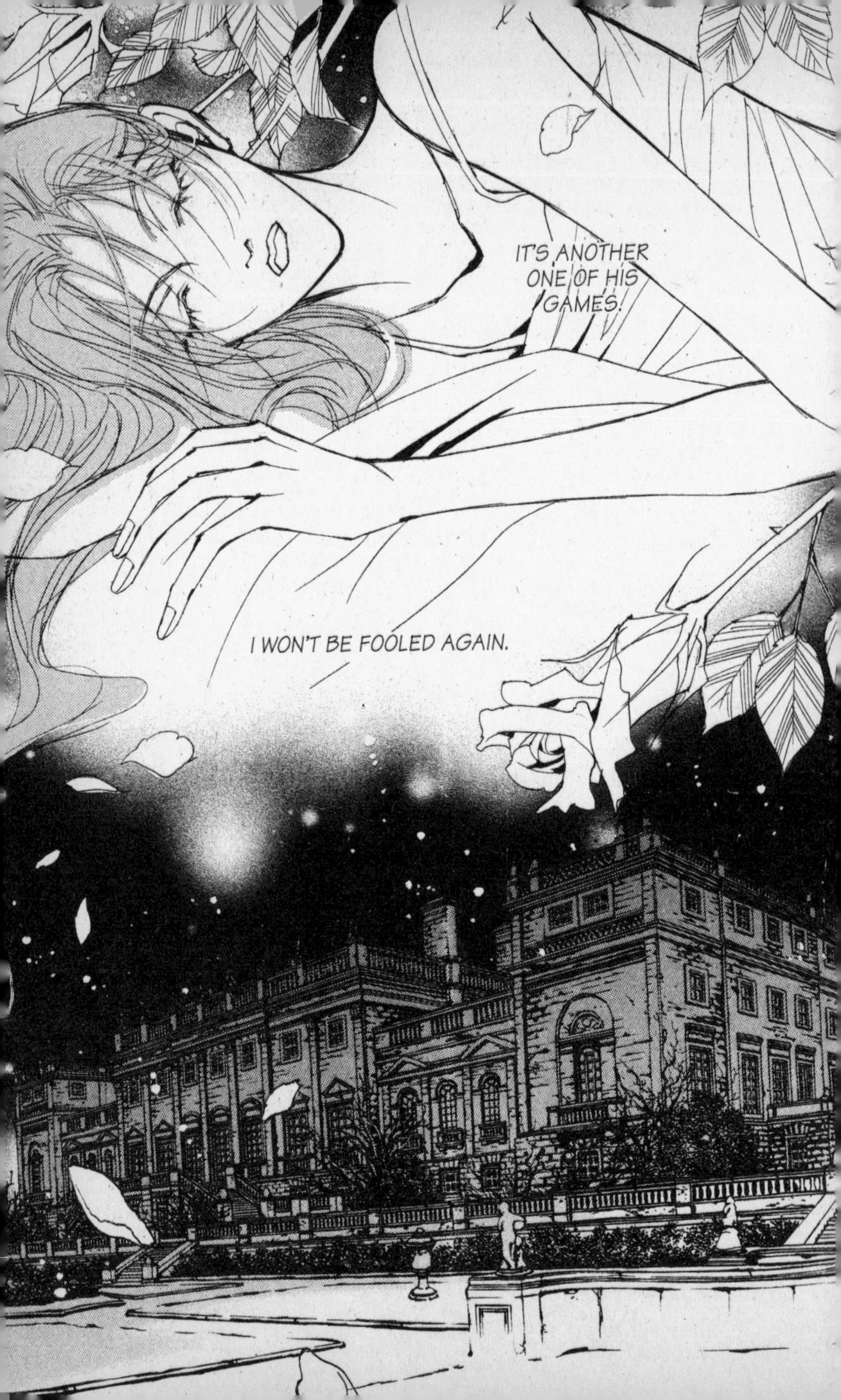
IT'S ANOTHER ONE OF HIS GAMES!
I WON'T BE FOOLED AGAIN.

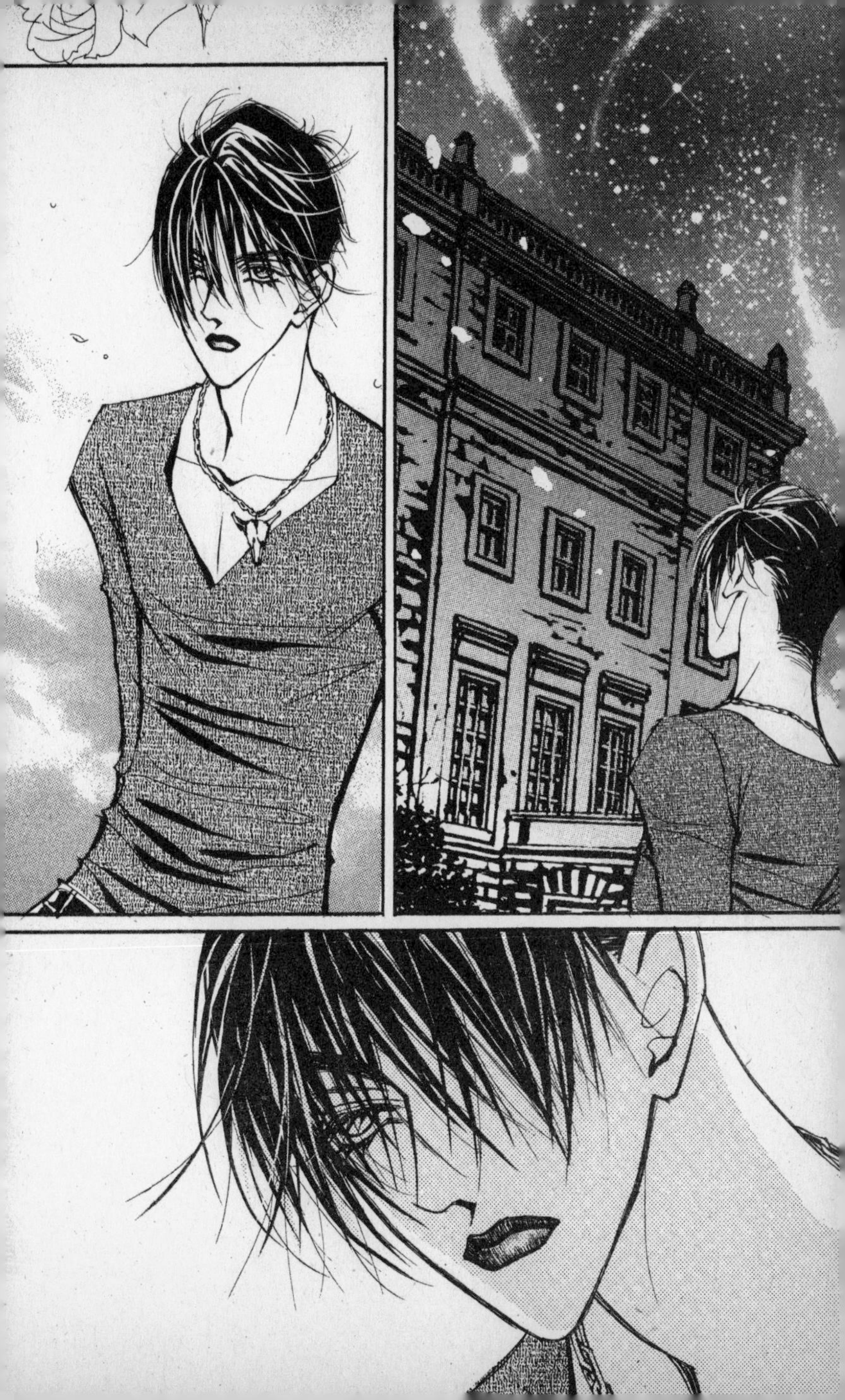

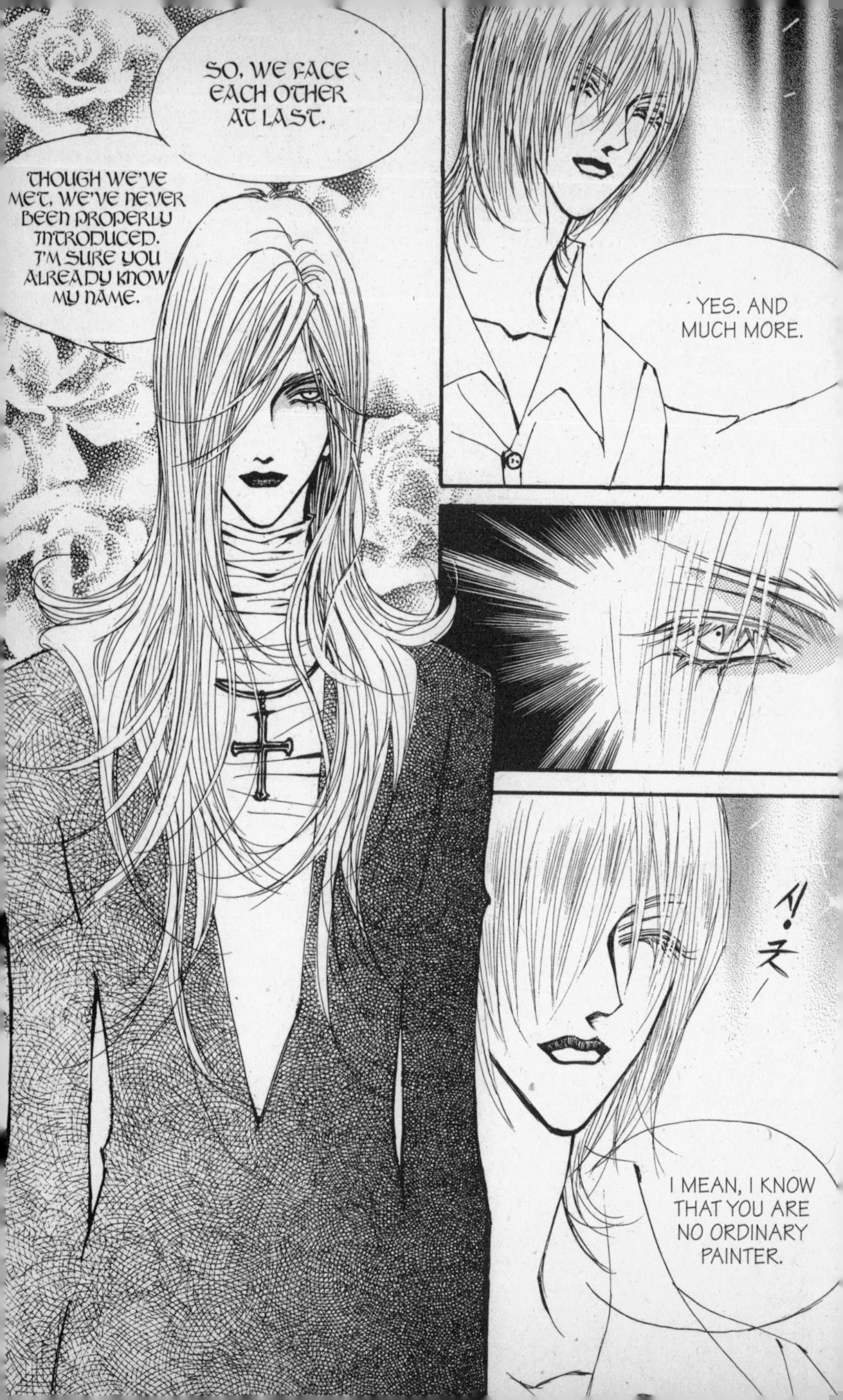
SO, WE FACE EACH OTHER AT LAST.
THOUGH WE'VE MET, WE'VE NEVER BEEN PROPERLY INTRODUCED. I'M SURE YOU ALREADY KNOW MY NAME.
YES. AND MUCH MORE.
시 긋
I MEAN, I KNOW THAT YOU ARE NO ORDINARY PAINTER.

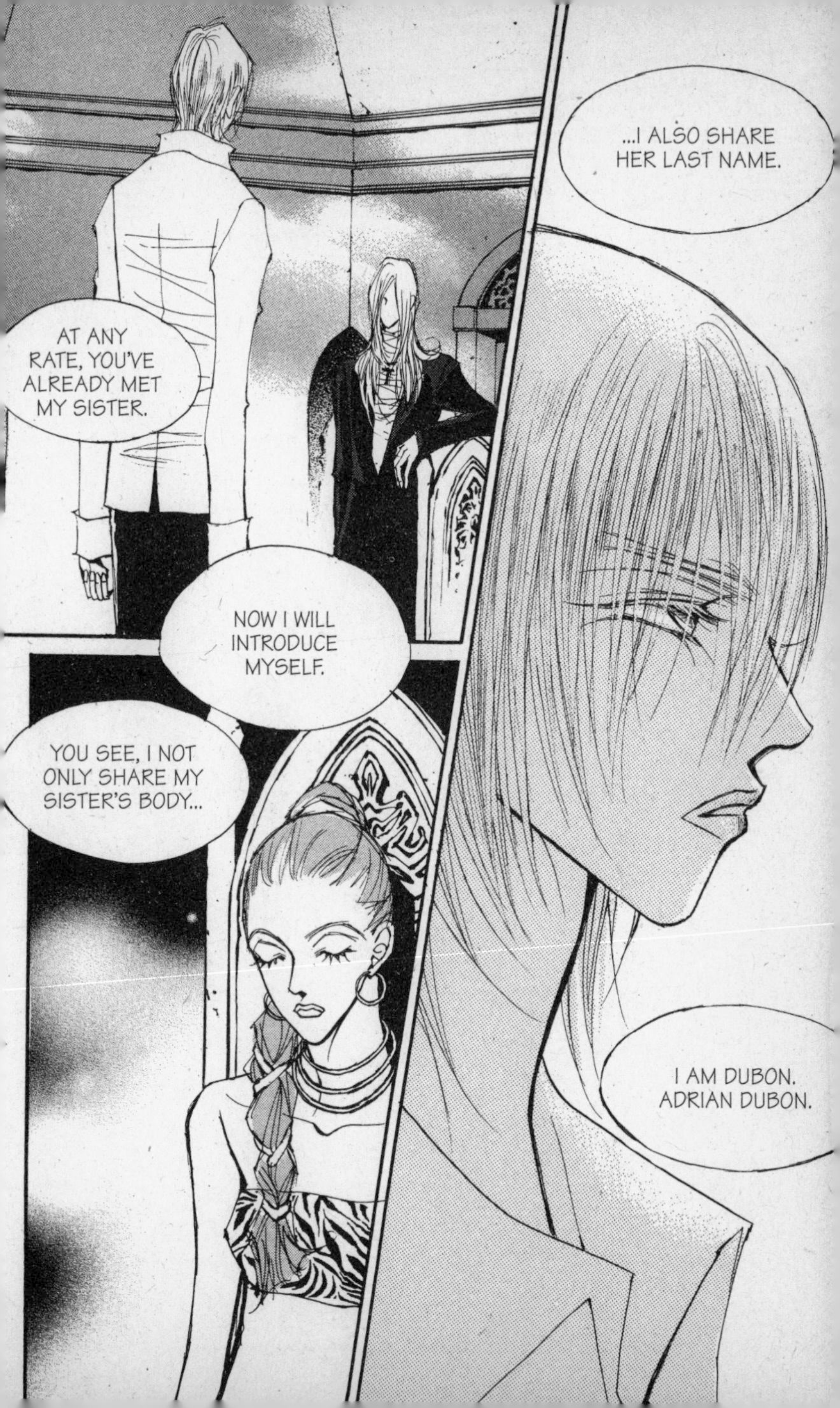
AT ANY RATE, YOU'VE ALREADY MET MY SISTER.
NOW I WILL INTRODUCE MYSELF.
YOU SEE, I NOT ONLY SHARE MY SISTER'S BODY...
...I ALSO SHARE HER LAST NAME.
I AM DUBON. ADRIAN DUBON.

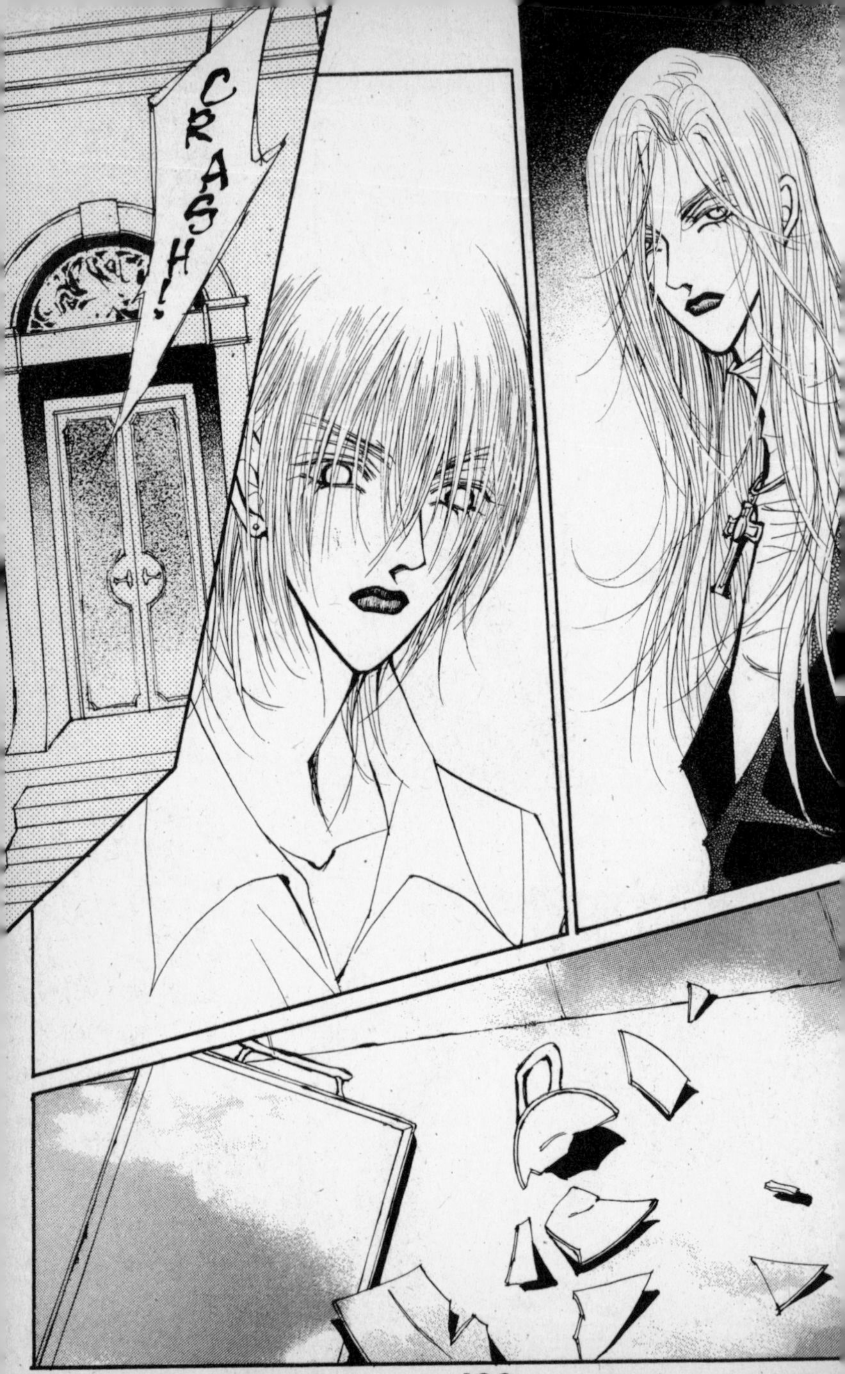
CRASH!

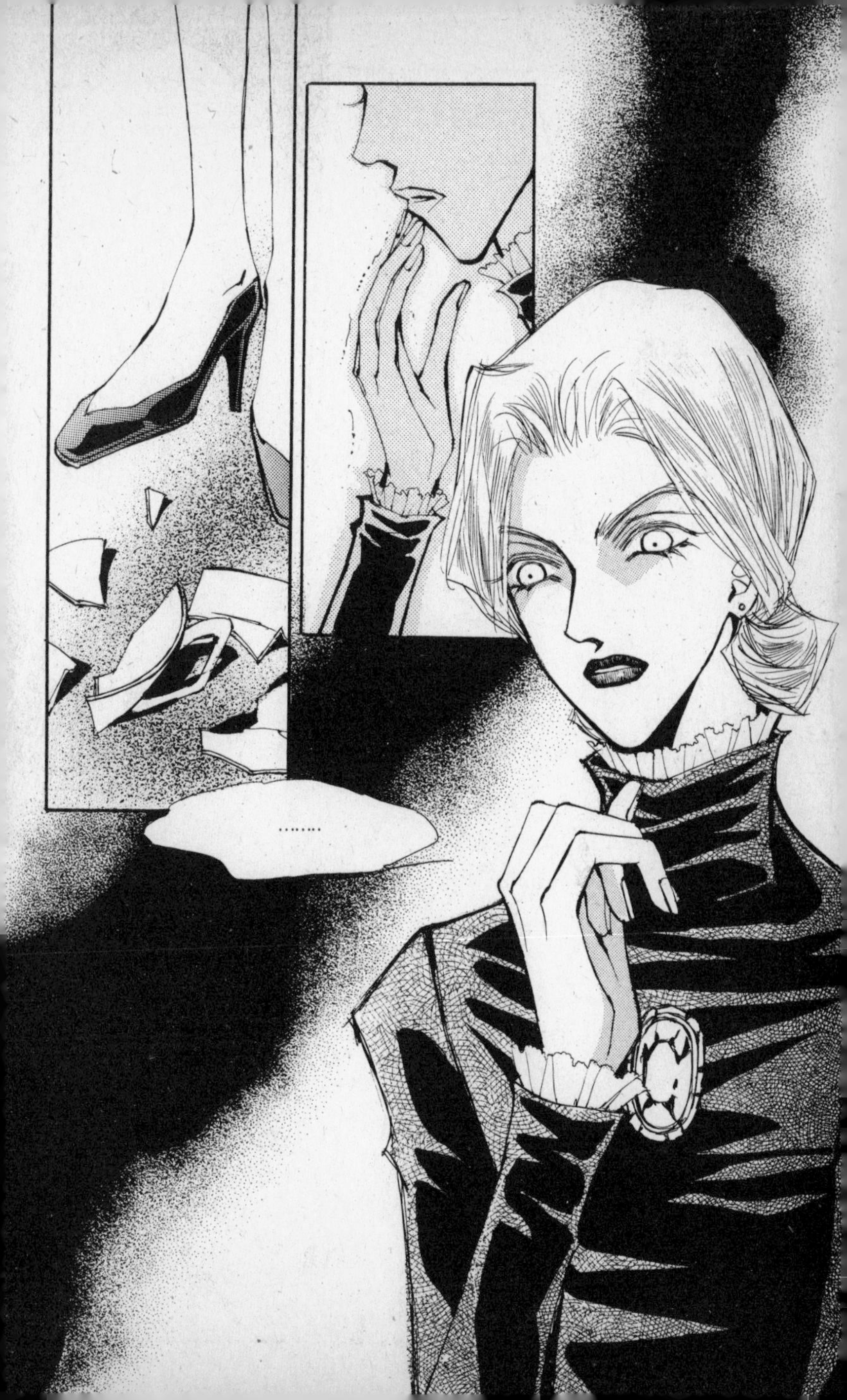
……

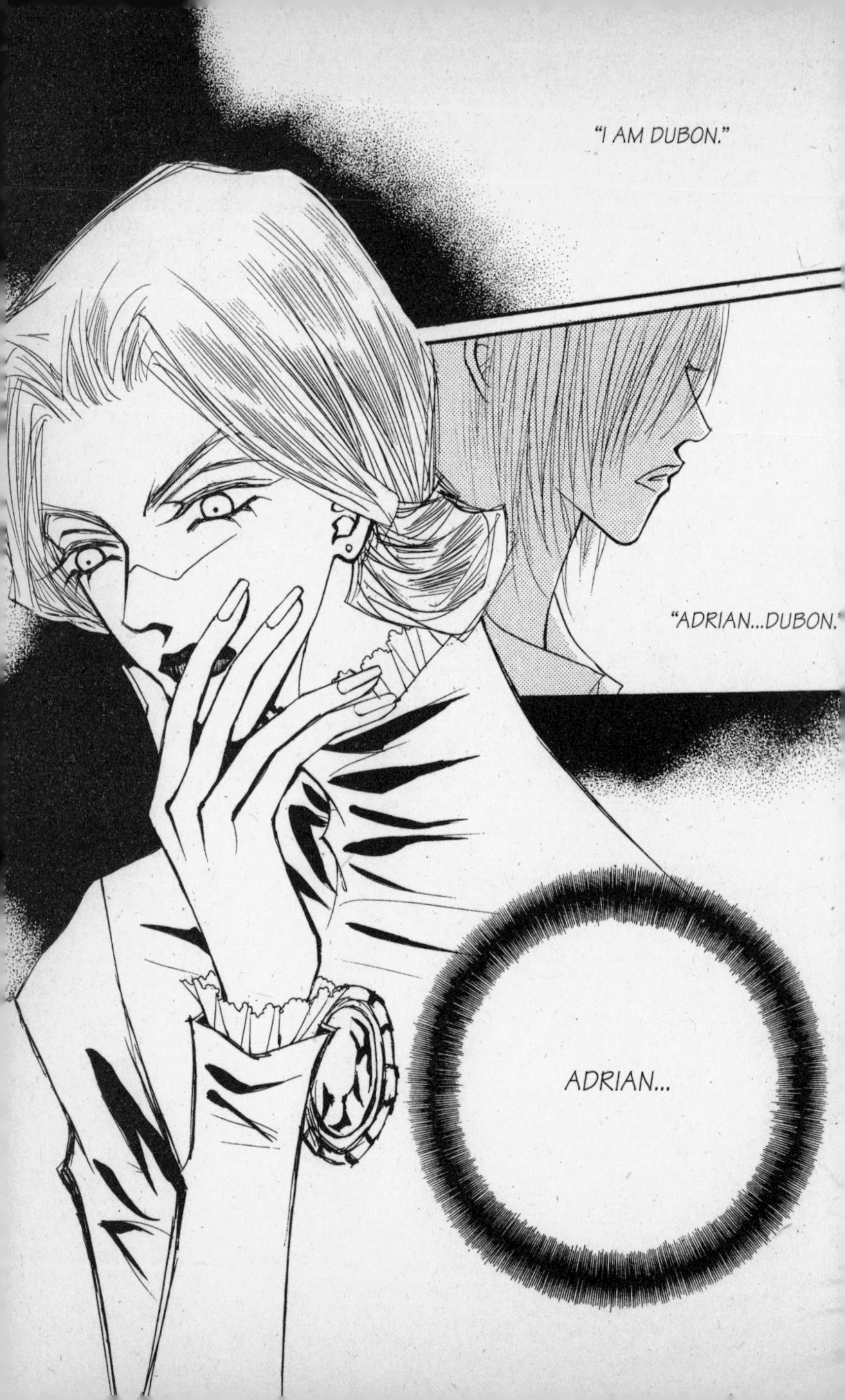
"I AM DUBON."
"ADRIAN...DUBON."
ADRIAN...

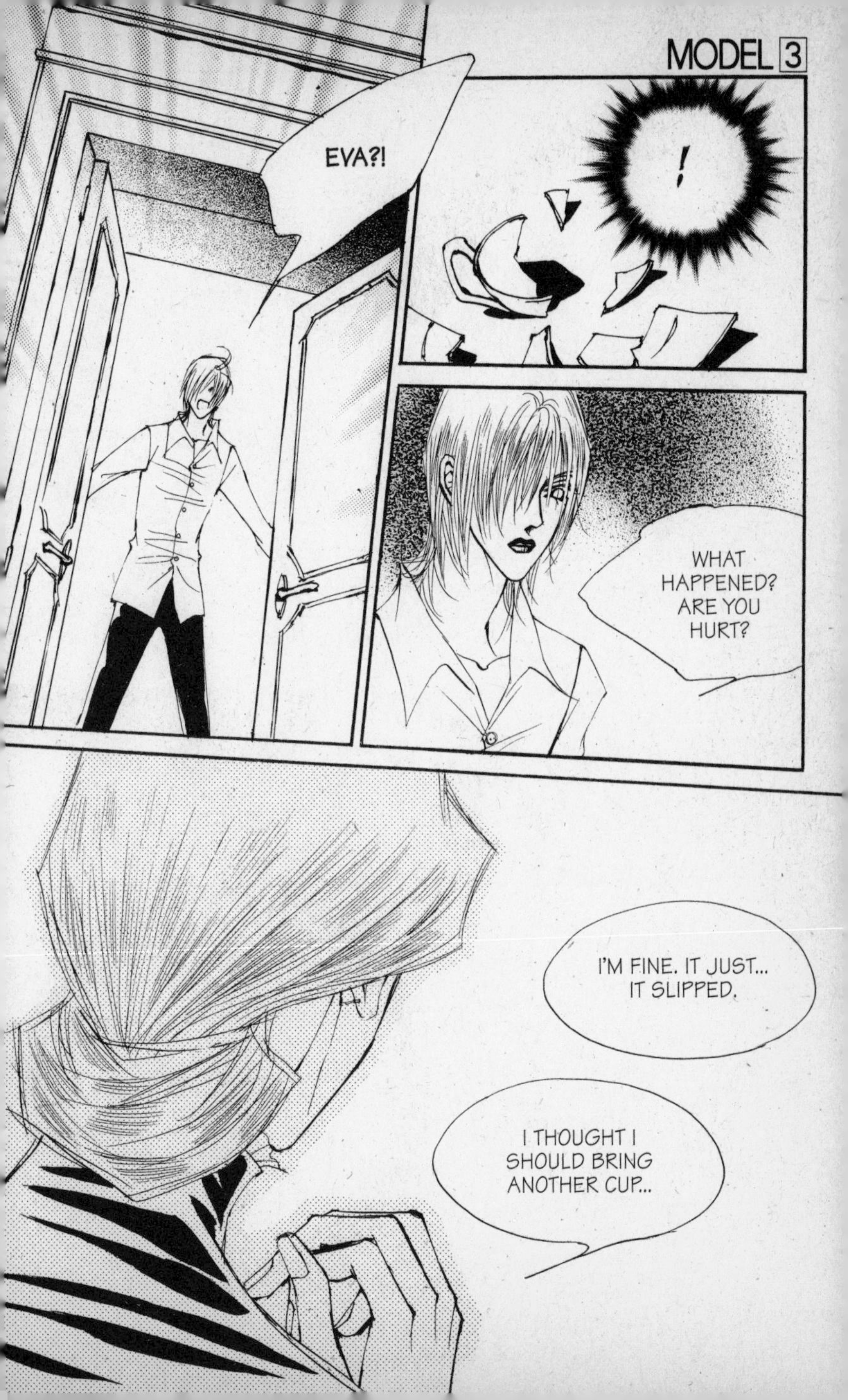
EVA?!
!
WHAT HAPPENED? ARE YOU HURT?
I'M FINE. IT JUST... IT SLIPPED.
I THOUGHT I SHOULD BRING ANOTHER CUP...

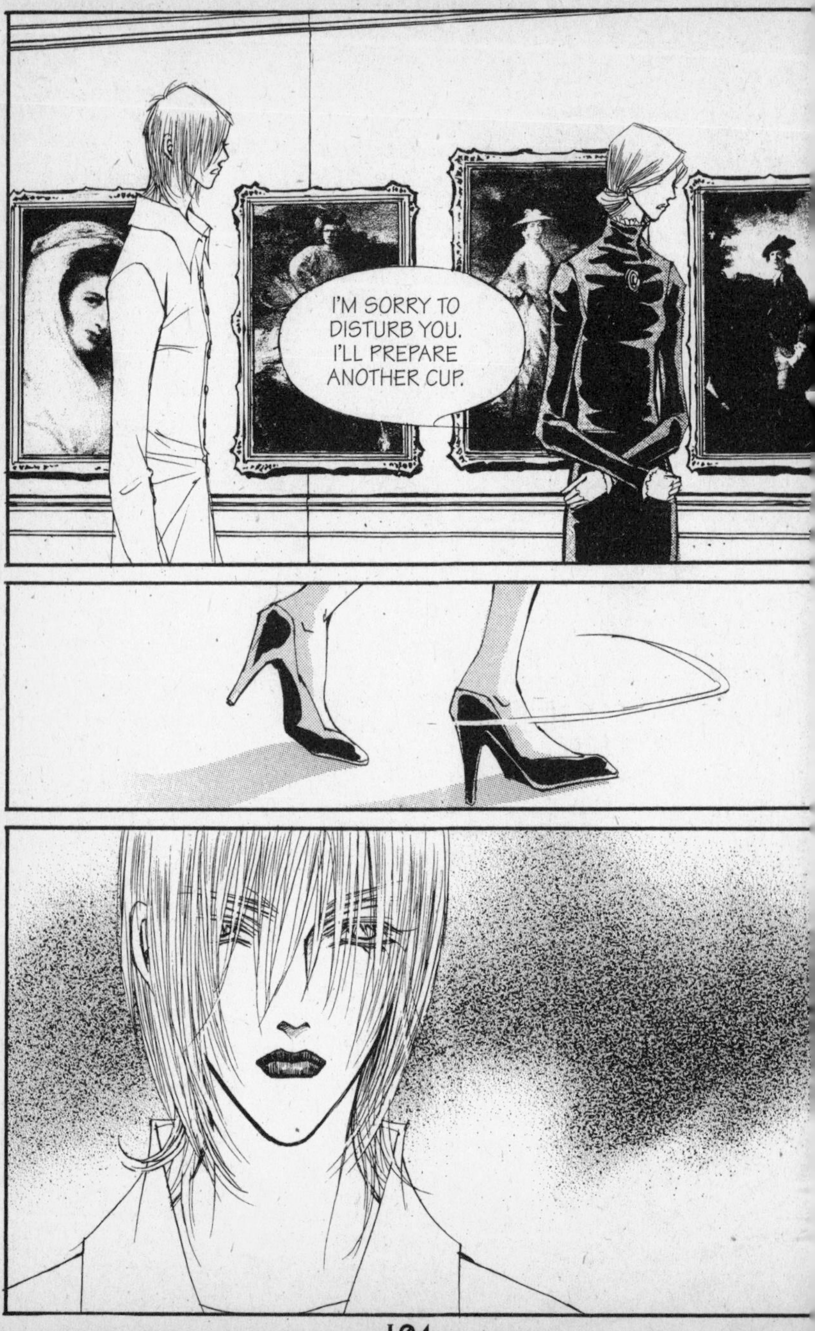
I'M SORRY TO DISTURB YOU. I'LL PREPARE ANOTHER CUP.

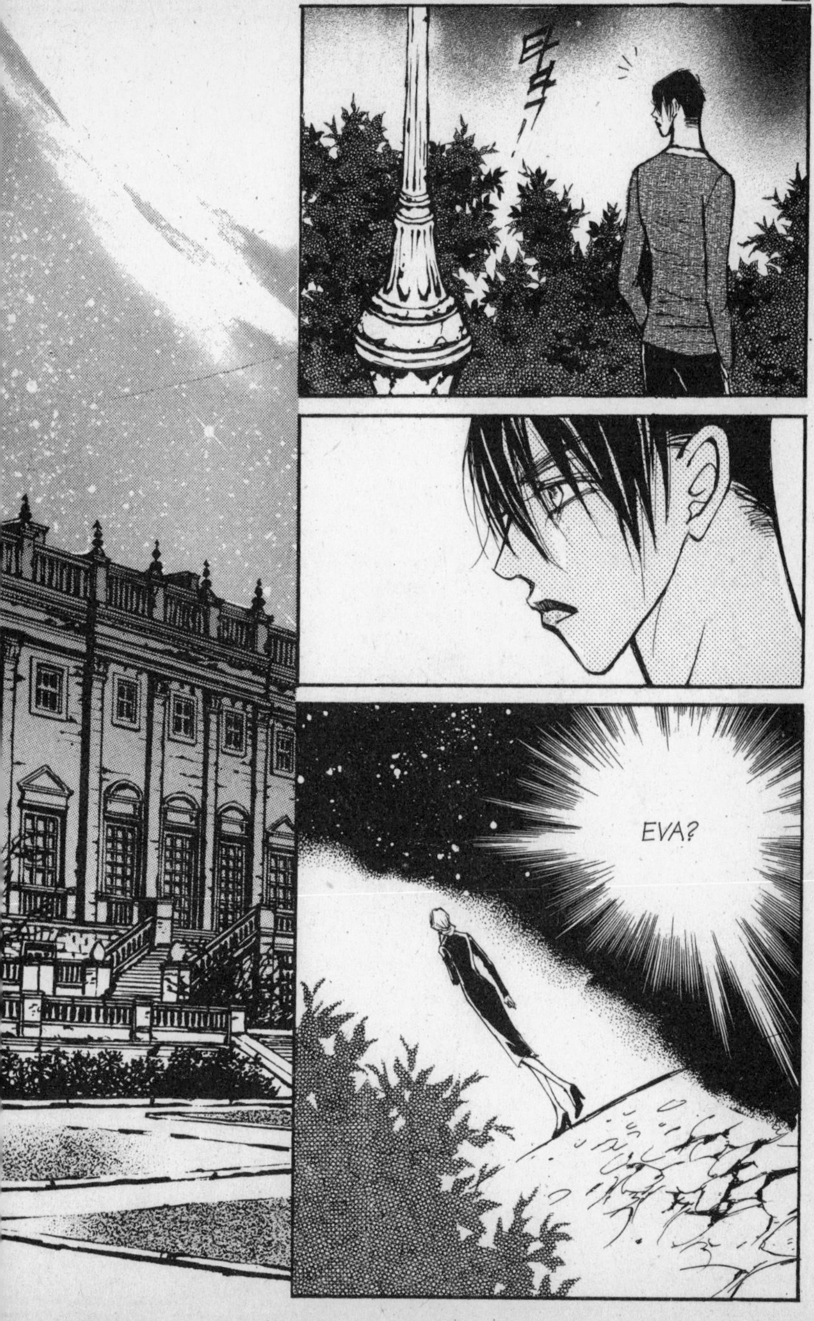
타닥..!
EVA?

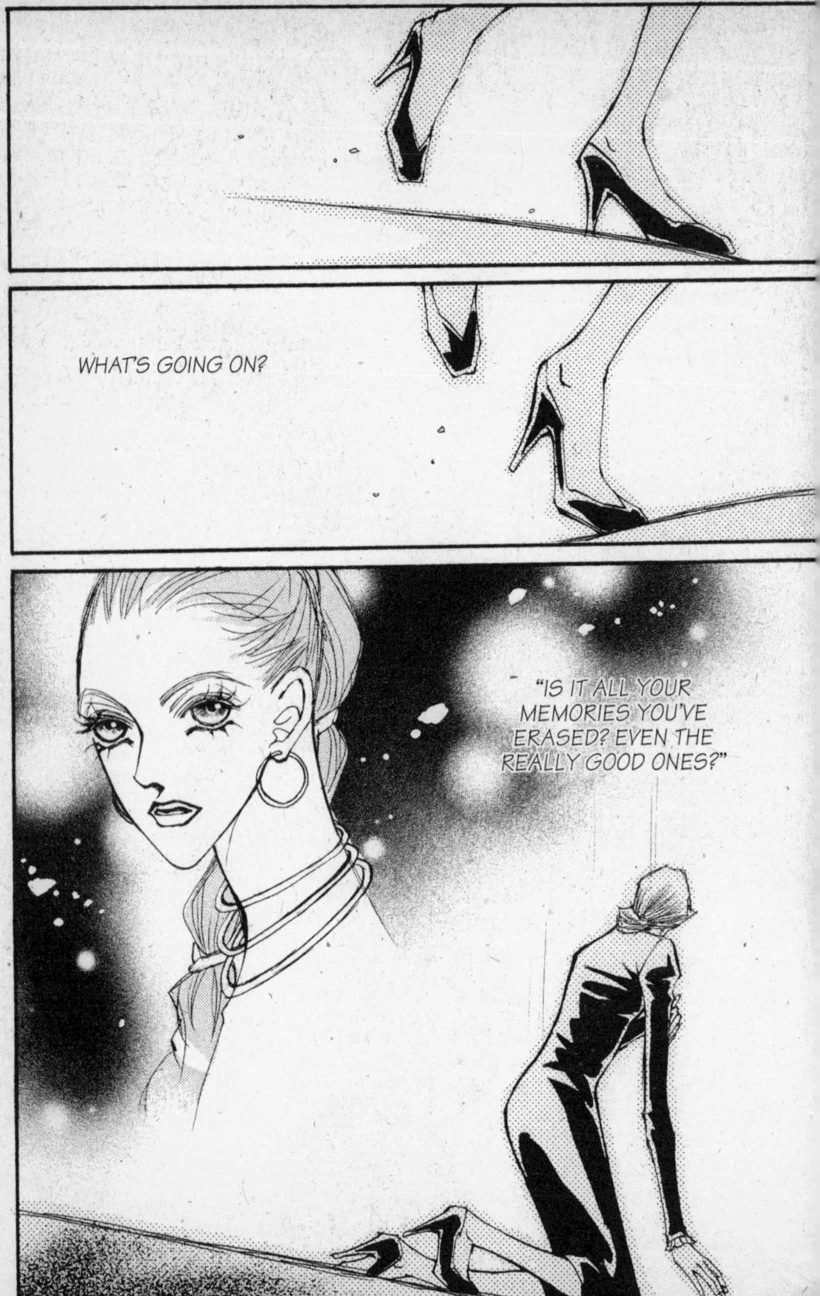
WHAT'S GOING ON?
"IS IT ALL YOUR MEMORIES YOU'VE ERASED? EVEN THE REALLY GOOD ONES?"

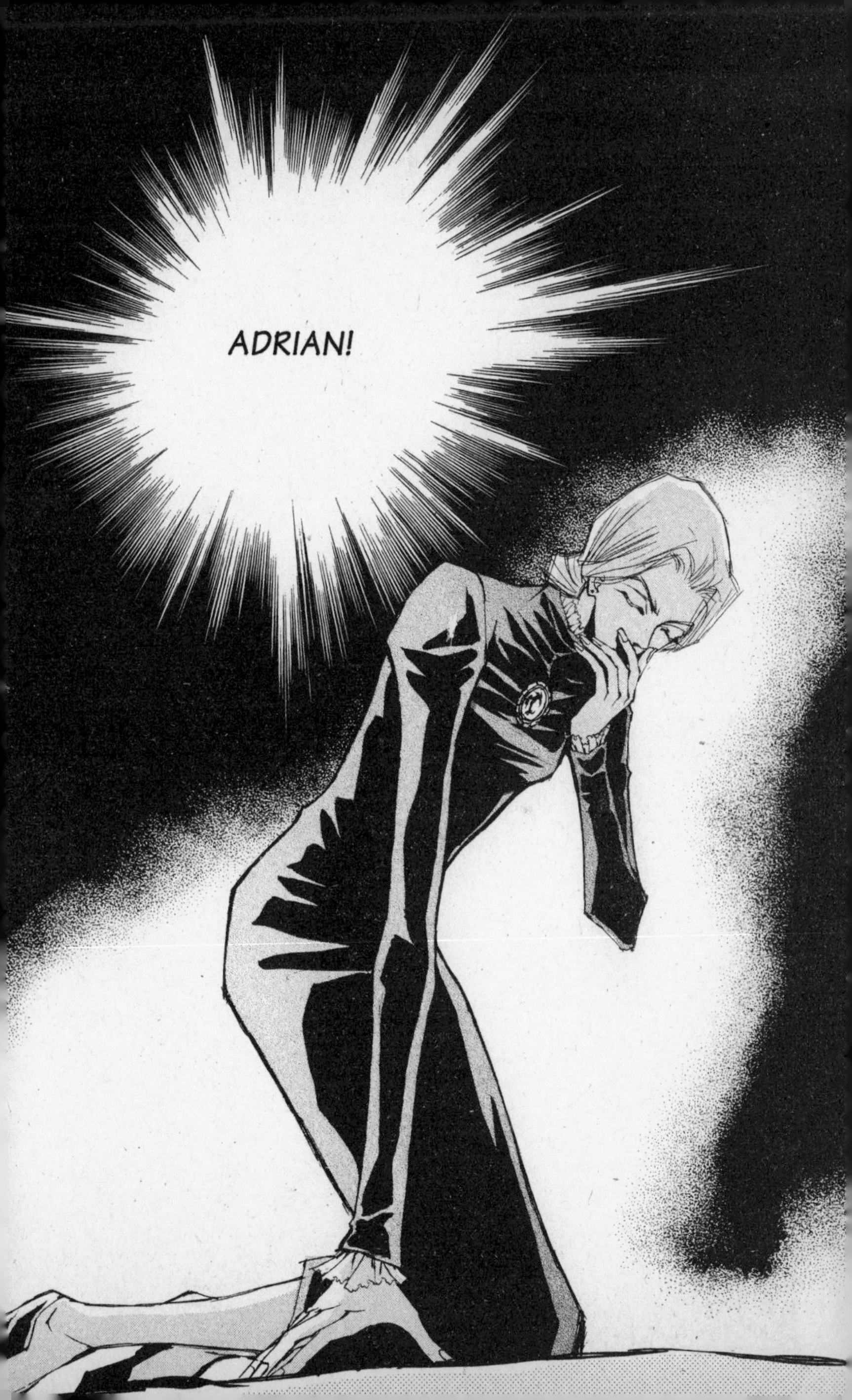
ADRIAN!

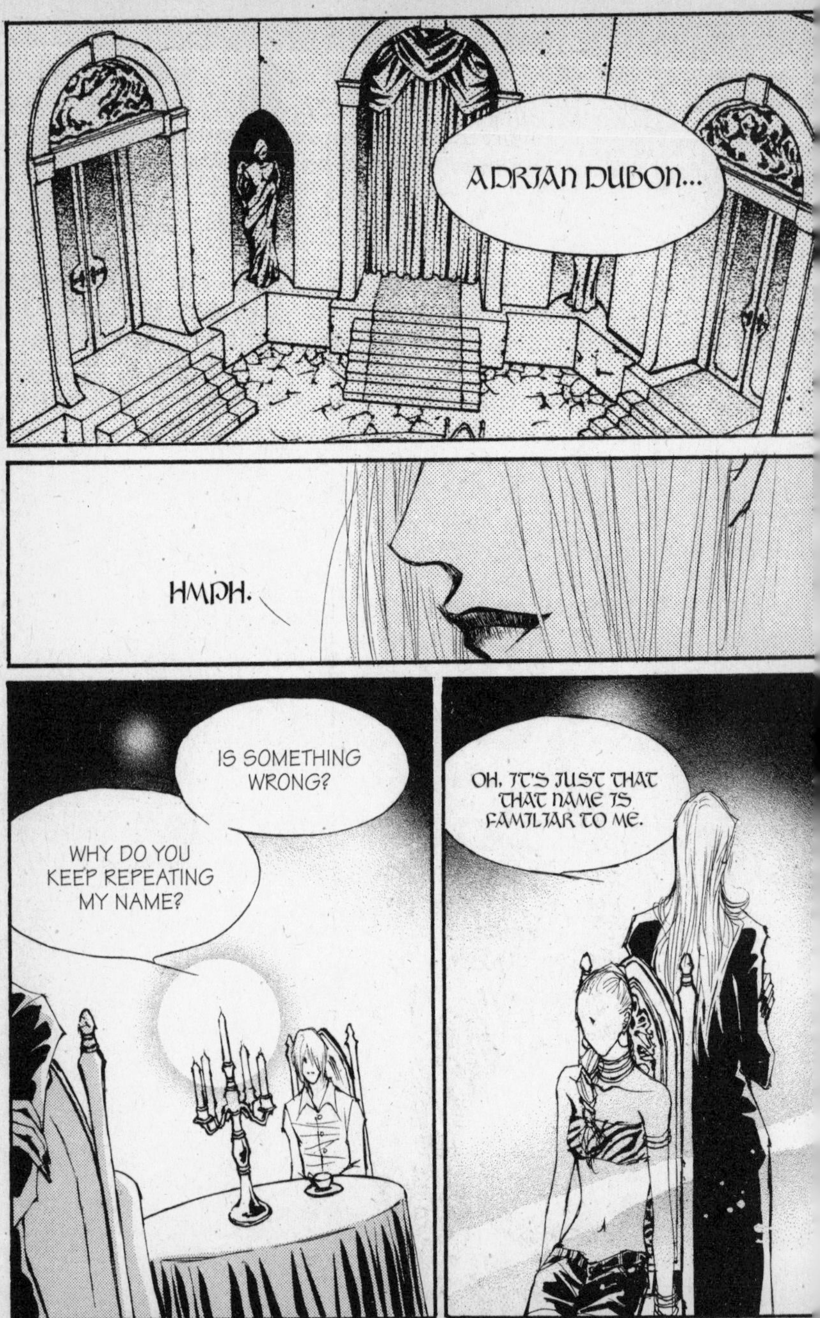
ADRIAN DUBON...
HMPH.
IS SOMETHING WRONG?
WHY DO YOU KEEP REPEATING MY NAME?
OH, IT'S JUST THAT THAT NAME IS FAMILIAR TO ME.

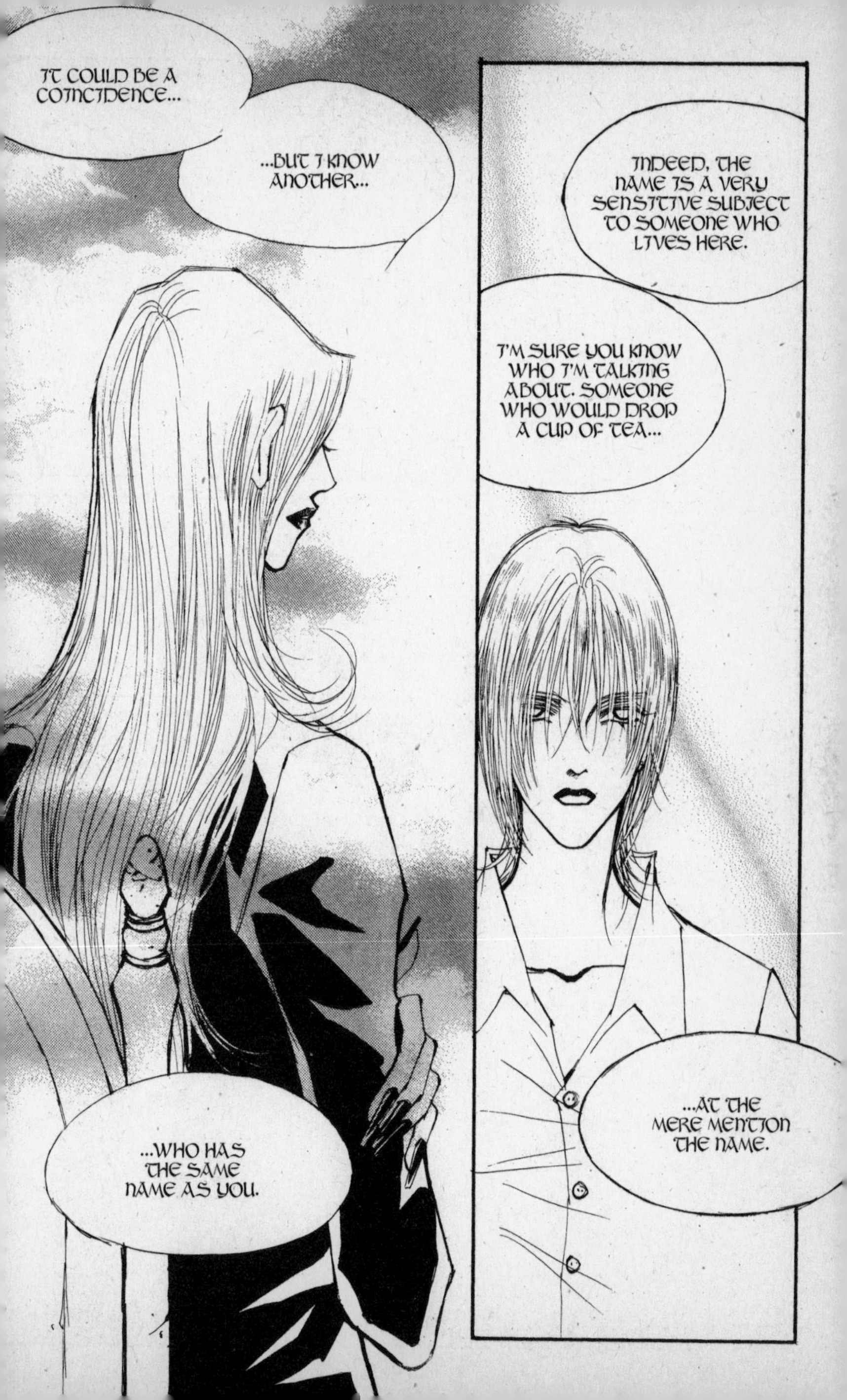
IT COULD BE A COINCIDENCE...
...BUT I KNOW ANOTHER...
...WHO HAS THE SAME NAME AS YOU.
INDEED, THE NAME IS A VERY SENSITIVE SUBJECT TO SOMEONE WHO LIVES HERE.
I'M SURE YOU KNOW WHO I'M TALKING ABOUT. SOMEONE WHO WOULD DROP A CUP OF TEA...
...AT THE MERE MENTION THE NAME.

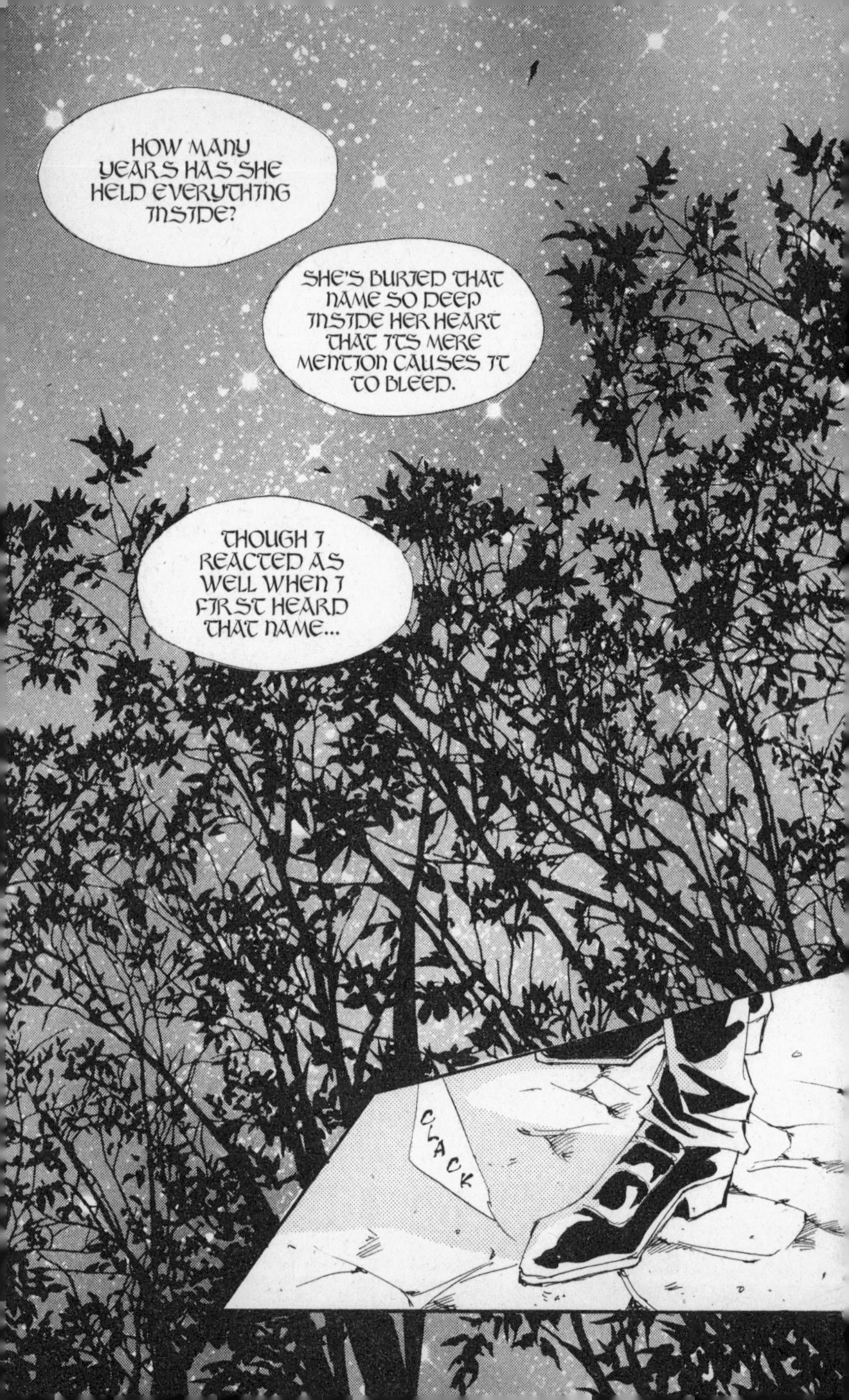
HOW MANY YEARS HAS SHE HELD EVERYTHING INSIDE?
SHE'S BURIED THAT NAME SO DEEP INSIDE HER HEART THAT ITS MERE MENTION CAUSES IT TO BLEED.
THOUGH I REACTED AS WELL WHEN I FIRST HEARD THAT NAME...
CLACK

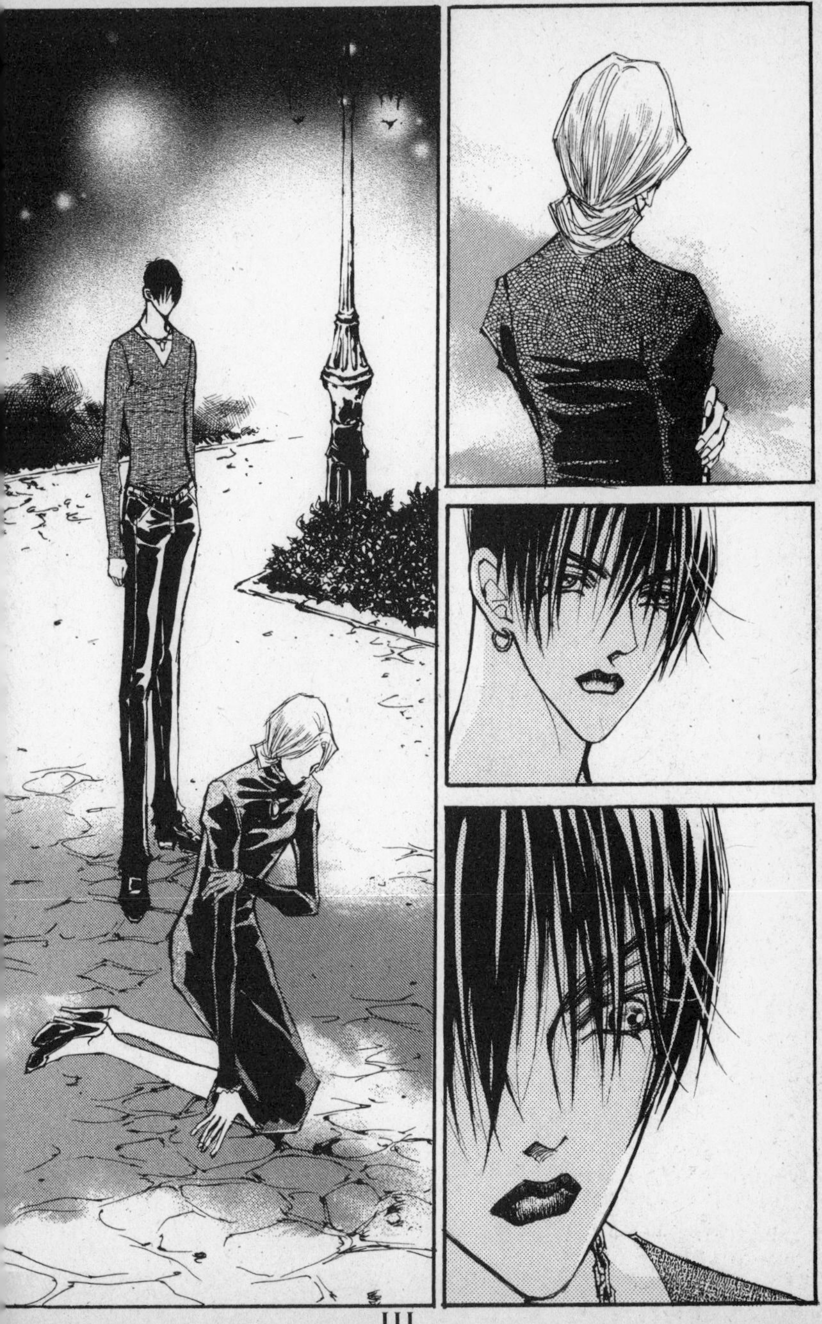

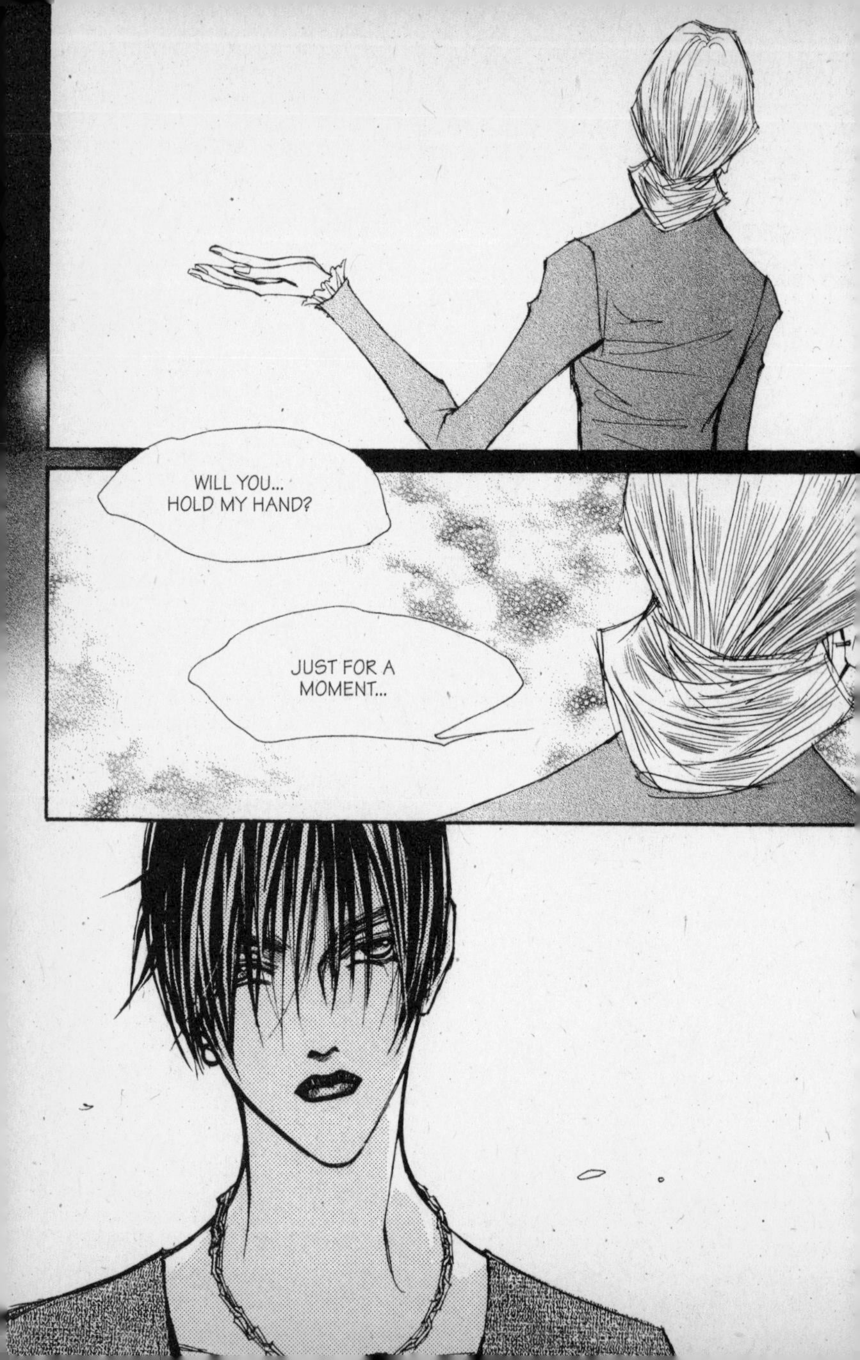
WILL YOU... HOLD MY HAND?
JUST FOR A MOMENT...

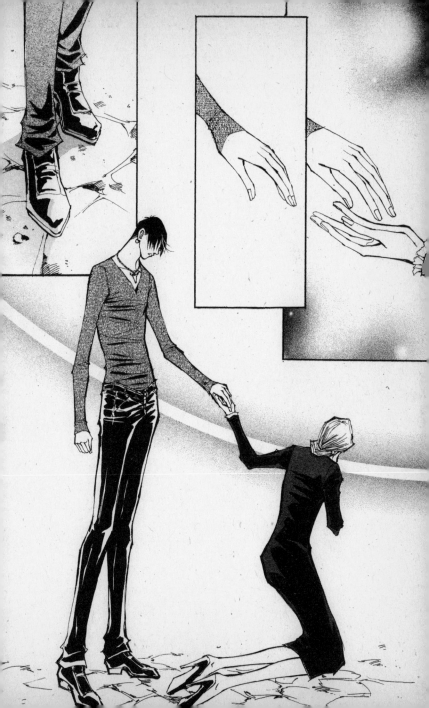

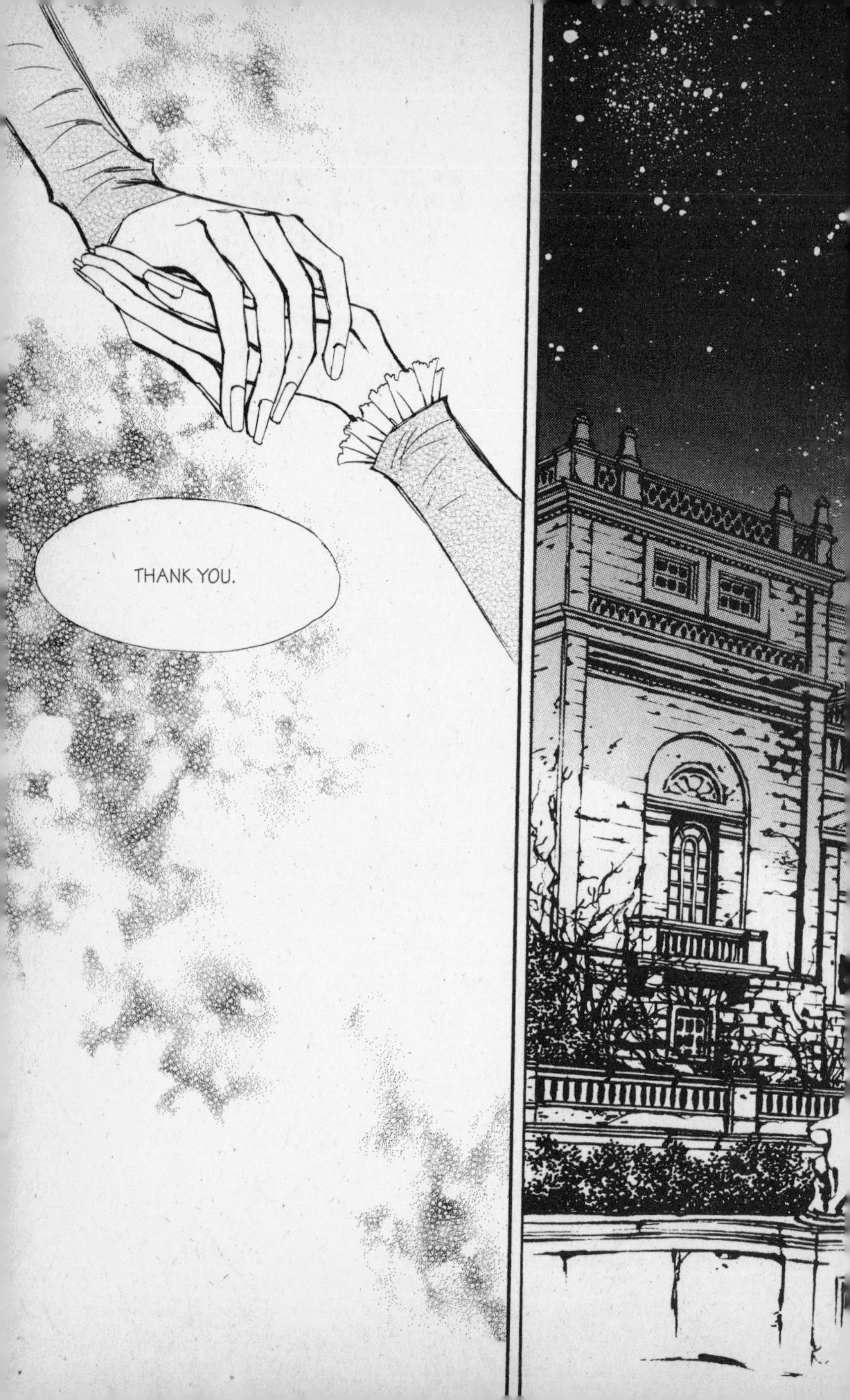
THANK YOU.

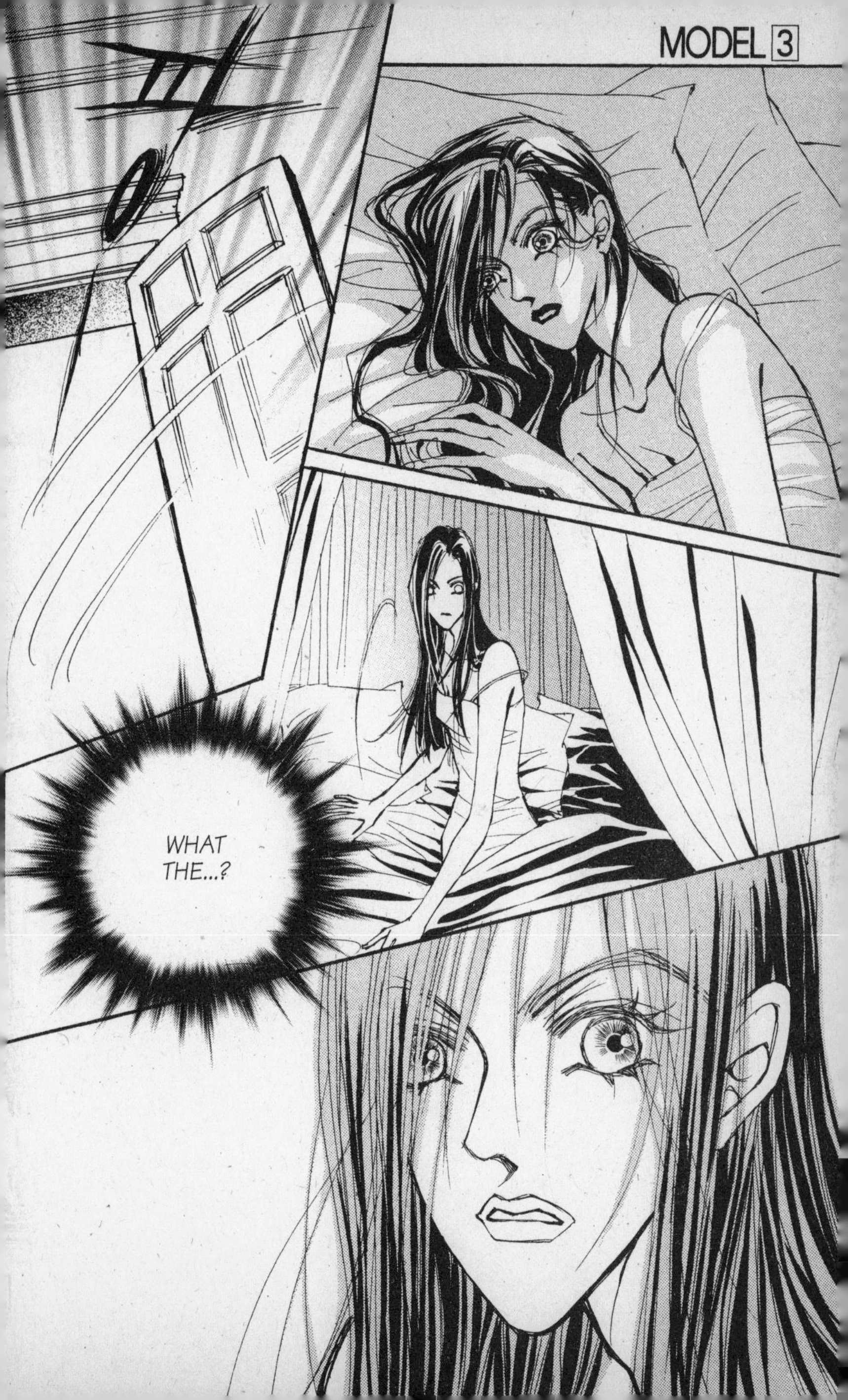
WHAT
THE...?

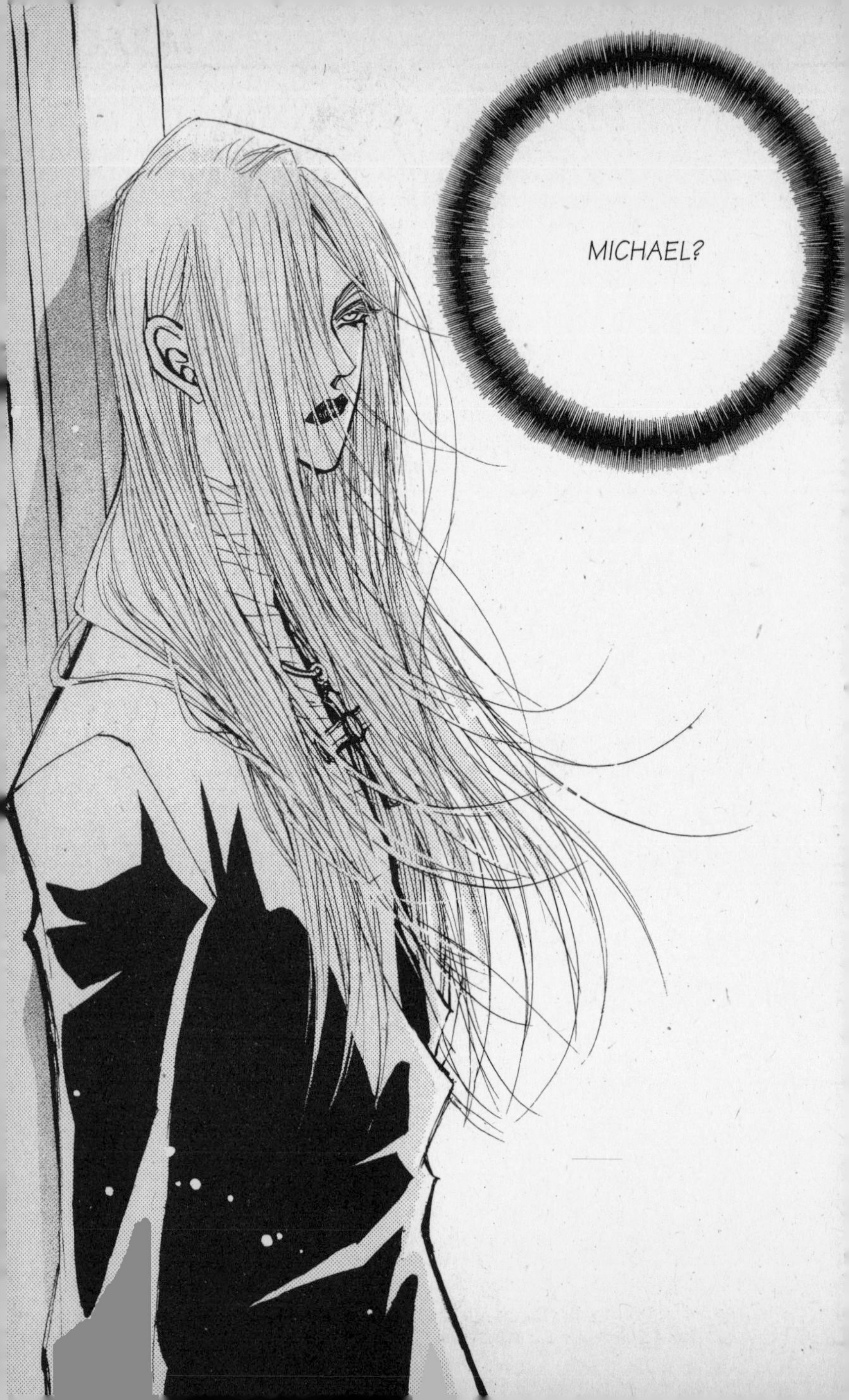
MICHAEL?

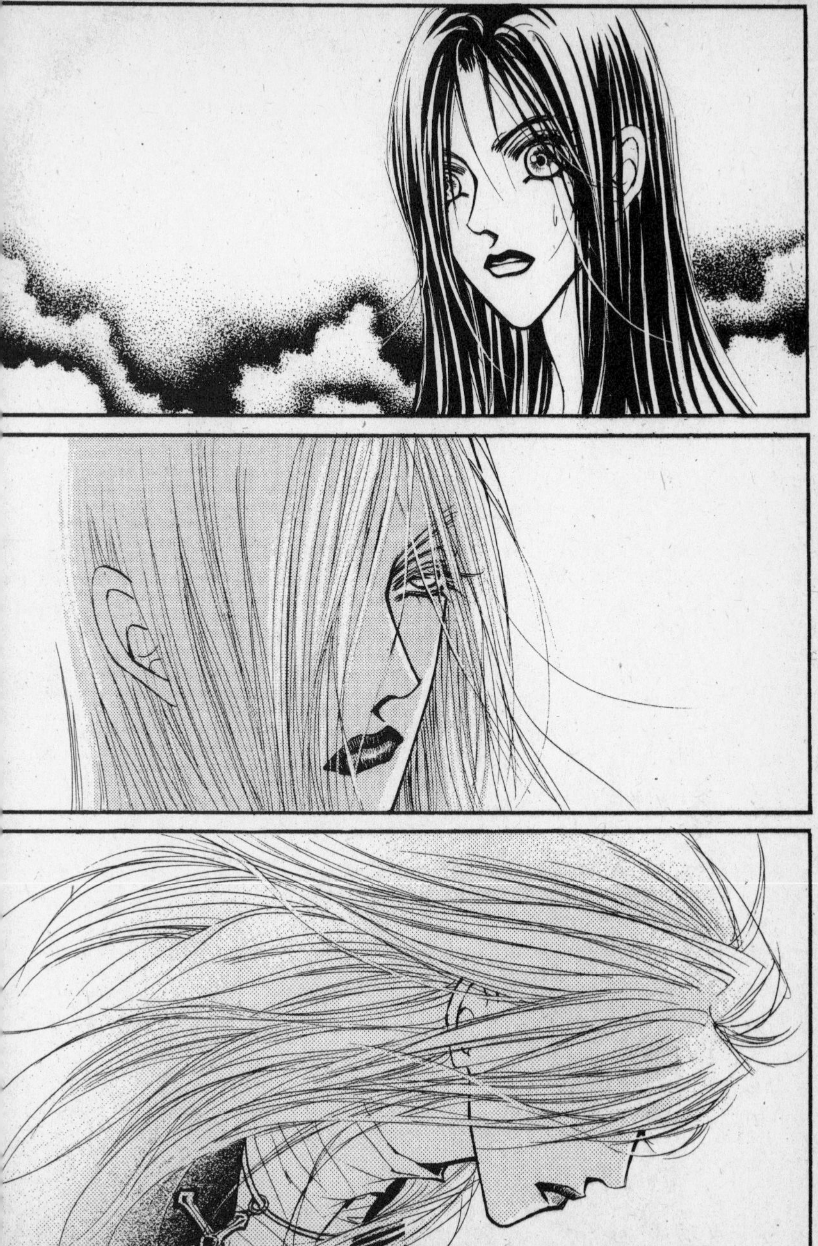

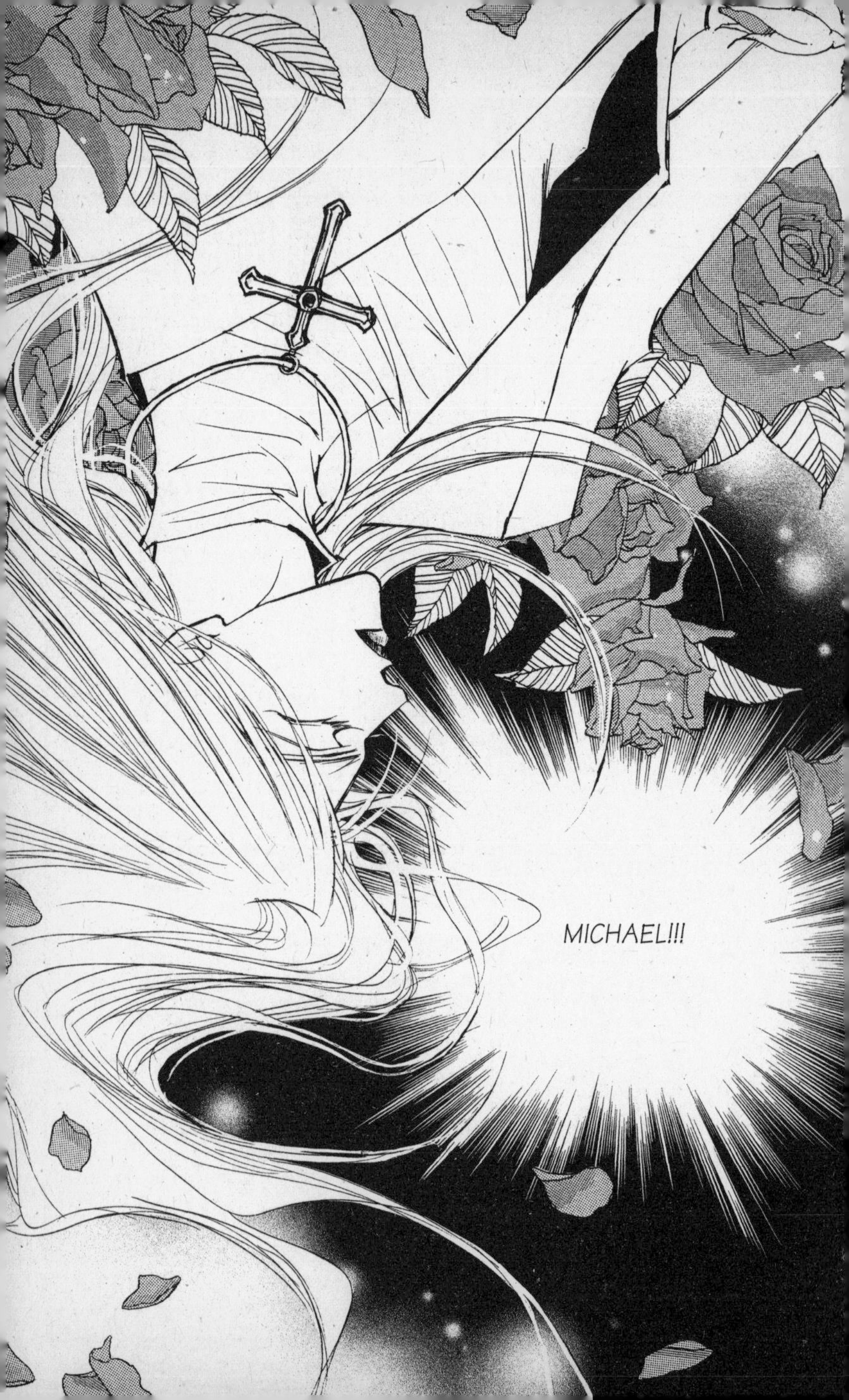
MICHAEL!!!

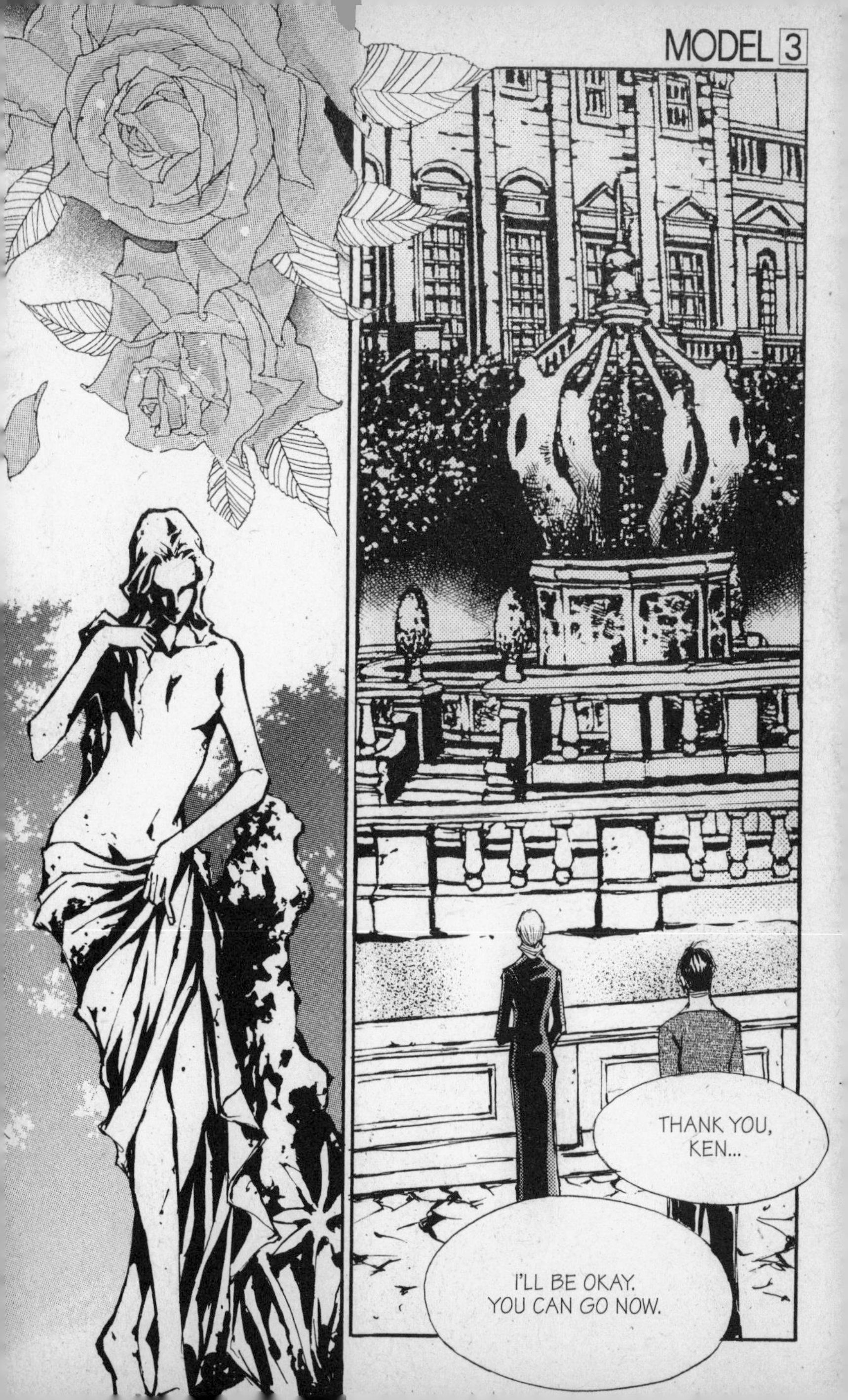
THANK YOU, KEN...
I'LL BE OKAY. YOU CAN GO NOW.

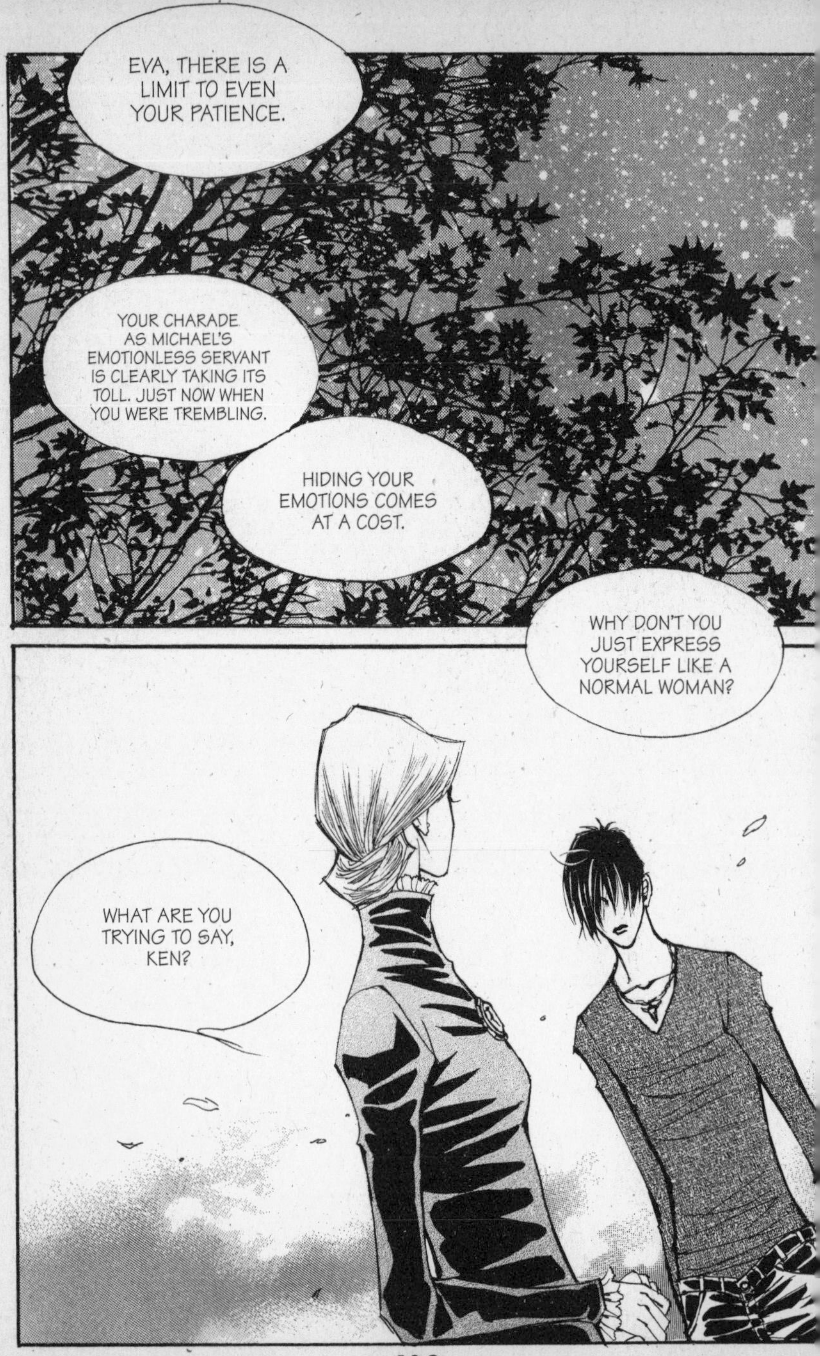
EVA, THERE IS A LIMIT TO EVEN YOUR PATIENCE.
YOUR CHARADE AS MICHAEL'S EMOTIONLESS SERVANT IS CLEARLY TAKING ITS TOLL. JUST NOW WHEN YOU WERE TREMBLING.
HIDING YOUR EMOTIONS COMES AT A COST.
WHY DON'T YOU JUST EXPRESS YOURSELF LIKE A NORMAL WOMAN?
WHAT ARE YOU TRYING TO SAY, KEN?

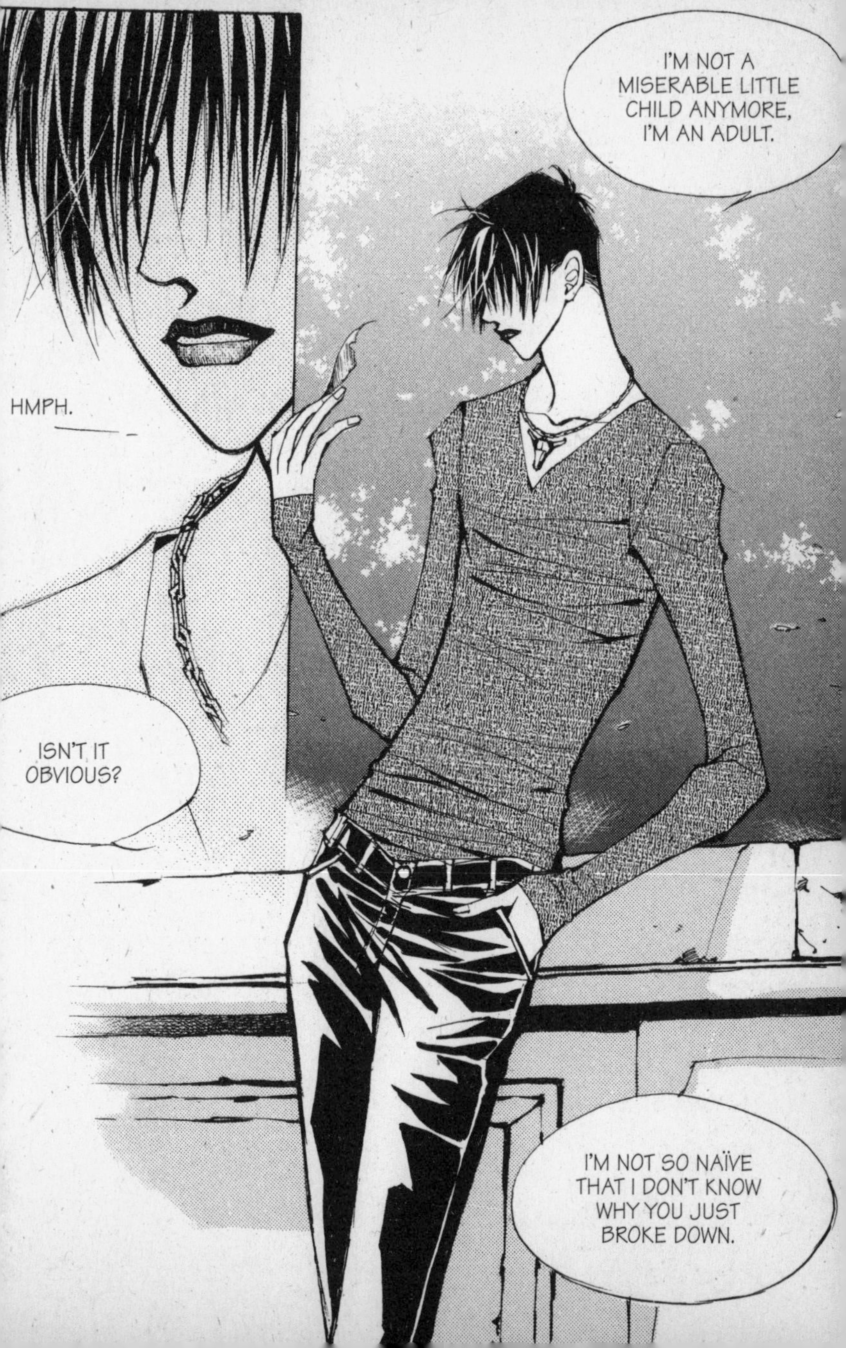
HMPH.
ISN'T IT OBVIOUS?
I'M NOT A MISERABLE LITTLE CHILD ANYMORE, I'M AN ADULT.
I'M NOT SO NAÏVE THAT I DON'T KNOW WHY YOU JUST BROKE DOWN.

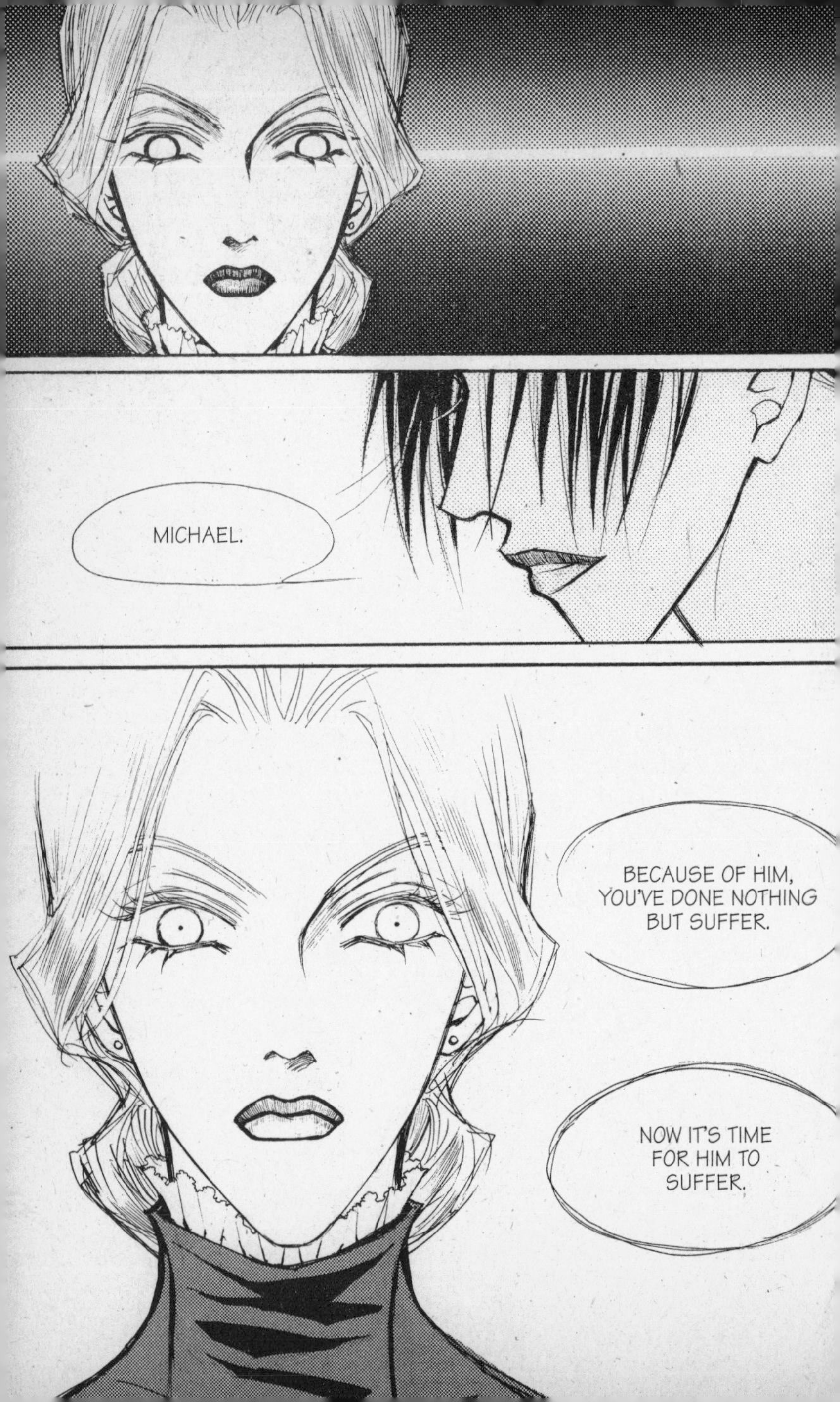
MICHAEL.
BECAUSE OF HIM, YOU'VE DONE NOTHING BUT SUFFER.
NOW IT'S TIME FOR HIM TO SUFFER.

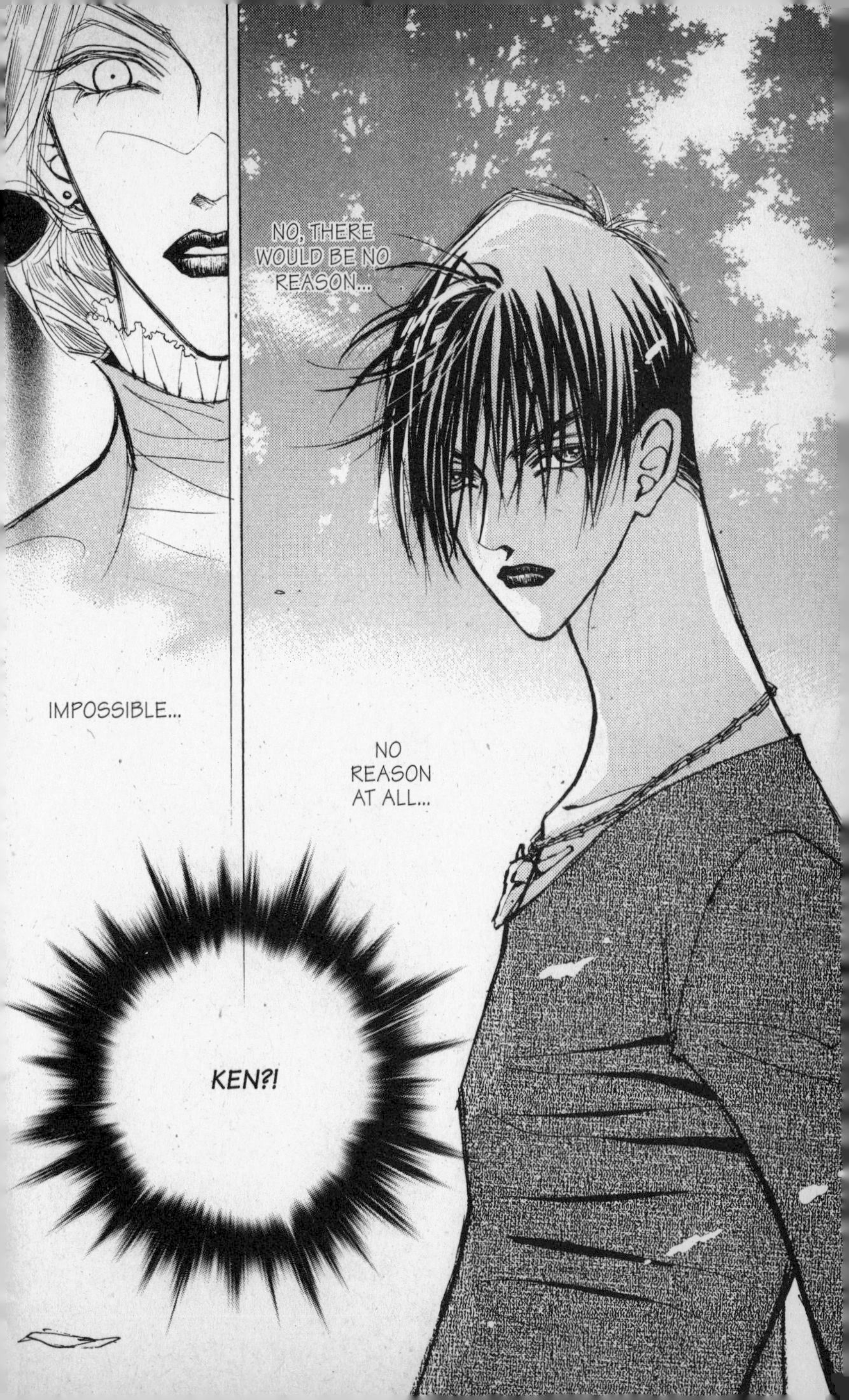
NO, THERE WOULD BE NO REASON...
IMPOSSIBLE...
NO REASON AT ALL...
KEN?!

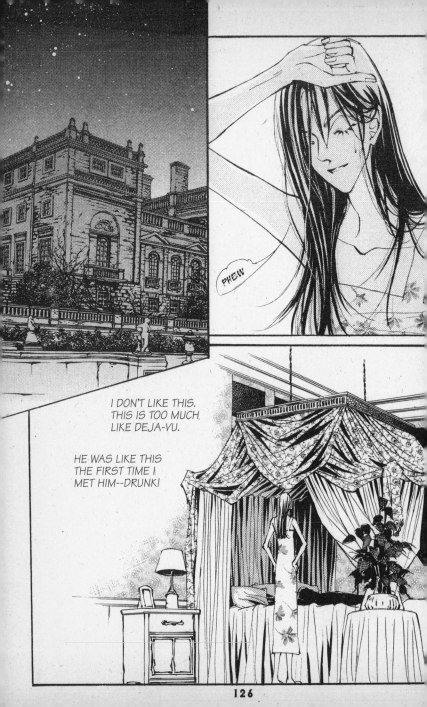

PHEW

I DON'T LIKE THIS.
THIS IS TOO MUCH
LIKE DEJA-VU.

HE WAS LIKE THIS
THE FIRST TIME I
MET HIM--DRUNK!

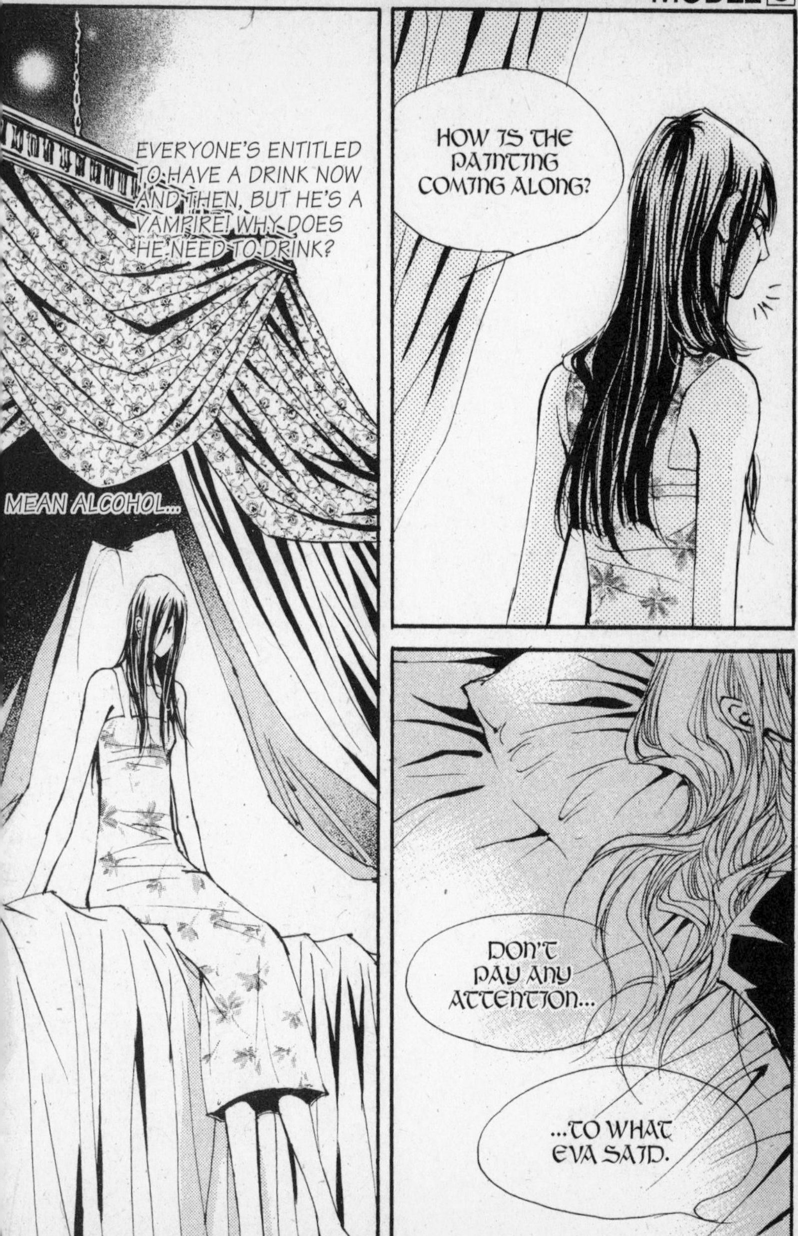
EVERYONE'S ENTITLED TO HAVE A DRINK NOW AND THEN, BUT HE'S A VAMPIRE! WHY DOES HE NEED TO DRINK?
MEAN ALCOHOL...
HOW IS THE PAINTING COMING ALONG?
DON'T PAY ANY ATTENTION...
...TO WHAT EVA SAID.

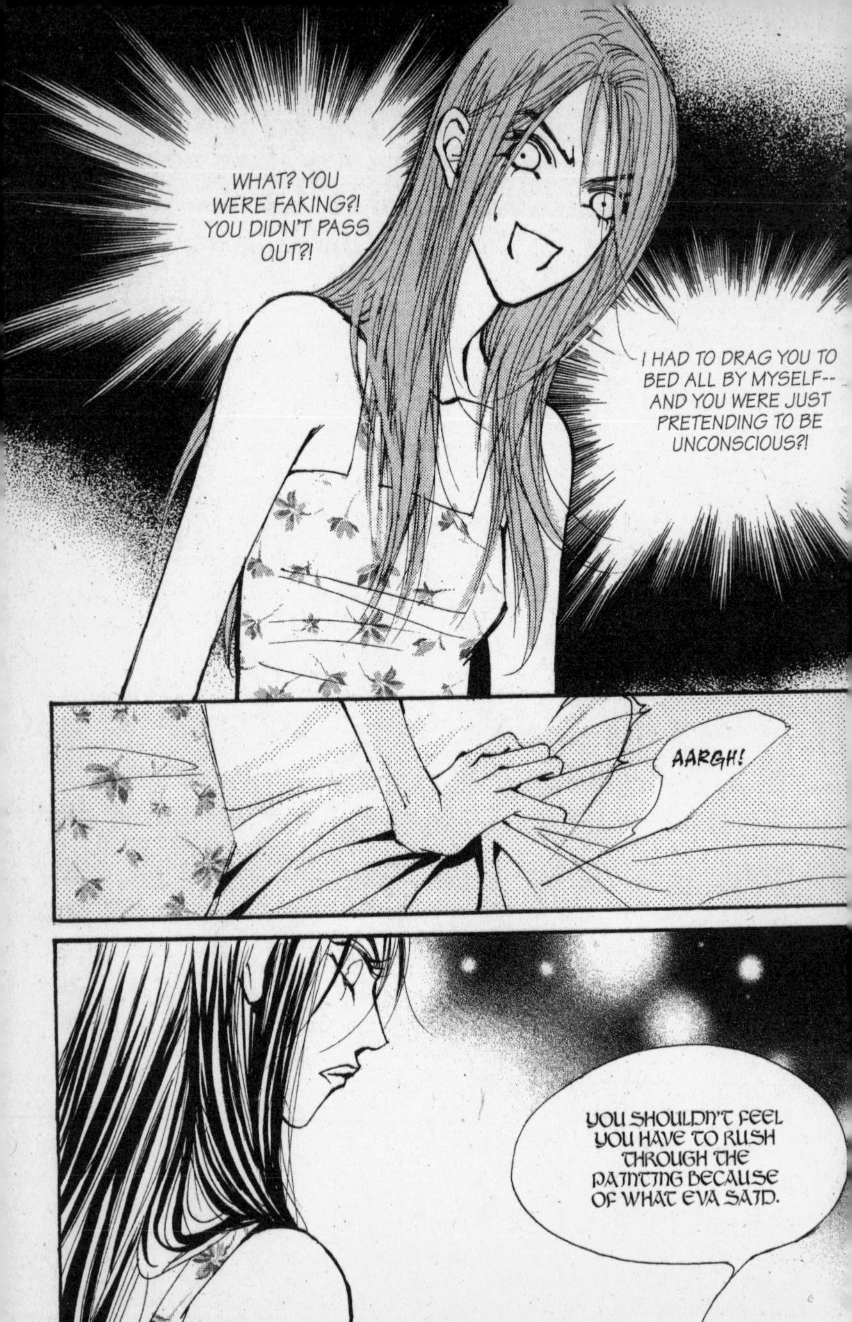
WHAT? YOU WERE FAKING?! YOU DIDN'T PASS OUT?!
I HAD TO DRAG YOU TO BED ALL BY MYSELF--AND YOU WERE JUST PRETENDING TO BE UNCONSCIOUS?!
AARGH!
YOU SHOULDN'T FEEL YOU HAVE TO RUSH THROUGH THE PAINTING BECAUSE OF WHAT EVA SAID.

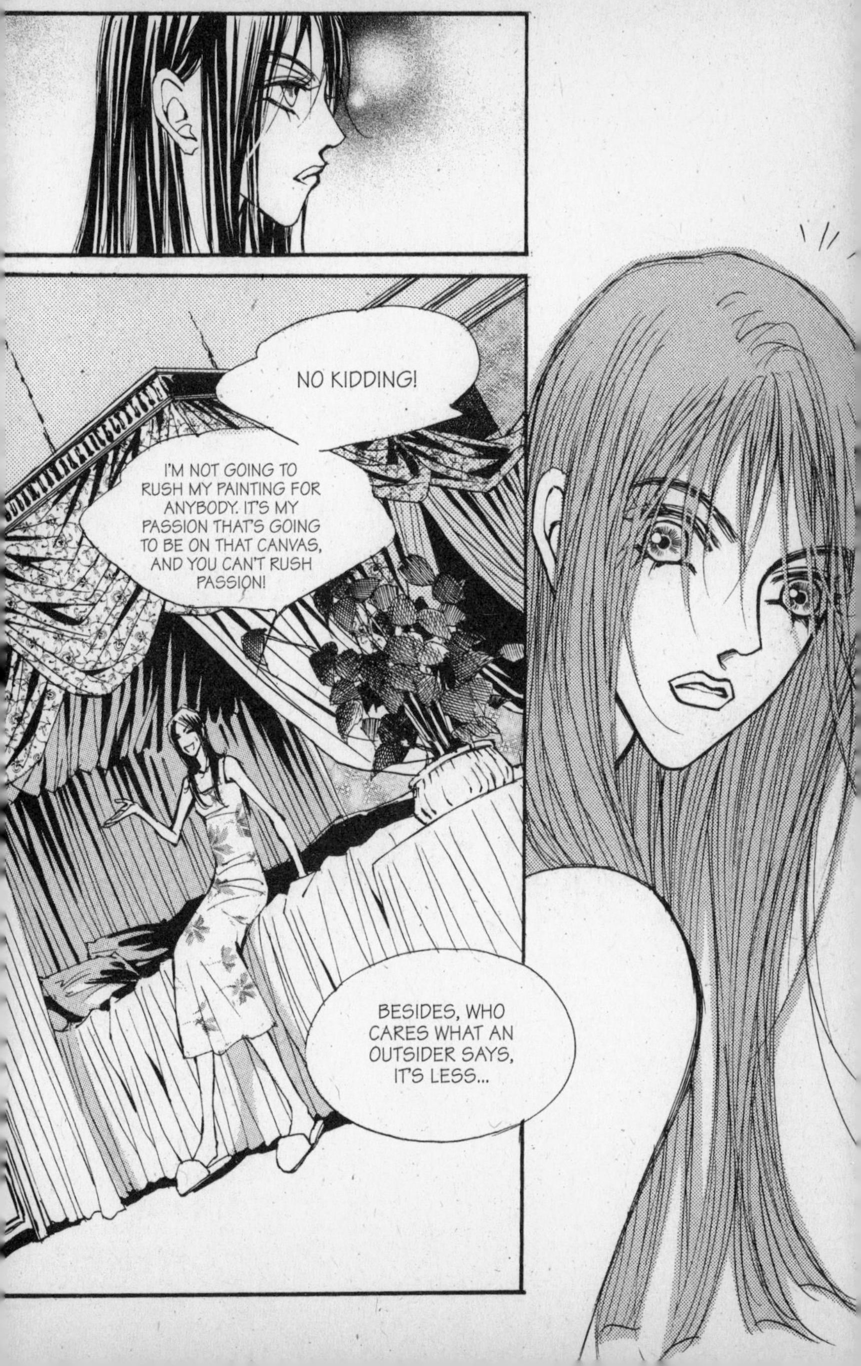
NO KIDDING!
I'M NOT GOING TO RUSH MY PAINTING FOR ANYBODY. IT'S MY PASSION THAT'S GOING TO BE ON THAT CANVAS, AND YOU CAN'T RUSH PASSION!
BESIDES, WHO CARES WHAT AN OUTSIDER SAYS, IT'S LESS...

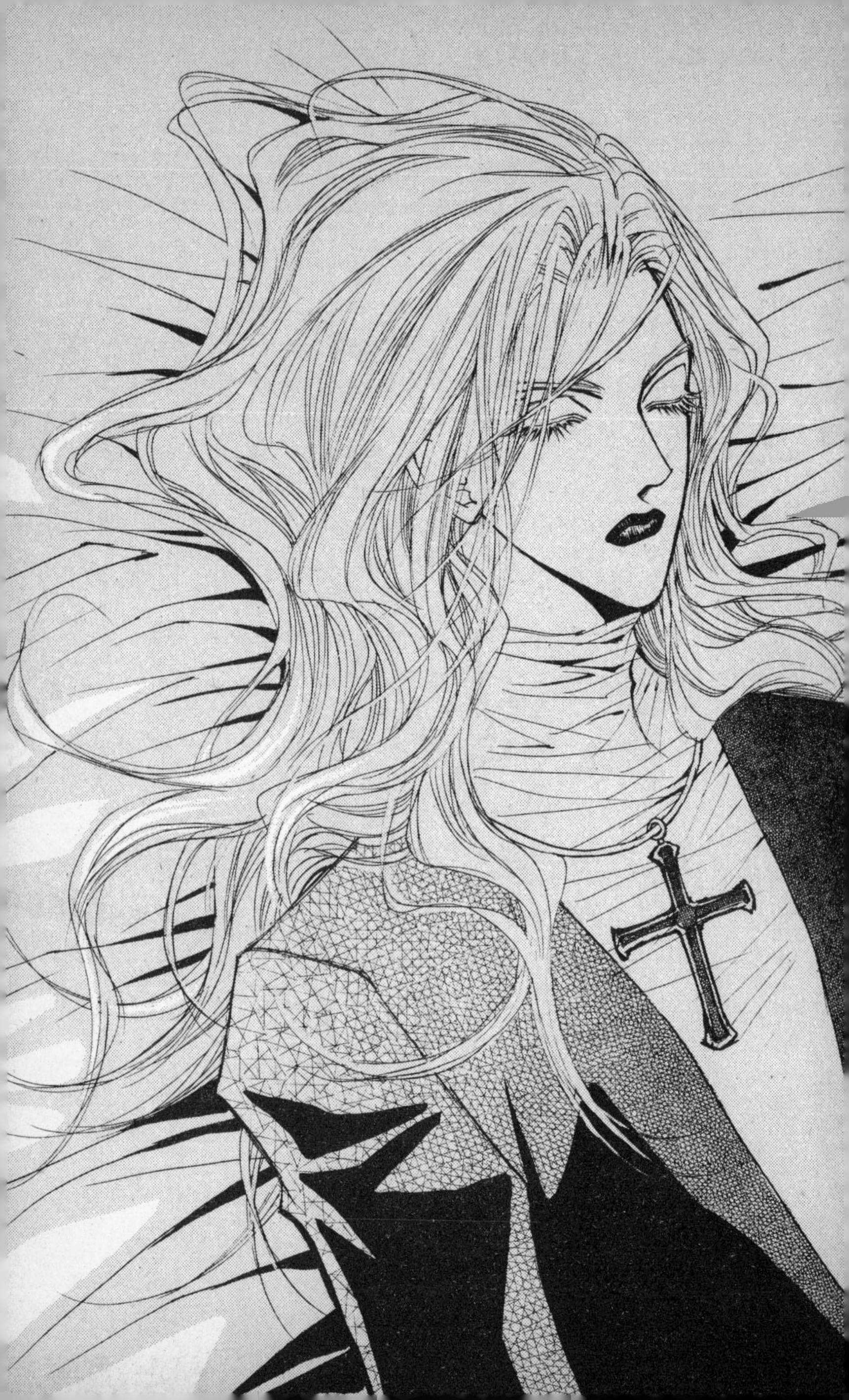

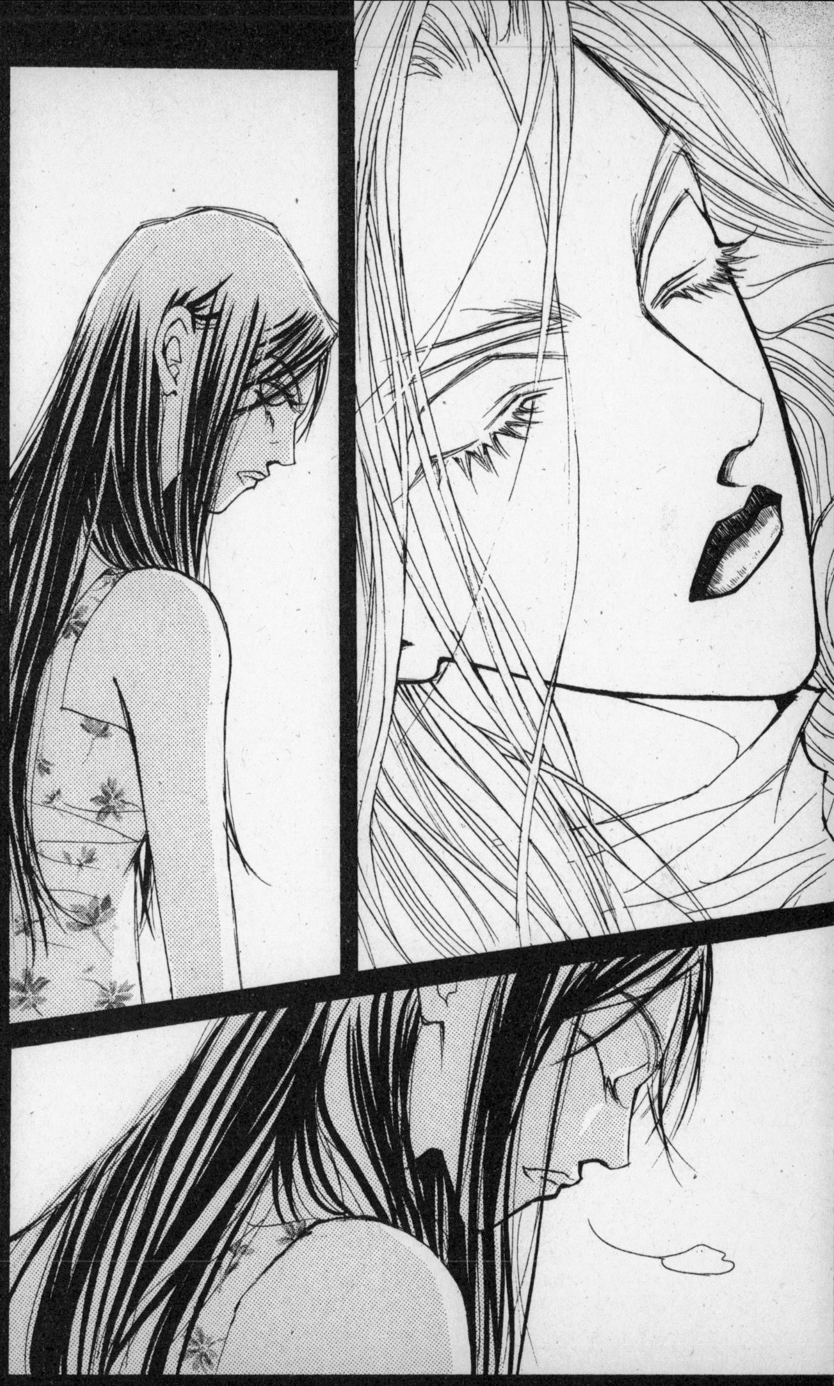

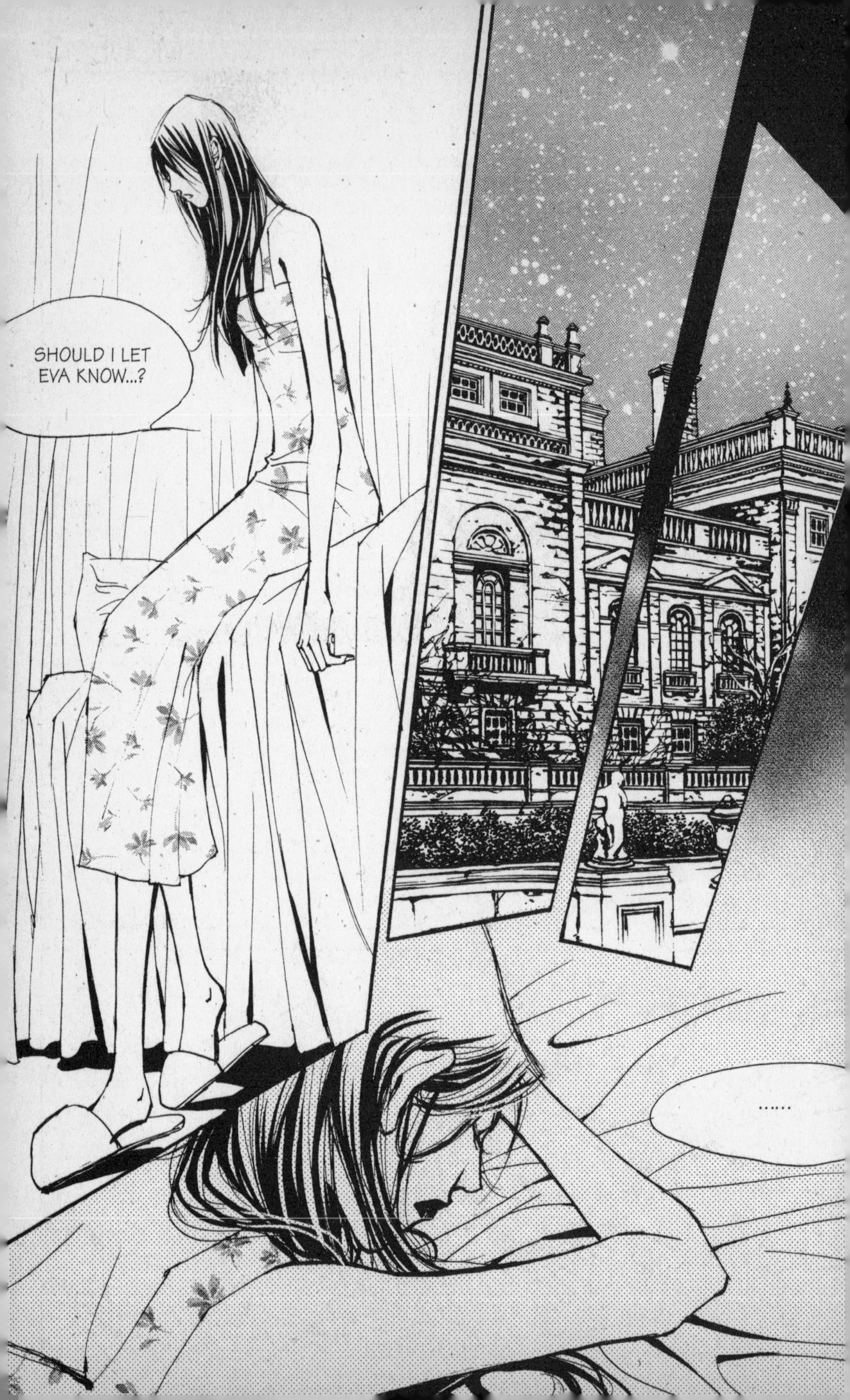
SHOULD I LET EVA KNOW...?
......

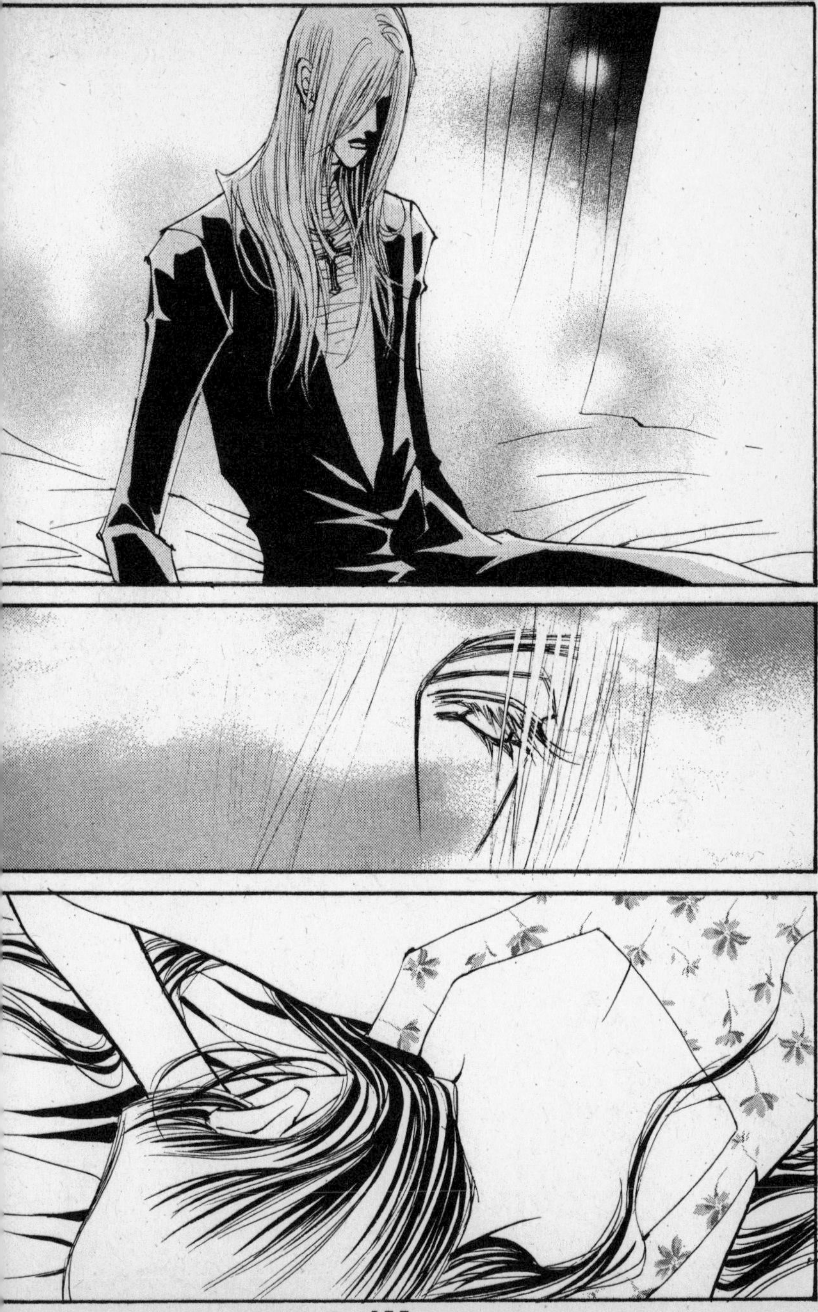

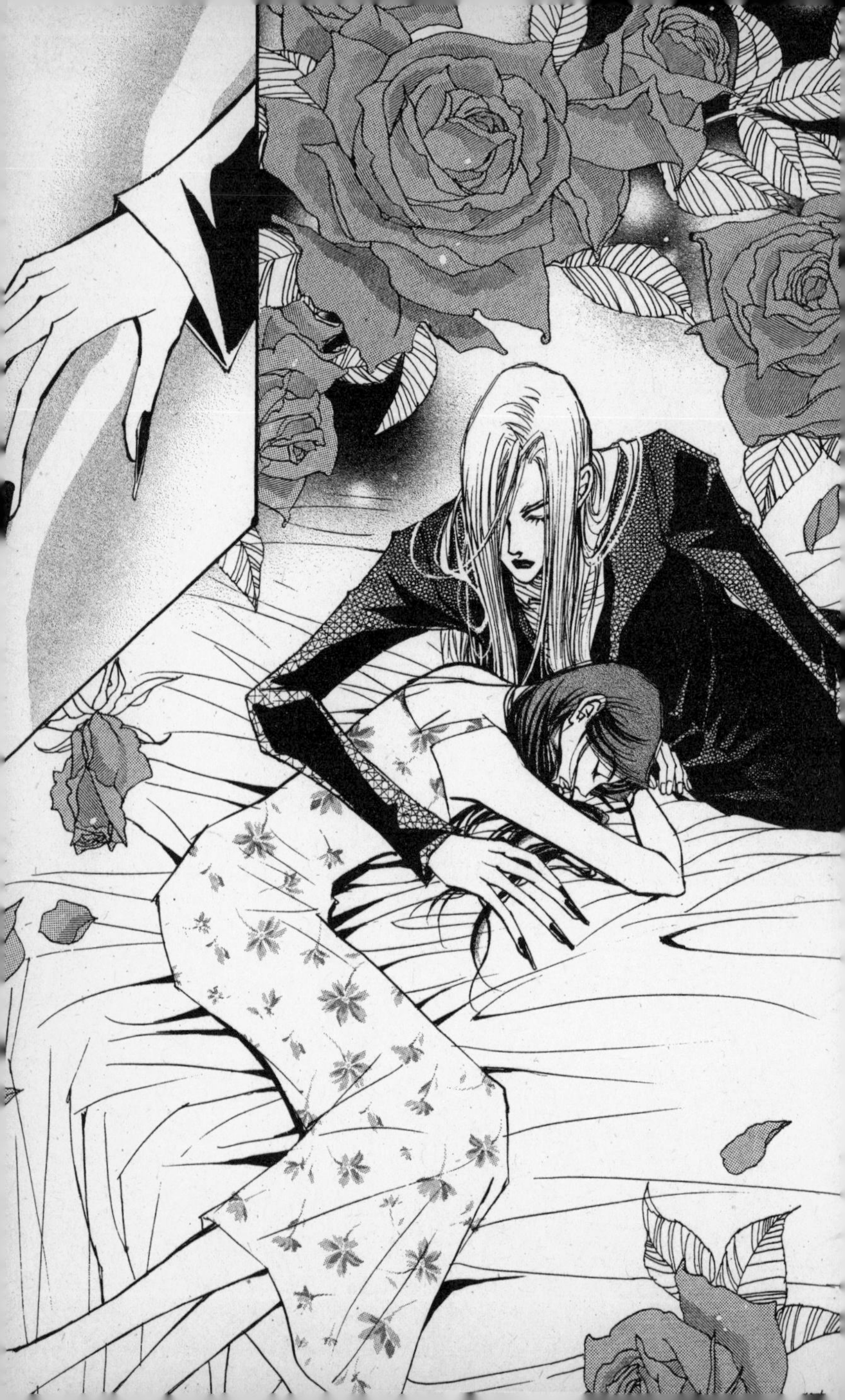

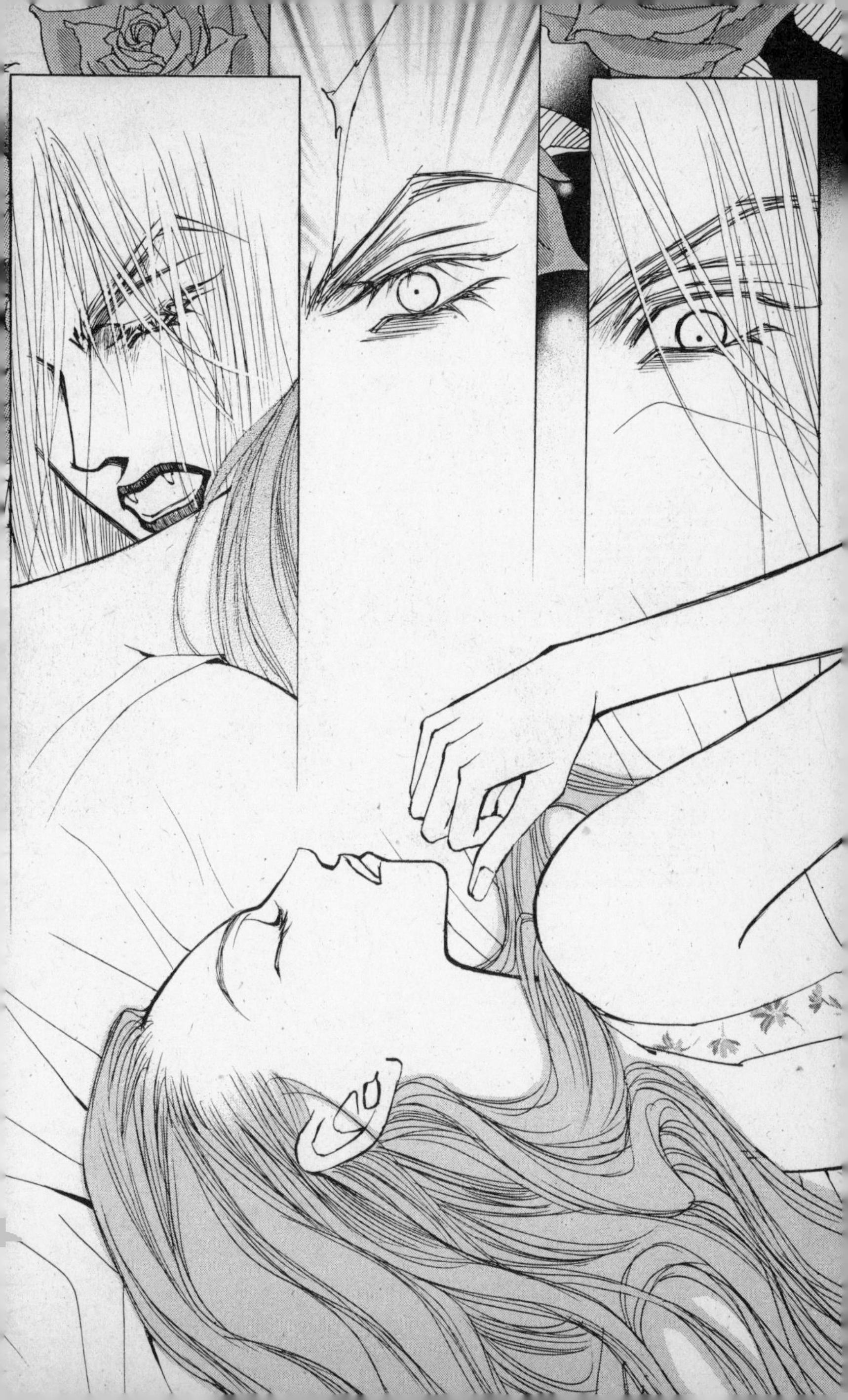

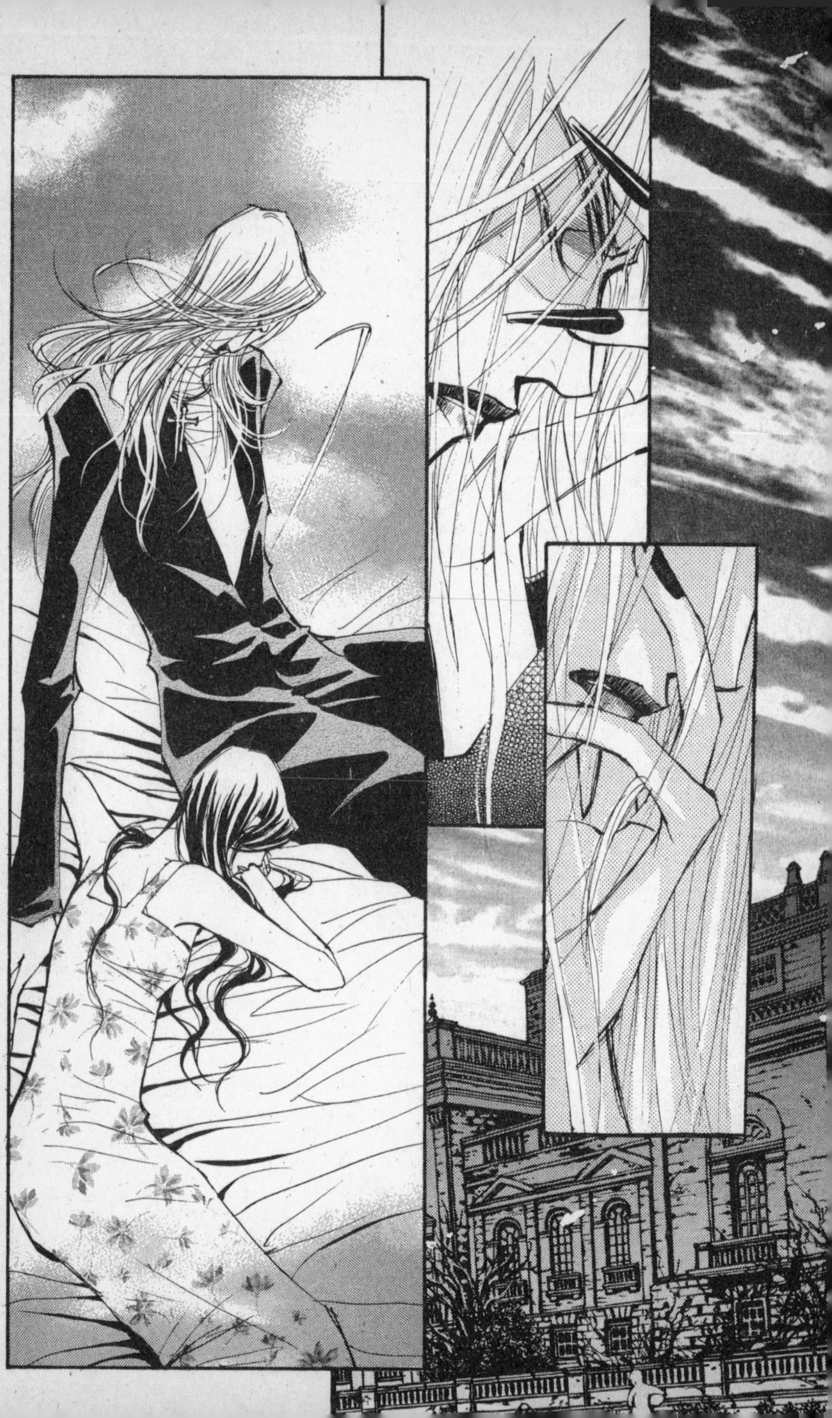

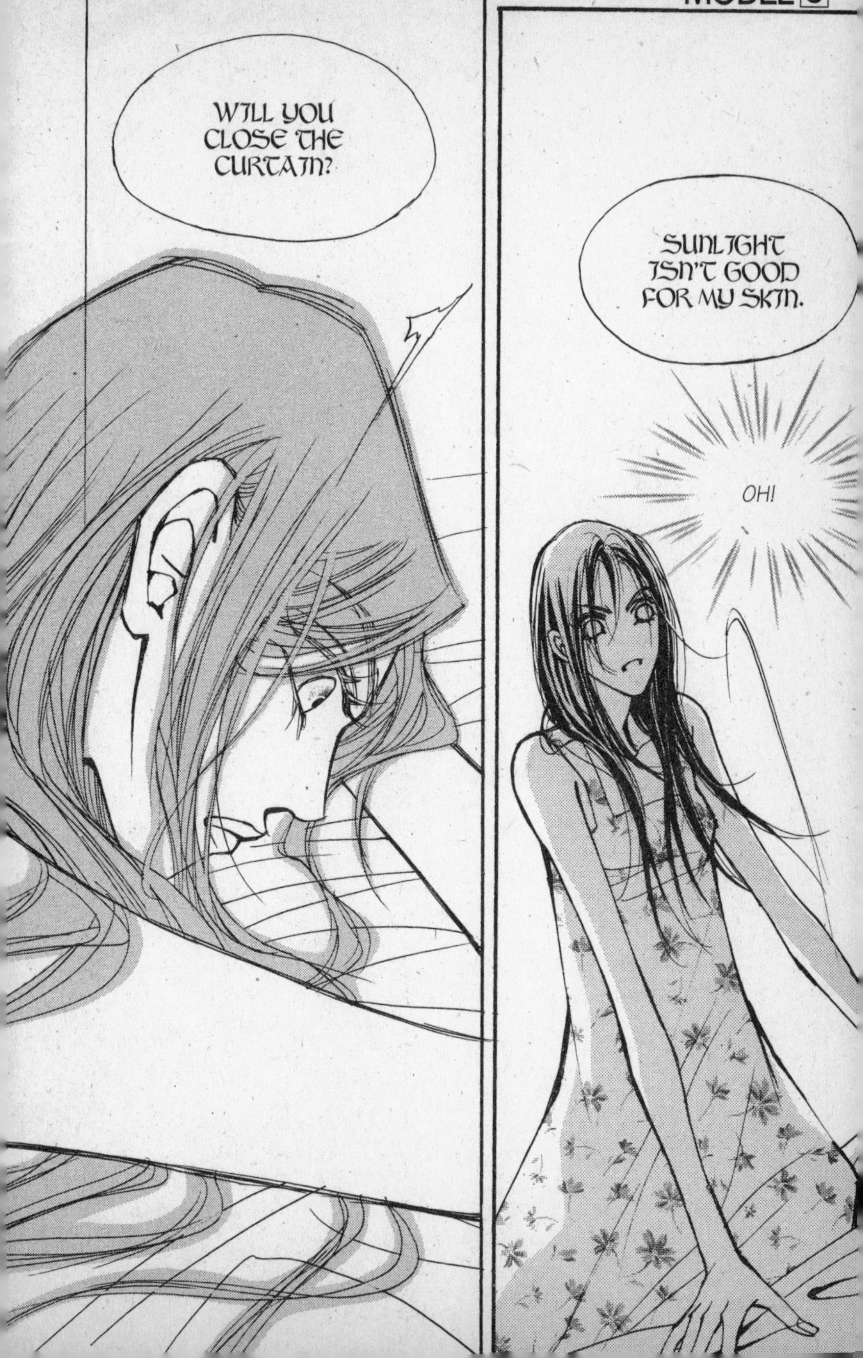
WILL YOU CLOSE THE CURTAIN?
SUNLIGHT ISN'T GOOD FOR MY SKIN.
OH!

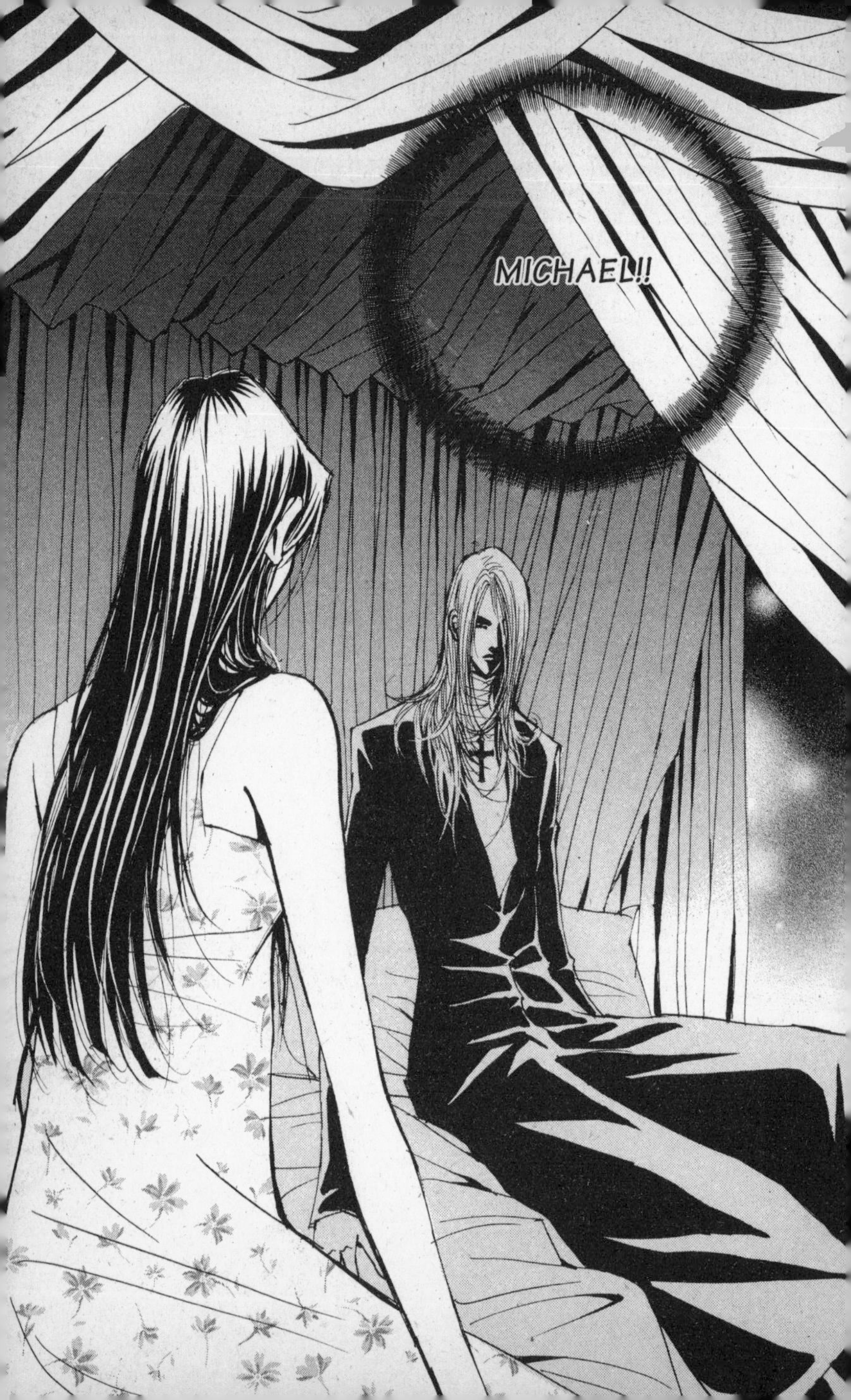
MICHAEL!!

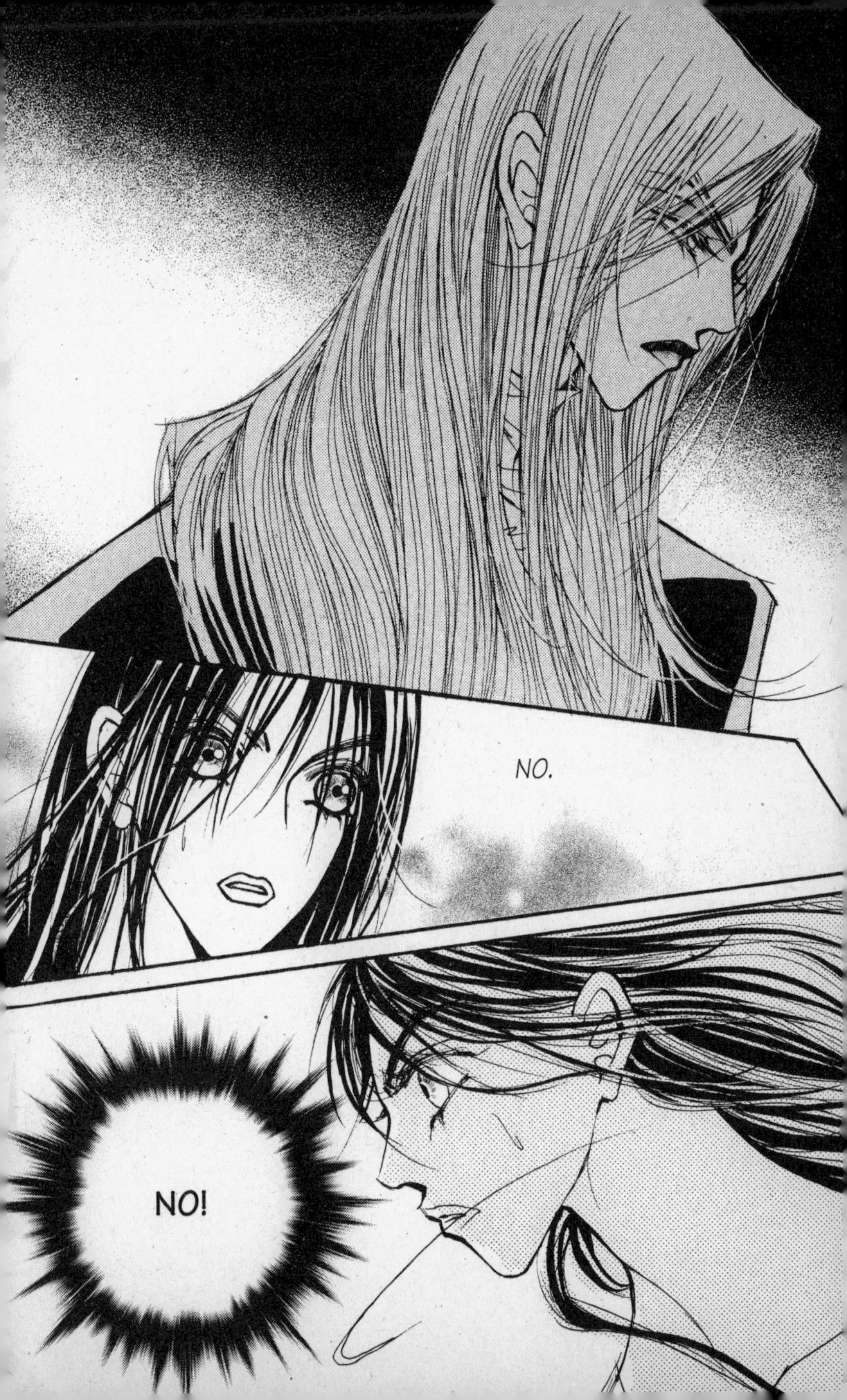
NO.
NO!

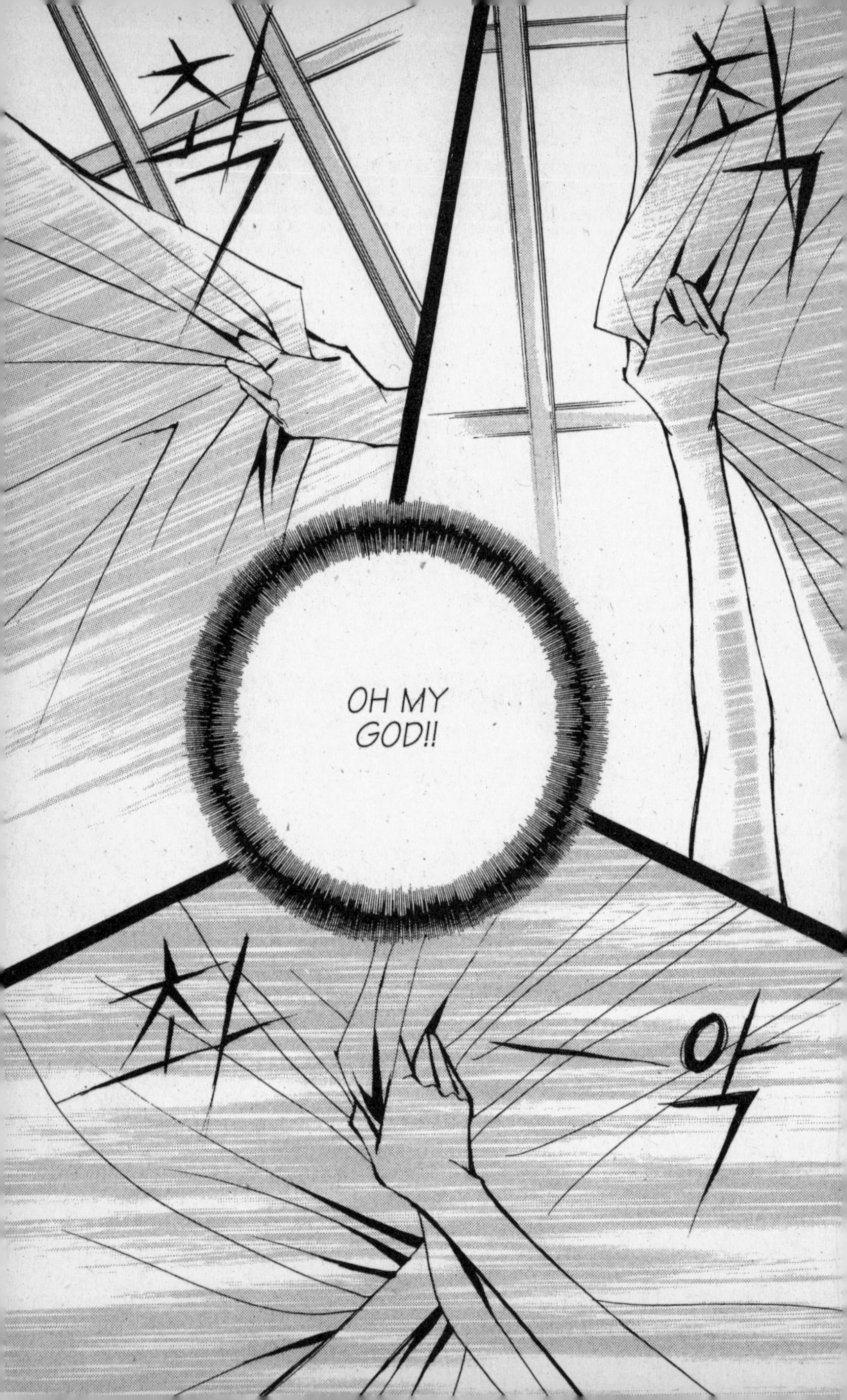
OH MY GOD!!

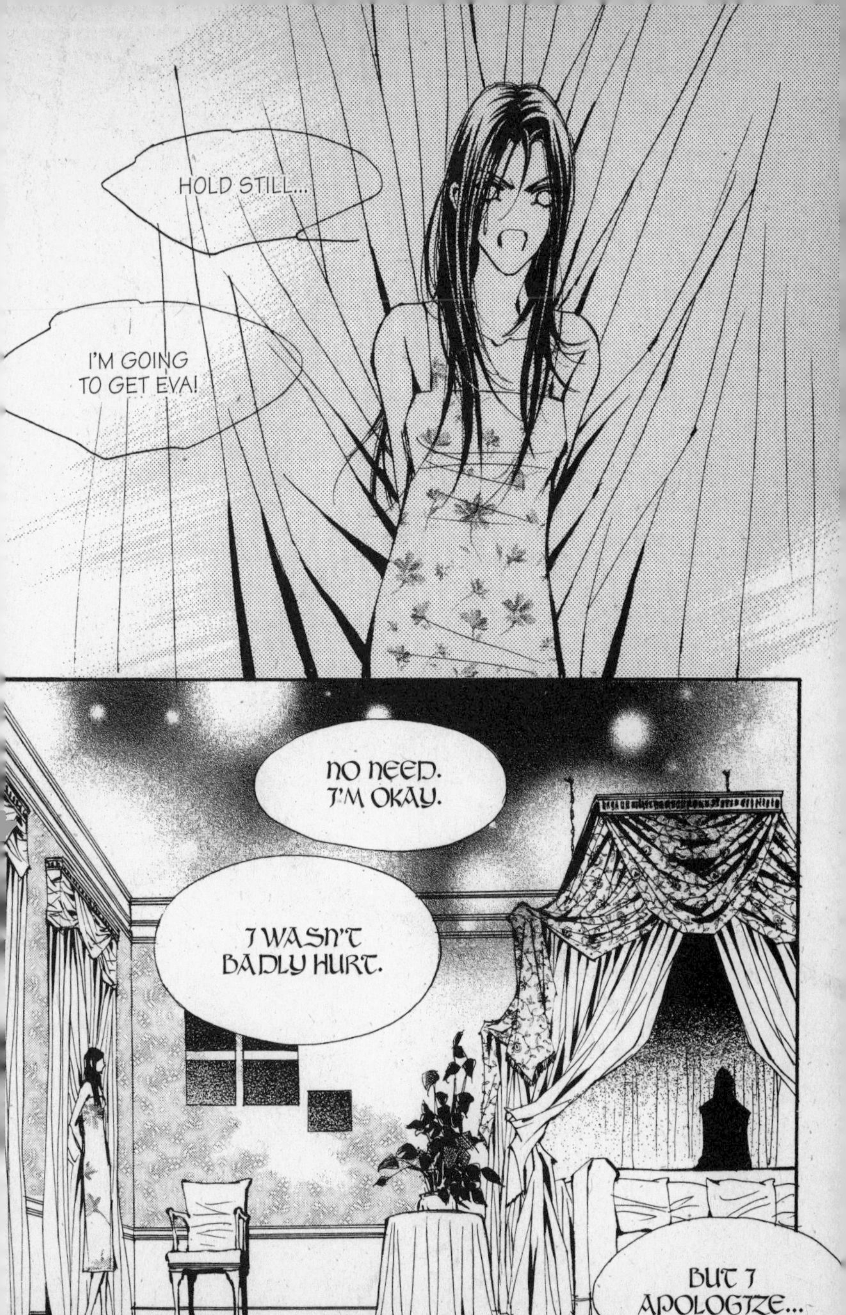
HOLD STILL...
I'M GOING TO GET EVA!
NO NEED. I'M OKAY.
I WASN'T BADLY HURT.
BUT I APOLOGIZE...

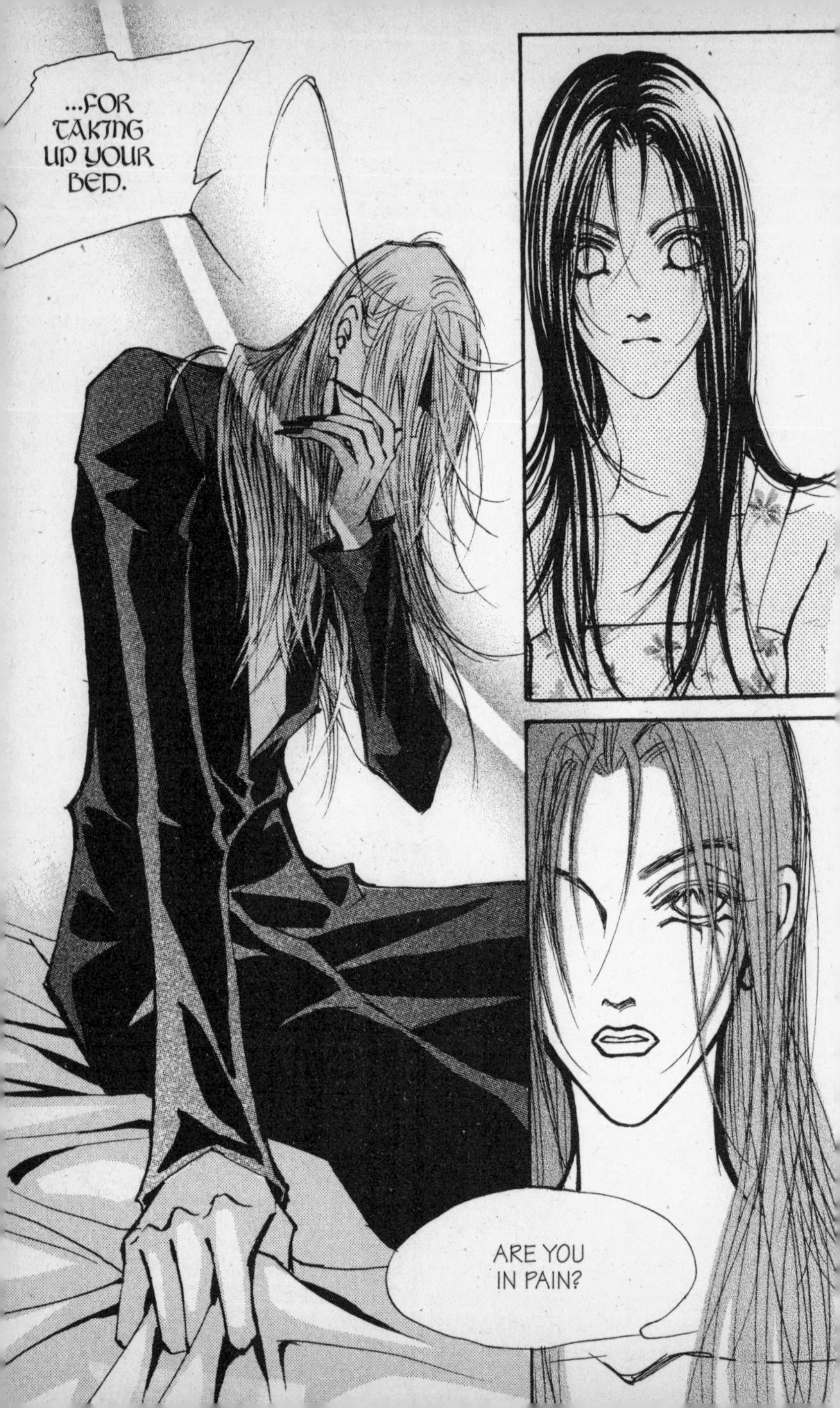
...FOR TAKING UP YOUR BED.
ARE YOU IN PAIN?

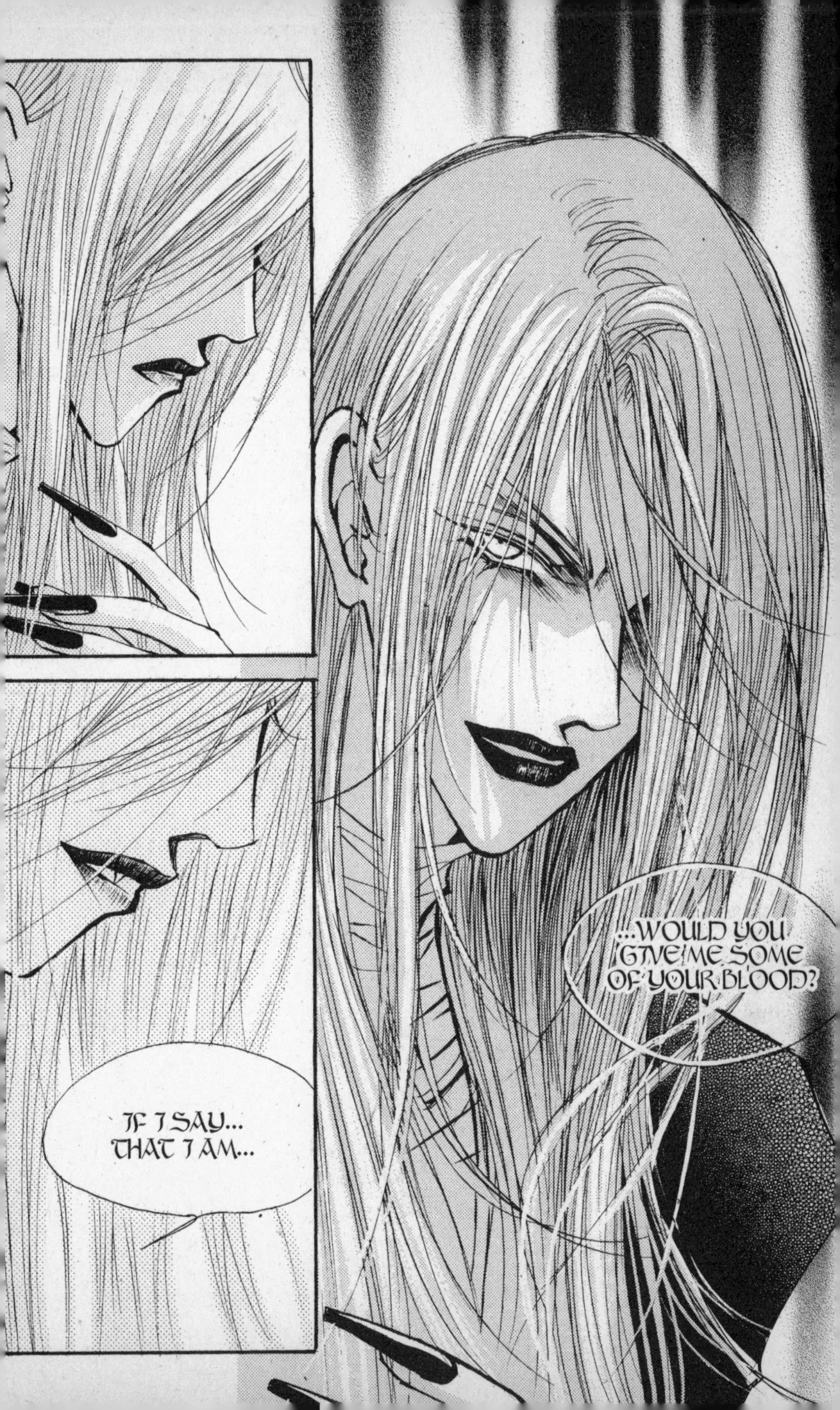
IF I SAY... THAT I AM...
...WOULD YOU GIVE ME SOME OF YOUR BLOOD?

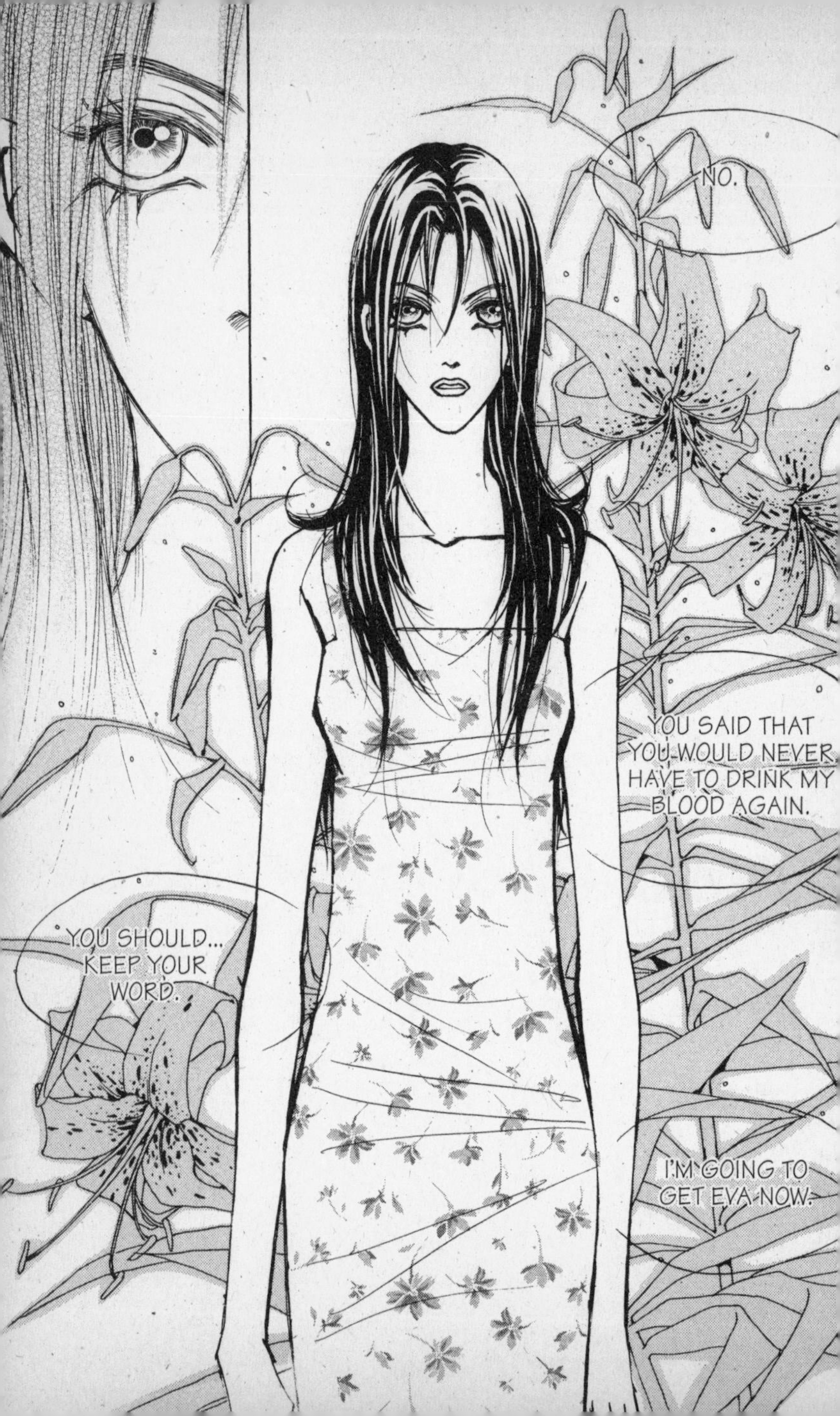
NO.
YOU SAID THAT YOU WOULD NEVER HAVE TO DRINK MY BLOOD AGAIN.
YOU SHOULD... KEEP YOUR WORD.
I'M GOING TO GET EVA NOW.

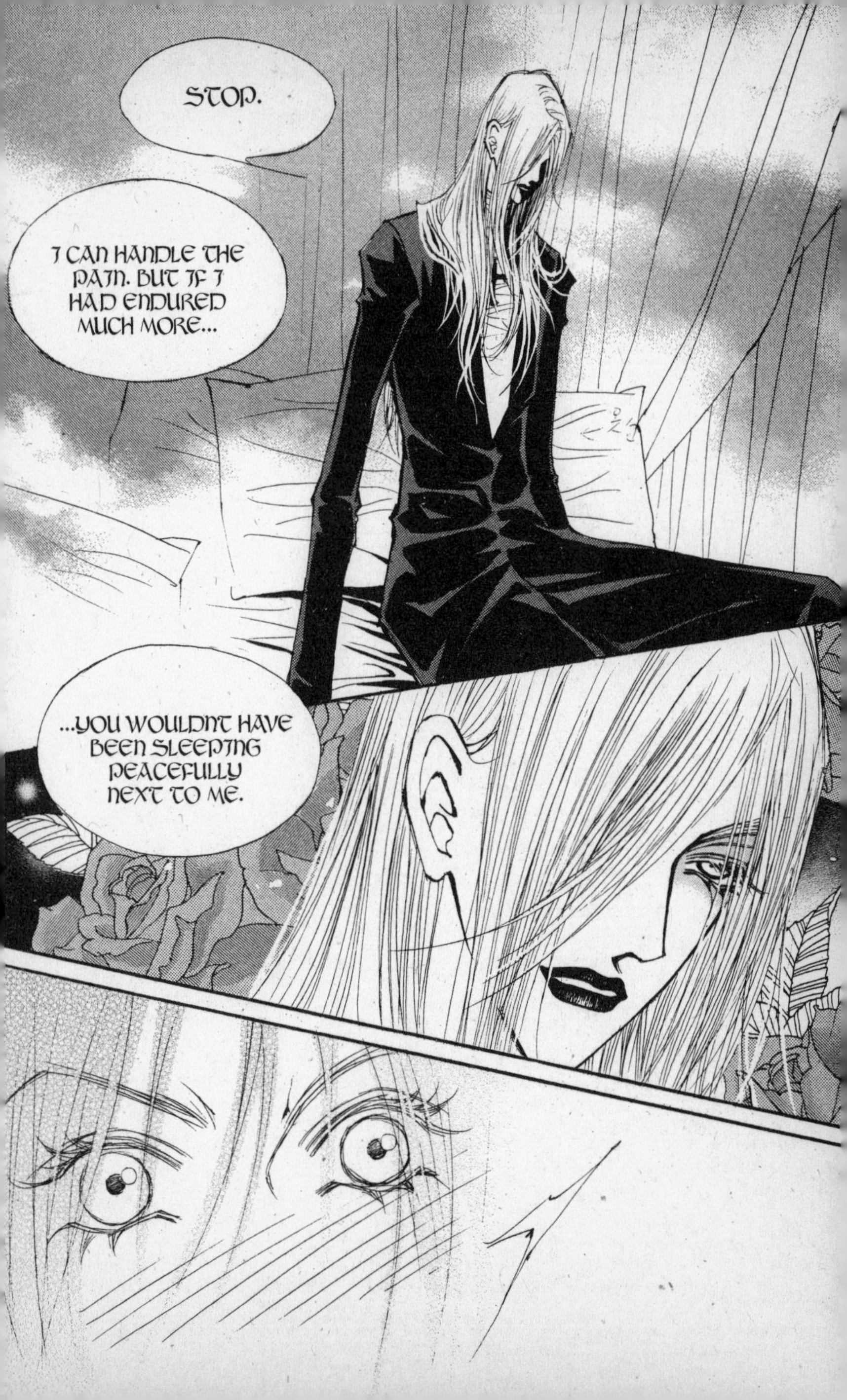
STOP.
I CAN HANDLE THE PAIN. BUT IF I HAD ENDURED MUCH MORE...
...YOU WOULDN'T HAVE BEEN SLEEPING PEACEFULLY NEXT TO ME.

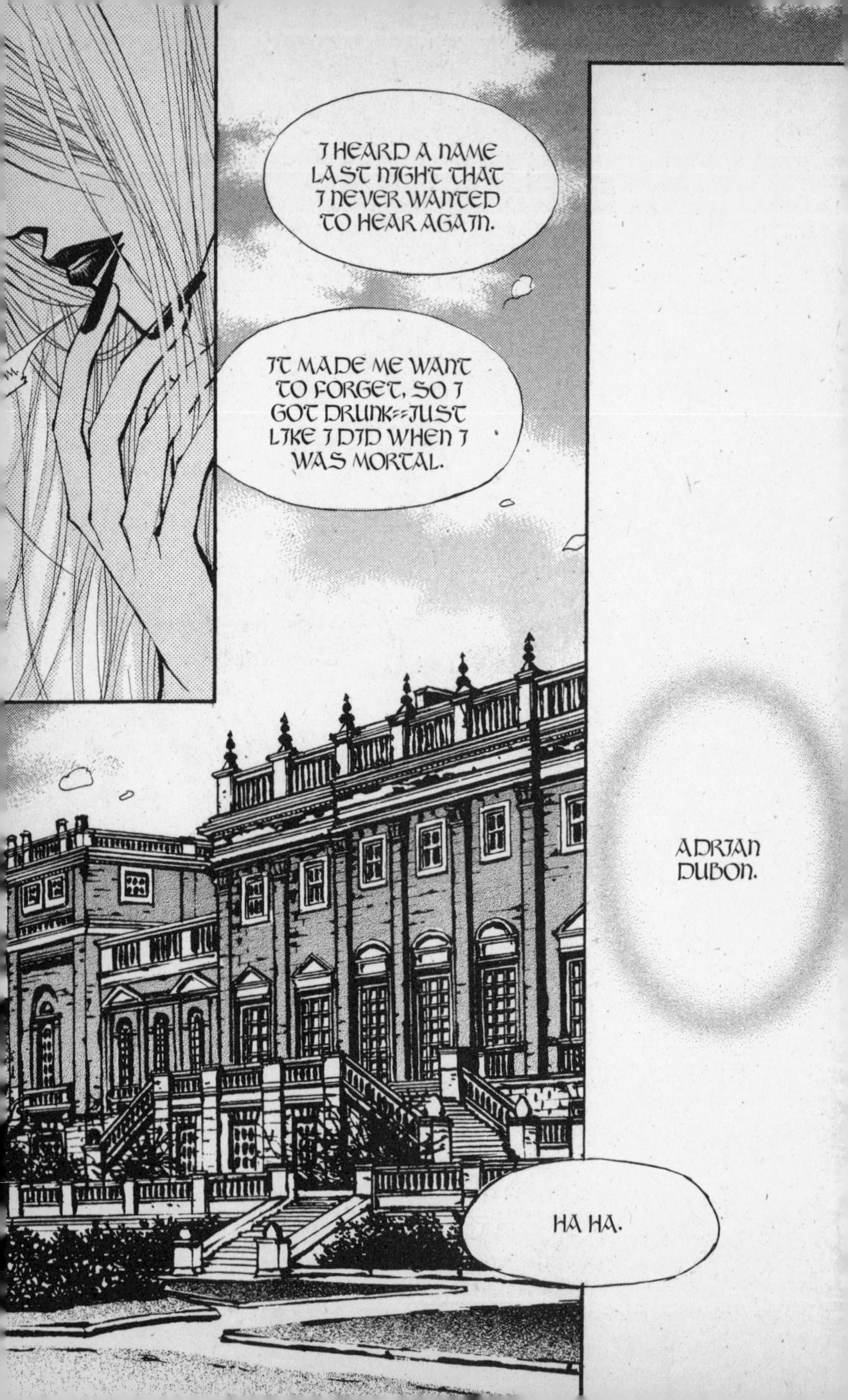
I HEARD A NAME LAST NIGHT THAT I NEVER WANTED TO HEAR AGAIN.
IT MADE ME WANT TO FORGET, SO I GOT DRUNK--JUST LIKE I DID WHEN I WAS MORTAL.
ADRIAN DUBON.
HA HA.

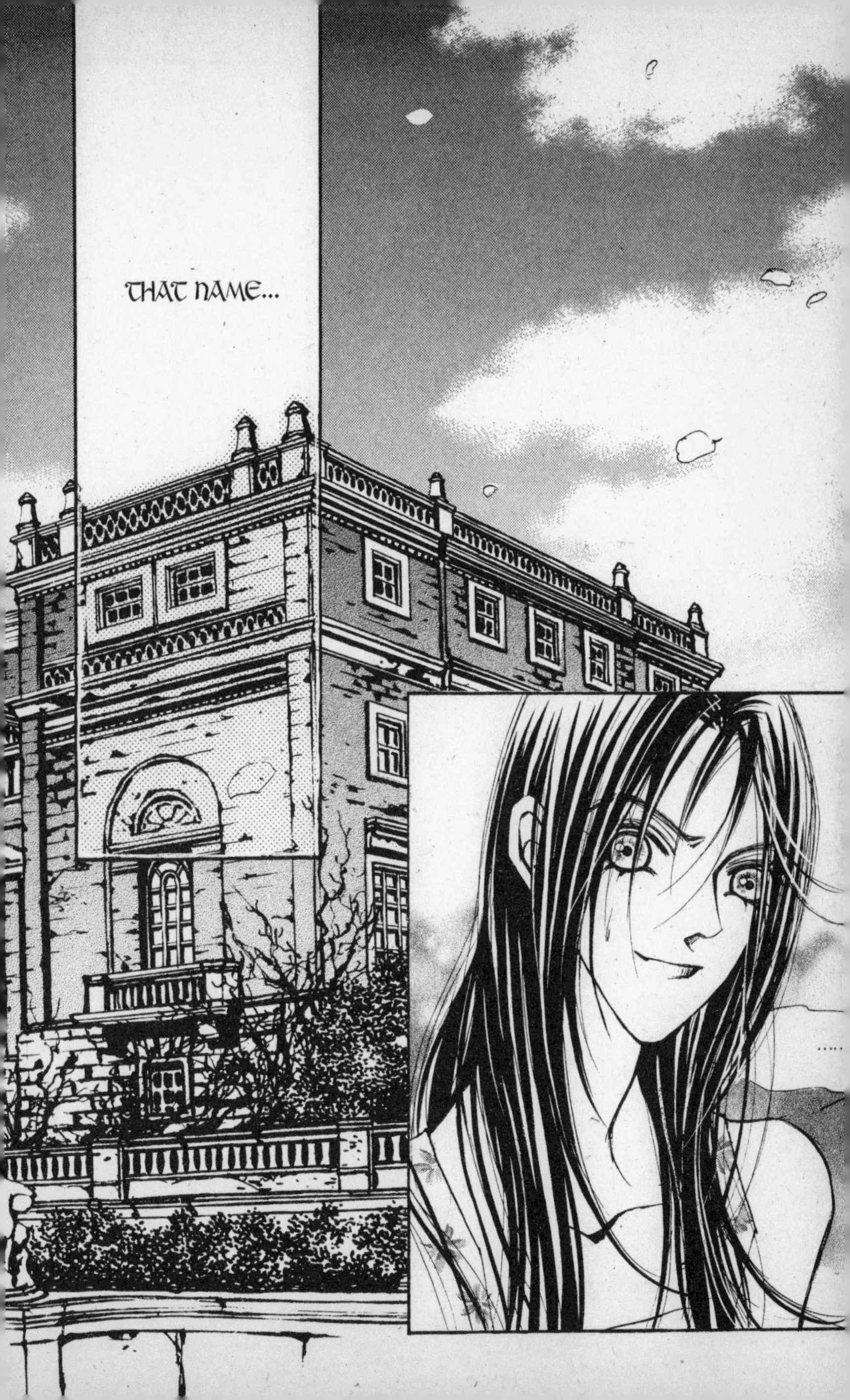
THAT NAME...
.....

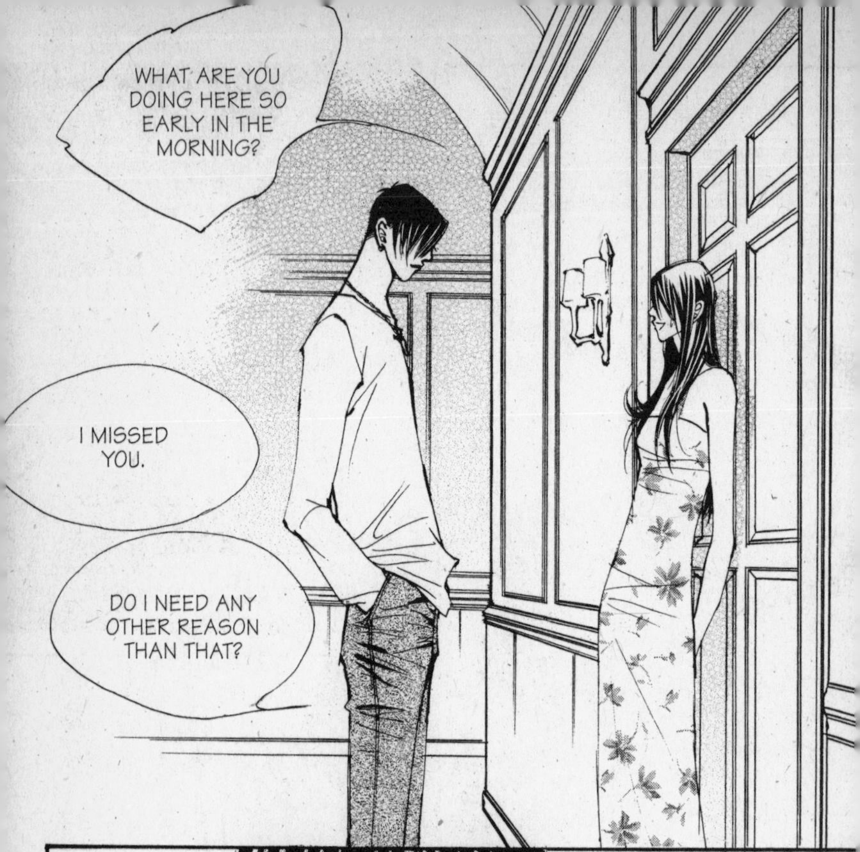
WHAT ARE YOU DOING HERE SO EARLY IN THE MORNING?
I MISSED YOU.
DO I NEED ANY OTHER REASON THAN THAT?
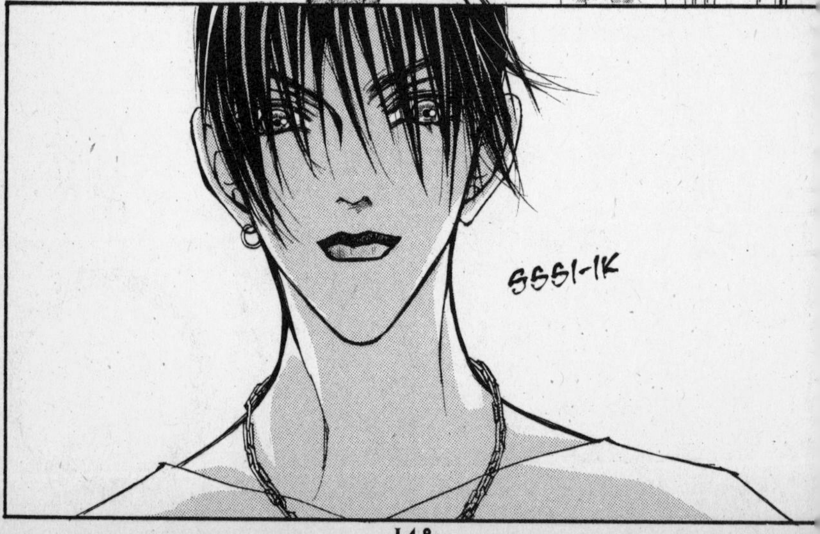
SSSI-IK

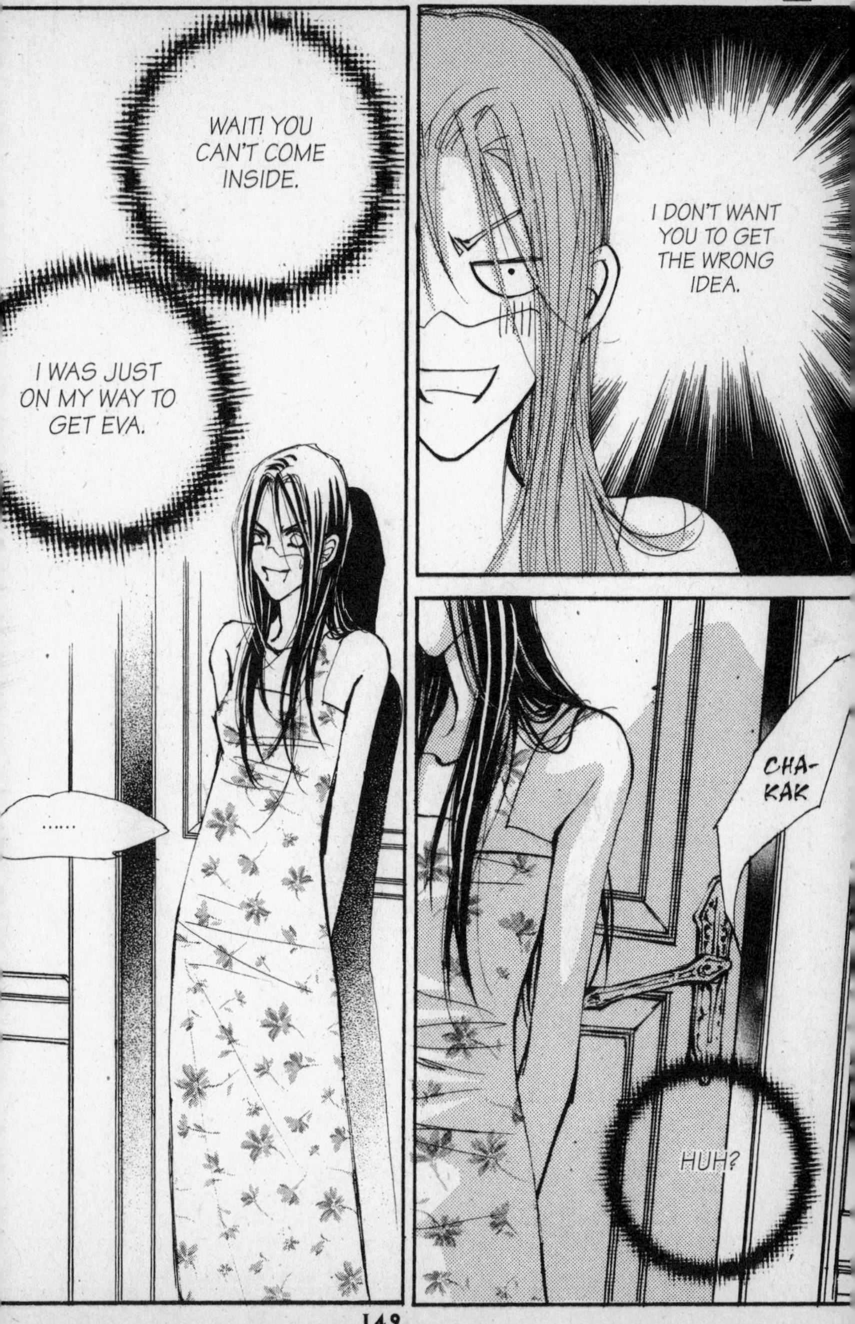
WAIT! YOU CAN'T COME INSIDE.
I WAS JUST ON MY WAY TO GET EVA.
......
I DON'T WANT YOU TO GET THE WRONG IDEA.
CHA-KAK
HUH?

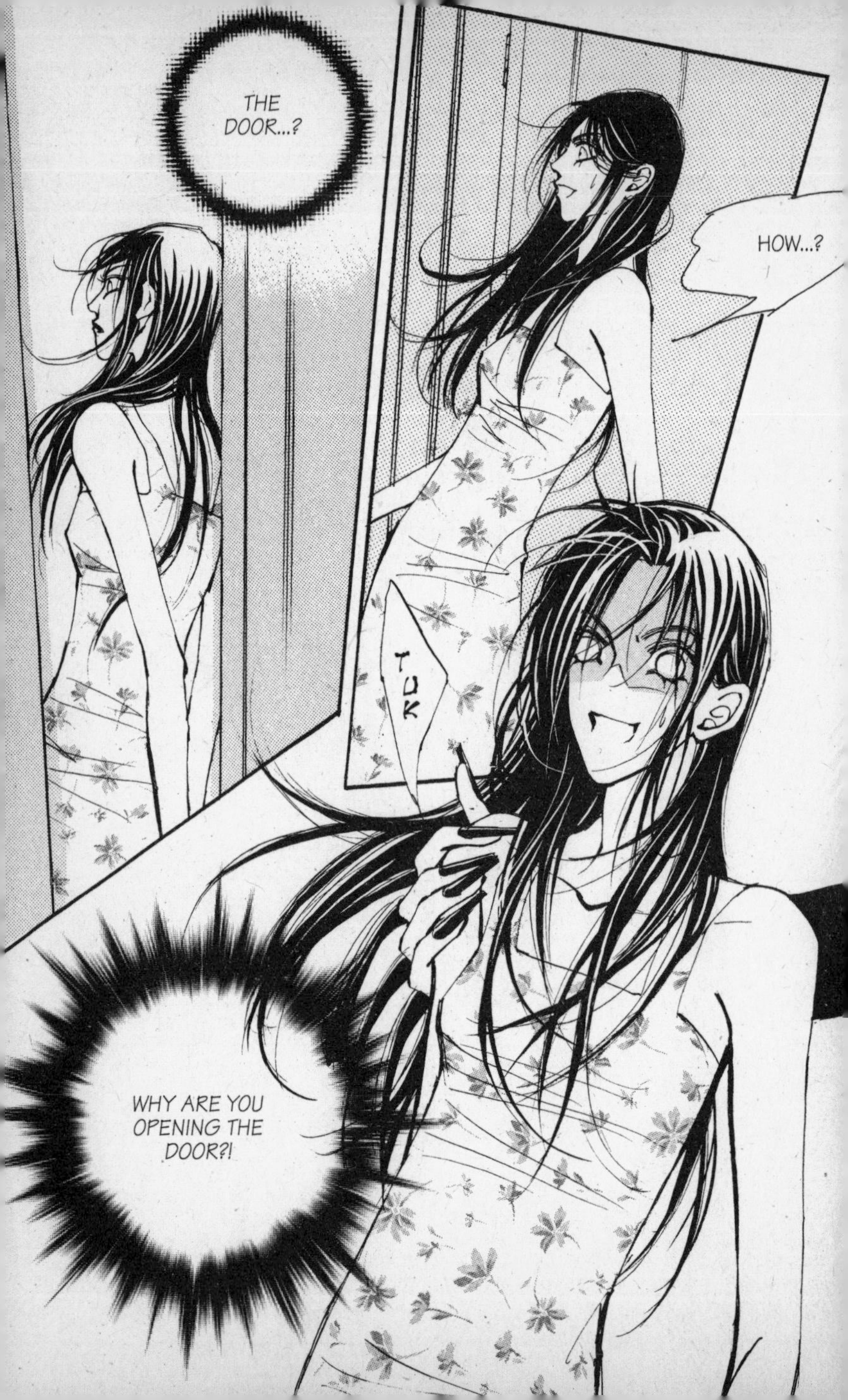
THE DOOR...?
HOW...?
TUK
WHY ARE YOU OPENING THE DOOR?!

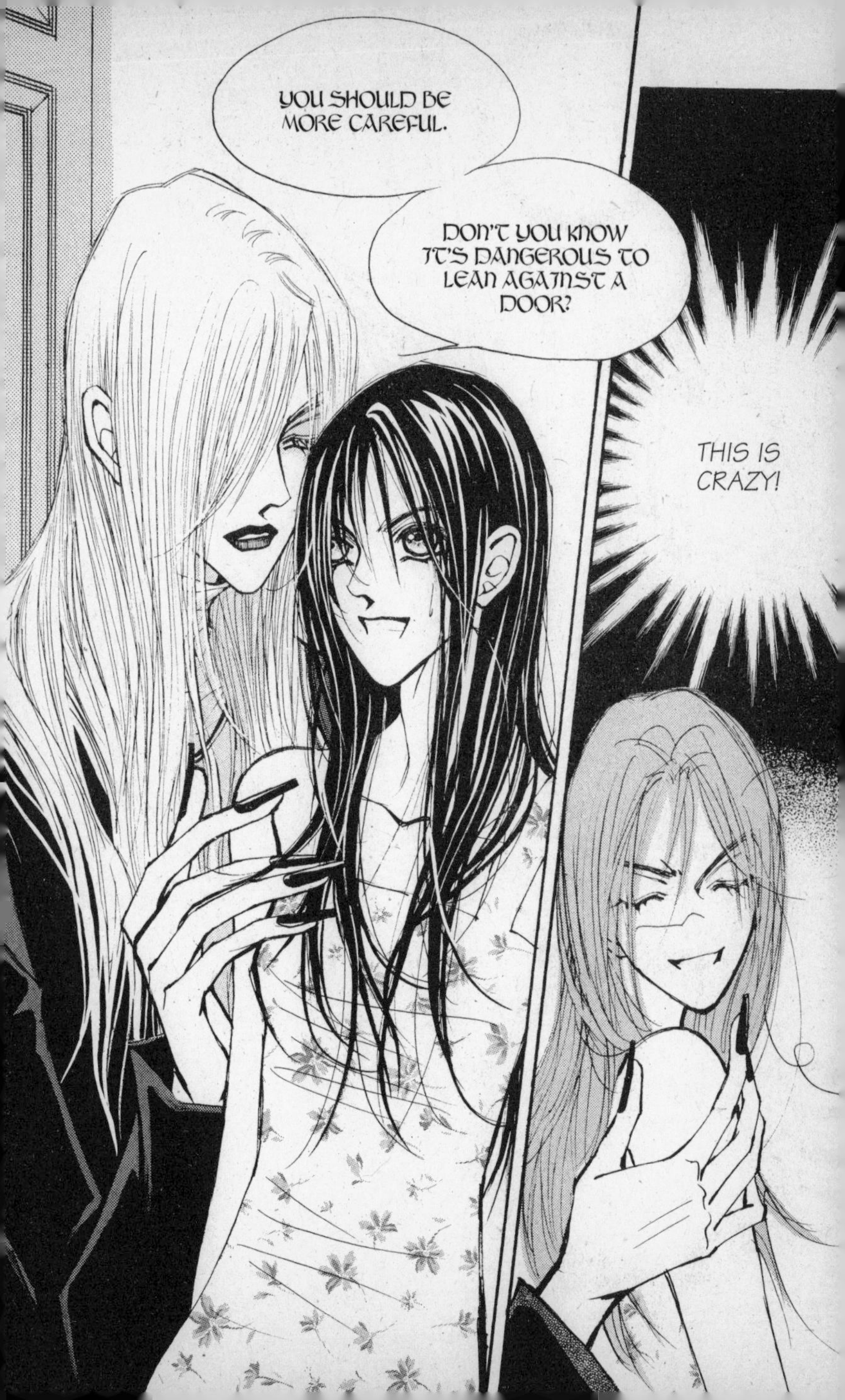
YOU SHOULD BE MORE CAREFUL.
DON'T YOU KNOW IT'S DANGEROUS TO LEAN AGAINST A DOOR?
THIS IS CRAZY!

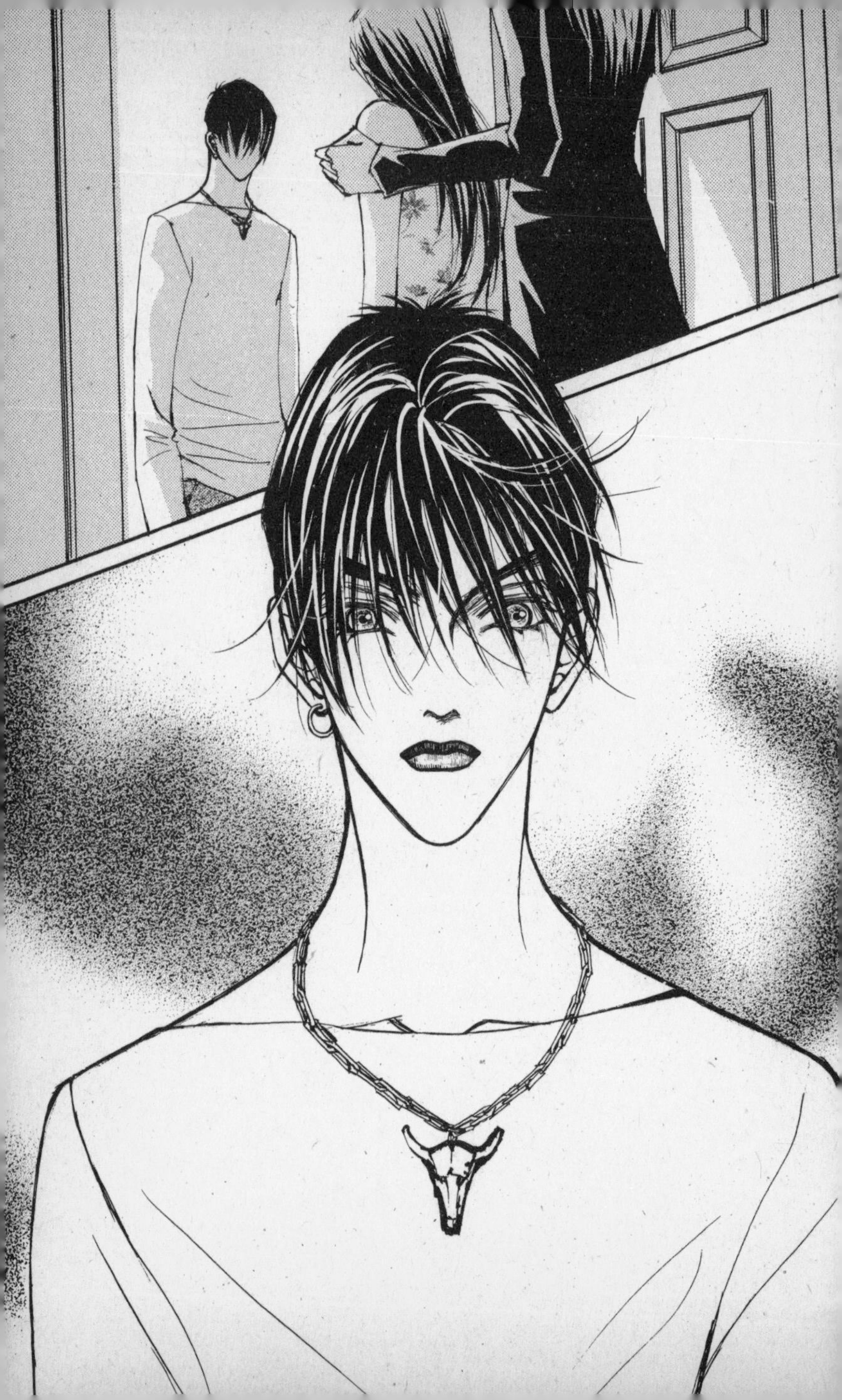

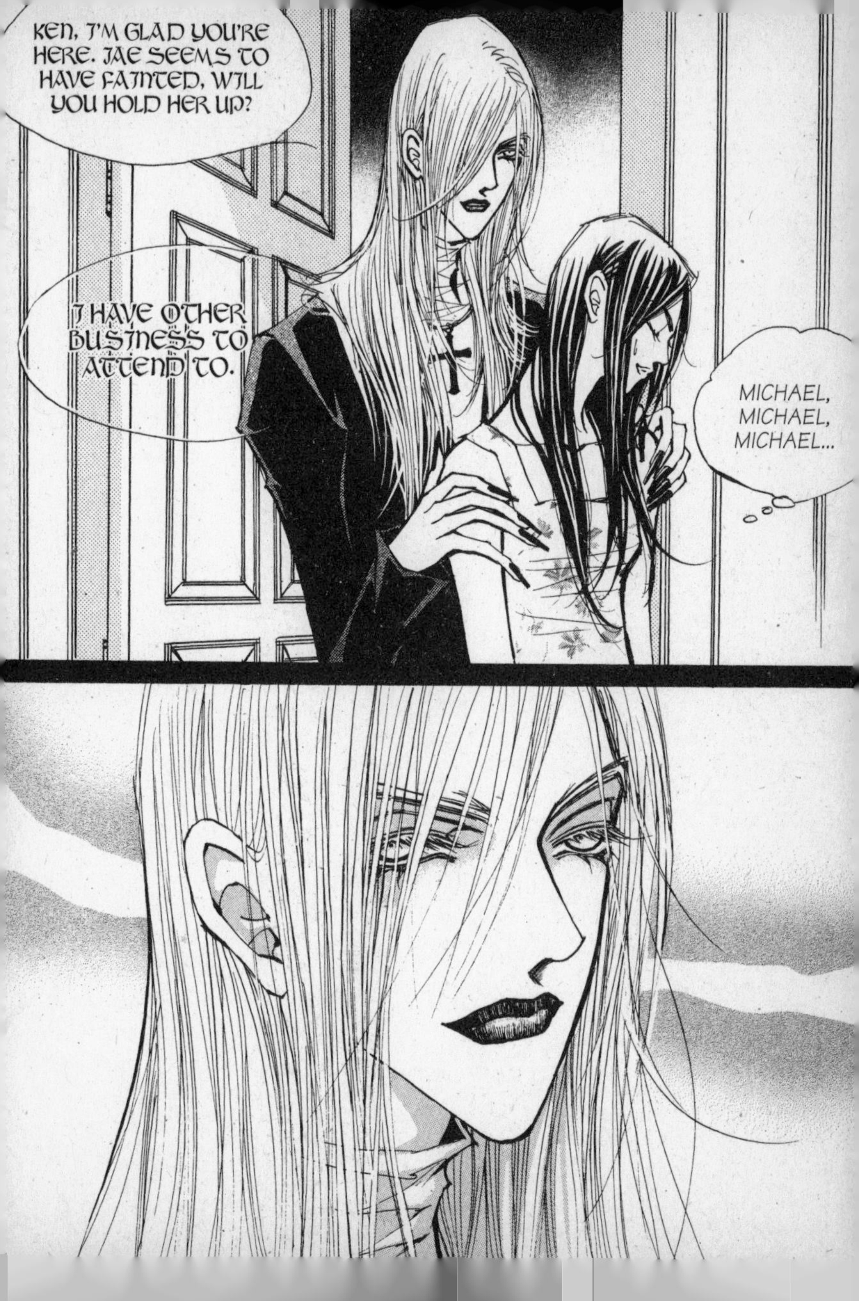
KEN, I'M GLAD YOU'RE HERE. JAE SEEMS TO HAVE FAINTED, WILL YOU HOLD HER UP?
I HAVE OTHER BUSINESS TO ATTEND TO.
MICHAEL, MICHAEL, MICHAEL...

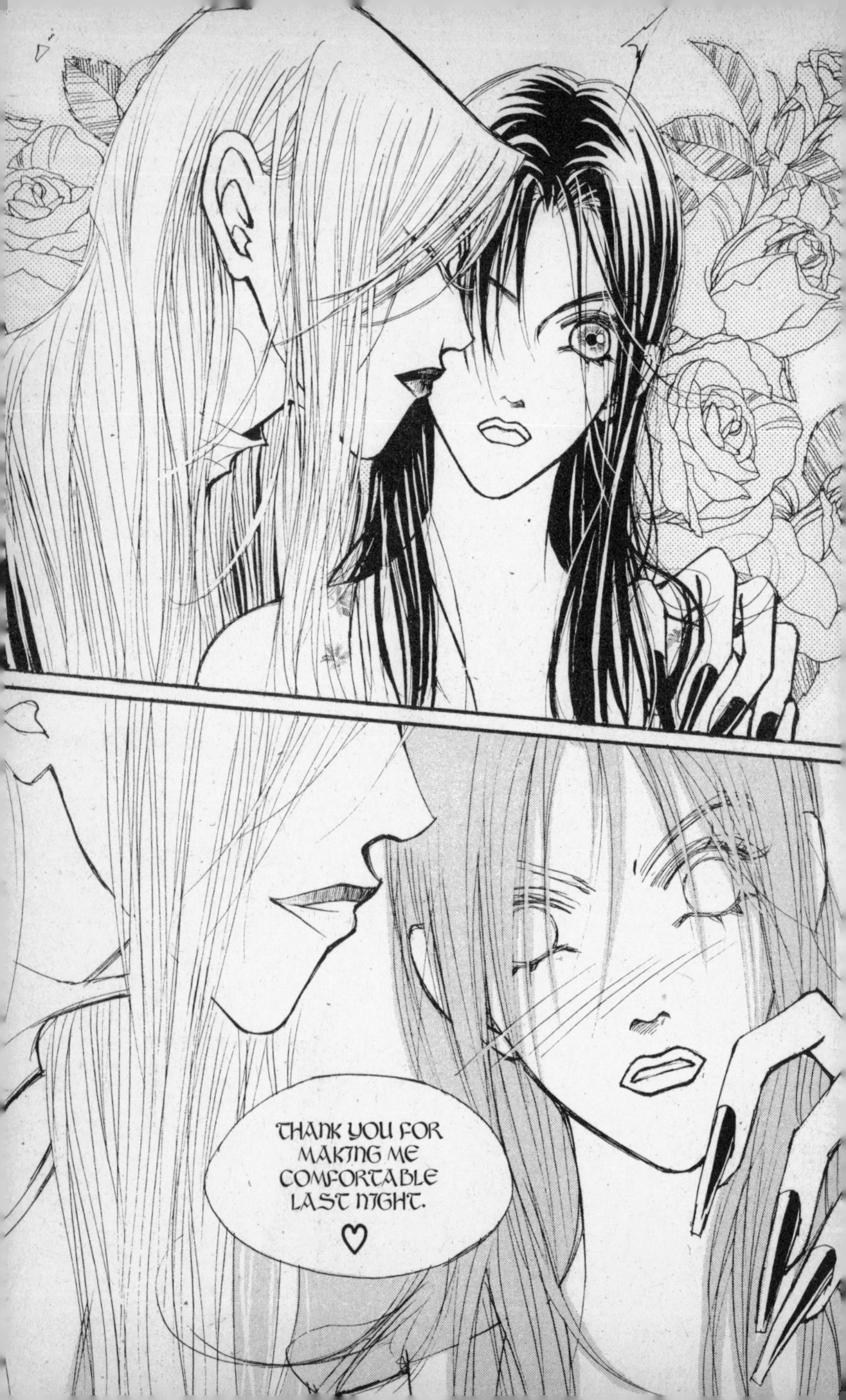
THANK YOU FOR MAKING ME COMFORTABLE LAST NIGHT. ♡

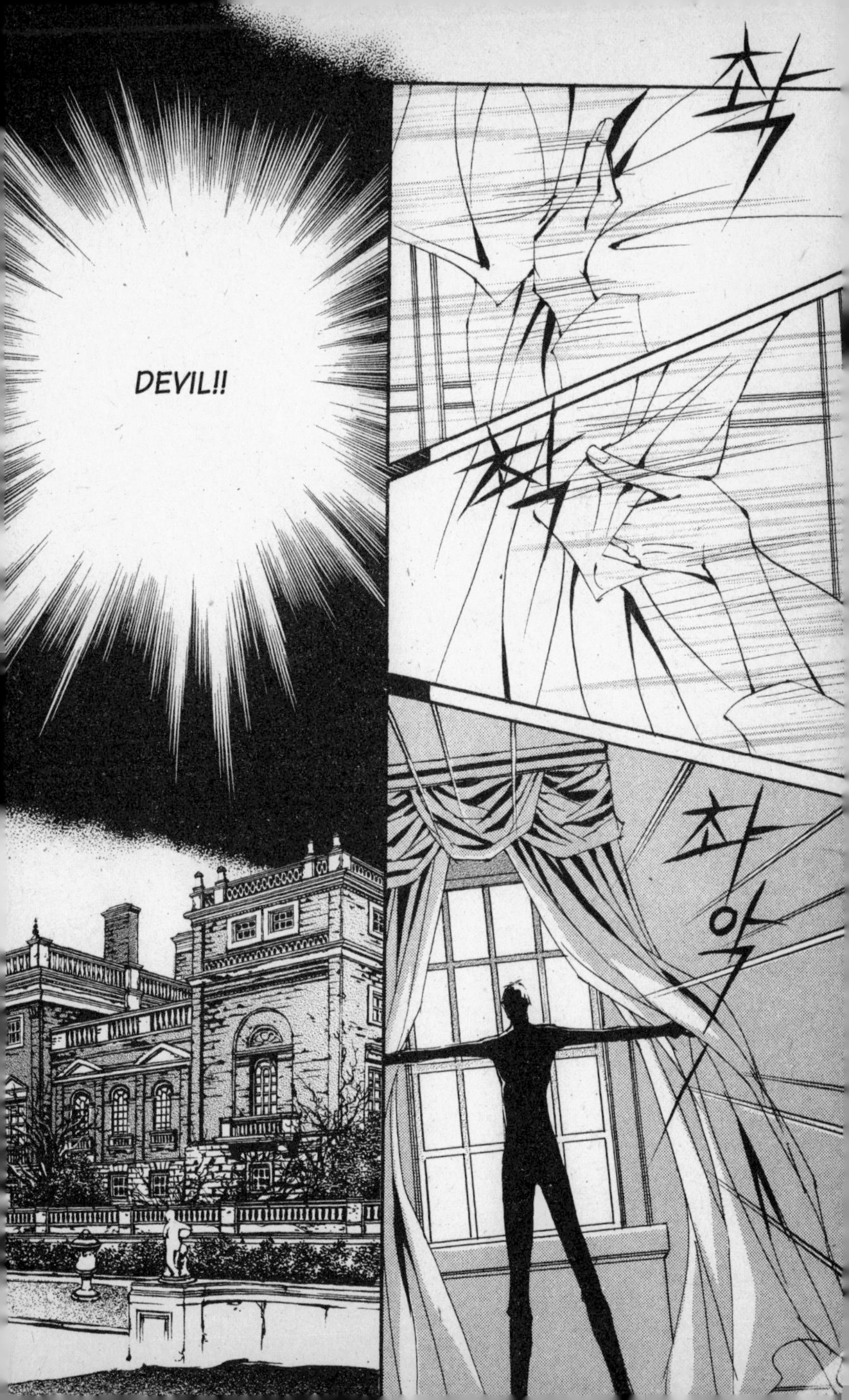
DEVIL!!
착
착
촤악

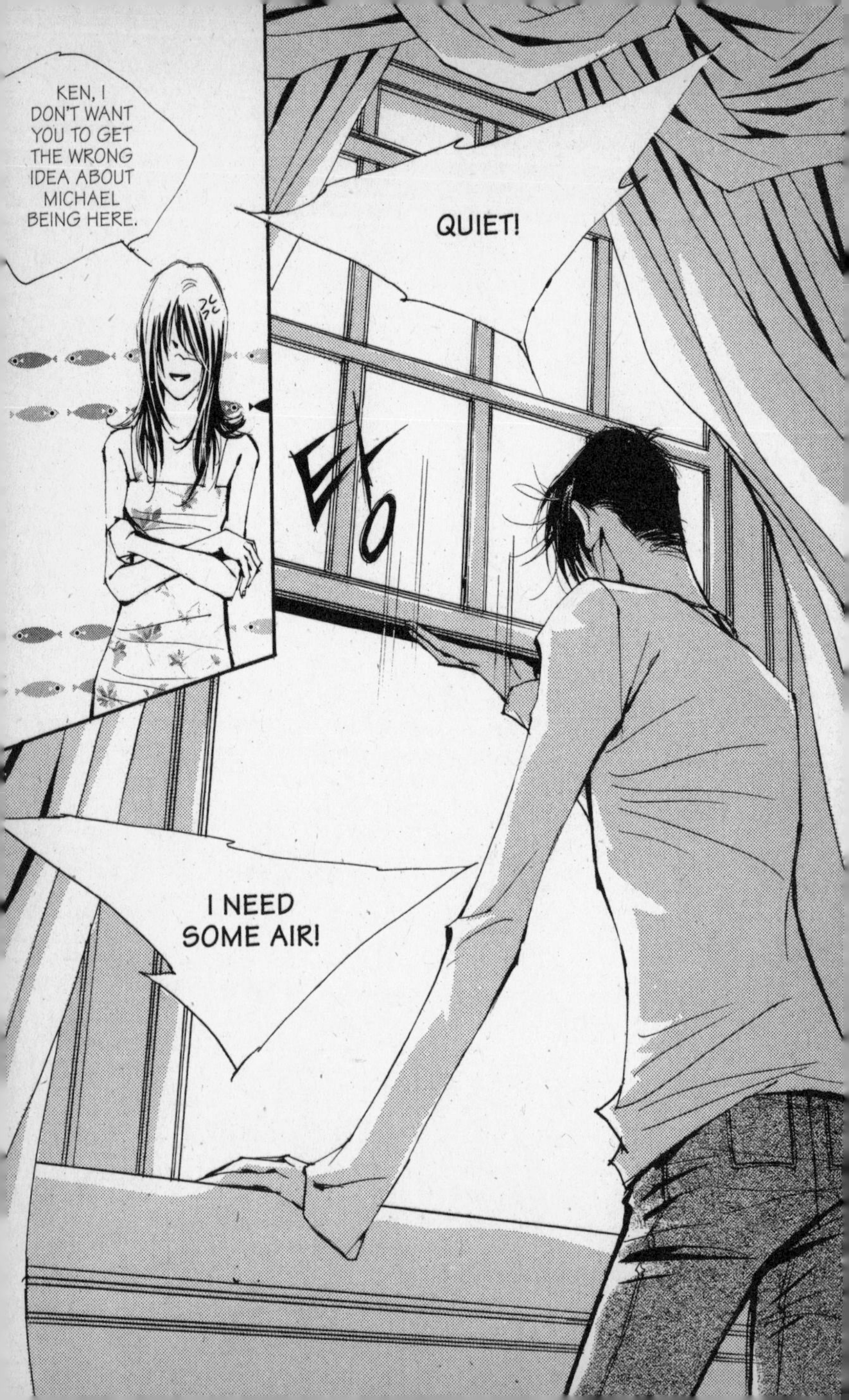
KEN, I DON'T WANT YOU TO GET THE WRONG IDEA ABOUT MICHAEL BEING HERE.
QUIET!
탕
I NEED SOME AIR!

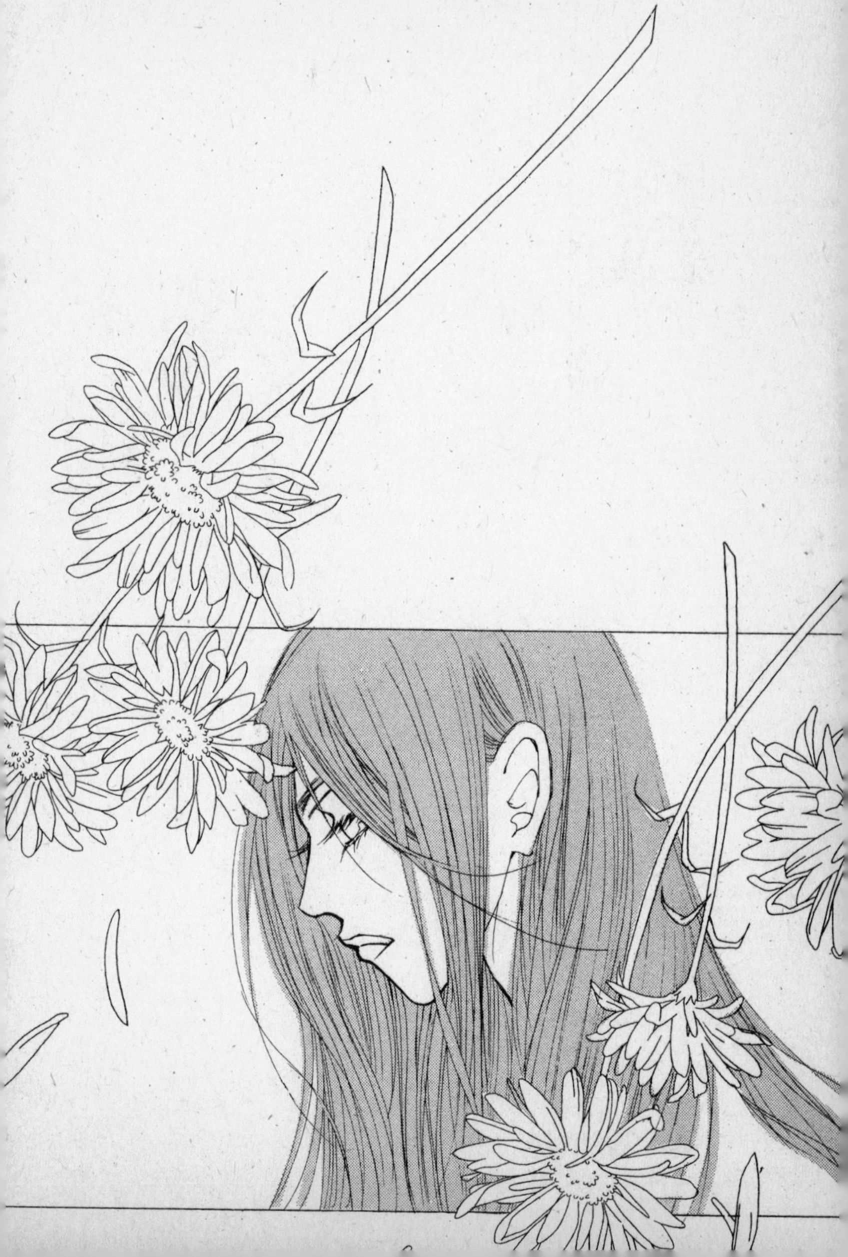

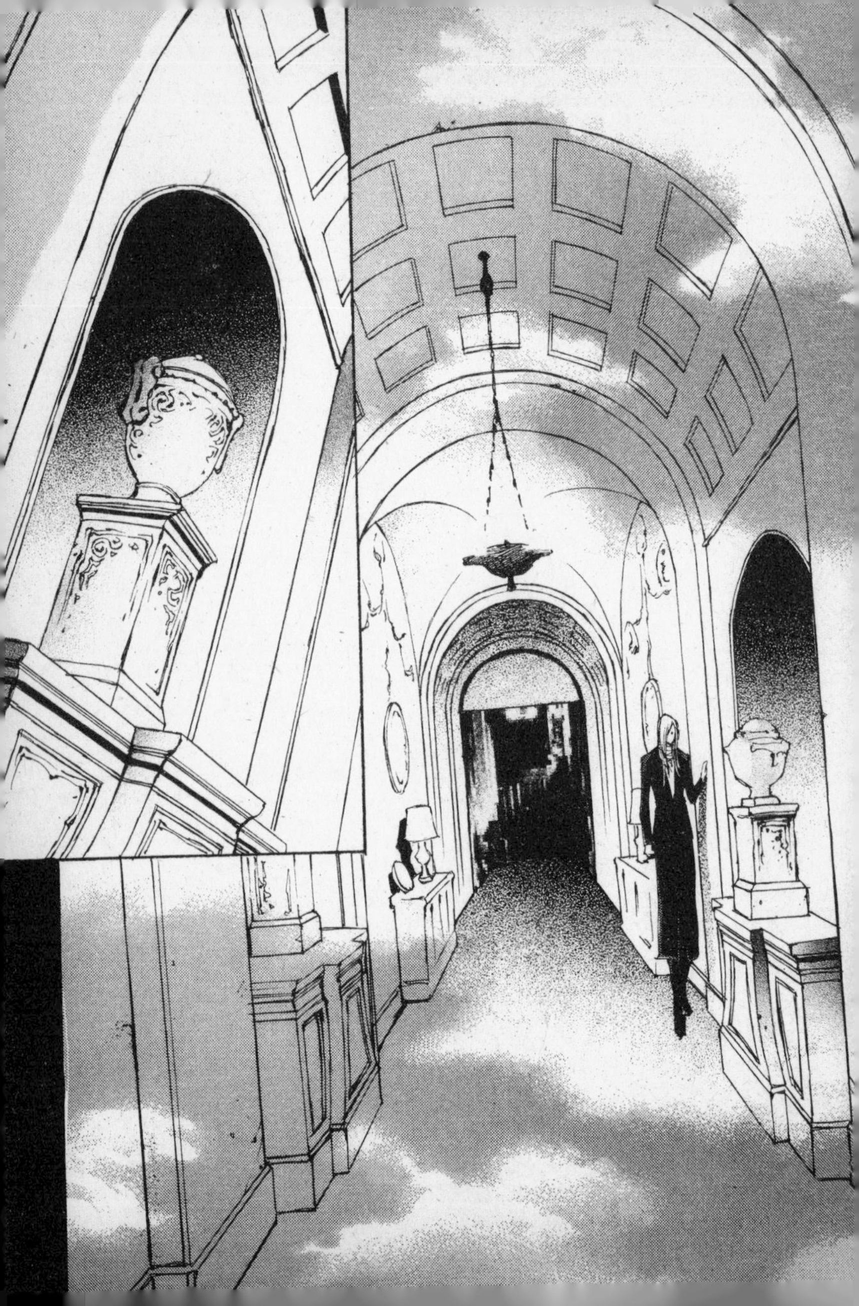

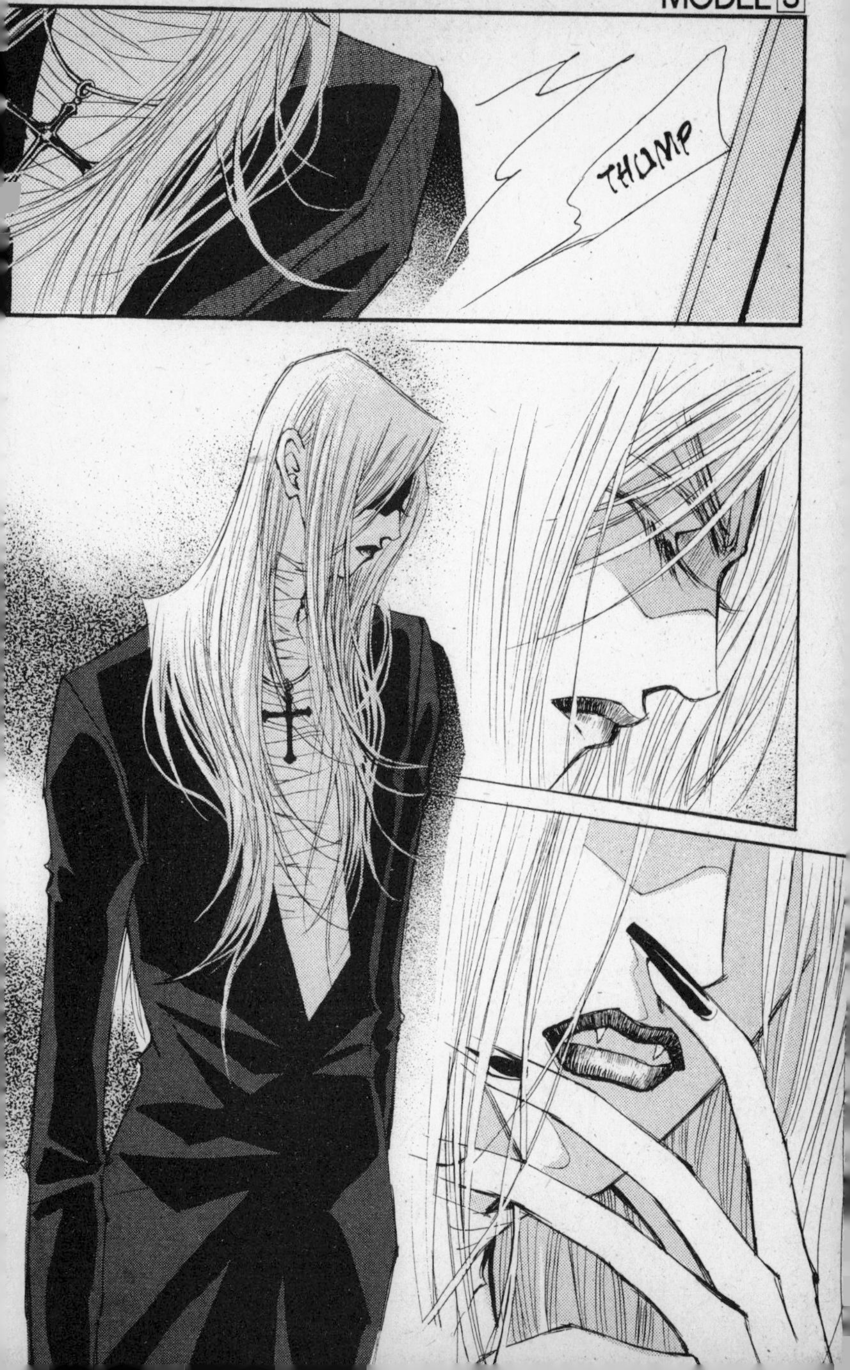
THUMP

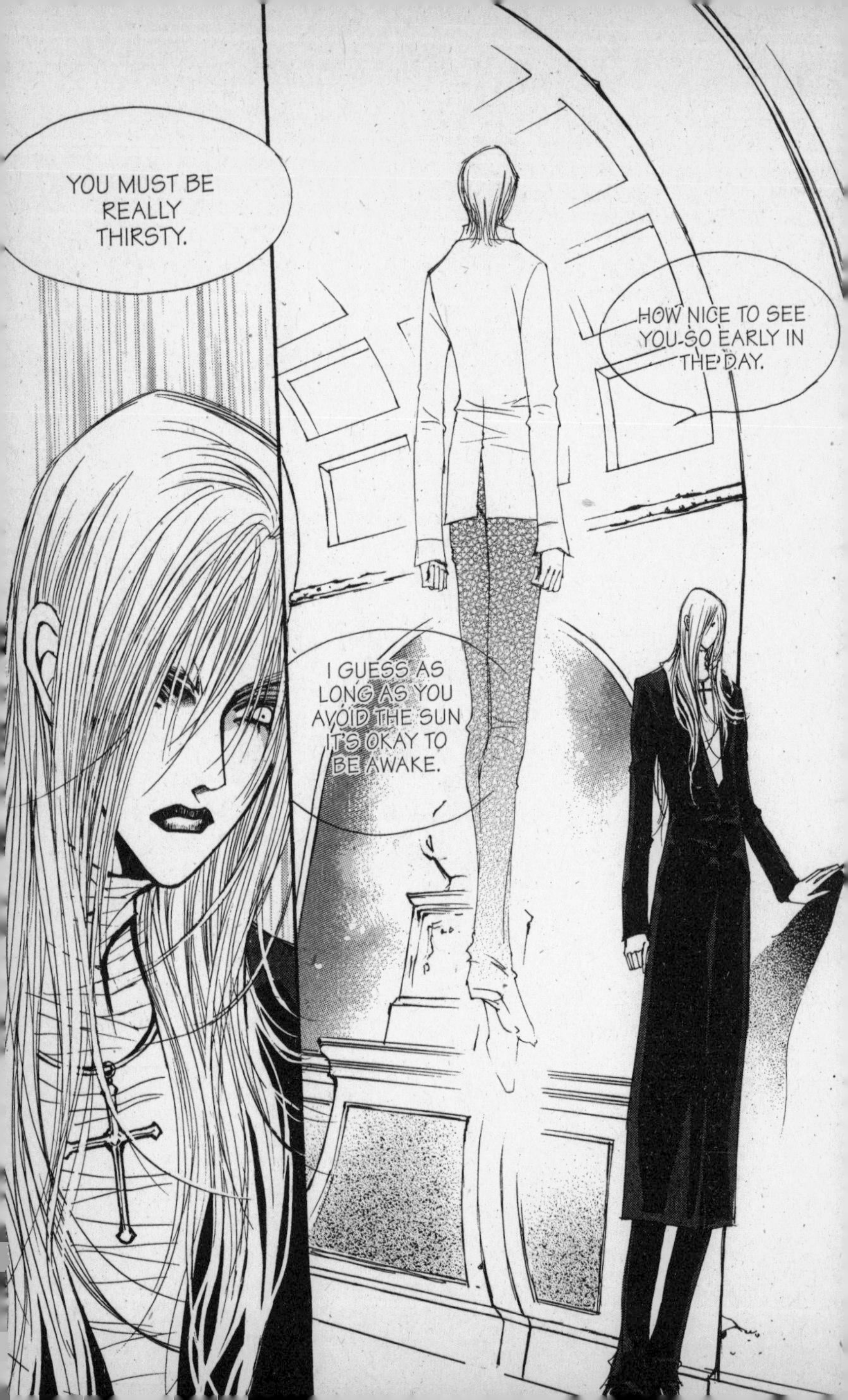
YOU MUST BE REALLY THIRSTY.
HOW NICE TO SEE YOU SO EARLY IN THE DAY.
I GUESS AS LONG AS YOU AVOID THE SUN IT'S OKAY TO BE AWAKE.

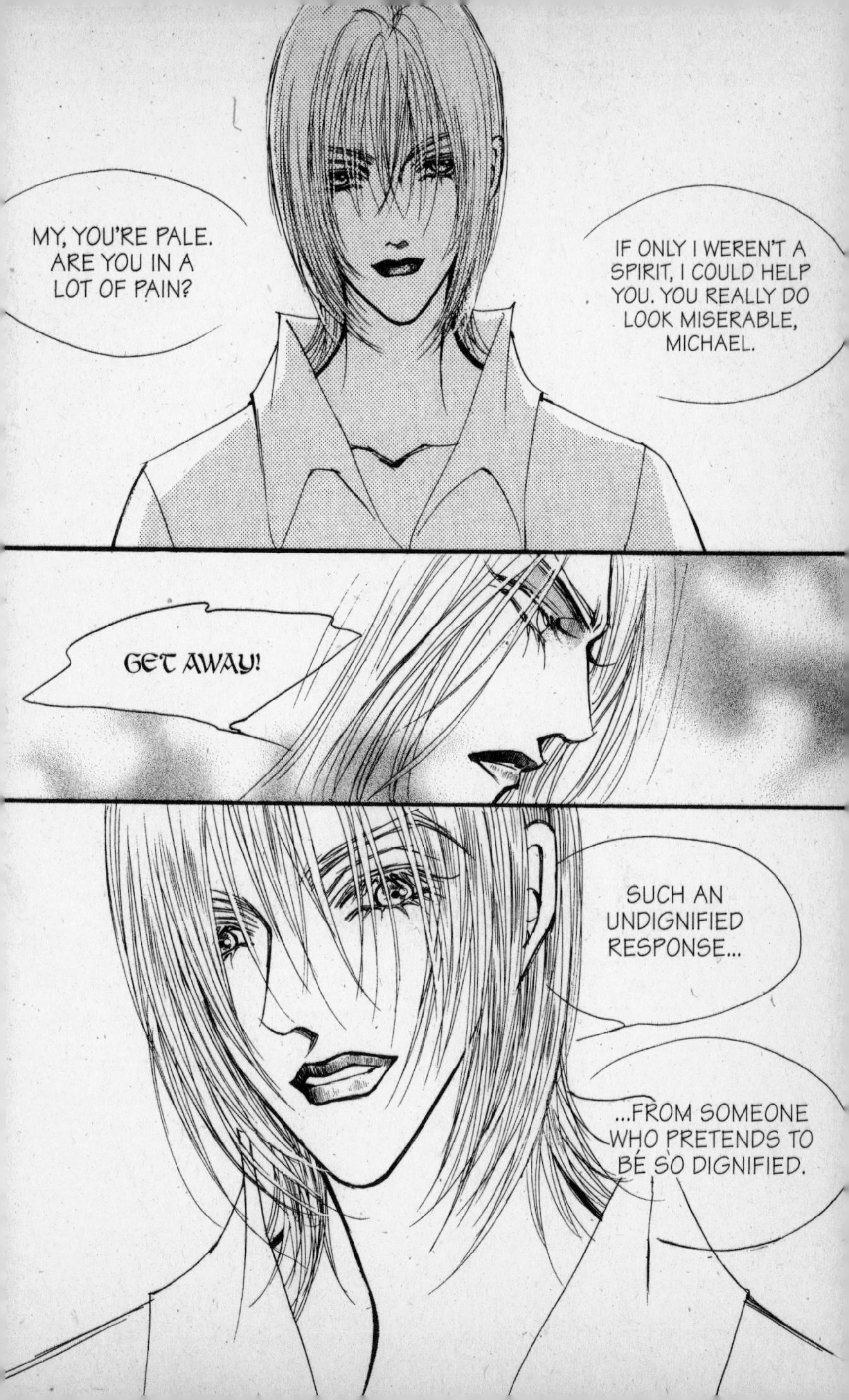
MY, YOU'RE PALE. ARE YOU IN A LOT OF PAIN?
IF ONLY I WEREN'T A SPIRIT, I COULD HELP YOU. YOU REALLY DO LOOK MISERABLE, MICHAEL.
GET AWAY!
SUCH AN UNDIGNIFIED RESPONSE...
...FROM SOMEONE WHO PRETENDS TO BE SO DIGNIFIED.

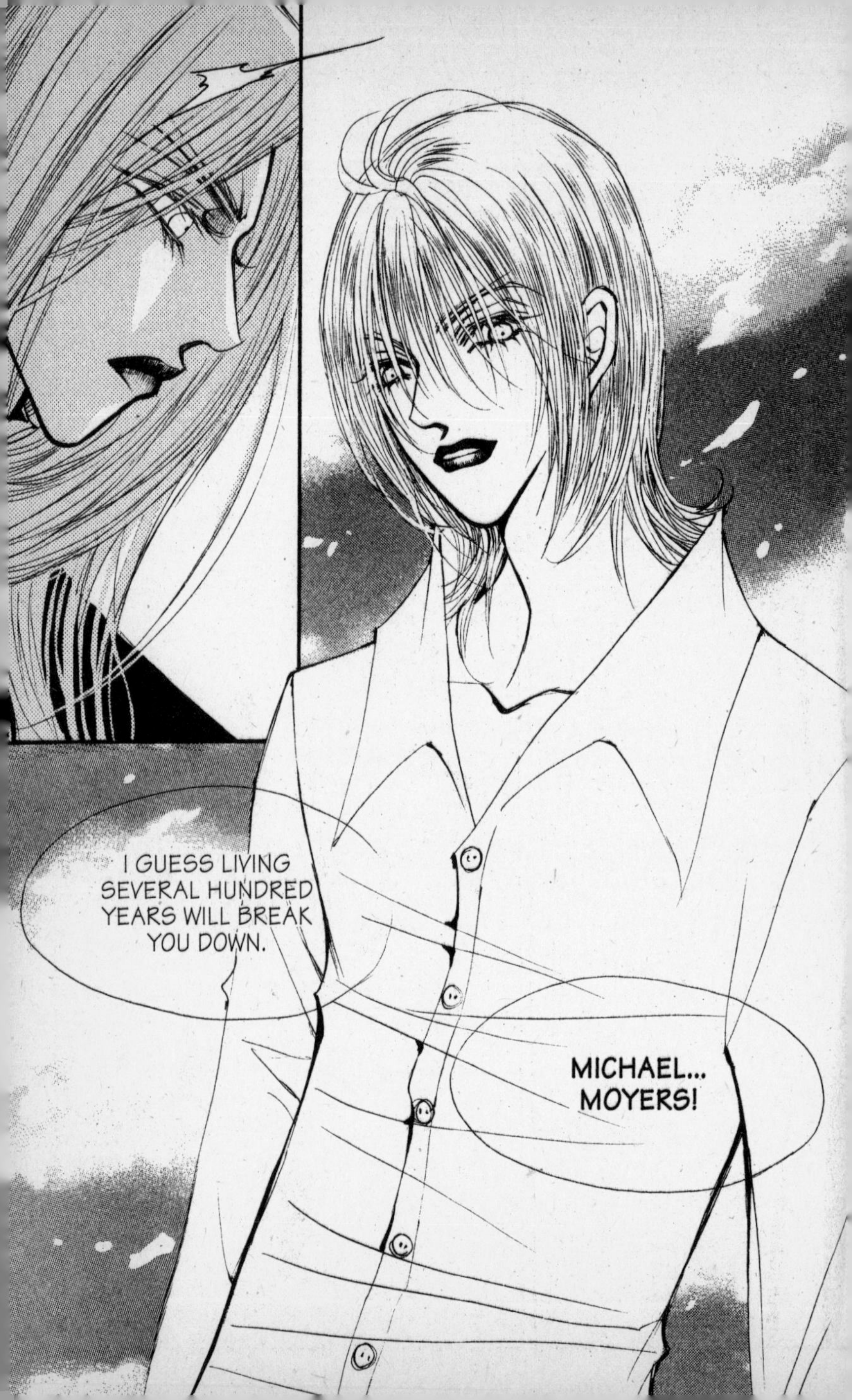
I GUESS LIVING SEVERAL HUNDRED YEARS WILL BREAK YOU DOWN.
MICHAEL... MOYERS!

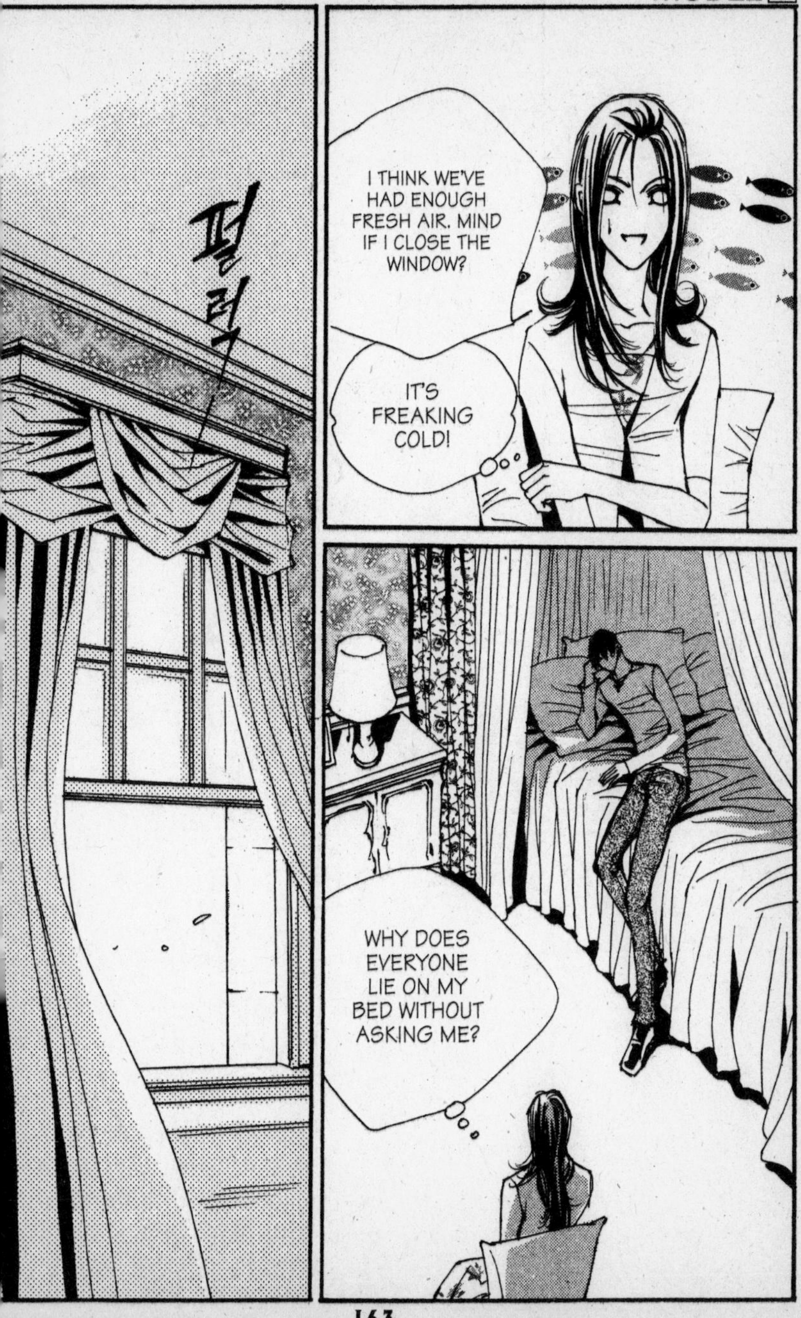
펄럭
I THINK WE'VE HAD ENOUGH FRESH AIR. MIND IF I CLOSE THE WINDOW?
IT'S FREAKING COLD!
WHY DOES EVERYONE LIE ON MY BED WITHOUT ASKING ME?

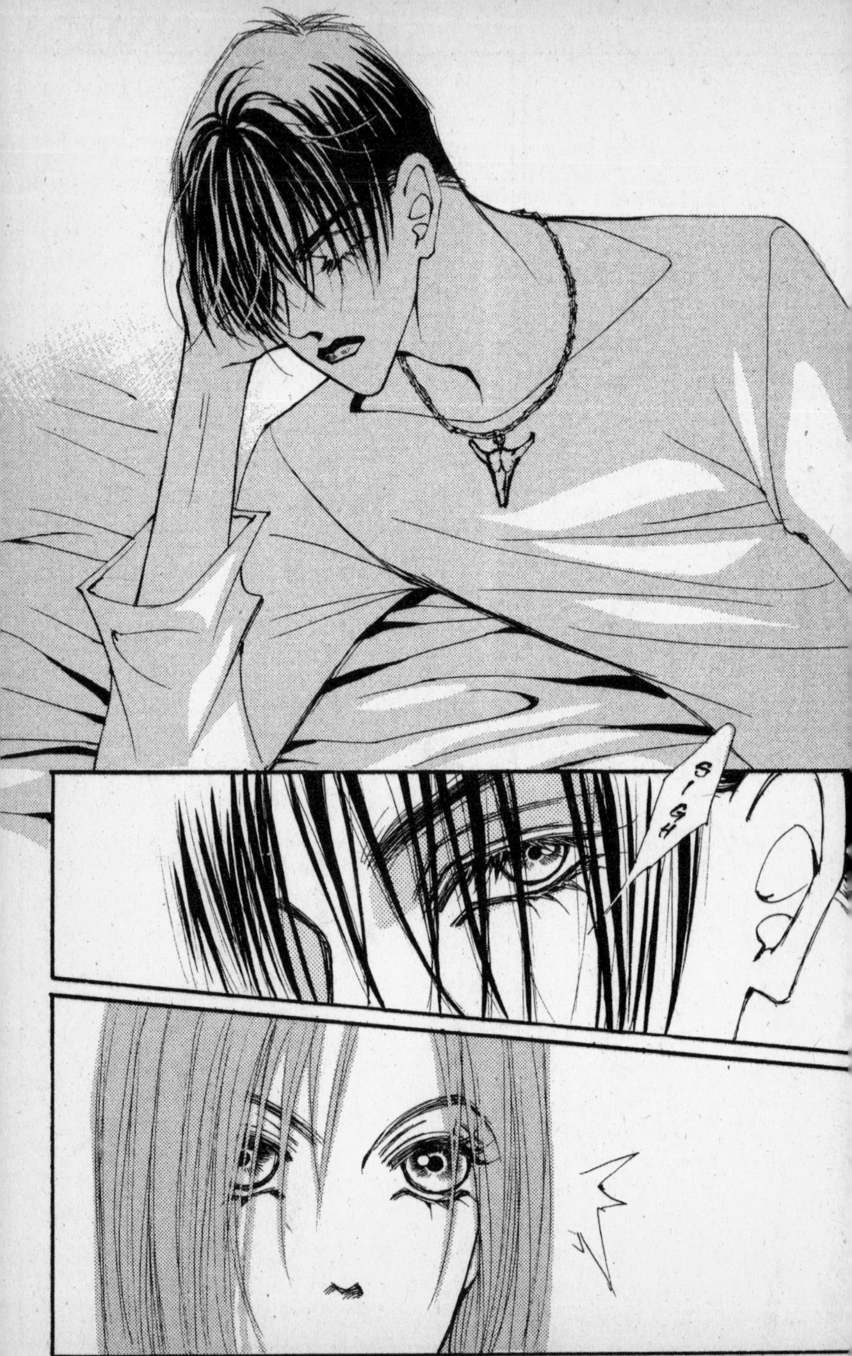
SIGH

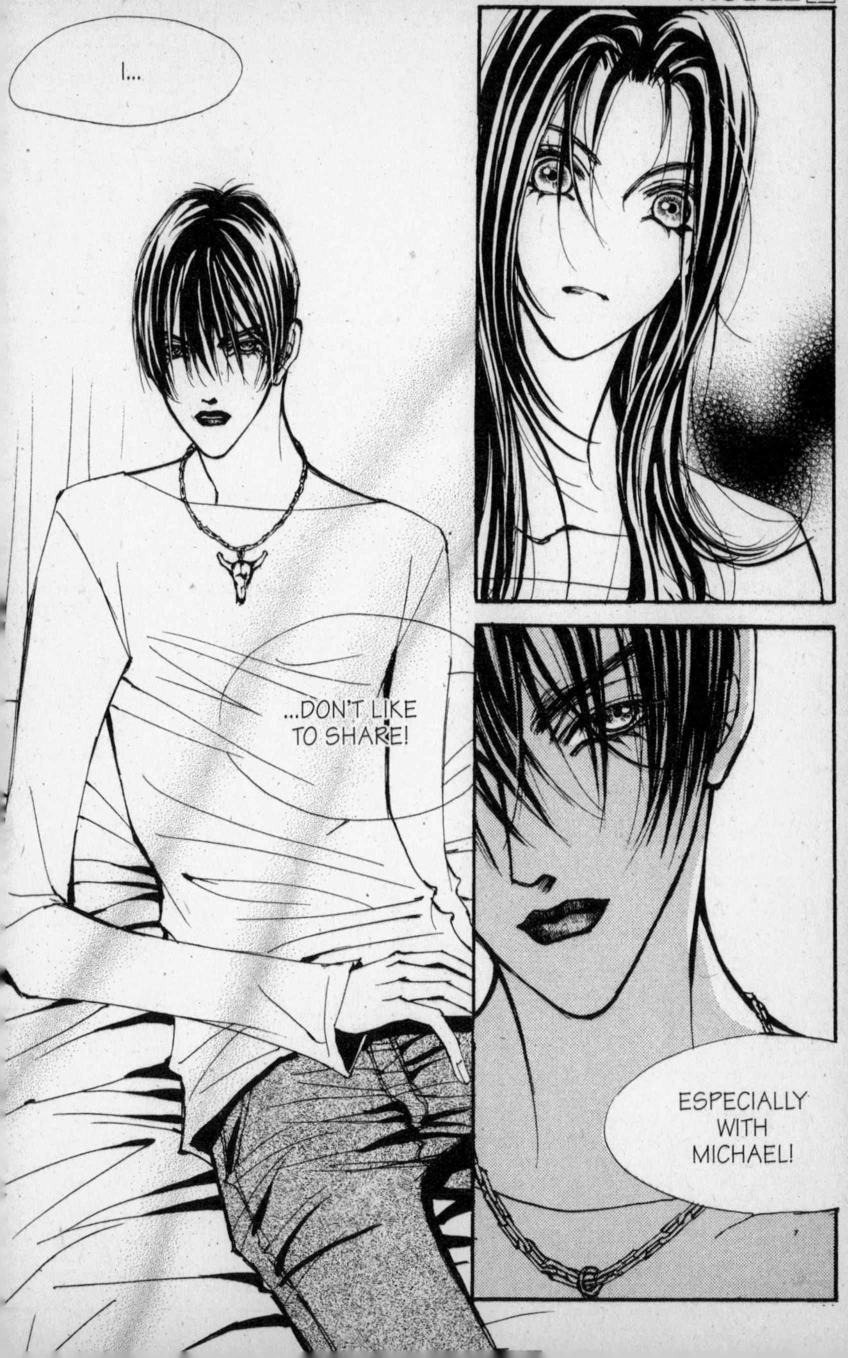
I...
...DON'T LIKE TO SHARE!
ESPECIALLY WITH MICHAEL!

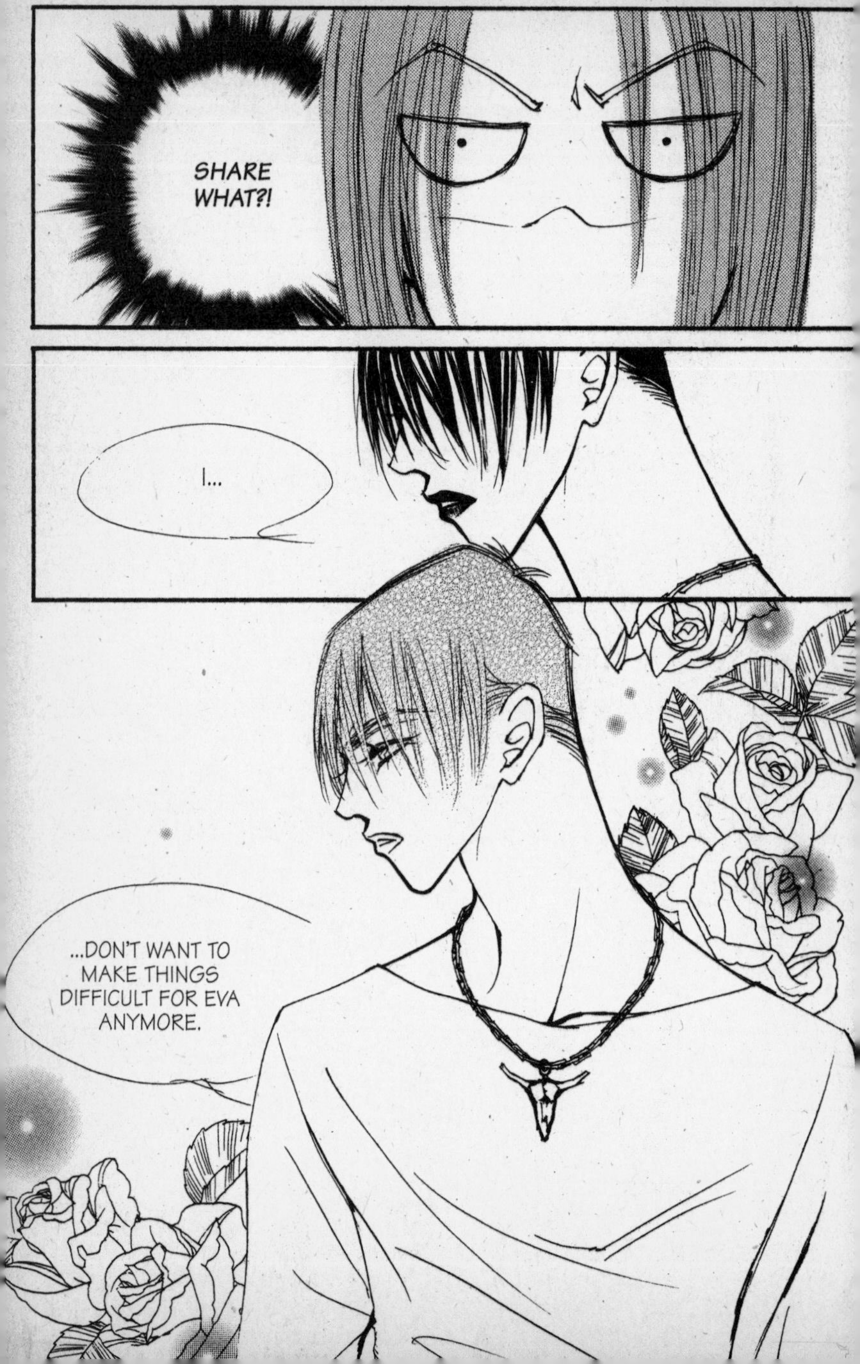
SHARE WHAT?!
I...
...DON'T WANT TO MAKE THINGS DIFFICULT FOR EVA ANYMORE.

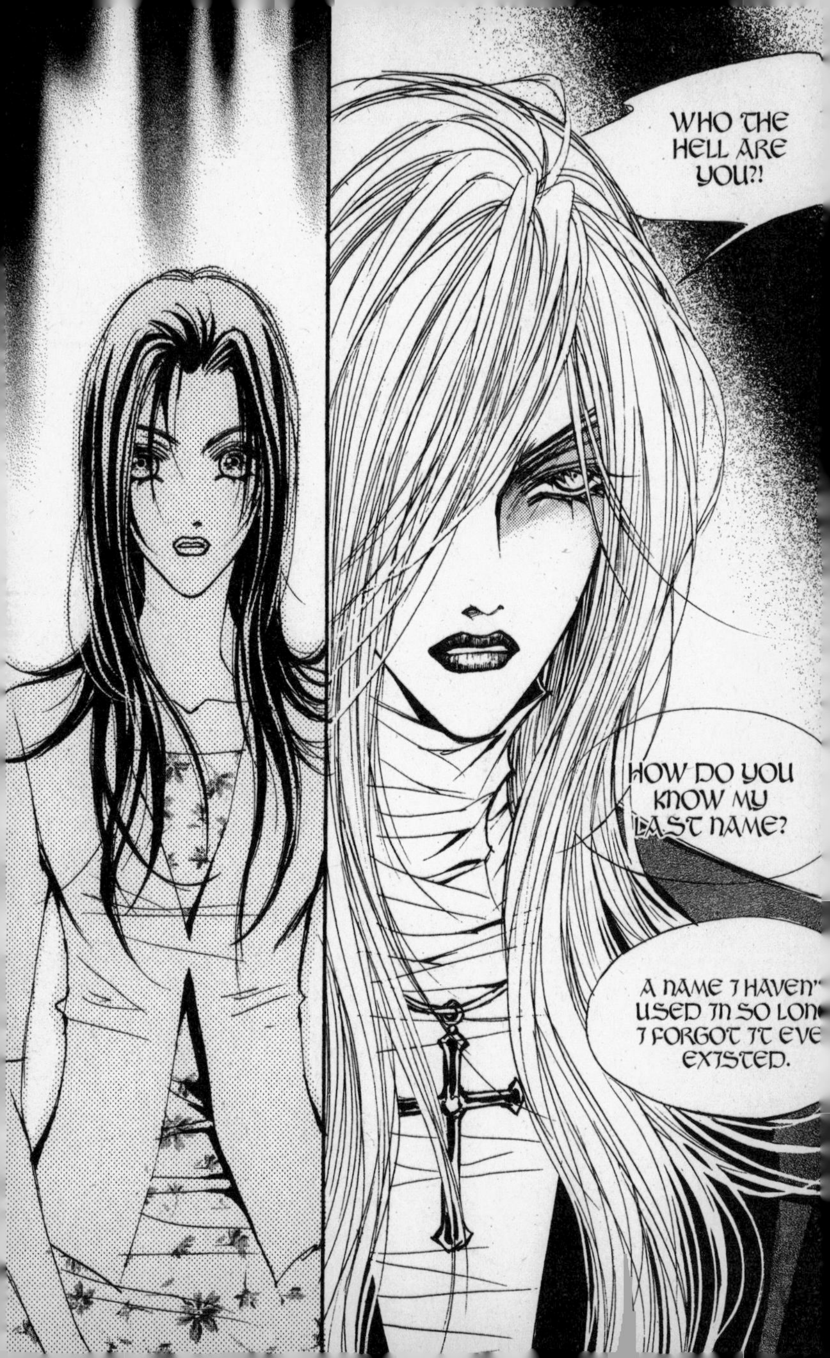
WHO THE HELL ARE YOU?!
HOW DO YOU KNOW MY LAST NAME?
A NAME I HAVEN'T USED IN SO LONG I FORGOT IT EVE EXISTED.

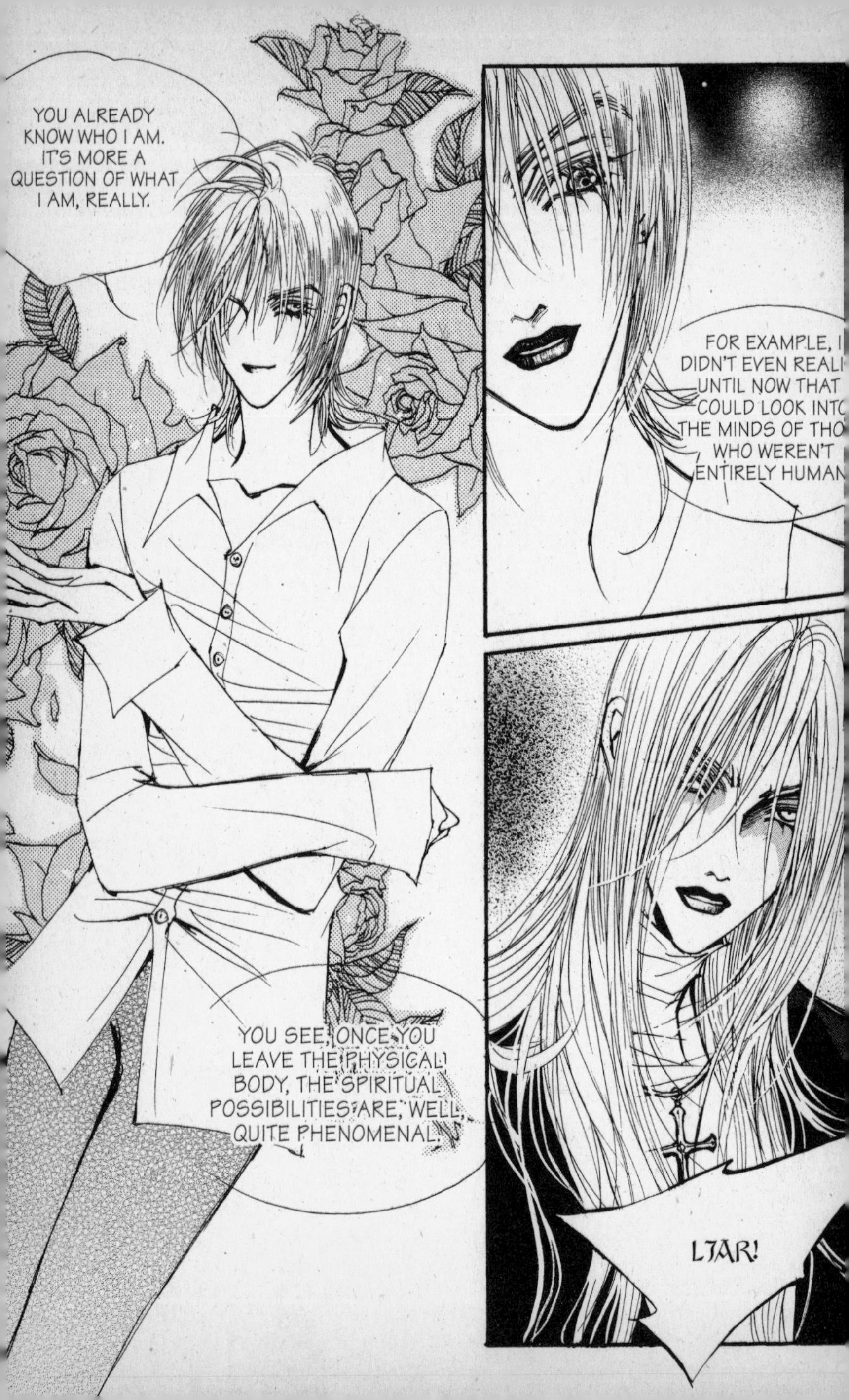
YOU ALREADY KNOW WHO I AM. IT'S MORE A QUESTION OF WHAT I AM, REALLY.
YOU SEE, ONCE YOU LEAVE THE PHYSICAL BODY, THE SPIRITUAL POSSIBILITIES ARE, WELL, QUITE PHENOMENAL.
FOR EXAMPLE, I DIDN'T EVEN REALI UNTIL NOW THAT COULD LOOK INTO THE MINDS OF THO WHO WEREN'T ENTIRELY HUMAN
LIAR!

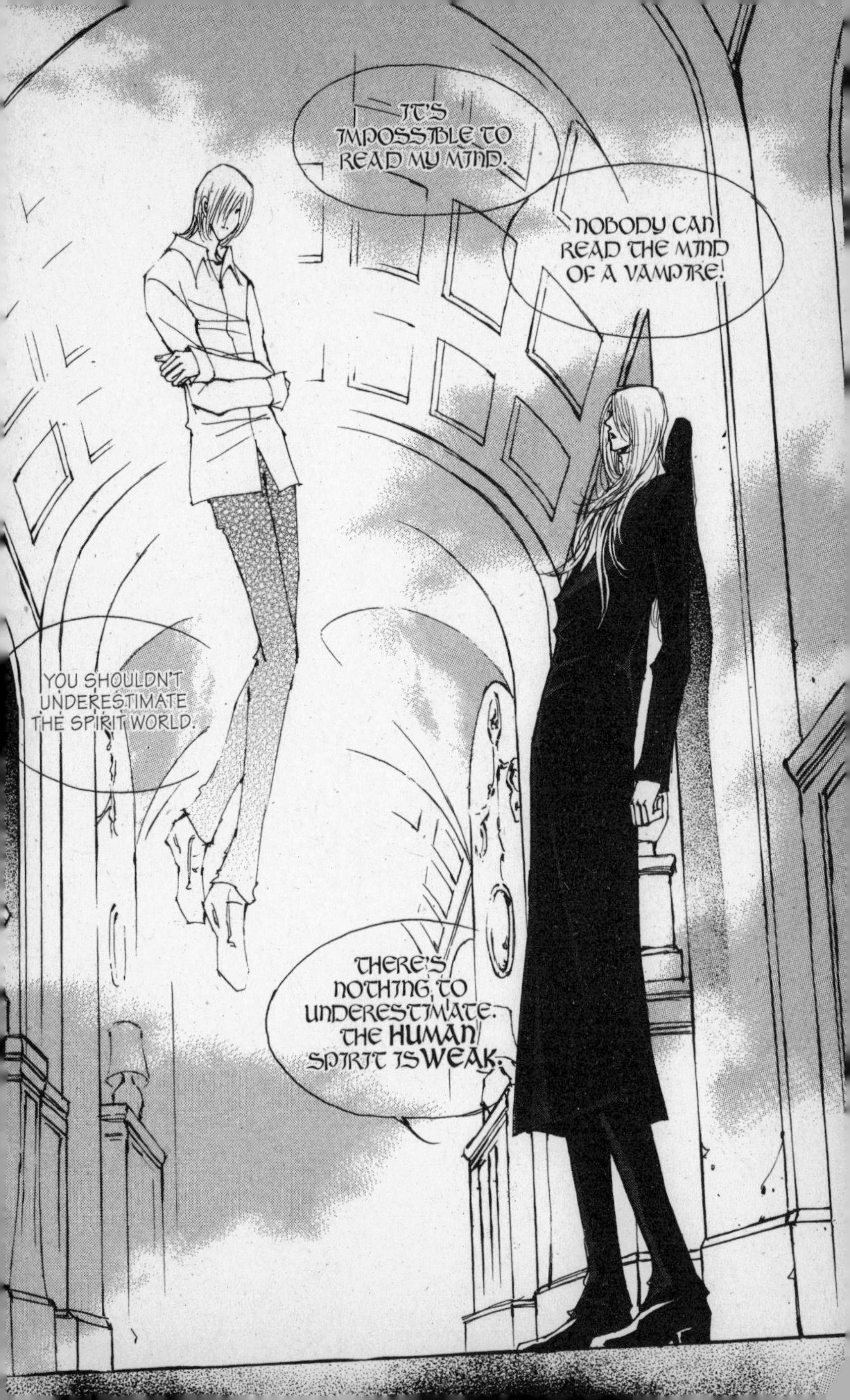
IT'S IMPOSSIBLE TO READ MY MIND.
NOBODY CAN READ THE MIND OF A VAMPIRE!
YOU SHOULDN'T UNDERESTIMATE THE SPIRIT WORLD.
THERE'S NOTHING TO UNDERESTIMATE. THE HUMAN SPIRIT IS WEAK.

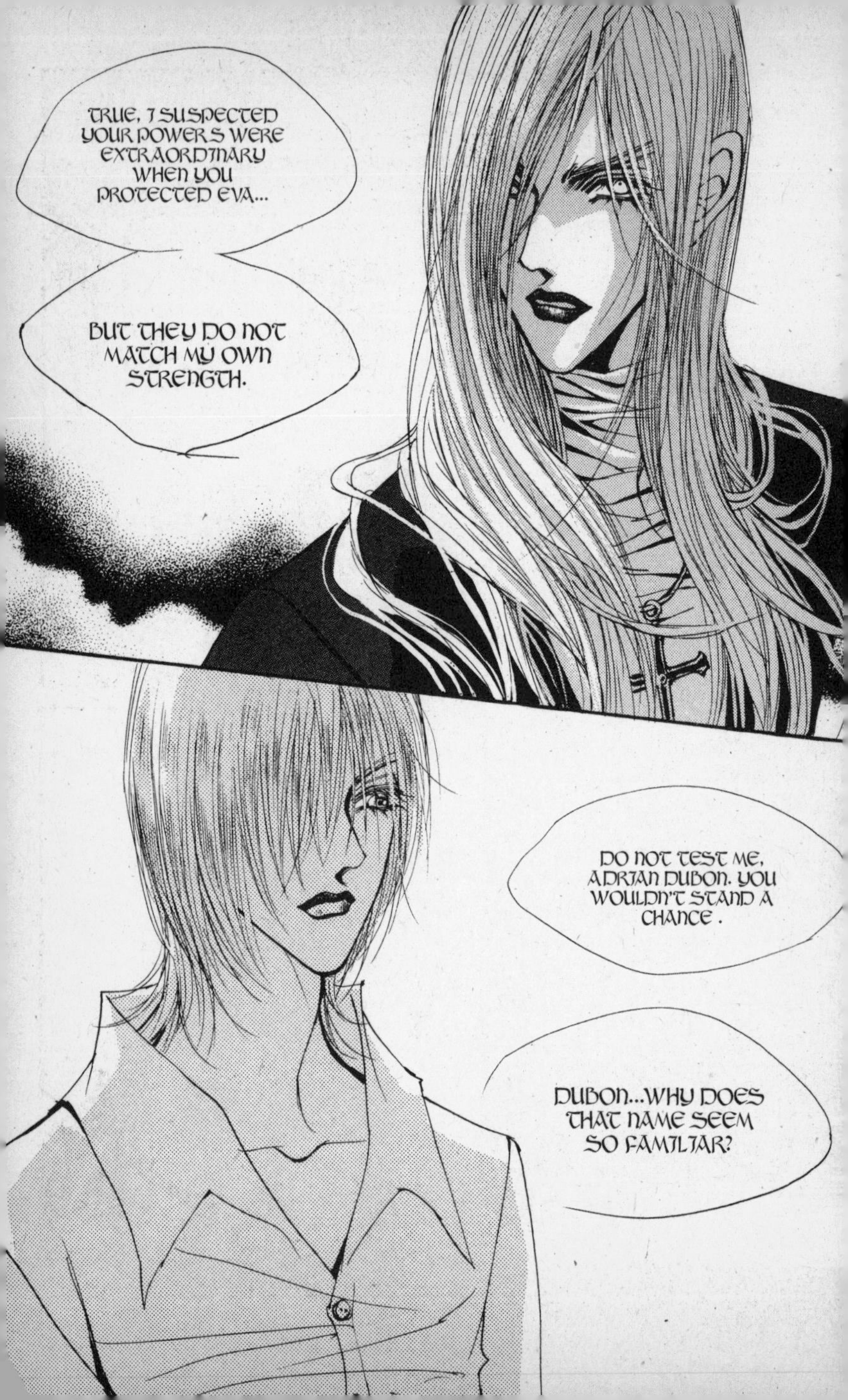
TRUE, I SUSPECTED YOUR POWERS WERE EXTRAORDINARY WHEN YOU PROTECTED EVA...
BUT THEY DO NOT MATCH MY OWN STRENGTH.
DO NOT TEST ME, ADRIAN DUBON. YOU WOULDN'T STAND A CHANCE .
DUBON...WHY DOES THAT NAME SEEM SO FAMILIAR?

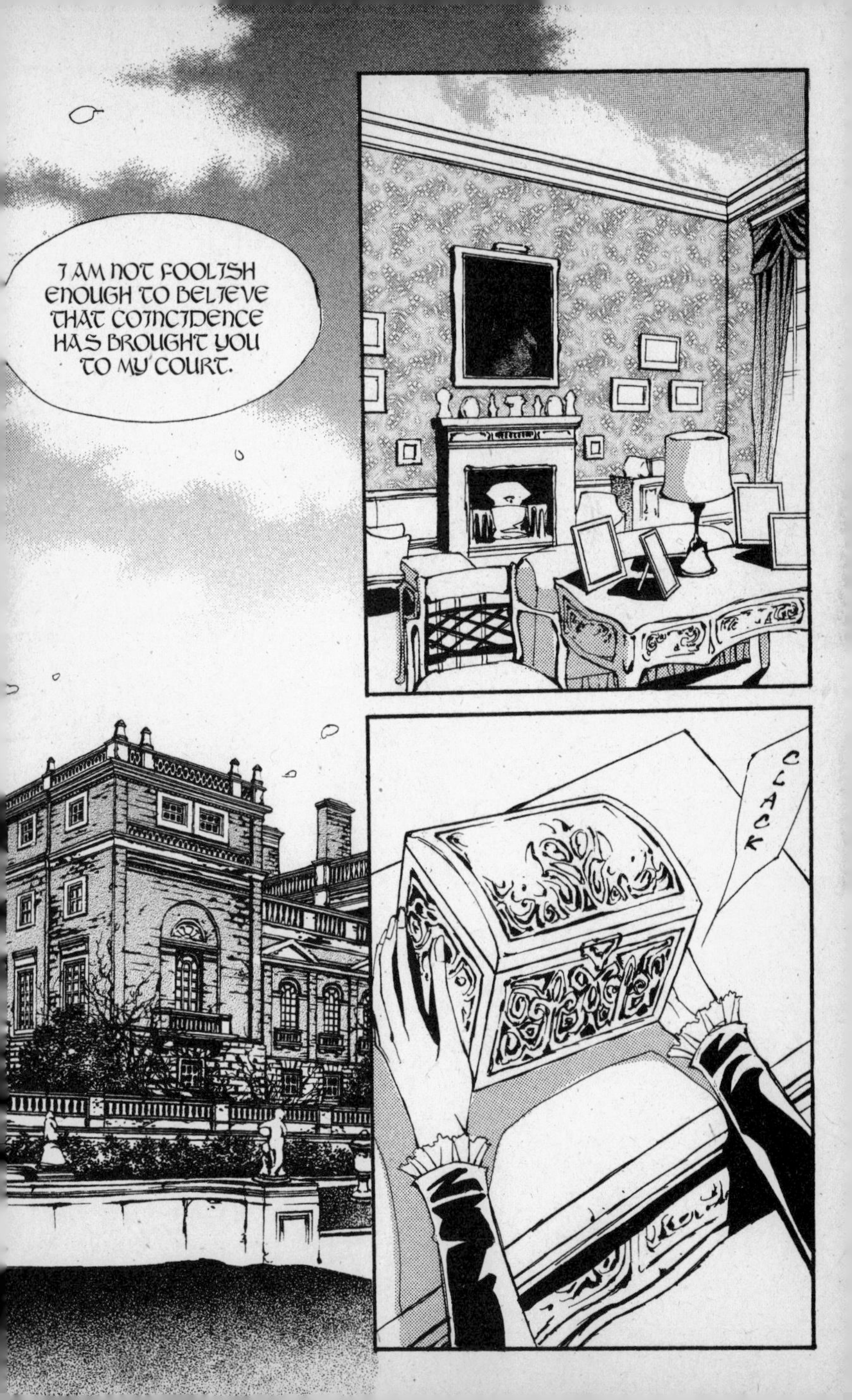
I AM NOT FOOLISH ENOUGH TO BELIEVE THAT COINCIDENCE HAS BROUGHT YOU TO MY COURT.
CLACK

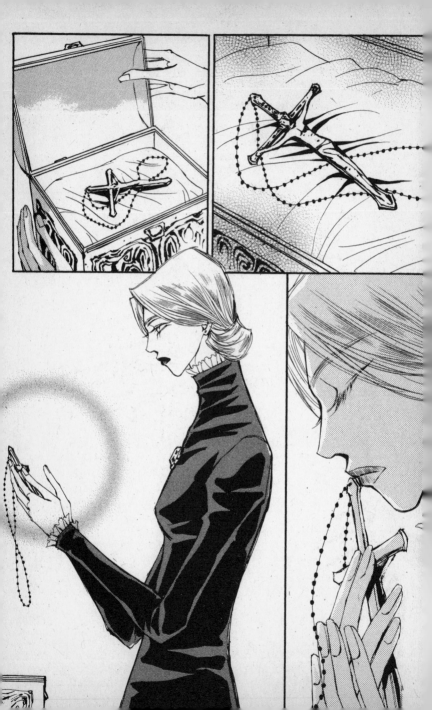

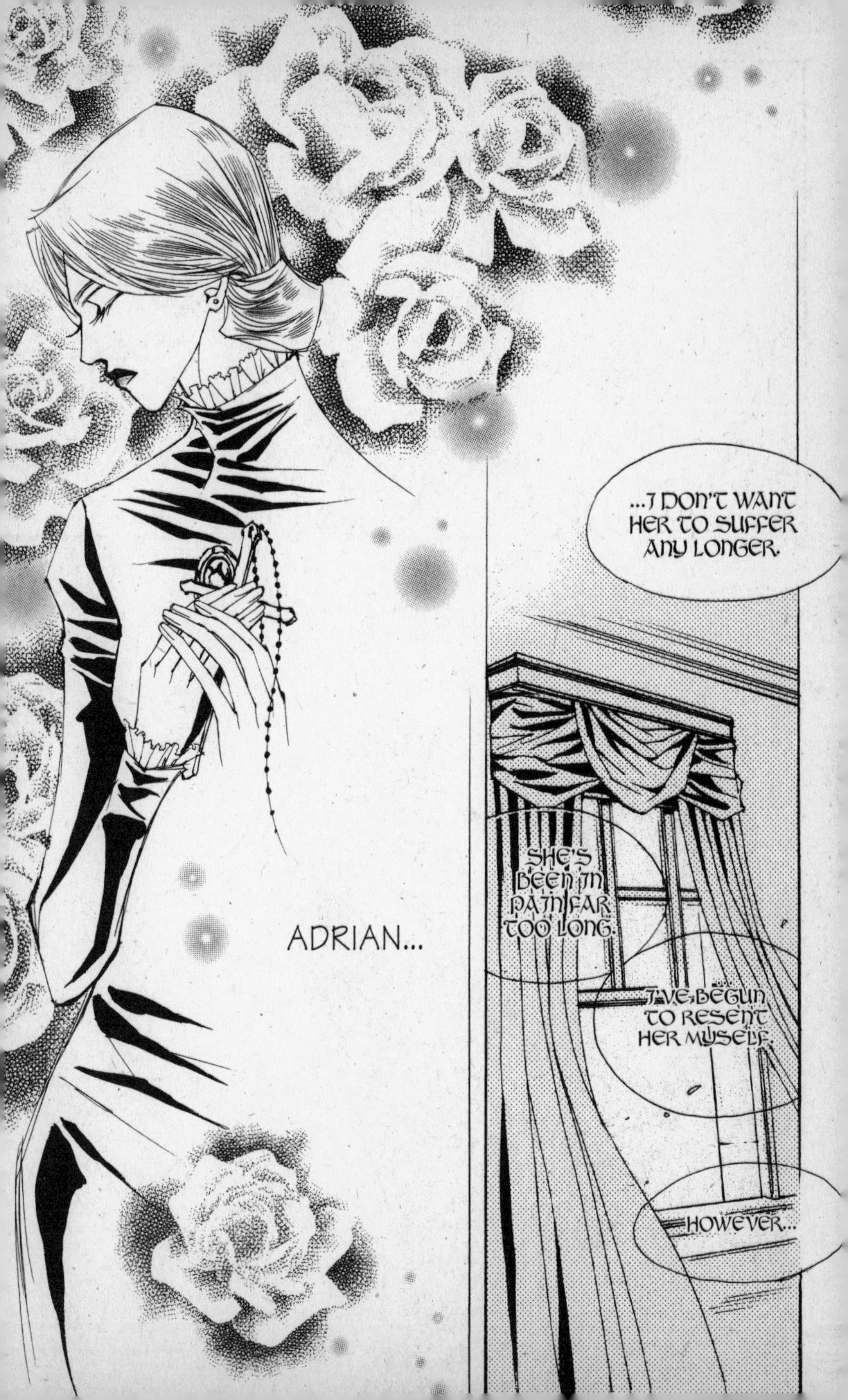
ADRIAN...
...I DON'T WANT HER TO SUFFER ANY LONGER.
SHE'S BEEN IN PAIN FAR TOO LONG.
I'VE BEGUN TO RESENT HER MYSELF.
HOWEVER...

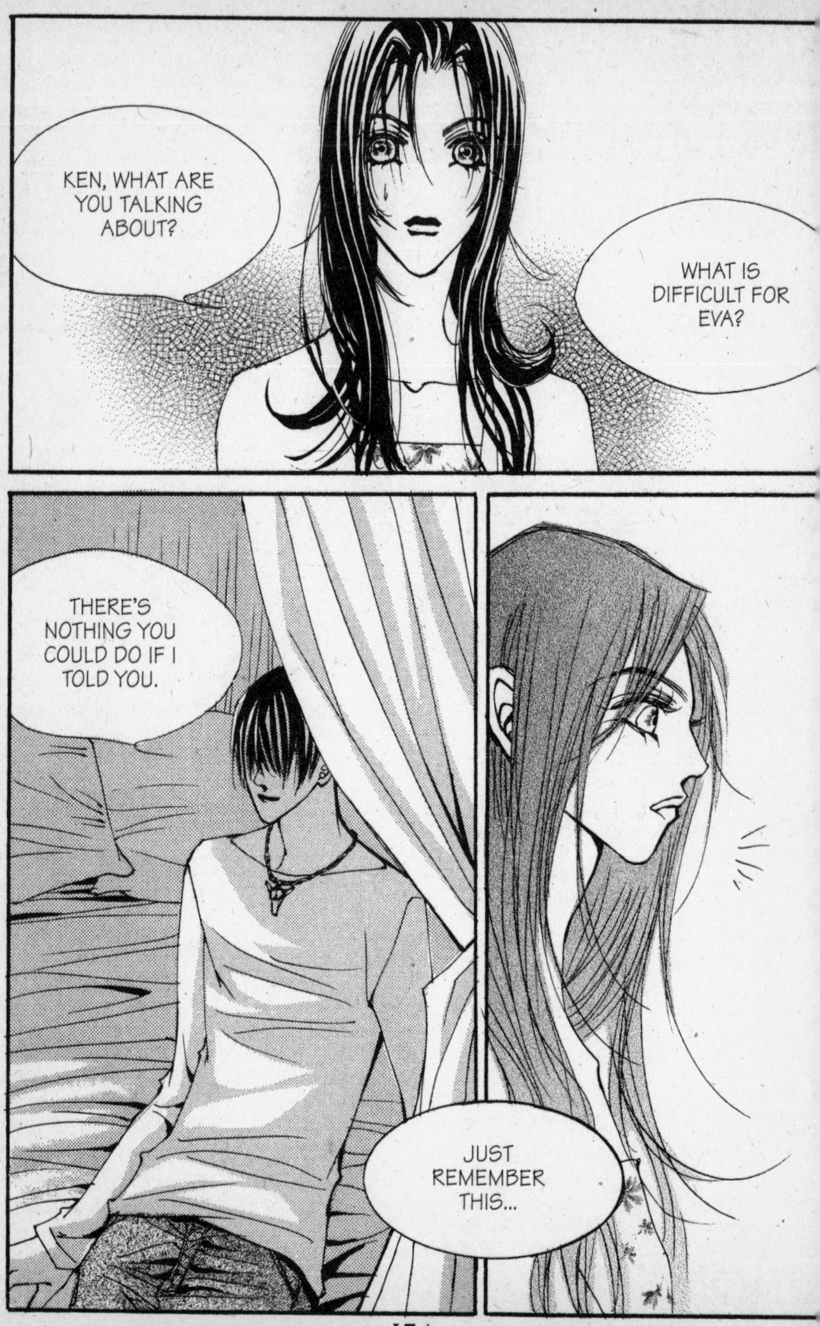
KEN, WHAT ARE YOU TALKING ABOUT?
WHAT IS DIFFICULT FOR EVA?
THERE'S NOTHING YOU COULD DO IF I TOLD YOU.
JUST REMEMBER THIS...

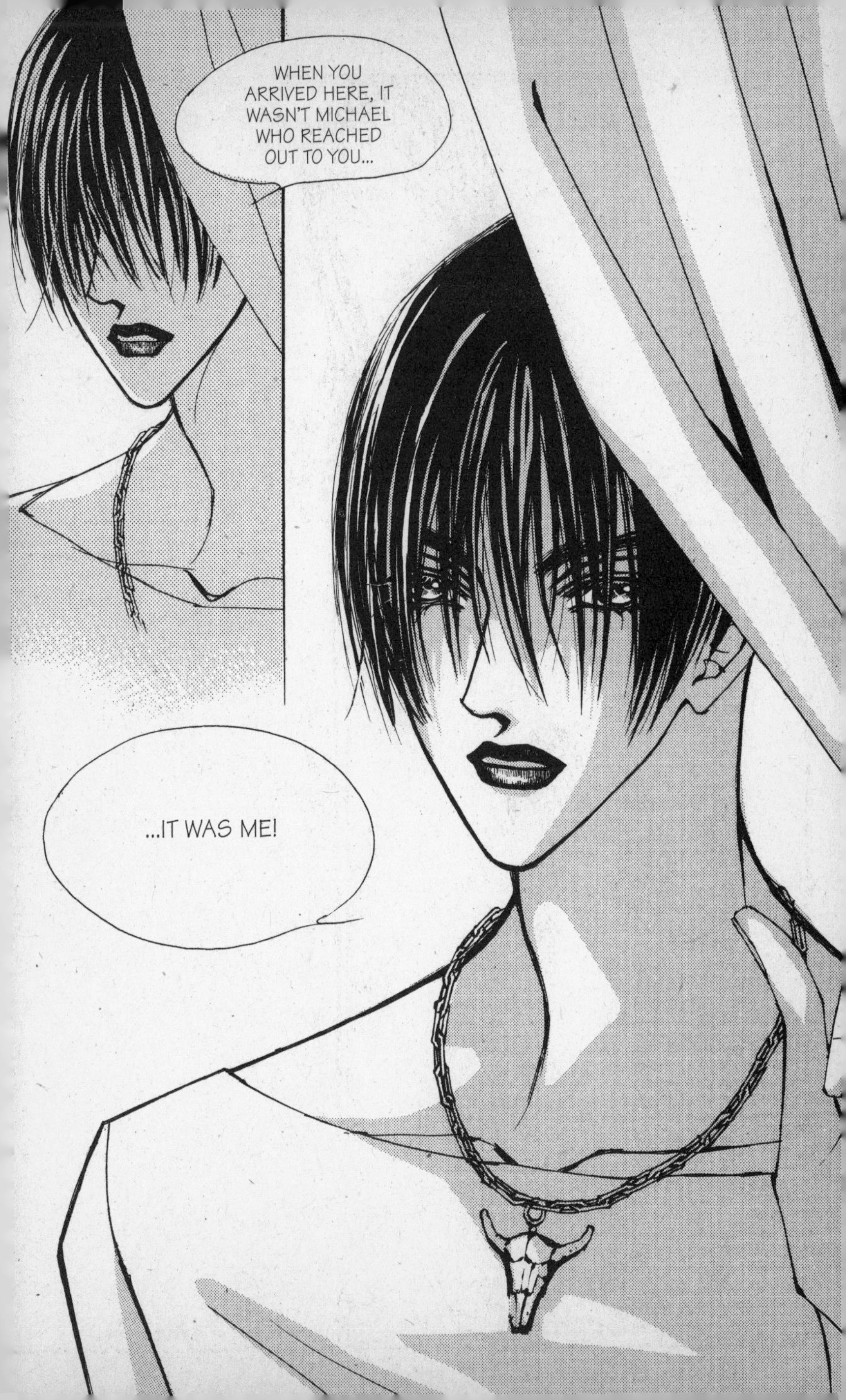
WHEN YOU ARRIVED HERE, IT WASN'T MICHAEL WHO REACHED OUT TO YOU...
...IT WAS ME!

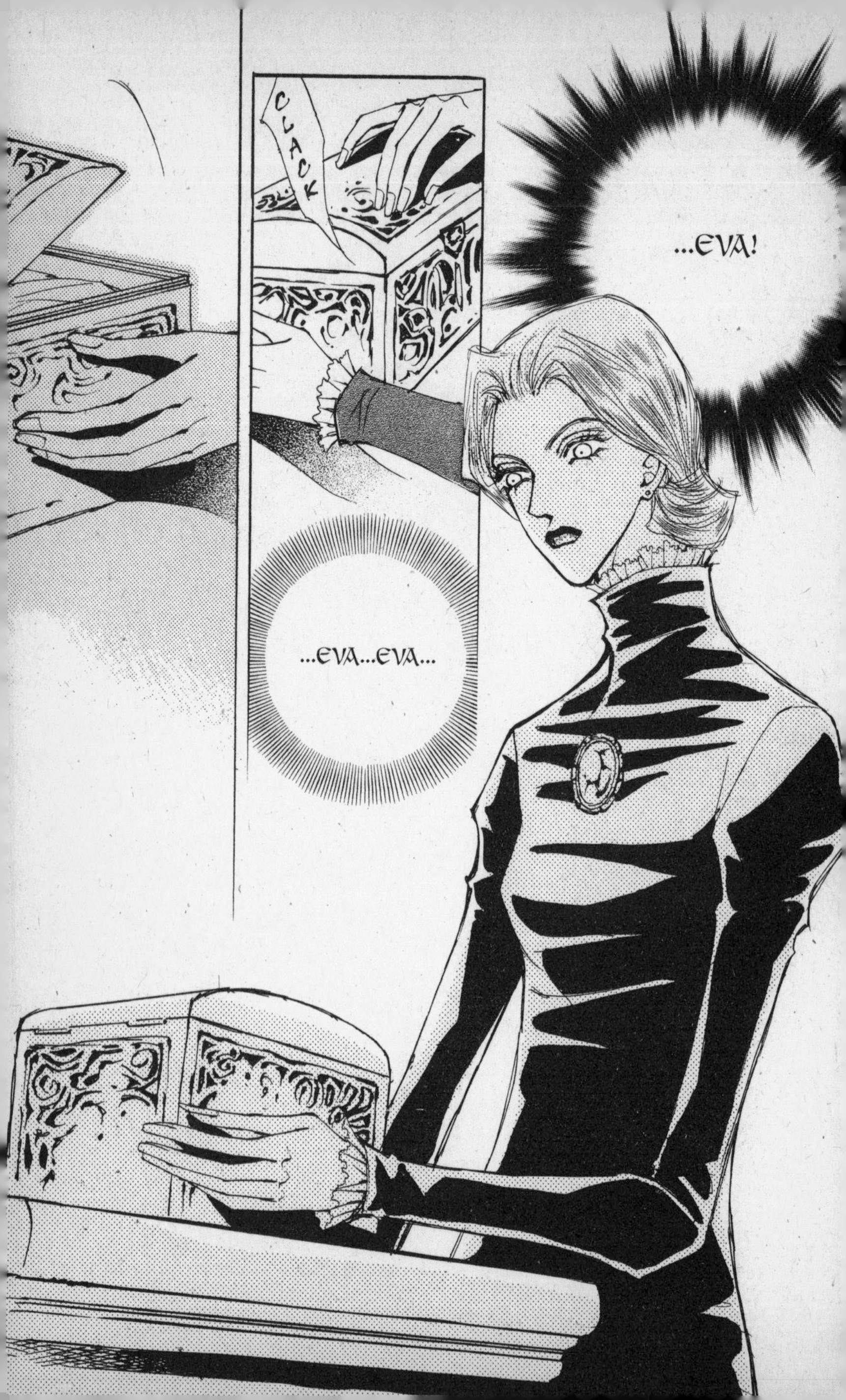
CLACK
...EVA!
...EVA...EVA...

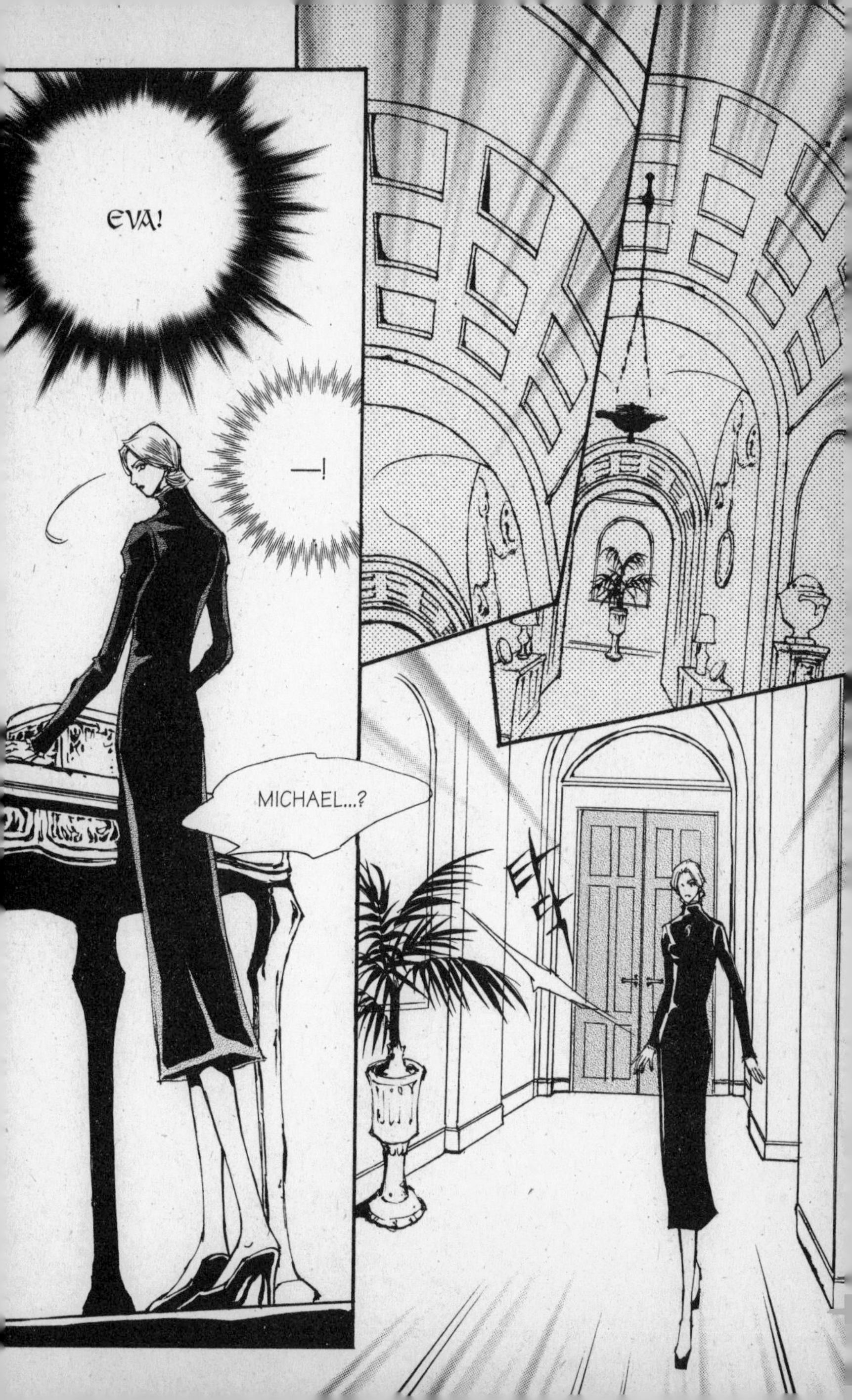
EVA!
—!
MICHAEL...?

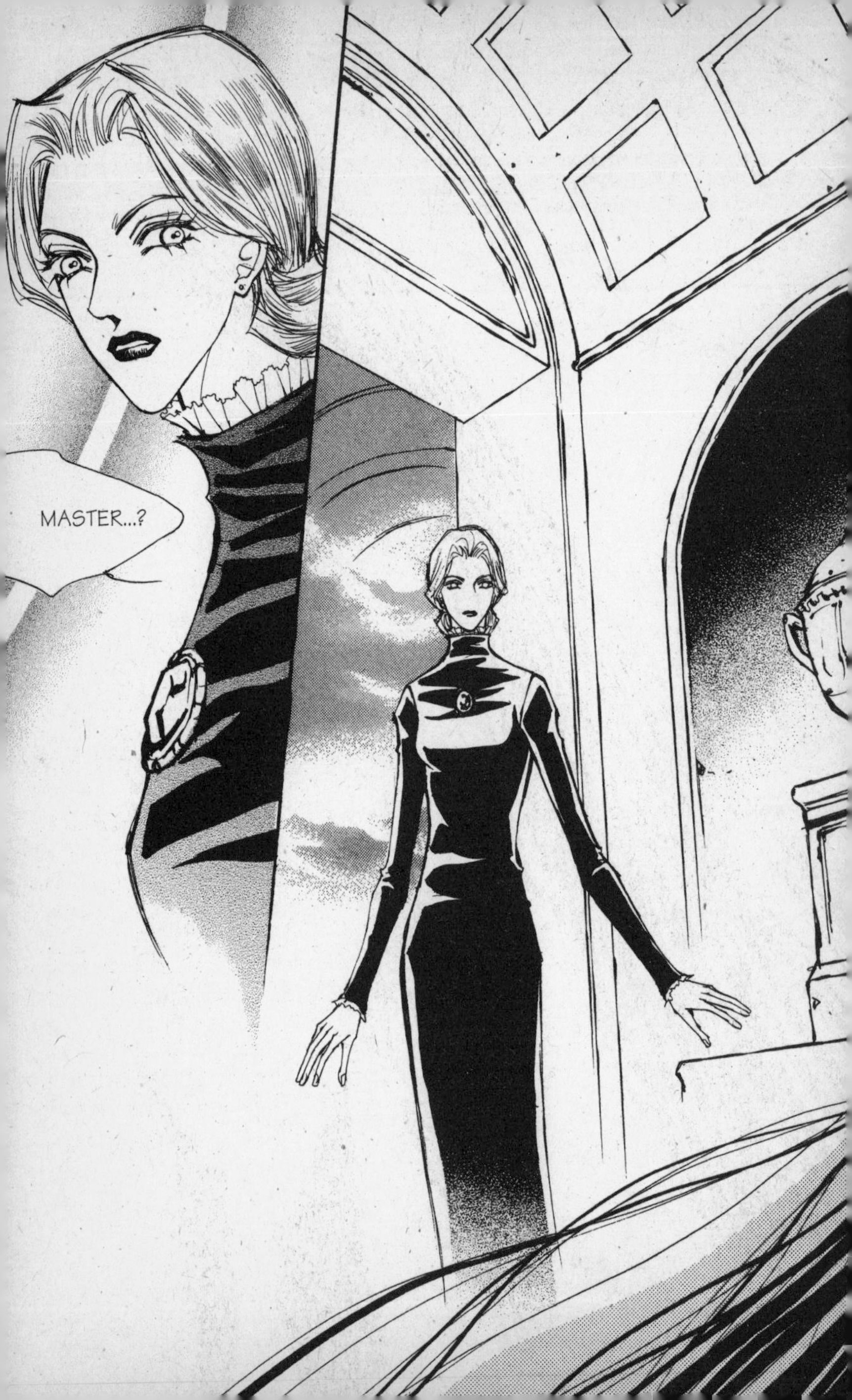
MASTER...?

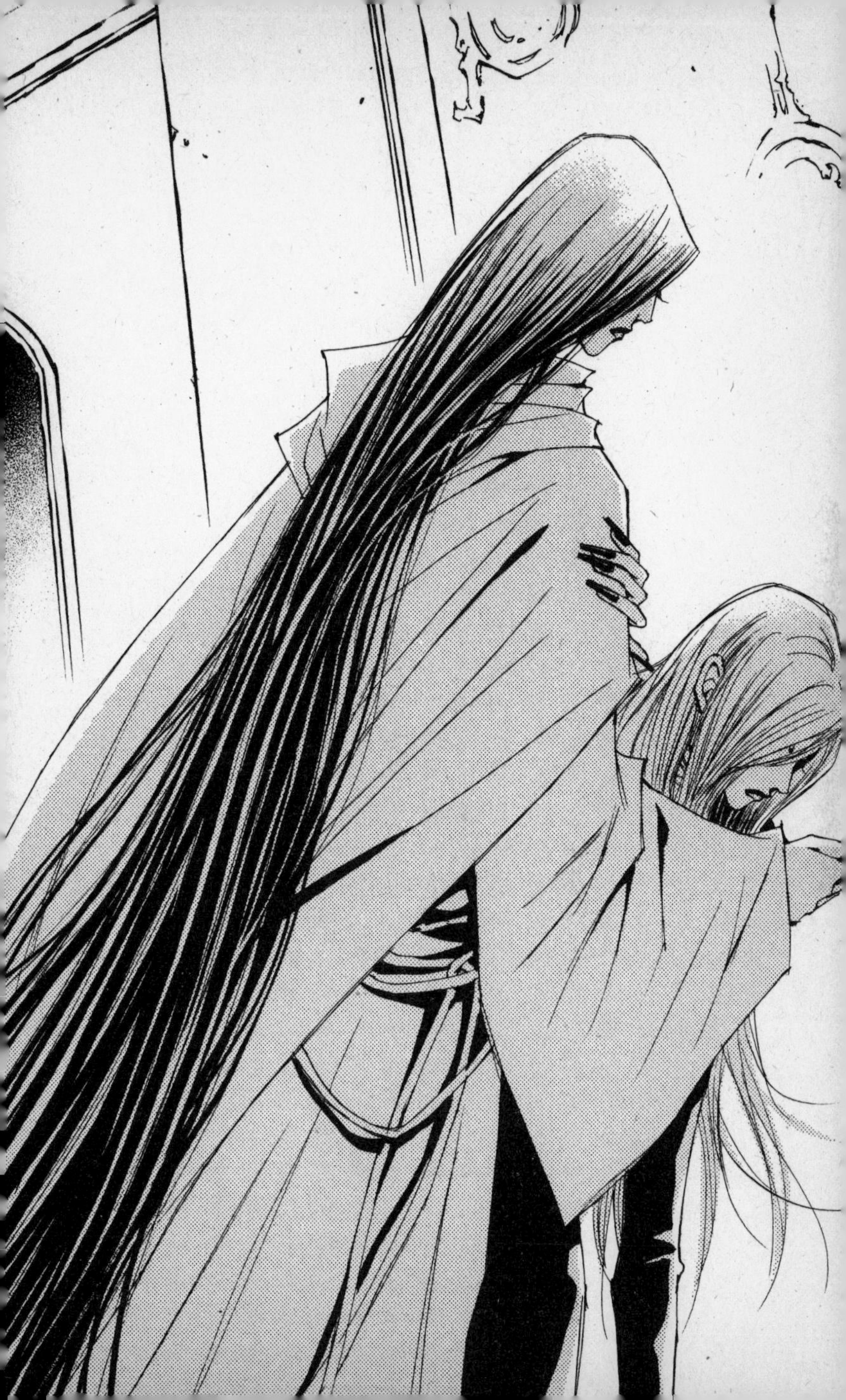

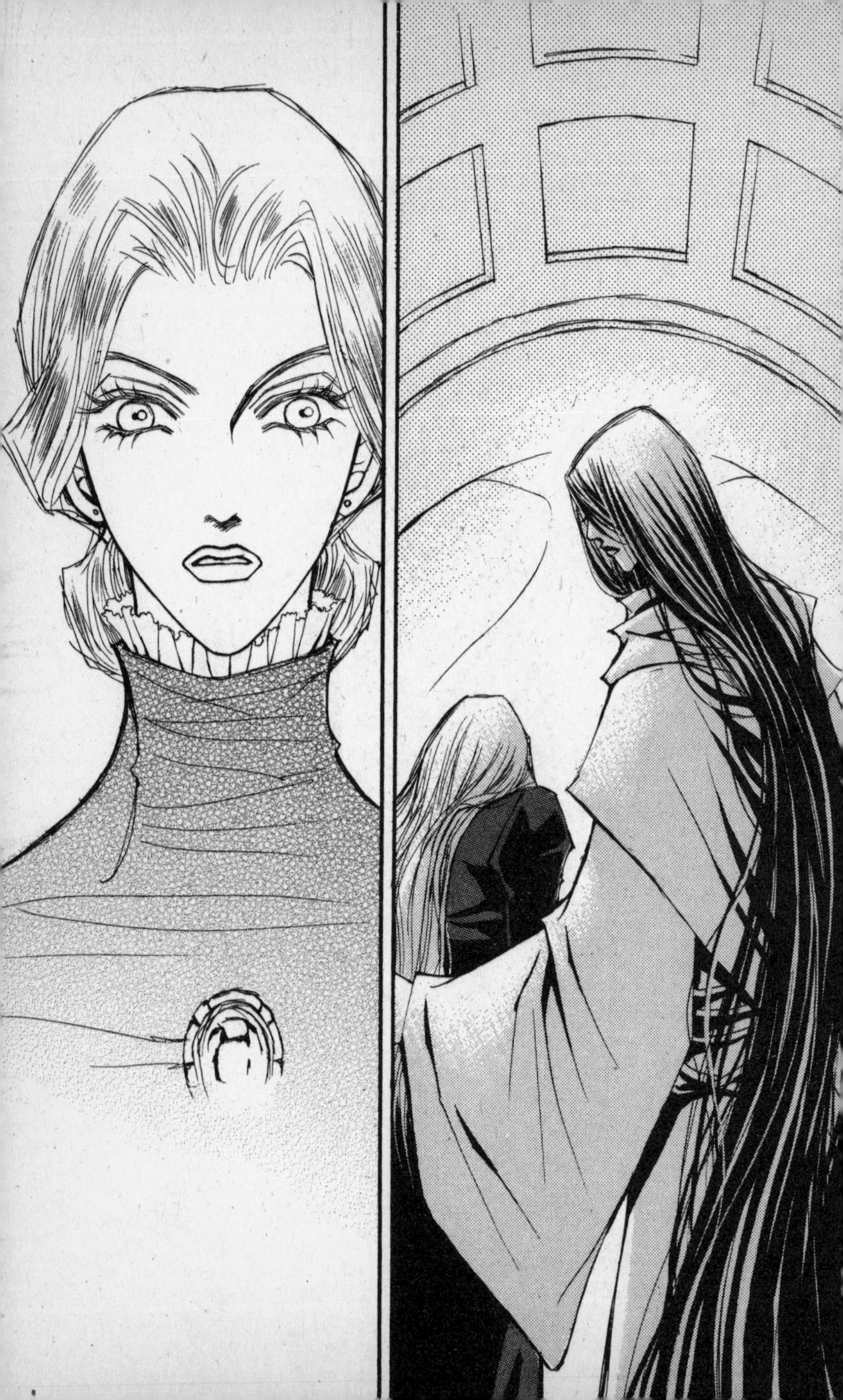

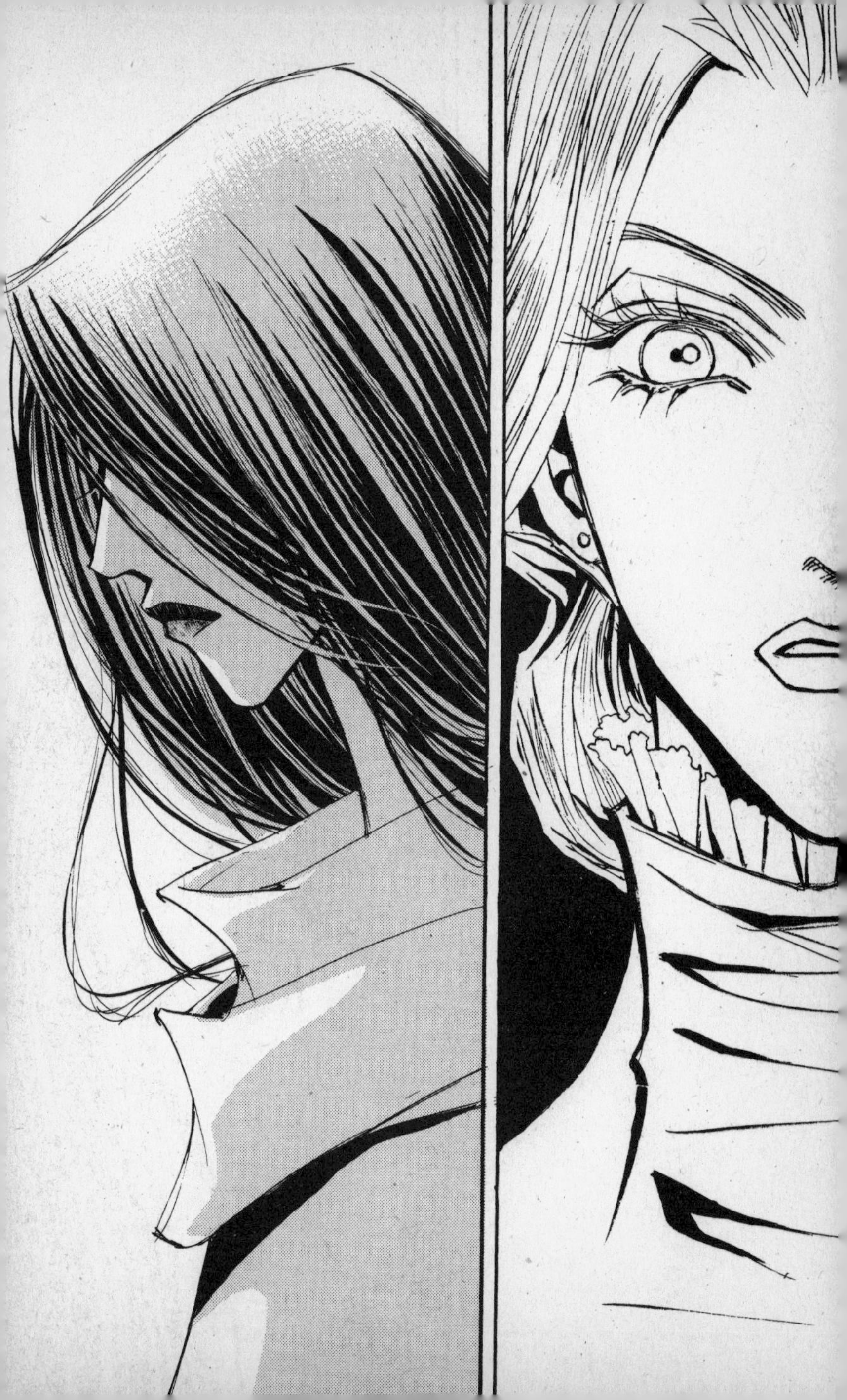

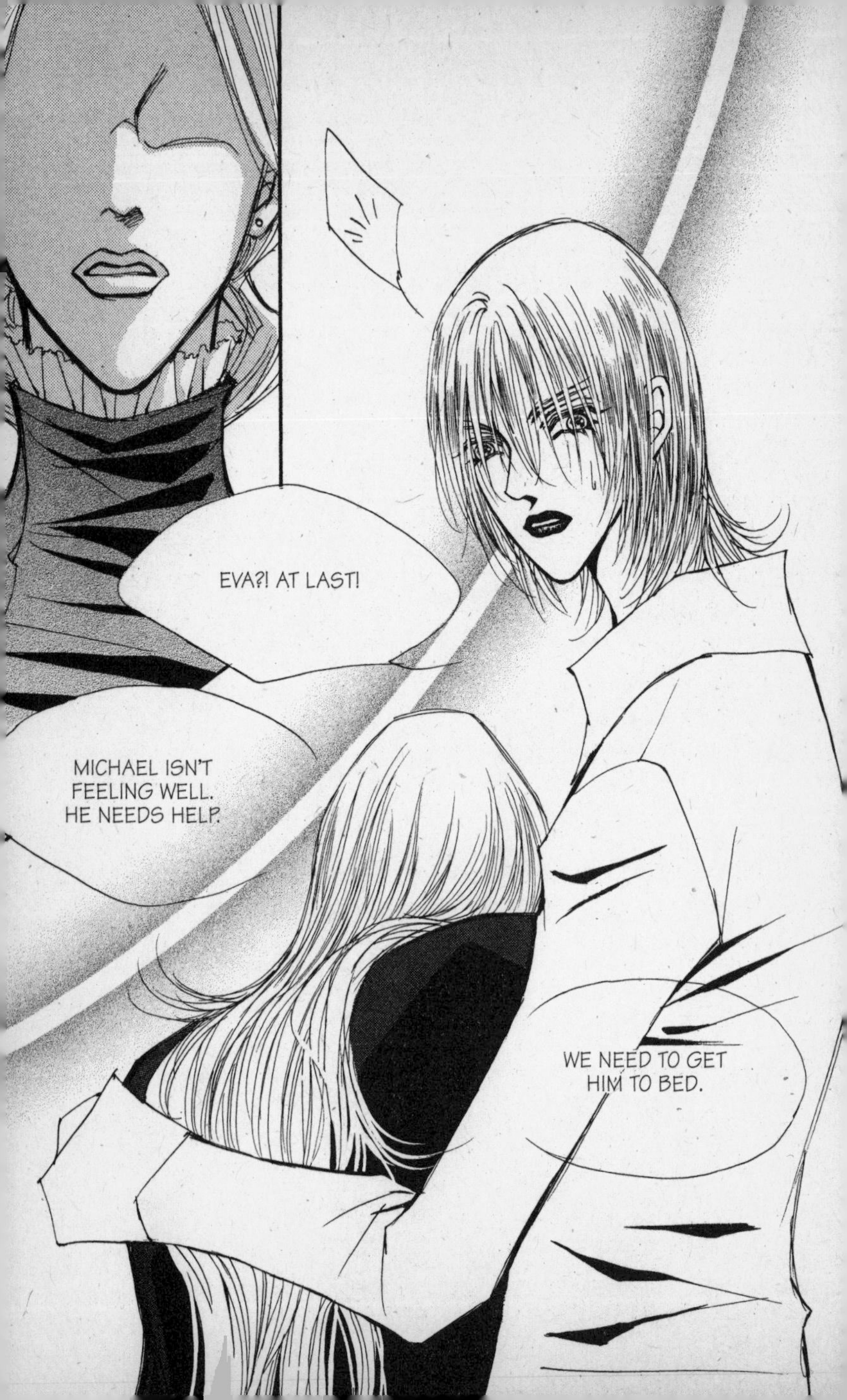
EVA?! AT LAST!
MICHAEL ISN'T FEELING WELL. HE NEEDS HELP.
WE NEED TO GET HIM TO BED.

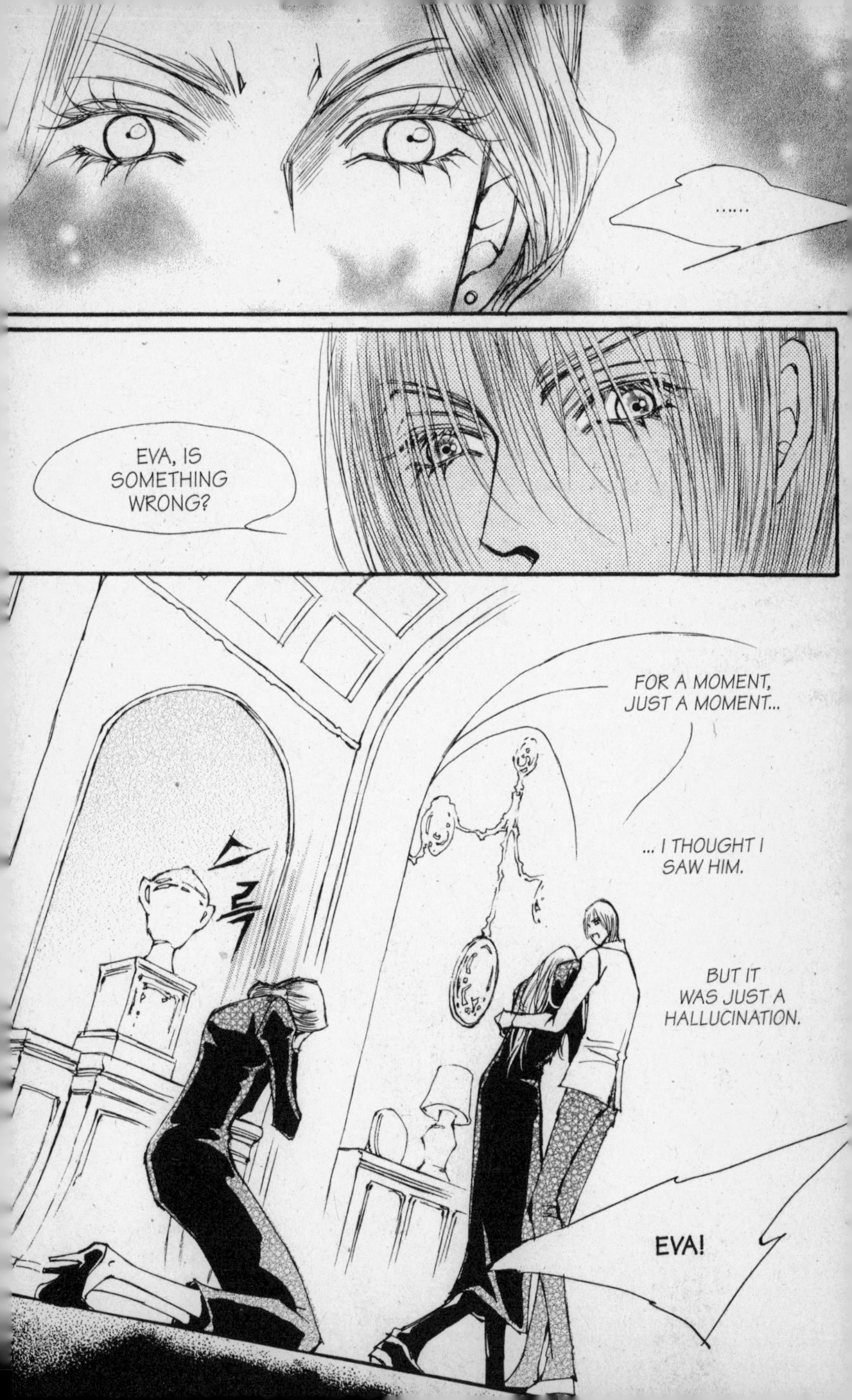
......
EVA, IS SOMETHING WRONG?
FOR A MOMENT, JUST A MOMENT...
... I THOUGHT I SAW HIM.
BUT IT WAS JUST A HALLUCINATION.
EVA!

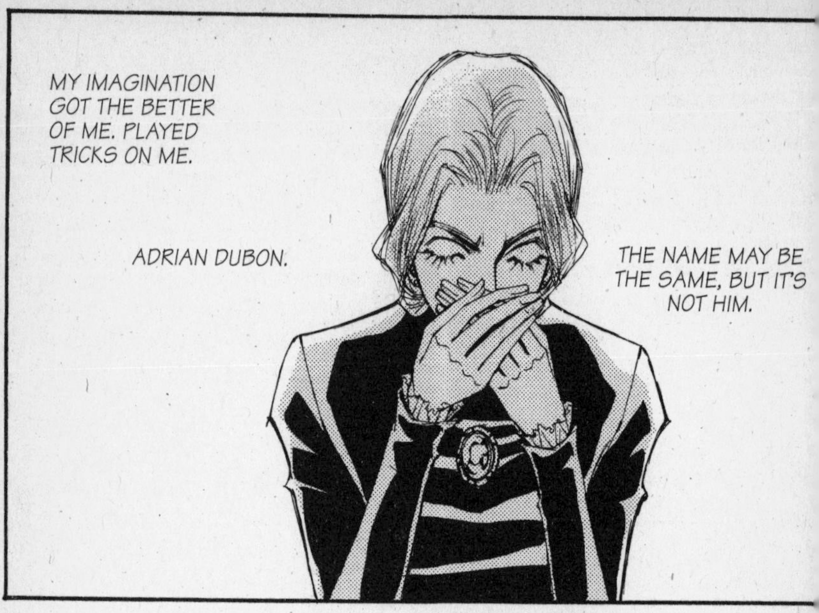
MY IMAGINATION GOT THE BETTER OF ME. PLAYED TRICKS ON ME.
ADRIAN DUBON.
THE NAME MAY BE THE SAME, BUT IT'S NOT HIM.

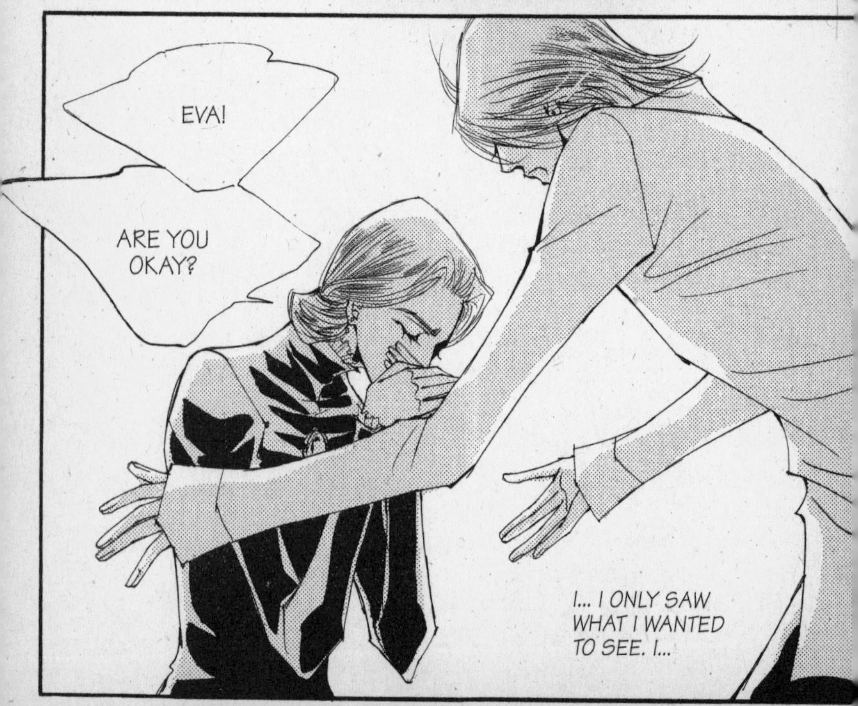
EVA!
ARE YOU OKAY?
I... I ONLY SAW WHAT I WANTED TO SEE. I...

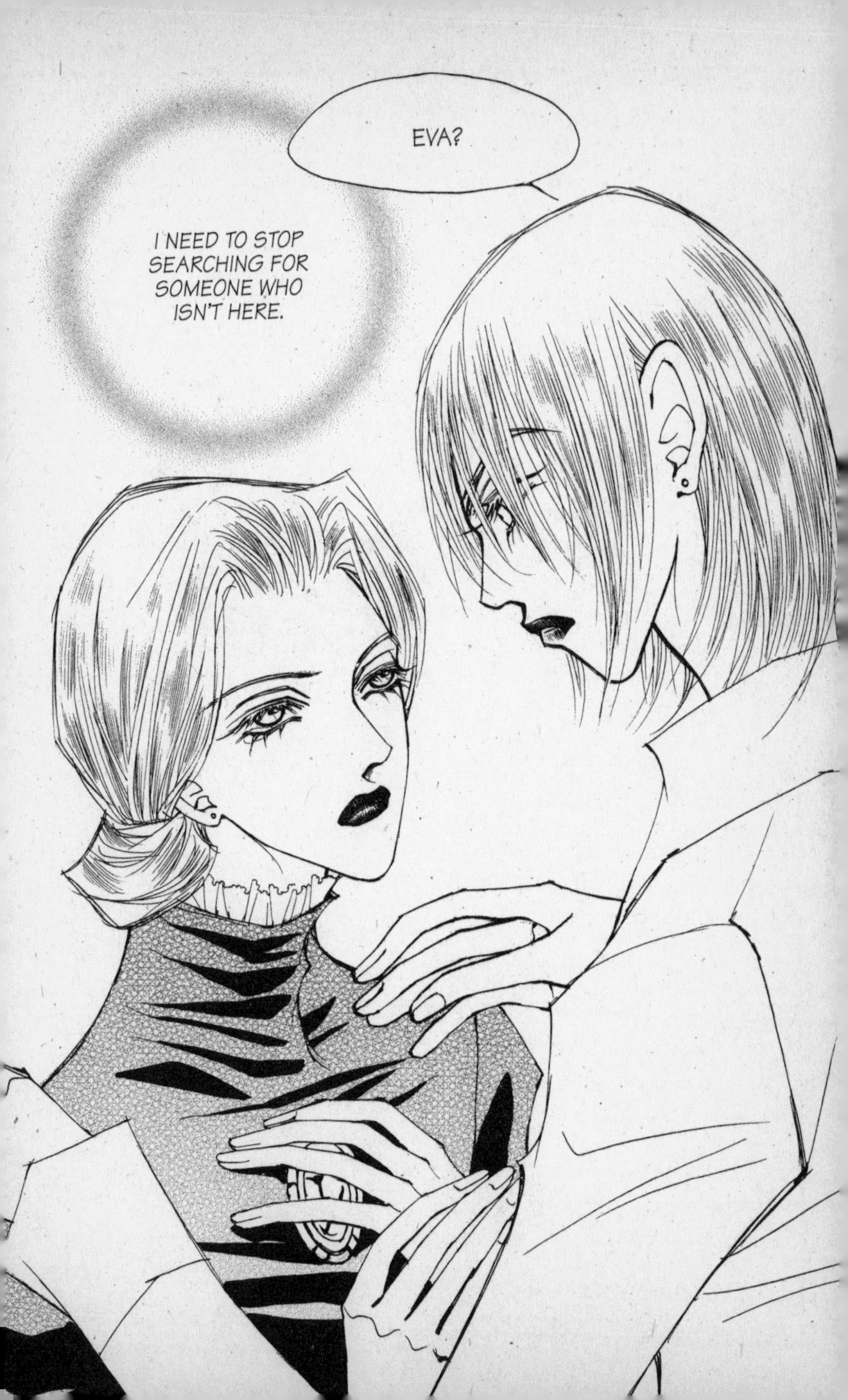
EVA?
I NEED TO STOP SEARCHING FOR SOMEONE WHO ISN'T HERE.

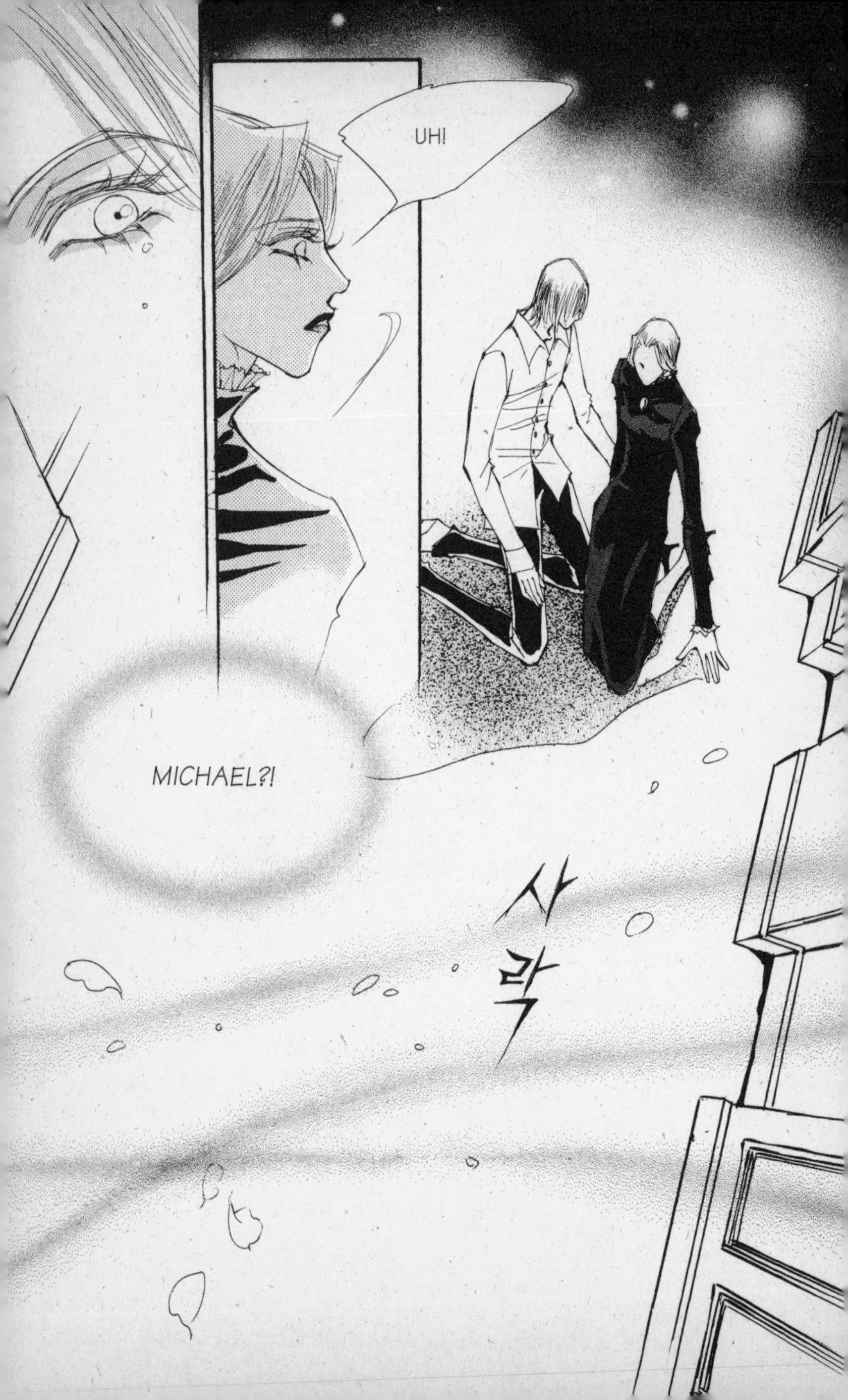
UH!
MICHAEL?!
사락

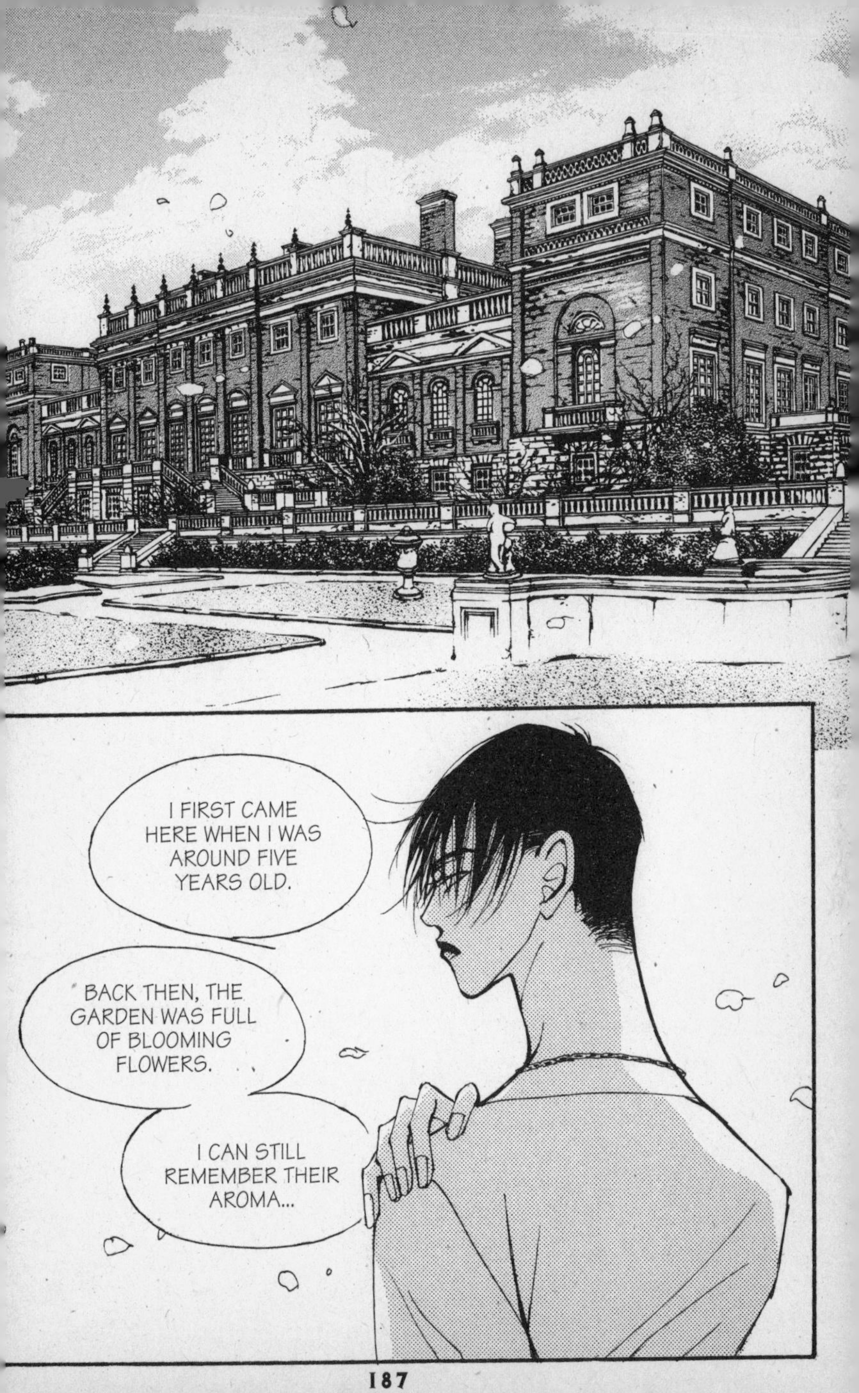
I FIRST CAME HERE WHEN I WAS AROUND FIVE YEARS OLD.
BACK THEN, THE GARDEN WAS FULL OF BLOOMING FLOWERS.
I CAN STILL REMEMBER THEIR AROMA...

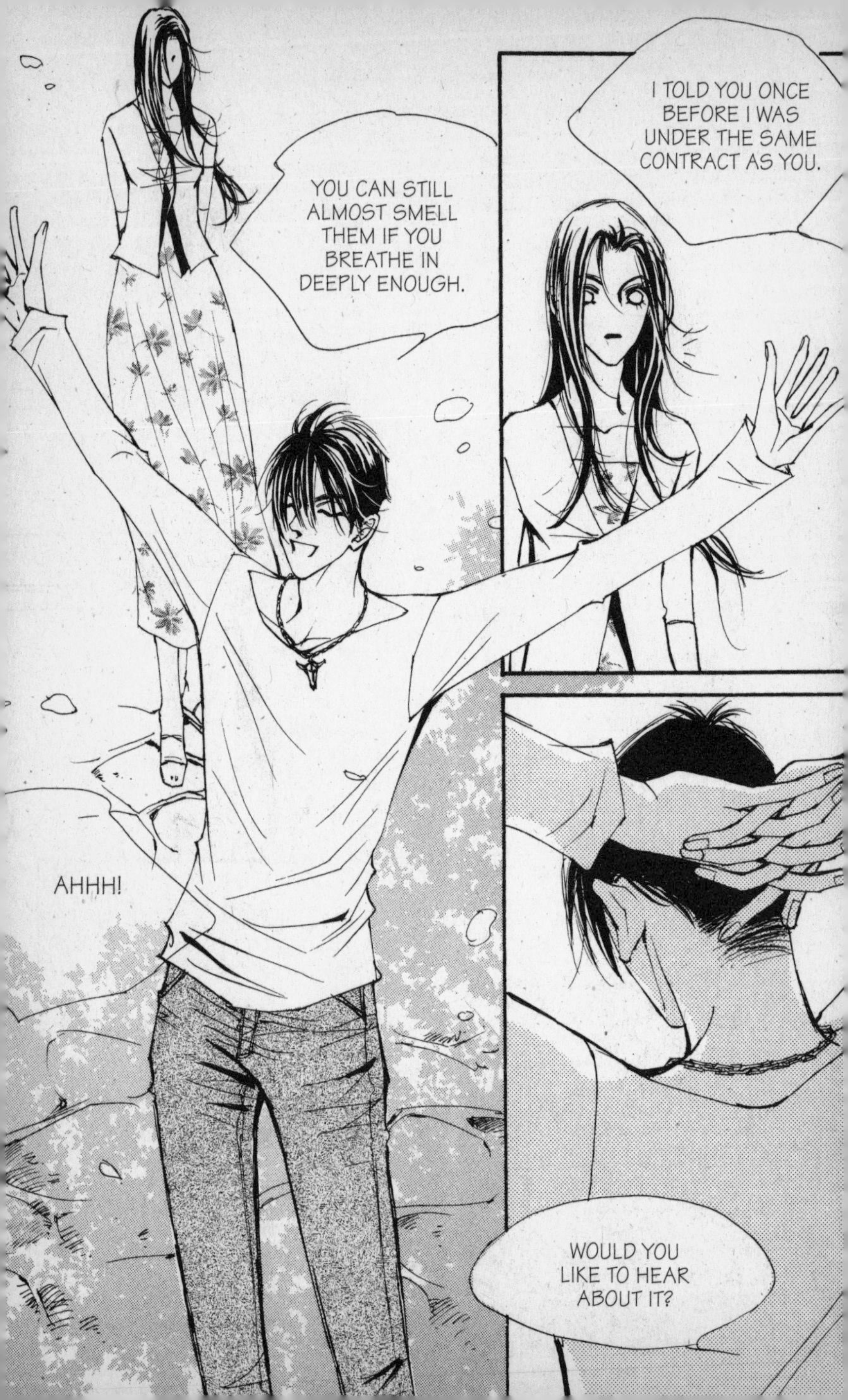
YOU CAN STILL ALMOST SMELL THEM IF YOU BREATHE IN DEEPLY ENOUGH.
AHHH!
I TOLD YOU ONCE BEFORE I WAS UNDER THE SAME CONTRACT AS YOU.
WOULD YOU LIKE TO HEAR ABOUT IT?

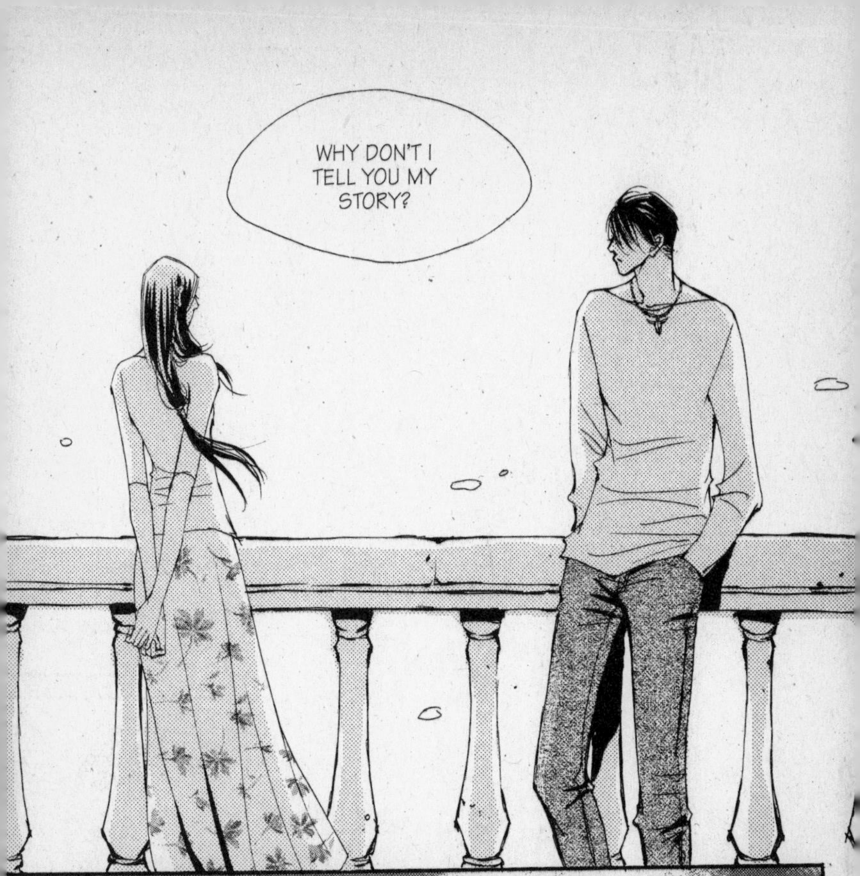
WHY DON'T I TELL YOU MY STORY?
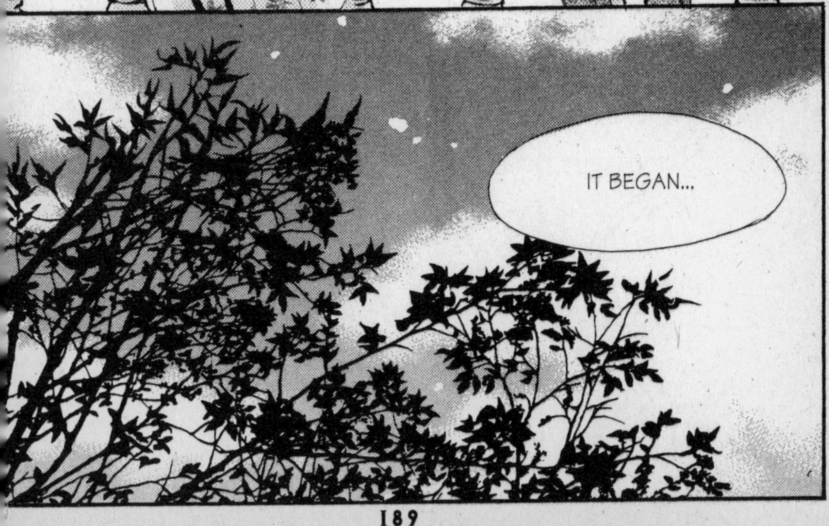
IT BEGAN...

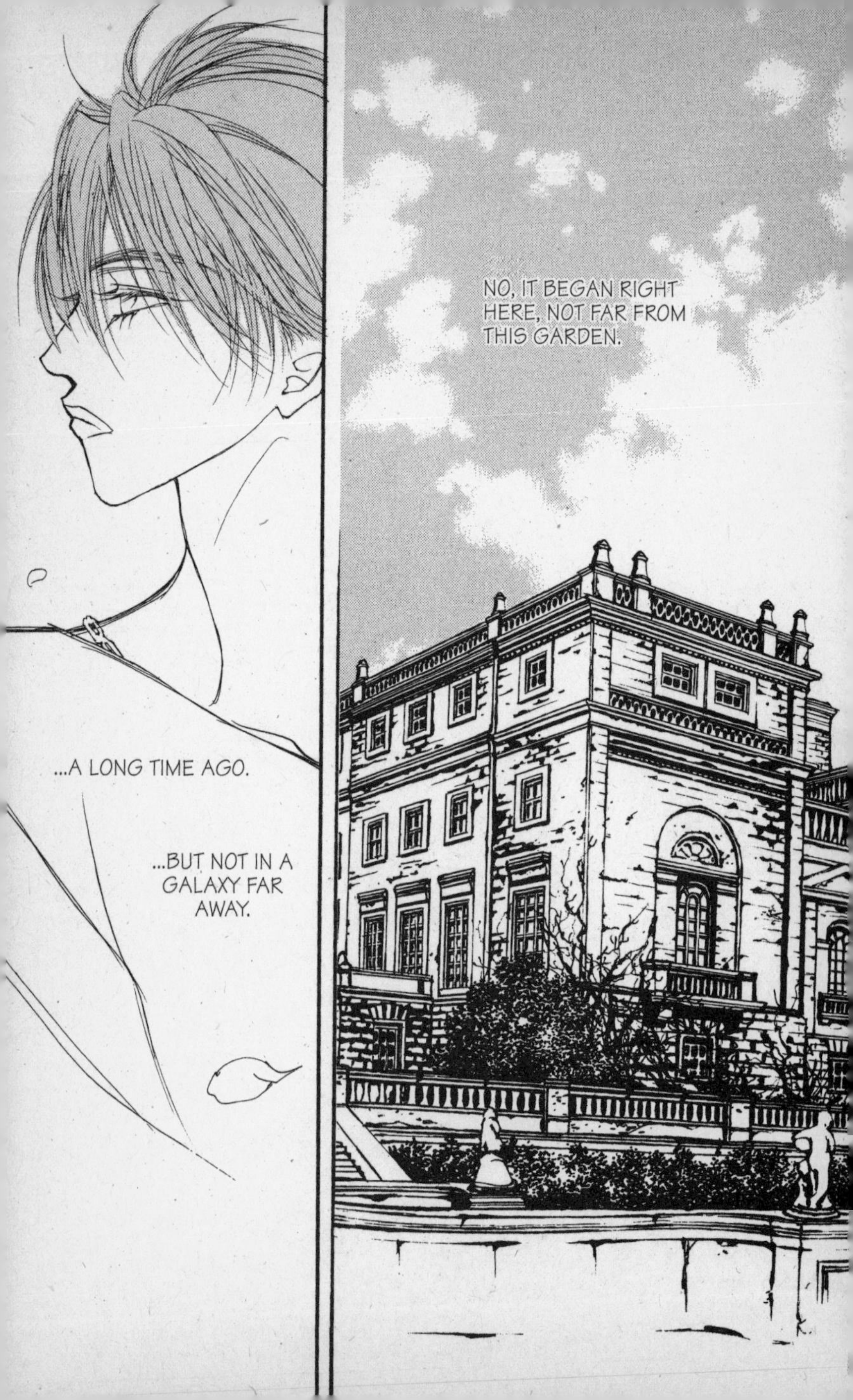
...A LONG TIME AGO.
...BUT NOT IN A GALAXY FAR AWAY.
NO, IT BEGAN RIGHT HERE, NOT FAR FROM THIS GARDEN.

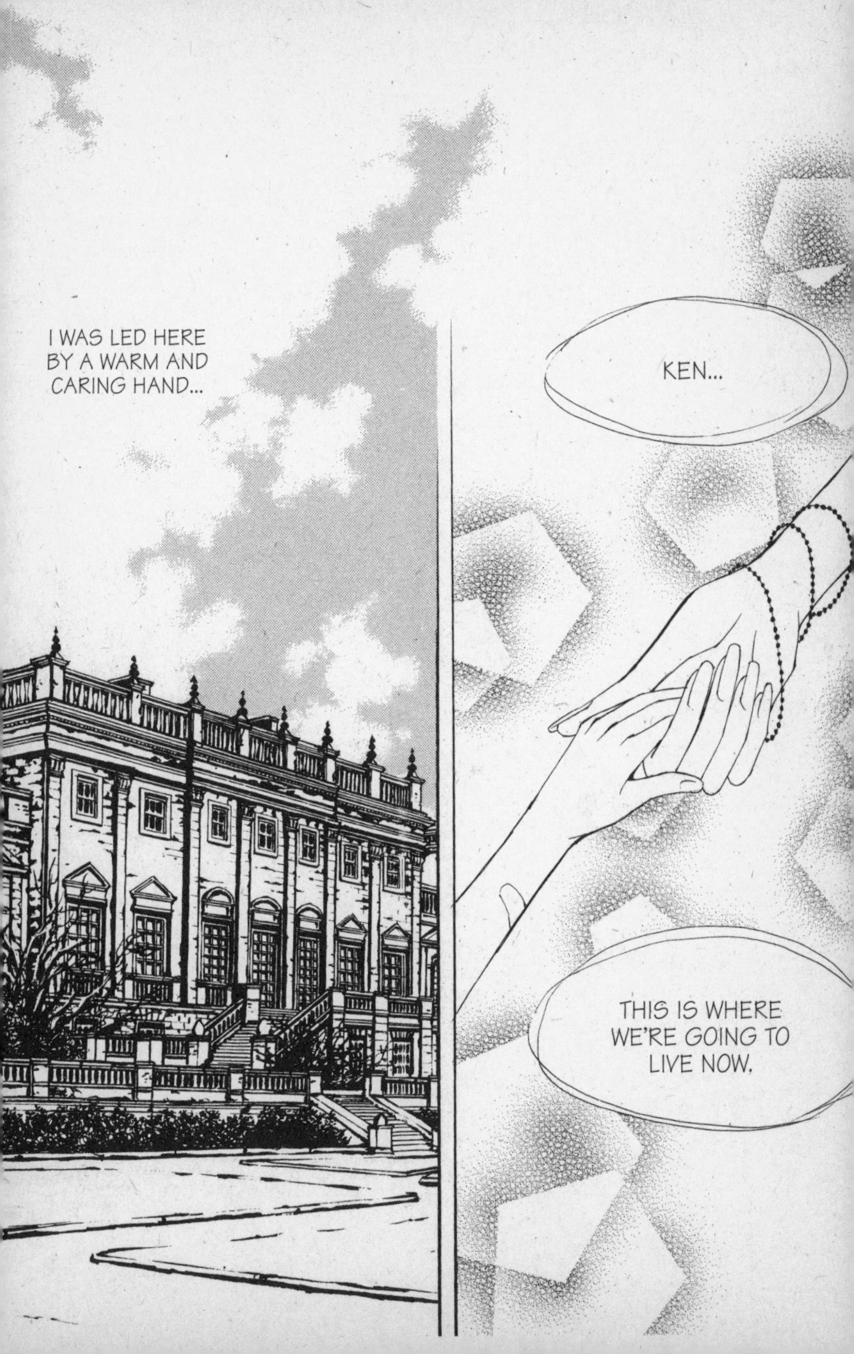
I WAS LED HERE BY A WARM AND CARING HAND...
KEN...
THIS IS WHERE WE'RE GOING TO LIVE NOW.

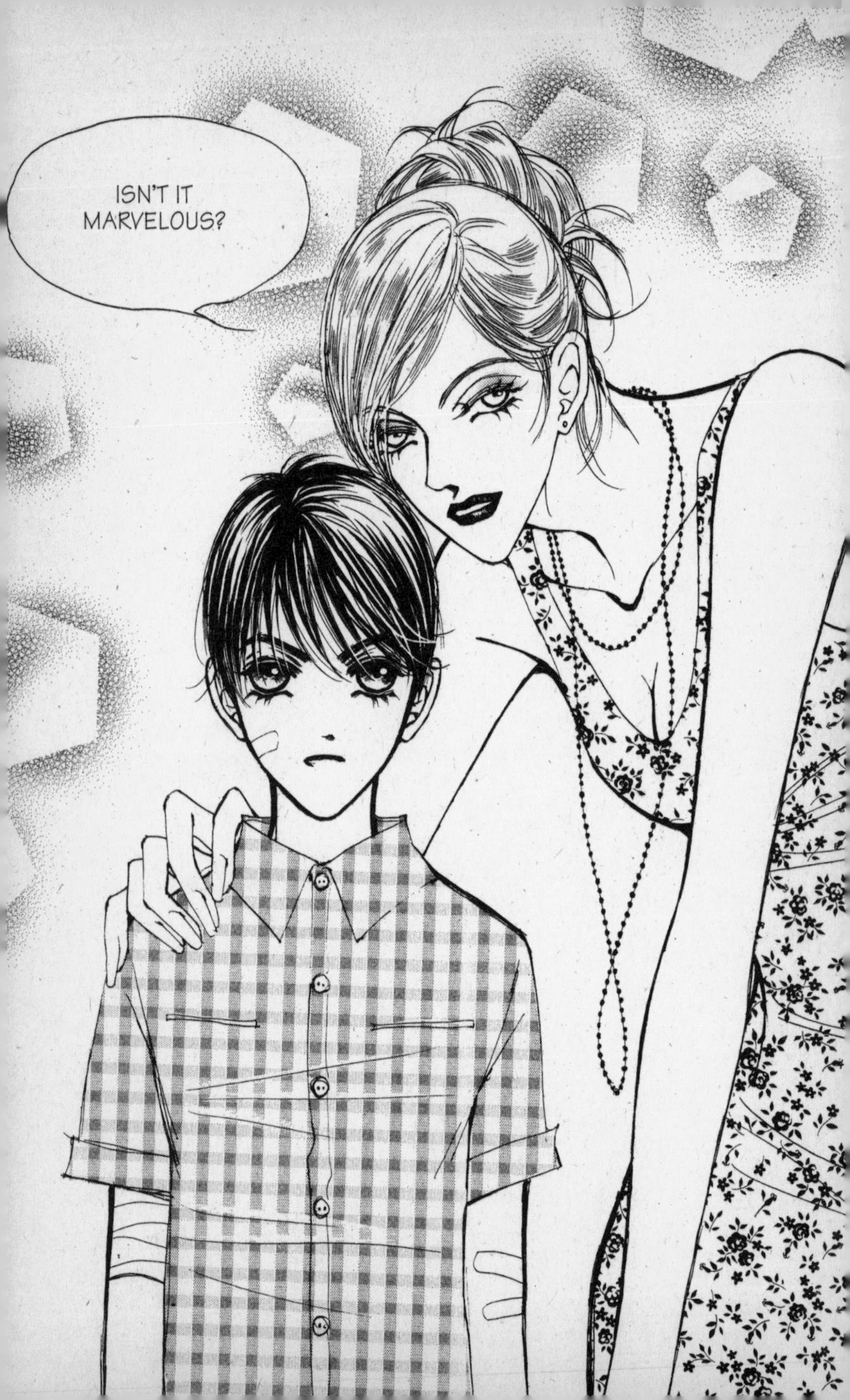
ISN'T IT MARVELOUS?

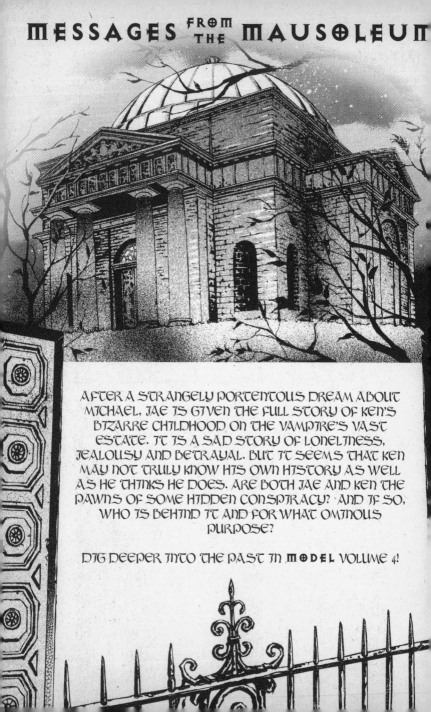

# MESSAGES FROM THE MAUSOLEUM

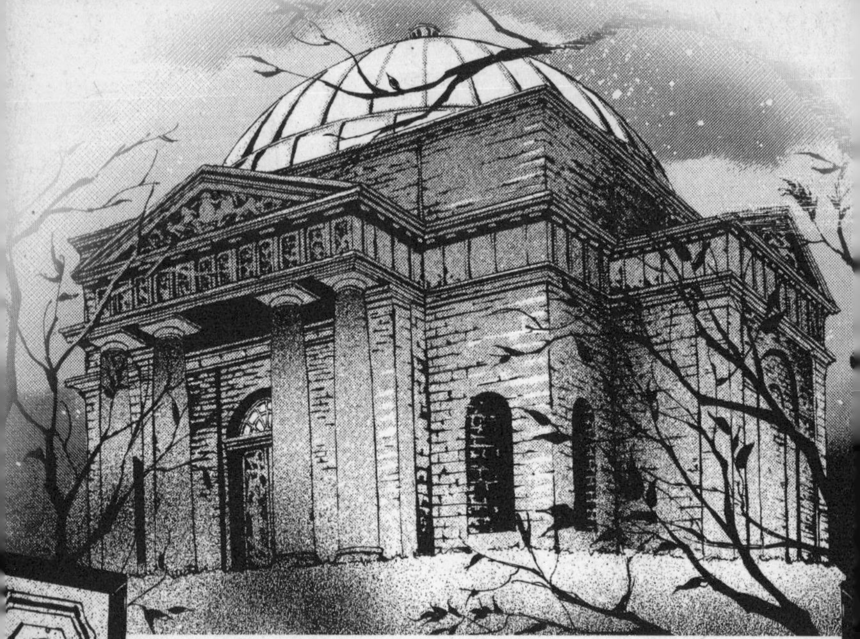

AFTER A STRANGELY PORTENTOUS DREAM ABOUT MICHAEL, JAE IS GIVEN THE FULL STORY OF KEN'S BIZARRE CHILDHOOD ON THE VAMPIRE'S VAST ESTATE. IT IS A SAD STORY OF LONELINESS, JEALOUSY AND BETRAYAL. BUT IT SEEMS THAT KEN MAY NOT TRULY KNOW HIS OWN HISTORY AS WELL AS HE THINKS HE DOES. ARE BOTH JAE AND KEN THE PAWNS OF SOME HIDDEN CONSPIRACY? AND IF SO, WHO IS BEHIND IT AND FOR WHAT OMINOUS PURPOSE?

DIG DEEPER INTO THE PAST IN **MODEL** VOLUME 4!

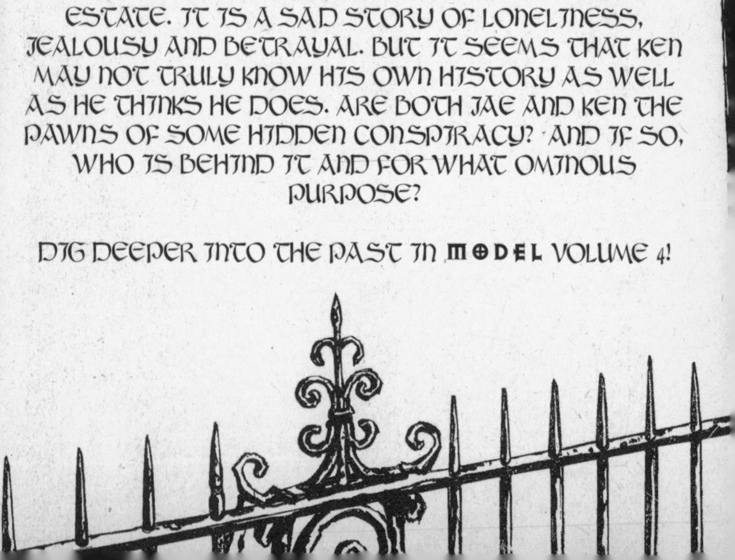

FROM CLAMP, CREATORS OF CHOBITS.

# TOKYO
# BABYLON™

Welcome to Tokyo.
The city never sleeps.
May its spirits rest in peace.

# ALSO AVAILABLE FROM TOKYOPOP®

## MANGA

.HACK//LEGEND OF THE TWILIGHT
@LARGE
ABENOBASHI: MAGICAL SHOPPING ARCADE
A.I. LOVE YOU
AI YORI AOSHI
ANGELIC LAYER
ARM OF KANNON
BABY BIRTH
BATTLE ROYALE
BATTLE VIXENS
BRAIN POWERED
BRIGADOON
B'TX
CANDIDATE FOR GODDESS, THE
CARDCAPTOR SAKURA
CARDCAPTOR SAKURA - MASTER OF THE CLOW
CHOBITS
CHRONICLES OF THE CURSED SWORD
CLAMP SCHOOL DETECTIVES
CLOVER
COMIC PARTY
CONFIDENTIAL CONFESSIONS
CORRECTOR YUI
COWBOY BEBOP
COWBOY BEBOP: SHOOTING STAR
CRAZY LOVE STORY
CRESCENT MOON
CROSS
CULDCEPT
CYBORG 009
D•N•ANGEL
DEMON DIARY
DEMON ORORON, THE
DEUS VITAE
DIABOLO
DIGIMON
DIGIMON TAMERS
DIGIMON ZERO TWO
DOLL
DRAGON HUNTER
DRAGON KNIGHTS
DRAGON VOICE
DREAM SAGA
DUKLYON: CLAMP SCHOOL DEFENDERS
EERIE QUEERIE!
ERICA SAKURAZAWA: COLLECTED WORKS
ET CETERA
ETERNITY
EVIL'S RETURN
FAERIES' LANDING
FAKE
FLCL
FLOWER OF THE DEEP SLEEP
FORBIDDEN DANCE
FRUITS BASKET
G GUNDAM

GATEKEEPERS
GETBACKERS
GIRL GOT GAME
GIRLS EDUCATIONAL CHARTER
GRAVITATION
GTO
GUNDAM BLUE DESTINY
GUNDAM SEED ASTRAY
GUNDAM WING
GUNDAM WING: BATTLEFIELD OF PACIFISTS
GUNDAM WING: ENDLESS WALTZ
GUNDAM WING: THE LAST OUTPOST (G-UNIT)
GUYS' GUIDE TO GIRLS
HANDS OFF!
HAPPY MANIA
HARLEM BEAT
HYPER RUNE
I.N.V.U.
IMMORTAL RAIN
INITIAL D
INSTANT TEEN: JUST ADD NUTS
ISLAND
JING: KING OF BANDITS
JING: KING OF BANDITS - TWILIGHT TALES
JULINE
KARE KANO
KILL ME, KISS ME
KINDAICHI CASE FILES, THE
KING OF HELL
KODOCHA: SANA'S STAGE
LAMENT OF THE LAMB
LEGAL DRUG
LEGEND OF CHUN HYANG, THE
LES BIJOUX
LOVE HINA
LUPIN III
LUPIN III: WORLD'S MOST WANTED
MAGIC KNIGHT RAYEARTH I
MAGIC KNIGHT RAYEARTH II
MAHOROMATIC: AUTOMATIC MAIDEN
MAN OF MANY FACES
MARMALADE BOY
MARS
MARS: HORSE WITH NO NAME
MINK
MIRACLE GIRLS
MIYUKI-CHAN IN WONDERLAND
MODEL
MOURYOU KIDEN
MY LOVE
NECK AND NECK
ONE
ONE I LOVE, THE
PARADISE KISS
PARASYTE
PASSION FRUIT
PEACH GIRL
PEACH GIRL: CHANGE OF HEART